Irwin Taylor

Public Schools a Law Treatise on the Rights, Powers, Duties and Liabilities of School Boards, Officers and Teachers

Irwin Taylor

Public Schools a Law Treatise on the Rights, Powers, Duties and Liabilities of School Boards, Officers and Teachers

ISBN/EAN: 9783337811297

Printed in Europe, USA, Canada, Australia, Japan

Cover: Foto ©Suzi / pixelio.de

More available books at **www.hansebooks.com**

PUBLIC SCHOOLS

A LAW TREATISE

ON THE

RIGHTS, POWERS, DUTIES AND LIABILITIES OF SCHOOL BOARDS, OFFICERS AND TEACHERS.

WITH APPENDIX
CONTAINING SYNOPSES OF PRINCIPAL STATUTES OF EACH STATE.

By IRWIN TAYLOR,
AUTHOR OF PLEADING AND PRACTICE, COLORADO DIGEST, ANNOTATED CODE, GENERAL STATUTES OF KANSAS, TAX LAWS, KANSAS DIGESTS, ETC., ETC.

CHICAGO:
IRWIN TAYLOR, PUBLISHER, 13 SOUTH ASHLAND AVENUE.
1893.

COPYRIGHT, 1893,
BY IRWIN TAYLOR, CHICAGO, ILLINOIS.

TABLE OF CONTENTS.

Preface — p. 3.
Appeals — p. 5, §§1 – 4.
Bonds — p. 10, §§5 – 9.
Buildings — Contract, Control, Repair, Use — p. 16, §§10 to 28.
Colored Schools — p. 36, §§29 – 33.
Contracts — Attorney, Notes, Officer Interested, Officer Liability, Power, Ratification — p. 44, §§34 – 42.
Corporation — p. 53, §43.
Crime — p. 54, §44.
Districts — Alteration, Boundary, Dissolution, Library, Organization, Union — p. 54, §§45 – 73.
Election — p. 91, §74.
Funds — Apportionment, Appropriation Bonds, Constitution, Fines, Interest, Investing, Liquor, Loan, Officer, Use — p. 92, §§75 – 96.
Grammar and High Schools — p. 113, §97.
Judgment — p. 114, §98.
Legislature — p. 116, §99.
Mandamus — p. 116, §100.
Mechanic's Lien — p. 116, §101.
Meeting — Notice — p. 117, §§102 – 110.
Normal — p. 127, §111.
Officer — Compensation, Contract, District Election, Liability, Power, Qualification, Tax, Term, Treasurer, Vacancies — p. 128, §§112 – 137.
Parochial School — Bible, Sectarian, Religion — p. 157, §§138 – 148.
Pupil — Admission, Chinese, Discharge, Dismissal, Expulsion, Punishment, Residence, Tuition — p. 171, §§149 – 163.

Record — p. 195, §§164–166.
Rules — p. 197, §167.
Site — Addition, Condemnation, Contract, Conveyance, Election, Injunction, Notice, Officers, Place, Sale, Tax Title, Trust — p. 200, §§168–180.
Statute — p. 208, §181.
Suits — District Party — p. 209, §§182–186.
Superintendent — Public Instruction, County, Schools — p. 214, §§187–191.
Supplies — p. 222, §§192–195.
Surety — p. 226, §§196–198.
Tax — p. 228, §§199–237.
Teacher — Certificate, Compensation, Contract, Dismissal, Discharge, Institutes, Liability — p. 262, §§238–265.
Term — p. 296, §266.
Text-Books — Adoption, Change, Free, German, Studies, Pupil — p. 296, §§267–279.
Title — p. 312, §280.
Town — p. 313, §§281–282.
Treasurer — p. 313, §283.
Trespass — p. 313, §284.
Truant — p. 314, §§285–286.
Trust — p. 316, §287.
Universities — Colleges — p. 317, §§288–291.
Vaccination — p. 323, §292.
Voters — p. 323, §293.
Warrants — p. 324, §§294–297.
Women — Officers, Voters — p. 328, §§298–299.
Appendix — Synopses, School Laws of the Different States — pp. 331–399.
Teachers' Certificates — Effect in other States — pp. 400–404.
Index — pp. 405–411.

PREFACE.

In presenting a law book on the subject of Public Schools, I claim that this is one of the most important subjects that come under the supervision of courts, and is farther reaching than any other—covering in its scope, social, business, religious and official relations.

I have quoted largely on prominent subjects from the leading cases, and it has been a task of pleasure to prepare the volume for publication, knowing that while many decisions may appear conflicting, yet they are presented in such a manner that those who use this book can readily distinguish and apprehend the law applicable to the system in their State. I trust that Teachers, School Officers and the Bar will appreciate the effort to unravel and present in a tangible form the law of the land, taken from nearly 5,000 cases in the courts.

IRWIN TAYLOR.

CHICAGO, ILLINOIS.
1893.

PUBLIC SCHOOL LAW.

§ 1. **Appeals.**—Ordinarily an appeal does not lie, the sole purpose of which is to determine the validity of a claim against the district, and the right of appeal is confined to the party affected by the decision. It is generally an adequate remedy from the exercise of discretionary powers imposed on an officer, but often where the obligation on the officer is mandatory the courts of law give speedier relief by the writ of mandamus. "Where the right of appeal is given, and the record shows that this right was attempted to be exercised, that the appellate tribunal took jurisdiction of the matter, that the parties interested appeared before such tribunal, that no objection was made to its jurisdiction of the appeal, the regularity of the steps taken to perfect such appeal will, in any collateral inquiry, be presumed."[1] Under Ind. Law of 1855 an appeal would lie to the state superintendent from action of trustees on location of school-house;[2] and under law of 1861, if trustee refused to locate, appeal would be to examiner, and trustee would be compelled to locate site by mandamus.[3] In R. I. the school commissioner cannot reverse decision of school committee of town on location of site, but appeal is confined to redress of grievances violating rights,[4] and there is no appeal in a dispute between tax officers as to payments of moneys.[5] The decision of the supreme court judge on appeal from school commission-

[1] Bd. Ed. v. Campbell, 17 Kas. 541.
[2] State v. Custer, 11 Ind. 210.
[3] Trager v. State, 21 Ind. 317.
[4] Gardner's Appeal, 4 R. I. 602.
[5] Appeal of James, 5 R. I. 602.

(5)

ers is final,[1] and the jurisdiction on appeal is comprehensive in its character, and settles many controversies and disputes. In Md. the question decided on appeal is considered as *res adjvdicata*.[2] The remedy by appeal is one more suited to settle the questions there involved, and often gives more satisfactory, cheaper and speedier relief.[3] Under N. J. L. 28, all appeals must be to the county superintendent.[4] In Wis. the state superintendent has appellate power over the decision of town boards on division of districts, and he may make his own rules, requiring evidence to be in form of affidavits, and briefs to be filed without oral argument;[5] and when not required by statute, it is not always necessary that the board or officer hearing matters in dispute should require the witness to be sworn;[6] and in the delicate questions of teachers' fitness, it seems best sometimes that it is advisable not to pursue the same strictness required in court as to evidence.[7] The county superintendent in Ind. cannot compel the building of a school-house on a site when the land does not belong to a township,[8] and no appeal will lie to the superintendent from action of trustee making contracts or dismissing teacher in a city or town,[9] but appeals should exclusively relate to school matters, and in certain cases the decision of the superintendent is final;[10] and when the school law is doubtful, the opinions of the officials having power to pass on school questions is of great weight,[11] and the decisions of the state superintendent are entitled to great weight.[12] In fact, the decision by the tribunals having jurisdiction are always *prima facie* proper, and must be overthrown by the appellant.

[1] Smith's Appeal, 4 R. I. 590.
[2] Wiley v. Sch. Comm'rs, 51 Md. 401.
[3] Wiley v. Comm'rs, 51 Md. 406; Appeal of Cottrell, 10 R. I. 618.
[4] State v. Gloucester City, 45 N. J. L. 100.
[5] State v. Whitford, 54 Wis. 150.
[6] People v. Bd. Ed., 3 Hun (N. Y.), 177.
[7] People v. Bd. Ed., 3 Hun (N. Y.), 177.
[8] Koontz v. State, 44 Ind. 323; State v. McWhinney, 67 Ind. 397.
[9] Crawfordsville v. Hayes, 42 Ind. 206.
[10] Fogle v. Gregg, 26 Ind. 345.
[11] Appeal of Cottrell, 10 R. I. 615.
[12] State v. Burton, 45 Wis. 150.

§ 2. **Appeal.**—In N. Y. the county judge under the act of 1864 can only review cases arising under § 8, and cannot review refusal of a district to vote a tax to reimburse trustee for costs in endeavoring to recover a penalty imposed under § 14 of that act,[1] and the power of the board of education to hear appeals in removal of teacher by trustees is discretionary, and the supreme court cannot reinstate.[2] When teacher's certificate is annulled and he appeals to the state superintendent, his decision is final,[3] and under act of 1864 the manner of investigating the appeal is left to the discretion of the board of education.[4] In Mich. an appeal from the action of inspector to the town board on arrangement of districts, is a waiver of the questions requiring judicial review.[5] In Cal. certiorari was refused to review the action of board of education in adopting text-books, it being held that the adoption was legislative and not judicial.[6] On reviewing the decision of state superintendent on appeal, the proceedings by certiorari only go to the extent of ascertaining whether the officer having jurisdiction has acted according to the law; errors and irregularities will be corrected,[7] but the writ will not warrant reviewing questions of fact, where there is conflict of evidence or judgment on the merits.[8]

§ 3. **Appeal.**—It was held that where appeal was given, that precluded the right to apply for mandamus,[9] and an appeal respecting location of school-house does not give the president of a district power to employ counsel at the expense of the district; such an appeal is not a suit.[10] Where pupil is expelled, the party is not relegated to his right of appeal to county super-

---

[1] People v. Hatch, 60 Barb. (N. Y.), 298.
[2] People v. Bd. Ed., 3 Hun (N. Y.), 178.
[3] People v. Collins, 34 How. (N. Y.), 336; 11 Wend. 90.
[4] People v. Bd. Ed., 3 Hun (N. Y.), 177.
[5] Brody v. Tp. Bd., 32 Mich. 272.
[6] People v. Oakland Bd., 54 Cal. 375.
[7] Milwaukee Iron Co. v. Schubee, Clerk, 29 Wis. 444; Brody v. Tp. Bd., 32 Mich. 272.
[8] State v. Whitford, 54 Wis. 154.
[9] Marshall v. Sloan, 35 Iowa, 445.
[10] Templin v. Dist. Tp., 46 Iowa, 411.

intendent, but he may maintain action of mandamus,[1] and no pupil can be suspended except as a punishment for breach of discipline or an offense against good morals.[2] Where a teacher was wrongfully discharged for incompetency, it was held the remedy was appeal, and that he could not maintain an action on his contract.[3] The refusal of an annual meeting to act on a proposed change of boundary cannot stop an appeal,[4] and on appeal from change of boundary-line the commissioner must confine himself to the question whether the change proposed at said election shall be made.[5] In Mich. the approval of the appeal bond is essential to the appeal,[6] and the township board there will entertain appeal on apportionment of debts on division of a district.[7] On selection of site by trustees, one-third of the electors may appeal in Ky. to county superintendent, whose decision is final,[8] and his decision cannot be disturbed unless it is shown he acted on improper motives.[9] The removal of an assessor by the township board is reviewable on certiorari,[10] but its proceedings can only be reviewed in courts of law on questions of law,[11] and its action in removing a director is final unless speedily brought up for review.[12]

§ 4. **Appeal.**—It was held in *Knight v. Woods* (Ind. Sup.), 28 N. E. 306: "Under Rev. St. Ind. 1881, § 4537, providing that appeals shall be allowed from the decisions of the township trustees relative to school matters to the county superintendents, and their decision of all local questions relating to the establishment of schools and the location of school-houses, etc., shall be final, the decision of the county superintendent prohibiting the

---

[1] Clark v. Bd. Dir., 24 Iowa, 266; Smith v. Ind. Dist., 40 Iowa, 518; Dove v. Same, 41 Iowa, 689; Perkins v. Dirs., 56 Iowa, 476.
[2] Perkins v. Dirs., 56 Iowa, 476.
[3] Kirkpatrick v. Ind. Dist., 53 Iowa, 585.
[4] 85 Mo. 156.
[5] 85 Mo. 156; 89 Mo. 23; 94 Mo. 612.
[6] Clement v. Everest, 29 Mich. 19.
[7] Sch. Dist. v. Wilcox, 48 Mich. 404.
[8] Stiles v. Beall, 11 Ky. L. R. 486.
[9] Brinsmore v. Cottingham, 12 Ky. L. R. 720.
[10] Merrick v. Tp. Bd., 41 Mich. 630.
[11] Tp. Bd. v. Holiham, 46 Mich. 127.
[12] Geddes v. Tp., 46 Mich. 316.

erection of a school-house on a location selected by the trustee is within his jurisdiction, and is final and binding on the trustee; and it is immaterial whether the selection has been made by the trustee on his own motion, or by proceedings instituted by the voters. . . . It is immaterial at what time the superintendent's decision in such case is entered on his record."

"By § 4537, Rev. St. Ind. 1881, appeals lie in matters of this character from the decision of the township trustee to the county superintendent, and the decision of the superintendent is made final. In so far as the decision of the county superintendent related to the condemning and prohibiting the erection of the school-house on the site designated by the trustee, it was within his jurisdiction, and was valid and binding upon the trustee, and took from the trustee all authority to build a school-house on that site. The finding of facts shows that this decision was made upon the 29th day of October, 1889, and that the trustee had full knowledge of the decision when he let the contract to Williams; though it appears that such portion of the decision was not entered on the superintendent's record until after Nov. 5th. The decision was binding, though not entered until afterwards. (*Tufts v. State*, 119 Ind. 232.)

"It is contended by counsel for appellant that the duty of building and providing proper school-houses is enjoined on the trustee by § 4444, Rev. St. 1881; that it is exclusively within the discretion of the trustee, and cannot be affected by an appeal to the county superintendent; that the right of appeal lies only when proceedings are instituted by the voters of the school district, as provided by § 4499, Rev. St. 1881; and that in no event can the sound discretion of the trustee be controlled as declared in the proviso to § 4499, *supra*. The proviso appended to § 4499, *supra*, relates to the action taken by the voters in relation to repairs, removing or erecting school-houses, and costs thereof, and provides that the action taken by the voters shall not be conclusive, and prevent the trustee from exercising a sound discretion; while § 4537, *supra*, gives the right of appeal in such matters to the county superintendent, and makes his decision final. There is no inconsistency in these sections of the statute. The trustee first determines in regard to the location, building, or removing of school-houses, and from his decision there is an appeal to the county superintendent, and his decision is made final. The decision of the superintendent in this case went beyond his power in ordering the school-house erected on another site not owned by the township, and that portion of his decision is probably void; but that question is not involved in this case.

"It is further contended that the appeal was not taken from the trustee within the proper time, but it is not shown by the finding of facts the date when the trustee made his decision. No entry of it was made of record, and the voters of the district and patrons of the school were in no way notified of his having made it. He paid for the land Oct. 1st, and afterwards gave notice that he would let a contract for the building of a school-house. When those steps were taken, the appellees took immediate steps to preserve their rights. The trustee granted the appeal, and appeared and submitted the question to the county superintendent for decision, and by such decision he was bound. The judgment is affirmed, with costs."

§ 5. **Bonds.**—In an election, "the" omitted from the words "for the bonds" on the ballot does not invalidate the election,[1]

[1] State v. Metzger, 26 Kas. 395.

and mere irregularities will not invalidate.¹ A vote was required by a majority of all the inhabitants of a district entitled to vote; it was held that a vote in favor of bonds by a majority of those voting was sufficient, though this was less than half the voters at that meeting;² but it was held, where bonds may be voted for at special or at regular city election, and must have a majority of votes polled, if voted for at a regular city election all the votes cast at such election for any officer must be considered to determine the issue of the bonds;³ and where bonds were voted and sold, and proceeds used by district, on petition to compel the officers of the district to report the amount of debt, the court will not investigate the regularity of the election when the same was held in good faith by *bona fide* residents of the district.⁴ The successors of a school district, sued on a bond given by former district, are not estopped from making defense of non-incorporation of former and *ultra vires*.⁵ The right to recover on refunding bonds cannot be defeated because a part of the proceeds of their sale was misapplied;⁶ but where a board issued to one of its members a bond for an unauthorized purpose, a person who received the bond from the payee, knowing that he was a member, could not recover on the bond;⁷ but bonds issued under a law for a proper purpose are valid in the hands of innocent holders for value, notwithstanding the uses for which they were intended have been prevented.⁸ No authority is given school directors to issue bonds and place them on the market for anything less than their par value. If they

---

¹ State v. Ellwood, 12 Wis. 552; State v. Cavers, 22 Iowa, 343; Cattell v. Lowry, 45 Iowa, 478; Clark v. Robinson, 88 Ill. 498; Kirk v. Rhoads, 46 Cal. 398.
² Smith v. Proctor, N. Y. App., 29 N. E. 312; 6 N. Y. S. 212.
³ State v. Benton (Neb.) 45 N. W. 794.
⁴ State v. Adams Co. Sch. Dist., 13 Neb. 82.
⁵ Dartmouth etc. v. Sch. Dist., 6 Dak. 255.
⁶ Cummins v. Dist. Tp., 42 F. 644.
⁷ Hewitt v. Norm. Sch. Dist. Bd. etc., 94 Ill. 528.
⁸ Sherlock v. Village Winnetka, 68 Ill. 531.

do, they are liable in Ill. for any loss the school fund may sustain.[1]

§ 6. **Bonds.**—Ill. Rev. St. 1874, p. 47, conferring upon school directors the power to give bonds for money borrowed, enlarges the power they would otherwise have in connection with the power to borrow money.[2] The right of the secretary of state and auditor of public accounts, in La., to claim possession of the assets of the free-school fund, is not affected by the prescription of three years.[3] Payment of interest does not estop district from repudiating where it is not shown that the district officers and people had knowledge.[4] In action against directors in Ill., on a note, it must be alleged that the indebtedness was incurred for a purpose authorized by statute.[5] The Neb. statute that the submission of bonds to vote must also include a proposition to levy tax to pay interest on same, does not apply to act of March 31, 1887.[6] Bonds issued under a vote not authorized by law are not valid even when held by innocent purchaser,[7] but authority to issue a certain amount does not invalidate the issue of a lesser amount or levy of tax at lesser rate.[8]

§ 7. **Bonds.**—In an action against a district on refunding bonds, the burden is on defendant to show that at the date of the original issuance the outstanding indebtedness of the district exceeded its constitutional limitation,[9] but the refunding of an outstanding valid bonded indebtedness is not the creation of a debt, within the inhibition of Const. Iowa, art. 11, p. 3, providing that "no county shall be indebted in any manner exceeding

---

[1] Adams v. State, 82 Ill. 132.
[2] Folsom v. Sch. Dirs., 91 Ill. 402.
[3] Sun. M. Co. v. Bd. of Liquidation, 31 La. An. 175.
[4] Ashuelot Bk. v. Sch. Dist., 41 F. 514.
[5] Sch. Dist. v. Sippy, 54 Ill. 287.
[6] State v. Benton (Neb.) 45 N. W. 794.
[7] Ashuelot Bk. v. Sch. Dist., 41 F. 514.
[8] Rogers v. Trs., (Ky.) 13 S. W. 587.
[9] Cummins v. Dist. Tp., 42 F. 644.

five per centum on the value of the taxable property."[1] An act authorizing trustees of district to hold an election, subscribe stock, and issue bonds in aid of a railroad, is unconstitutional,[2] and the act which abolished the free-school fund, and ordered the bonds composing that fund to be sold, is unconstitutional, and no title is acquired at a sale made under said act.[3] In Kas. a school district irregularly created and organized may issue bonds that will be binding on that territory,[4] so a school district *de facto*, but not *de jure*, may issue bonds; its acts bind itself, third persons, and its successor,[4] and power to borrow money implies power to issue bonds therefor under Neb. statutes.[5]

§ 8. **Bonds.**—Under 1st Ind. Rev. St. 1876, p. 343, where trustees of incorporated town have filed a verified report showing contract to purchase land on which to erect building, and showing amount of debt and cost of building, and asking the issuance of bonds, the board may authorize sale of the city bonds not exceeding limit specified in the first section of the act;[6] but where bonds were issued to purchase a site and erect a building, and the bonds recited on their face that they were issued in exchange for a school-house and site, it was held that the issue of bonds for that purpose was not authorized by statute, and that they were not valid.[7] The official certificate of call for bond election to purchase a site and build a school-house, and of the posting of notices, and result and issuance of the bonds purporting to be by officers of the district, and of the election and registration of the bonds, are evidence of corporate existence of the school district.[8] The selection of an ineligible site, or the fact that a former election had resulted against their

---

[1] Cummins v. Dist. Tp., 42 F. 644.
[2] Trustees of School v. People, 63 Ill. 299.
[3] State v. Bd. of Liquidators, 29 La. An. 77.
[4] Sch. Dist. v. State, 29 Kas. 57.
[5] State v. Adams Co. Sch. Dist., 13 Neb. 78.
[6] Williams v. Albion, 58 Ind. 329.
[7] State v. Sch. Dist., 16 Neb. 182; State v. Bd. Co. Com'rs, (Neb.) 48 N. W. 146.
[8] State v. Sch. Dist., (Neb.) 33 N. W. 266.

issue, does not invalidate the issue of bonds at a later election.[1] The St. Joseph (Mo.) board of public schools had power to issue bonds in 1868 and 1871 to build school-houses, and to refund same.[2] The leasing of a public school building for private school unauthorized by law, will not render the building bonds invalid.[3] Boards of education in cities of first class under law of 1879, in Kas., had no authority to issue bonds to raise funds to purchase a school-site, or to erect buildings.[4]

§ 9. **Bonds.**—In the case of *Gibbs v. Sch. D.* (Mich.), 50 N. W. 294, it was decided: "Under How. St. Mich., §§ 5104, 5105, which authorize the school-district board to issue bonds only in specified instances and on a vote of the school district, the question whether the proceedings to vote bonds are such as will authorize the board to issue them is one of fact, to be determined by the board, and hence a recital in a bond, signed by two of the three members of the board, that the bond is issued pursuant to a vote of the qualified electors at a special school meeting, held at a designated date and place in accordance with law, is sufficient evidence of the legality of the issue to protect a *bona fide* purchaser, though the records of the board do not show its authority to issue the bond.

"Purchasers of municipal bonds are bound to know the extent and limitations upon the authority of the corporation to issue the bonds. They are bound, in other words, to know the law under which the authority is exercised. Purchasers of such securities have a right to rely upon all facts asserted or appearing upon the face of the bonds, made by any person or body authorized by law to pass upon and determine the facts. In purchasing this bond the purchaser was bound to know that

---

[1] Taylor v. Brownfield, 41 Iowa, 264.
[2] St. Joseph Sch. Bd. v. Gaylord, 86 Mo. 401.
[3] Sherlock v. Winnetka, 68 Ill. 530.
[4] Bd. Ed. v. State, 26 Kas. 44.

school districts have no authority to issue bonds except for the purposes specified in the statute, and that their authority is limited by the number of scholars between five and twenty years then residing in the district; that there must be a two-thirds vote of the qualified electors in favor of their issue. The purchaser is chargeable with knowledge of the prerequisites of a legal special meeting, and of the provisions for a board of inspectors, and their duties, and of the requirement that the vote shall be by ballot. The recitals in this bond are made by the director and moderator, who compose a majority of the school board. Neither the school board nor the moderator and director are authorized to issue the bonds unless voted by the district at a lawful meeting; and under § 5104, before the board can act they have a function to perform, in its nature somewhat judicial, and that is as to their own authority to issue the bonds. The statute limits that authority to bonds voted by the school district, and consequently the question whether the proceedings to vote such bonds are such as will authorize the board to issue them must be passed upon by the board. A purchaser of the bonds, therefore, need look no farther back than the face of the bonds for the facts which show a compliance with the law. We think the assertion appearing upon the face of the bond is sufficient evidence to an innocent purchaser that the board ordered and directed the bond to be issued. The officers signing the bond are two of the three officers who constitute the board, and the director is the officer whom the statute requires should make a record of the proceedings of all district meetings, and the orders, resolutions and other proceedings of the board. It matters not, therefore, that the records kept by the board do not show the order of the board to execute the bonds. The title of a *bona fide* holder of the bond cannot be defeated by a neglect to enter the order in cases where the face of the bond upon which he has a right to rely recites the fact that such order was made.

"This case is not controlled by *Spitzger v. Village of Blanchard*, 82 Mich. 234. In that case there was a limitation upon the authority to borrow money in excess of a certain percentage upon the taxable property. In that case the law did not designate any body or board to pass upon the facts, and only permitted the bonds to be issued for 'loans lawfully made.' The bonds could only be issued upon the vote of the electors, and the bonds did not recite that such a vote was taken. In that case we said that 'where there is a total want of power, under the law, in the officers or board who issue the bonds, the bonds will be void in the hands of innocent holders, the distinction being between questions of fact and questions of law. If it is a question of fact, and the board or officers are authorized by law to determine the fact, then their determination is final and conclusive; and although it may be contrary to the fact, yet if recited in the bond that the necessary and proper steps required by law to be taken had been taken, then the municipality is estopped from denying that they were taken.'"

§ 10. **Building contract.**—Where a school district votes to purchase a building for a school-house, and raises funds, and a committee of the district make a bargain in behalf of the district for the purchase of the building at an agreed price, if the district afterwards uses the building for a school-house, in an action by the owner to recover the price the defendant cannot deny the authority of the committee, and is bound, in the absence of fraud or mistake, to pay the price agreed on by the committee, although they acted in making the purchase without any legal antecedent authority.¹ Where a school district contracted with a builder to erect a school-house for a certain sum, with liberty to build a public hall over the same, as the builder's property, the district to have the use of the hall free of charge, for meetings and for examinations of the schools, etc., and the house was so built, the district did not exceed its authority, and a tax therefor was legal.² Where a tax was raised to build a school-house, and a committee was appointed for this purpose, but, owing to some difficulty as to the land for the site the committee did not proceed, and a second meeting was called to take the whole matter into consideration, and the district was unable to elect a committee, but requested the selectmen to proceed and build the house, this was construed as neglect and refusal on the part of the district to give the selectmen jurisdiction.³

§ 11. **Building contract.**—A district authorized its school board to build a school-house, and to expend not to exceed $5,000 in building, and to procure plans for the house, which were to be presented at the next meeting. At that meeting plans were not accepted, but an architect was empowered to make other plans and specifications for a certain size building, and to have them ready at the next meeting. At that meeting no plans or specifications were presented, or adopted by the district, but the meeting appointed the school board a committee to carry out the previous vote of the district to build a school-house, and with power to act fully in the matter, limiting the board to a certain size for the building and the amount to be expended; the power thus conferred on the school board was full and complete, limited only as to size of school-house and

¹ Keyser v. Sch. Dist., 35 N. H. 477.
² George v. Meudon, 6 Metc., (Mass.) 497.

³ Blake v. Sturtevant, 12 N. H. 567.

the amount of money to be expended, and their acts were legal and binding.¹ The school board let the contract for building accordingly, and as the work progressed certain changes were necessary in order to make the building symmetrical and strong, which changes were made by order of the board, causing an additional outlay. Held, that so long as the changes were beneficial and necessary, and the additional cost, added to the original contract, did not exceed the amount limited to be expended, the board had the power to make them, and its acts are binding.¹ A committee with power to lease, executed a lease to A for five years; another committee, same year, subsequently executed a lease for the building to B for four years, which lease B accepted and had recorded; in an action by A against B, under Conn. Stat., title 56, ch. 1, § 12, against selling pretended titles, it was held that the first committee had authority to make the lease to A, and that A was rightfully in possession under it; but that as he was tenant of the society, claiming under it, the society were not ousted of their possession, and consequently B had not incurred the forfeiture of the statute.² The board of directors of a district township, having power to make contracts for the erection of school-houses in the sub-districts, may ratify a contract of this character,³ but where vote to raise money to build is absolutely void for want of power, no claim will lie against district, and cannot be made by ratification.⁴ The board of public schools in St. Louis, in contracting for building may take a bond from contractor to protect material and labor, and may sue in their behalf on said bond;⁵ and in Iowa, contract for building school-houses must be let to lowest bidder, who must give bond;⁶ and under Ohio Rev. Stat., § 3988, board of

---

¹ Edinburg Am. L. & M. Co. v. City of Mitchell, S. D., 48 N. W. 131.
² Emerson v. Goodwin, 9 Conn. 422.
³ Stevenson v. Tp. of Summit, 35 Iowa, 462.
⁴ Brown v. Sch. Dist., (N. H.) 10 A. 119.
⁵ St. Louis Sch. Bd. v. Woods, 77 Mo. 197.
⁶ Weitz v. Ind. Dist. of Des Moines, Iowa, 44 N. W. 696.

education can accept only the lowest responsible bid for improvement or repairs,[1] and a contract for building at larger cost than authorized is void.[2]

§ 12. **Building contract.**—In Ind. the school trustees cannot bind a township without an order from county commissioners, for erection of a school-house, when the debt of a township already exceeds the money in hands of trustees and that to be raised by taxes for the next year;[3] but Mich. Comp. Law, § 3618, in providing that the township school director shall keep the necessary school-house furniture in proper order, and that his expenses shall be subsequently audited and paid, does not intend that money must be put into his hands beforehand.[4] A provision in a building contract that a board may retain in their hands a certain fund to meet the demands of material-men is valid,[5] and equity will treat the transaction as an assignment of the fund, to the exclusion of any other creditors of the original contractor.[5] Contracts should be made with reference to the funds in the treasury for that purpose, and the district board has no authority to draw orders on a fund which has been proposed, but not raised by taxation.[6]

§ 13. **Building contract.**—A school district having voted a certain sum toward purchasing land and erecting a school-house, it is no defense to an action against them on a contract with their committee, that the committee expended a larger sum than that named in the vote, nor that the school-house was worth no more than that sum;[7] and where the district voted to build a school-house, and located it, and chose a committee to superintend the building thereof, and the committee employed

---

[1] State v. Bd. Ed., 42 Ohio St. 374.
[2] App. Luburg, 23 W. N. C. 454, Pa; 17 A. 245.
[3] Middletown v. Greeson, 106 Ind. 18; Roseboom v. Jeff. Sch. Tp., 122 Ind. 377.
[4] Hantranck v. Holikan, 46 Mich. 127.
[5] Luthy v. Woods, 6 Mo. App. 67.
[6] Sch. Dist. v. Stough, 4 Neb. 357.
[7] Junkins v. Union Sch. Dist., 39 Me. 220.

the plaintiffs to build the house, and they built it where the committee directed, but not where the district had voted to locate it, and on land owned by the district, the plaintiffs acting in good faith under the direction of the committee, the district was held liable.[1] In a suit on a building contract against trustees, where there was no allegation that they were trustees and had contracted as such, or were so authorized, a recovery could not be had.[2] Where a school-house was used to keep all the schools of the district, without objection from anyone, and the district at its annual meeting, after the house was built, voted to sell the old house to help pay for the new one, and also voted to raise money to pay for the house and land, the evidence was competent to show a ratification of what had been done by the plaintiff and an acceptance of the house by the district, notwithstanding an informality in the notice of the meeting.[3]

§ 14. **Building contract.**—The inhabitants cannot empower a building committee to advertise or make a contract for building a school-house, or do any other act binding upon the trustees, without their assent.[4] In Ind. the township trustees may levy a tax to build school-houses; and their contracts for building such houses are binding on the township.[5] Where a district erected a school-house with a hall on the second floor, on a petition praying for an injunction against the collection of tax for same, on the ground that such expenditure was illegal, the court found that the house, with the exception of the hall, was not more than the convenience of the district required for school purposes; it was held, that aside from any question as to the propriety of erecting said hall, the proceedings of the

---

[1] Baker v. Sch. Dist. No. 2, 46 Vt. 189; Norris v. Sch. Dist., 12 Me. 293.
[2] Shuler v. Meyers, 5 Lans. N. Y. 170.
[3] Chapin v. Sch. Dist. No. 2 in Walpole, 30 N. H. (10 Fost.) 25.
[4] People v. Banfield, 6 How. (N. Y.) Pr. 437.
[5] Heal v. Jefferson, 15 Ind. 431; Rose v. Bath, 10 Ind. 18.

district were not illegal;[1] and where the expense of such hall was about one-fifth of that of the whole building, and it would be useful and convenient for holding district meetings and exhibitions, these were legitimate objects; and the vote authorizing the building of such school-house was not void, because it specified, among other uses of the hall, that of holding school society meetings and lectures therein.[1]

§ 15. **Building contract.**—The board of directors of district have no power to employ one of their number to oversee the completion of a school-house abandoned by the contractor, nor can he recover from the district for services so rendered.[2] Under the Iowa law which empowers the electors to vote a tax "for the payment of any debts contracted for the erection of school-house, and for procuring district libraries," etc., they cannot be incurred by the directors before a tax has been voted upon.[3] A warrant in W. Va. against sheriff for material and labor furnished for school-house is a novation, and after acceptance an action of assumpsit will not lie against board, but holder must sue sheriff.[4] Where board of education does not take bond required from contractor for building school-house, the board will be liable for labor and material, but the payments thereon will be a set-off in action by contractor on the contract.[5] Where land is held by city in trust for public school, the board of education may build thereon, (the law of Neb. forbidding building of brick or stone school-house without at first obtaining title in fee.)[6] In Ill. the board of education cannot contract to build school-house without petition of majority of voters of district.[7]

[1] Sheldon v. Centre Sch. Dist., 25 Conn. 224.
[2] Moore v. Toledo City Dist., 55 Iowa, 654; Weitz v. Ind. Dist. Iowa, 42 N. W. 577.
[3] Manning v. Van Buren, 28 Iowa, 332.
[4] Canby v. Sleepy Creek D. B., 19 W. Va. 93.
[5] Wells v. Bd. Ed., (Mich.) 44 N. W. 267.
[6] State v. Benton, (Neb.) 45 N. W. 794.
[7] Bd. Ed. v. Roehr, 23 Ill. App. 629.

(They may now on petition of 500 voters, or one-fifth the voters.) In assumpsit to recover pay for building a school-house and finding materials therefor, the district cannot object to the absence of proof of a legal meeting to determine upon the building and the raising of the money therefor, unless they have raised such objection by their specifications of defense,[1] and a contract for school-house building not authorized by vote required by statute is void; but the district cannot recover money advanced to the contractor.[2]

§ 16. **Building contract.**—Where at a meeting it was voted to build a school-house, and the committee was directed to make a contract proposed, and the meeting adjourned to a certain day, and before that day another meeting was legally called, and the district voted at that time to build on a plan proposed by another party, the second meeting rescinded the first;[3] and where the meeting notice was not legal, and a committee was chosen who superintended the erection of a school-house, it did not thereby bind the district.[4] A contract to build a school-house for an amount in excess of funds on hand, or subject to collection for that purpose, and the amount that could be realized by the maximum tax which could be levied by the inhabitants for the current year and used for that purpose, is void, and could not be ratified.[5]

§ 17. **Building contract.**—Where one contracts to build a school-house in a particular manner, to the acceptance of a district, and erects one thereon which is not built according to the contract, and the committee do not unreasonably refuse to accept it, and there is no acceptance, he cannot recover;[6] nor because defects were waived, unless the subsequent work is done

---

[1] Collins v. School Dist., 52 Me. 522.
[2] Fluty v. Sch. Dist., 49 Ark. 94.
[3] George v. Mendon, 6 Metc., (Mass.) 497.
[4] Jordon v. Dist., 38 Me. 164.
[5] Cap. Bk. v. School Dist., (N. D.) 48 N.W. 363.
[6] Hill v. Sch. Dist. No. 2, 17 Me. 316.

conformably to the contract, or accepted.[1] Boards of school commissioners in cities of more than 30,000 inhabitants, under Ind. Rev. Stat., § 4460, may contract for building school-house and give its notes for deferred payments.[2] Where contract is required to be let by township board to lowest responsible bidder, this power cannot be delegated to sub-district officers.[3]

§ 18. Under Vt. Gen. Stat., ch. 22, § 43, it is within the province of a school district to build a hall in connection with a school-house, designed to accommodate the school and the inhabitants of the district for the purpose of examinations and exhibitions, and such other things as are proper and customary in connection with district schools.[4] Mandamus lies to compel trustees to erect a school-house, according to the superintendent's decision in Ind.;[5] (but see § 1, *ante*.) No power is given in Wis. R. S., § 434, to the district board to build a school-house and then afterward impose the cost on the district, and Laws 1883, ch. 116, do not imply a ratification.[6] The normal-school authorities, having accepted the buildings erected by plaintiff and leased to them, which buildings were erected in pursuance of the authority granted by vote of the citizens, cannot retain the buildings and repudiate the conditions attached to the grant;[7] and the plaintiffs' recovery is not defeated because their contract was with a committee styled the "building committee of the district," instead of a "committee to superintend the laying out and expending of the moneys raised by the district," such a committee being the only one authorized by Laws 1850, art. 2, ch. 193, § 9, Me.[8] A sub-contractor can recover, in a suit against

[1] Hill v. Sch. Dist. No. 2, 17 Me. 316.
[2] Fatout v. Indianapolis S. C., 102 Ind. 223.
[3] Stock Bd. &c. v. Mills, 38 Ohio, 383.
[4] Greenbanks v. Boutwell, 43 Vt. 207.
[5] State v. Custer, 11 Ind. 210.
[6] Nevil v. Clifford, 63 Wis. 435.
[7] City Emporia v. Partch, 21 Kas. 206.
[8] Collins v. Sch. Dist., 52 Me. 522.

the district and the principal contractor, only an indebtedness of the contractor to him to the amount due such contractor from the district.[1]

§ 19. **Building contract.**—Under act of 1853, since repealed by act of 1857, a school-house erected in a sub-district formed from two townships was to be paid for solely by the part of the sub-district included in the township in which it is erected.[2] The Ohio statute authorizes the committee to assess "such portion" of the cost as they deem just upon the sub-district, and under that they may assess the whole upon the sub-district, and their certificate to the auditor need only state the amount, and not their reasons therefor.[3] The school board has no power to contract for work upon a school-house, unless authorized by voters of the district, under Neb. Gen. Stat., 966, §§ 29, 30.[3] A district at special meeting can vote to raise money to build school-house, notwithstanding a previous failure of such vote the same year.[4] Under N. J. Law, a majority vote of those present at a meeting is binding, except in regard to condemning land.[4] In Ga. a purchase of an interest in a building for public school purposes, where it is not kept up for private gain, is not illegal.[5] By the Ill. act of 1857, a tax to erect school-houses must be voted by the people.[6] Resolution to raise a single sum for building and furnishing a school-house is not bad for uncertainty because the amounts are not separately stated.[7] An order of a board of Ind. township trustees, signed by the clerk and president, on the treasurer, for the building of a school-house, was a valid demand, upon which an action might be maintained.[8]

[1] Radeunz v. Sch. Dist., 42 Wis. 397.
[2] Bryant v. Goodman, 9 Ohio St. 471.
[3] Gehling v. Sch. Dist., 10 Neb. 239.
[4] State v. Clark, (N. J.) 19 A. 462.
[5] Danully v. Cabaniss, 52 Ga. 211.
[6] Beverly v. Labin, 20 Ill. 357.
[7] State v. Clark, (N. J.) 19 A. 462.
[8] Heal v. Jefferson, 15 Ind. 431.

§ 20. **Building contract.**—It was held in *Capital Bank of St. Paul v. School Dist. No. 53 of Barnes County*, 48 N. W. Rep. 363 (N. D.)—opinion by Corliss, C. J.:

"A contract authorized by the inhabitants of a school district at a district meeting, to build a school-house for an amount in excess of funds on hand or subject to collection for that purpose and the amount that could be realized from the maximum tax which could be levied by the inhabitants for the current year and used for that purpose, is void. Therefore, held, that such a contract, void because the district board had no authority to make it, could not be made binding upon the district by subsequent ratification by the inhabitants. Whether there was sufficient evidence of such ratification, not decided.

"Such contract being impliedly prohibited by statute, the receipt by the district of the fruits thereof creates no liability either under the contract or for the value received.

"A warrant creates no greater liability than the debt it represents, whether in the hands of the original party or of a purchaser before maturity and for value. . . .

"That the action of the district board in making the contract to construct the building was wholly unauthorized and void, cannot well be disputed. (See *Farmers &c. Bank v. School Dist. No. 53*, [Dak.] 42 N. W. Rep. 767.) The power to designate a site and to authorize the building of a school-house is vested exclusively in the inhabitants. But it is urged that, although not originally binding upon the district, the contract has been ratified by the conduct of the inhabitants since the erection of the school-house and the issuing of the warrants representing the alleged contract price therefor. While we do not wish to be considered as assenting to this view of the evidence, we will assume, for the purpose of this opinion, that there was sufficient evidence of ratification to submit to the jury: still we think the court would have been justified in rendering judgment for defendant. Nay, we hold it would have been the duty of the court to give such judgment. Ratification is equivalent only to original authority, and we are of the opinion that the inhabitants, under the statute, had no authority to direct the building of a school-house whose cost would exceed the funds provided for that purpose. We hold that this contract was void, not only for want of power in the district to make it, but because prohibited by the spirit and necessary implication of the statute.

. . . .

"Our views find support in the decision of the territorial supreme court in *Farmers' &c. Bank v. School Dist. No. 53*, (Dak.) 42 N. W. Rep. 767. We find nothing in *Capital Bank v. School Dist. No. 85*, id. 774, decided by the same court at the same term, at war with the other decision. It is true that in the first case the court, while favoring the construction we adopt, limited the scope of its decision to the denial of the right to create a present indebtedness by the issue of warrants, payable immediately, in excess of the amount of tax that could be levied during the year the debt was contracted. This is the doctrine of Minn. under a similar statute, but we cannot give it our assent. . . .

"The language of the supreme court of Wis., in *Kane v. School District No. 3*, 52 Wis. 502, meets our full approval: 'We entertain very grave doubts whether the board and the voters of the district combined can make a contract payable out of funds not intended to be voted or raised by taxation during the current year, except by taking such proceedings in the particular cases authorized as are necessary, under the statute, to make a loan in behalf of the district. If they can, then it would be wholly unnecessary to make any loans on behalf of a district, and the district might during any current year incur such an amount of indebtedness, to be charged upon the funds of succeeding years, as to absorb all the taxes which could be lawfully collected in such years, and leave the district wholly without resources, except by a repetition of the same system of mortgaging the future for the necessities of the present. Either this result would follow, or, if such liabilities were held to be debts lawfully incurred by the district, then the tax-payers of the district could be compelled to raise the necessary amount to pay the same at the time agreed upon for their payment, notwithstanding such sum might exceed the limit fixed by the statutes for raising money by taxation for the purposes for which the debt was incurred. It seems to be the policy of the laws of this state to restrict the expenditures of the towns, cities, counties, and school districts within certain specified limits; and in the case of school districts it has put a very effectual restraint upon such expenditures by fixing a limit to the amount which can be lawfully collected from the tax-payers of the district for school purposes in any one year. To give proper force to these legislative restrictions, it would seem necessary to restrain the districts, as well as their officers, from contracting debts drawing interest which can become a lawful charge upon the future resources thereof.'"

§ 21. **Building contract.**—In the case of *Sullivan v. School District*, 39 Kas. 347, it was decided: "A contract for building a school-house, void because made by only one member of the school board, may afterward be ratified and made binding upon the school district by the full school board, or by the school district. The evidence in the present case tended to prove such a contract and such a ratification. Held, sufficient when attacked by a demurrer to the evidence. . . .

"It is admitted that the original contract with Eley was at the time it was made void, for the reason that it was not made by the entire school board, but only by a portion thereof. (*Aikman v. Sch. Dist.*, 27 Kas. 129; *Mincer v. Sch. Dist.*, 27 id. 253.) But it is claimed by the plaintiffs that the evidence introduced in the court below tended to show a ratification of the contract by the entire school board, and also by the entire school district. We think such a contract might be ratified and might be made binding upon the school district. (*Fisher v. Sch. Dist.*, 4 Cush. 494; *Keyser v. Sch. Dist.*, 35 N. H. 477; *Kimball v. Sch. Dist.*, 28 Vt. [2 Williams] 8; *Jordan v. Sch. Dist.*, 38 Me. 164; *Cory v. Somerset*, 45 N. J. Law, 445; *National Bank v. Albany*, 92 N. Y. 363; same case, 2 Am. & Eng. Corp. Cases, 61; *Read v. Plattsmouth*, 107 U. S. 568; *Corwin v. Wallace*, 17 Iowa, 374; *Humphrey v. Mercantile Association*, 50 id. 607; *Cook v. Tullis*, 18 Wall. 332; *City of Conyers v. Kirk*, [Ga.] 3 S. E. Rep. 442; *Sherman v. Fitch*, 98 Mass. 59; *Pinches v. Lutheran Church*, 55 Conn. 183; *Brown v. City of Atchison*, 39 Kas. 37, and the numerous cases there cited. See also *Walworth County Bank v. Farmers' Loan and Trust Co.*, 16 Wis. 629; *Supervisors v. Schenck*, 5 Wall. 77.)"

§ 22. **Building control.**—Under Gen. Stat. Ky., pp. 1155, 1167, § 7, arts. 6, 8, providing that it shall be the duty of the county superintendent to condemn dilapidated school buildings, and of the trustees, when notified by the superintendent of the condemnation, to repair the old building or erect a new one, the superintendent and the trustees are the judges of the necessity for a new building, and their action cannot be questioned by the tax-payers of the district;[1] and where a town is incorporated within the limits of a school township, a school-house situated within the limits of a town passes under the control of the school trustees of the town.[2] Under laws of Ind., state school property is held in trust for school purposes by the persons or corporations authorized for the time being to control the same, and it is within the power of the legislature at any time to change the trustee.[3] The inhabitants of school district having the power of determining the kind of houses requisite for their use and the amount necessary to defray the expenses, courts ought not to interfere, except in cases where it has been manifestly abused.[3] Injunction, and not mandamus, is the proper remedy to restrain the erection of a school-house, against parties claiming right to control the same.[4] The city is entitled to possession of normal-school building, where the rent is unpaid, built by bonds and rented to pay interest on the bonds.[5] In Ga., where the mayor and council of a city had power to levy tax for and control school, and a school was built by subscription, an injunction was granted, preventing the teacher retained by citizens from interfering or taking possession of building.[6]

§ 23. **Building control.**—Rev. Stat., ch. 11, § 22, Me., empowers school districts to sell and dispose of any school-house or other property, if necessary, and the school district is the judge of this necessity;[7] and before school districts were specially authorized to do so by statute, they might make sale of

[1] Trustees Sch. Dist. v. Jamison, (Ky.) 15 S. W. 1.
[2] Carson v. State, 27 Ind. 465.
[3] Sheldon v. Centre Sch. Dist., 25 Conn. 224.
[4] State v. Custer, 11 Ind. 210.
[5] City Emporia v. Partch, 21 Kas. 202.
[6] Pattison v. City of Butler, 83 Ga. 006.
[7] Sch. Dist. No. 6 v. Ætna Ins. Co., 54 Me. 505.

their old school-houses which had become unfit for the use of the district.[1] By statute Wis. (Laws 1863, ch. 155, § 48) the district board of school directors has the care of a school-house belonging to the district, and must be deemed to have authority to bring a suit for an injury to the school-house, without any direction from the electors;[2] and among the powers conferred on school trustees is that of taking care of the district property, and for that purpose they may maintain suits at law.[3] A complaint against a township for money for building a school-house should be against the school township, and not against the civil township.[4]

§ 24. **Building repairs and appendages.**—A school district is bound for repairs furnished for the school-house, notwithstanding the sum voted for specified repairs at the annual meeting had been expended,[5] and where a town voted to raise money for repairs of a school-house, which, in their opinion, the district unreasonably neglects to make, it would not be affected by the fact that the selectmen had unlawfully removed the house from the lot, or that the tax had been illegally collected.[6] But a district cannot be considered as promising to pay for unauthorized repairs upon school-house by using it afterwards,[7] and a vote of a school district to authorize laying out a certain sum for repairing the school-house, "does not authorize expending a greater sum, although it might require more to put the house in good repair."[7] In Iowa, contracts for "repairs" are under the control of the board of directors of the district township, and are payable out of the "contingent fund" (Laws 1862, ch. 172, § 44), and no vote of the electors of a sub-

[1] Whitmore v. Hogan, 22 Me. 564.
[2] Sch. Dist. No. 8 v. Arnold, 21 Wis. 657.
[3] Rapelye v. Van Sickler, 1 Edm. (N. Y.) Sel. Cas. 175.
[4] Carmichael v. Lawrence, 47 Ind. 554.
[5] Conklin v. Sch. Dist., 22 Kas. 521.
[6] Knowles v. Sch. Dist., 63 Me. 201.
[7] Davis v. Sch. Dist., 24 Me. 349.

district is necessary.[1] A committee appointed by the school district according to statute, to purchase and repair a school-house, are public officers, and a majority may act for the whole.[2] To recover for erecting necessary out-buildings for a school-house, a contract made by the board in regular session need not be shown, where the buildings were erected and used with the knowledge of directors.[3] In R. I., the power to insure the school-house and its appendages is vested in the district, and not in the trustee; but a legal vote of the district to raise money to pay the premium, would be a ratification.[4] It was competent for board school commissioners of the city of Baltimore to contract for heating apparatus, without a previous ordinance prescribing the formalities and the agencies by which such contract could be made,[5] and a contract for school-district out-house by trustee is authorized in N. Y. (Laws 1887.)[6] A well is necessary appendage to school-house,[7] and a line fence around the school-house is a necessary appendage,[8] and an inhabitant of a school district cannot, at his own pleasure, remove a fence erected by the trustees against their remonstrance.[9] A director may purchase new seats under a resolution adopted at annual meeting directing that the school board fix the school-house ready for the winter term.[10] In Ky., where trustees are notified by superintendent that a better house is required, and that the old one has been condemned, it is not necessary that they see the order of condemnation before taking action;[11] but a prudential committee cannot recover from the district the money expended for slight occasional repairs; such repairs

[1] Williams v. Peinny, 25 Iowa, 436.
[2] Keyser v. Sch. Dist., 35 N. H. 477.
[3] Bellows v. West F. D. T., 70 Iowa, 320.
[4] Holt's Appeal, 5 R. I. 603.
[5] Baltimore v. Weatherby, 52 Md. 442.
[6] Rauscher v. Cronk, (N. Y.) 3 N. Y. S. 470.
[7] Herne v. Sch. Dist., 30 Kas. 377.
[8] Creager v. Sch. Dist., 62 Mich. 101.
[9] Rapelye v. Van Sickler, 1 Edm. (N. Y.) Sel. Cas. 175.
[10] McLaren v. Town Bd., 48 Mich. 189.
[11] Trustees Sch. Dist. v. Jamison, (Ky.) 15 S. W. 1.

are to be made from the school-money assigned to the district.[1]

§ 25. **Building repairs.**—It was held in *School District of the City of Erie v. Fuess*, 98 Penn. St. 600: "A school district employed a contractor to repair and improve a school-house, under the direction of the architect of the improvements, who was employed by the district, as to the manner of executing the work. The contractor was not to begin work until vacation. By permission of the architect he began it before, and he negligently injured one of the pupils in the execution of it. Two of the school board visited the building after the work was begun, but did not order it stopped. In an action by the injured pupil against the district, held, (1) that the district was not liable for the contractor's negligence; (2) that the permission of the architect, being outside his authority, did not bind the district; (3) that the knowledge and inaction of the two members of the board did not render the district liable. . . .

"If the school district is to be treated strictly as a municipal corporation, the authorities settle that the employment of Shenk did not operate as a relief to the contractor, nor did it make the district liable as a master or principal for Hendry's trespass or carelessness. But school districts are corporations of lower grade and less power than a city, have less the characteristics of private corporations, and more of a mere agent of the state. They are territorial divisions for the purpose of the common-school laws, and their officers have no powers except by express statutory grant and necessary implication; and these are for the establishment and maintenance of the public schools. The common-school system partakes much of the nature of a public

[1] Giles v. Sch. Dist. No. 14 in Sanbornton, 31 N. H. (11 Fost.) 304.

charity, extends over the whole state, is sustained by the public moneys, and the directors, who devote much time and labor for the public benefit, receive no compensation for their services. Unless exempted by the act of incorporation or by law, a private corporation is liable for the wrongful acts and neglects of its officers done in the course and within the scope of their employment, the same as a natural person is for the acts and neglects of his servant or agent. A less stringent rule applies to public corporations, and least stringent of all should be applied to school districts, whose officers have limited and defined powers in a system exclusively for the free education of the children in the commonwealth. . . .

"The school board stipulated that possession of the building would be delivered at a date after the vacation of the schools. Before the schools had been closed some of the directors discovered that persons were making a dangerous excavation, and it would have been humane in them to have endeavored to stop it. The board might have been convened, and if necessary the schools suspended until the progress of the work could have been enjoined by legal process.

"But the directors omitted such action, and it is claimed that the district is liable in damages for the injury done to the plaintiff by the act of a trespasser or the unauthorized act of a contractor. Although the board of directors took no measures to prevent the excavation, we are of the opinion that the persons who caused the injury are liable, and not the school district." (*Wood v. Ind. Sch. Dist. of Mitchell*, 44 Iowa, 27; *Donovan v. Bd. Ed.*, 85 N. Y. 117; *Maximilian v. Mayor*, 62 N. Y. 160; *Donovan v. McAlpin*, 85 N. Y. 185.)

§ 26. **Building, use.**—A statute allowing school-house to

be used for religious purposes does not contravene Iowa constitution, art. 1, § 3, forbidding any law respecting the establishment of religion, or tax for maintaining a place of worship,[1] and the electors of school district may legally permit school buildings to be used for religious purposes.[2] The provision of Ill. Rev. Stat., 958, § 39, for granting the temporary use of a school-house for religious meetings and Sunday schools, is constitutional; no preference is thereby given by law to any religious denomination or mode of worship.[3] The trustees of a school district may, subject to the control of the district meeting, lawfully permit the district school-house to be used, out of school hours, for the purpose of private instruction in vocal music of the district scholars, and of others residing in the district; and it is no objection to such use that the teacher is compensated by private subscription or otherwise.[4] In Ind., a school-house built by township trustees may be used for township purposes, or a part appropriated therefor.[5] Under Ohio Stat. L. 1889, the use of school-houses may be allowed for literary meetings, school exhibitions, singing-schools, or religious meetings.[6] In Ind., the use of school-house for other purposes may be allowed on consent of majority of voters of the district.[7] In Ark., the use of building for private school may be allowed.[8] In Mass., the use is under supervision of school committee of town.[9]

§ 27. **Building, use.**—The question as to permission to use the buildings for other than public-school purposes is one on which the courts have largely differed, but the later statutes appear to be growing more liberal, and favor such use. But Mo. school law (2 Wagner's Stat., p. 1262) confers no authority

[1] Davis v. Blodget, 50 Iowa, 11.
[2] Townsend v. Hagan, 35 Iowa, 194.
[3] Nichols v. Sch. Dirs., 93 Ill. 61.
[4] Appeal of Barnes, 6 R. I. 591.
[5] Trustees &c. v. Osborne, 9 Ind. 458.
[6] Ohio Acts, 1889.
[7] Hurd v. Walters, 48 Ind. 148.
[8] Ark. L. § 6235.
[9] G. S. 38, § 40.

upon school directors to allow the school building to be used for a Sunday school.¹ The inhabitants of a school district have no right to use the school-house for religious meetings against the objection of any tax-payer of the district, even though the district may have voted to allow such use, and an injunction will be granted against such use.² A lessor demised land to the trustees of a school for the purposes of the school; the beneficiaries took a vested interest, and neither the lessor nor the trustees had any power to change the uses declared by the lease, that is, to provide that the school-house should be used for religious worship on Sundays;³ and in Kas., a tax-payer and patron of school may enjoin misuse of school-house for social, religious or political meetings, even though a majority of the tax-payers consent to such use;⁴ also, in Wis., a district board cannot authorize the use of the school-house for any other than school purposes.⁵

§ 28. **Building, use.**—A lease of public school-house for private school is invalid, and such use may be restrained;⁶ and a lease of a public school-house for a private school for a term of weeks is in violation of the trust imposed on the board of education by 70 Ohio Laws, 195, and such use of the house may be restrained at the suit of a resident tax-payer of the district.⁷ A prudential committee agreed to let H. the district school-house for a private school in vacation, and H. acted upon the agreement. The committee could not revoke it without cause, nor could he allege his want of legal authority to make the agreement, in an action of trespass against him for forcibly preventing H. from continuing the school.⁸ A lease made to

¹ Dorton v. Hearn, 67 Mo. 301.
² Schofield v. Eighth Sch. Dist., 27 Conn. 499.
³ McDonald v. Starkey, 42 Ill. 442.
⁴ Spencer v. Sch. Dist., 15 Kas. 259.
⁵ Sch. Dist. No. 8 v. Arnold, 21 Wis. 657.
⁶ 35 Ohio Stat. 143.
⁷ Weir v. Day, 35 Ohio Stat. 143.
⁸ Russell v. Dodds, 37 Vt. 497.

certain trustees and to their successors for a term of 99 years, "for and in consideration of the many advantages of a permanent school," and after the establishment of the present public-school system in this state, and not limited to private school purposes, will be presumed to be made with a view to that system; and the court, finding the premises in use of public-school directors as such trustees, will presume them to be the rightful possessors.[1] A district meeting voted to have a private school in the school-house, and nothing appeared but that if it had been permitted to proceed it would have answered all the purposes of a public school, and been open to all the children in the district, and taught all the branches of common-school instruction enumerated in the statute, and no others. There was nothing inconsistent with the rights of the district in allowing the school to continue there for the time being merely, but the district could not confer any exclusive right to the possession of the school-house for any definite time upon anyone.[1] By implication, the prudential committee of a school district must have the right to occupy the school-house when the school is in operation, but the statute does not give him the exclusive control of the school-house in his district; that power must be in the district.[2]

§ 29. **Colored schools.**—Where teacher refuses to accept colored school, but takes a white school, subject to the power of board to require teacher to take any school, and the board assigns her to a colored school, which she refuses to teach, she has no cause of action against the city.[3] "Taxation to sustain schools is permitted because the education of the children of a state is a recognized governmental purpose; if the state can

[1] McDonald v. Starkey, 42 Ill. 442.
[2] Chaplin v. Hill, 24 Vt. 528.
[3] Jacksonville v. Akers, 11 Ill. App. 393.

constitutionally exclude colored children from all benefits arising from this tax, because white people pay the tax, there is no good reason why the state may not limit and distribute the benefits of government in every respect according to race or color, and in proportion to the taxes paid by each race or color."[1] Where the statute of the state does not authorize separate schools for colored pupils, they will be entitled to a writ of mandamus for the purpose of obtaining admission to public schools, and shall have equal facilities and be entitled to attend the same school as the whites.[2] It is the duty of district officers to provide and furnish equal school facilities for blacks and whites, and they cannot claim immunity by apportioning to the pupils of each color their proportion of the fund.[3] The privilege of attending the public schools of a state is a right granted by the state, and when granted may be enforced by mandamus,[4] and since 1880, colored children cannot be refused admission in Cal. to the public schools, notwithstanding separate schools have been established for them by board of education or school trustees,[5] and the law of 1869-70, authorizing separate schools for colored pupils, was repealed in 1880.[6] A white person cannot enjoin the sale of bonds, in Ga., to be issued and sold, and proceeds divided according to *pro rata* of tax as to colored and white.[7] Where the state has not authorized separate schools for colored children, a city board of education has no right to establish them.[8] The directors cannot maintain a separate school solely to instruct three or four colored children of the district, when these can be accommodated at the school-house with the other scholars of district.[9] The law contemplates that

---

[1] Claybrook v. Owensboro, 23 Fed. R. 634.
[2] Knox v. Bd. Ed., 45 Kas. 156; Bd. Ed. v. Linnon, 26 Kas. 1; People v. Bd., 101 Ill. 308.
[3] Maddox v. Neal, 45 Ark. 121.
[4] Ward v. Flood, 48 Cal. 36.
[5] Wysinger v. Crookshank, 82 Cal. 588.
[6] Reid v. Town Eatonton, (Ga.) 6 S. E. 602.
[7] People v. Quincy Bd. Ed., 101 Ill. 308,— (Walker, J., dissenting.)
[8] Chase v. Stephenson, 71 Ill. 383.

all children within the district between the ages of six and twenty-one years, regardless of race or color, shall have equal and the same right to participate in the benefits of free schools;[1] and in Iowa, a person cannot be denied admission as a pupil in the public schools on account of his color, nor can he be compelled to attend a separate school for colored children.[2] The act of 1867 is applicable to the city of Detroit, and under it the school board of that city cannot exclude a resident of that city from any of its schools on account of color,[3] and mandamus will lie to compel the admission of a negro child to the public schools.[4] A declaration against school directors, "that the plaintiff is a resident of a district, having children which he is desirous of having taught in said school, and that the defendants, contriving to deprive him of the benefit of having his children therein educated, unlawfully admitted colored children into the school, whereby the plaintiff was deprived of the benefit and advantage of having his children taught in said school," is bad on demurrer, and states no cause of action.[5] Youth of negro, Indian and white blood, but of "more than half white blood," are entitled to the benefit of the school fund.[6] The children of a white mother and a father three-fourths white, are entitled to participate in the school fund.[7] Where the number of colored pupils in any district in Pa. is less than twenty, they cannot be excluded from the schools where white children are taught.[8]

§ 30. **Colored schools.**—A state has the power to provide by statute for separate schools for colored children.[9] It is now well settled that any classification which preserves substantially

[1] Chase v. Stephenson, 71 Ill. 383.
[2] Smith v. Sch. Dist. of Keokuk, 40 Iowa, 210; Dove v. Ind. Sch. Dist., 41 Iowa, 689; Clark v. Bd. Dirs., 24 Iowa, 266.
[3] People v. Bd. Ed., 18 Mich. 400.
[4] State v. Stoutmeyer, 7 Nev. 342.
[5] Stewart v. Southard, 17 Ohio, 402.
[6] Lane v. Baker, 12 Ohio, 237.
[7] Williams v. Drs., etc., Wright (Ohio) 579.
[8] Com. v. Williamson, 10 Phila. (Pa.) 490.
[9] Bd. Ed. v. Linnon, 26 Kas. 1; Cory v. Carter, 48 Ind. 327; State v. McCann, 21 Ohio St. 198; Ward v. Flood, 48 Cal. 36; Bertonmeau v. Dirs., 3 Woods, 177.

equal school advantages does not impair any right, and is not prohibited by the constitution of the U. S.[1] In suit of mandamus for school facilities for blacks as well as whites, the parents of the children are proper parties plaintiff.[2] Where there are white and colored scholars, the laws of Ark. contemplated separate schools.[3] In the case of *State v. McCann*, 21 Ohio St. 211, Judge Day, delivering the opinion of the court, says: "Equality of rights does not involve the necessity of educating white and colored persons in the same schools, any more than it does that of educating children of both sexes in the same school, or that different grades of scholars must be kept in the same school; any classification which preserves substantially equal school advantages is not prohibited by either the state or federal constitution, nor would it contravene the provisions of either."

§ 31. **Colored schools.**—Where the statute allowed the board of education to adopt regulations so that pupils could be assigned to schools affording equal advantages, and a colored man sought by mandamus to compel the admission of his children to a school where white children were taught, instead of that for colored children to which they were assigned by the board, the two schools affording equal advantages, the supreme court refused the mandamus;[4] and the right to enact laws as shall give to the children of the white and colored races equal educational advantages, but in separate schools, has been recognized and declared.[5] The Ohio act of Mar. 14, 1853, obliging towns to provide schools for both whites and blacks, is to be construed as a law of classification, and not a law of exclu-

[1] Bertonmeau v. Dirs., 3 Woods, 177.
[2] Maddox v. Neal, 45 Ark. 121.
[3] County Ct. v. Robinson, 27 Ark. 116.
[4] People v. Easton, 13 Abb. Pr. (N. S.) 164, 1C5.
[5] Puitt v. Comm'rs, 94 N. C. 709.

sion, though its practical effect may be exclusive where the number of black children is too small to fill a school;[1] and "white" and "black" are to be taken as commonly understood,[1] and under it a colored child regarded as such in the community, though more than half white, (and so far entitled to vote,) was not, as matter of right, entitled to admission to the white schools;[1] and it will be presumed that a person who was a slave before 1865, in this country, is a negro; and the word "generation," as used in the N. C. act, means a single succession of living beings in natural descent, and is not equivalent to "degree"; and an order from the board of education to admit a negro pupil to a school from which negroes are excluded does not require the school committee to admit him.[2] The Ark. law of 1868 required only districts containing both white and colored children to have separate schools.[3] In Ind. the complaint to obtain admission as a pupil was held defective unless it affirmatively showed that the person is between the ages of five and twenty-one years, is neither a negro nor mulatto, nor the issue of a mulatto, and is unmarried.[4] Where, under the laws of N. Y., a city or incorporated village of the state creates separate schools for white and colored children, a colored child has no right to attend a school established for white children.[5] A pupil may be refused admission, in Cal., to a public graded school if he has not sufficient education to enter the lowest grade of such school.[6] The Ohio act of 1849, "to authorize the establishment of separate schools for colored children," is constitutional.[7] A law authorizing the classification according to color of children for school purposes, and the es-

[1] Van Camp v. Bd. Ed., etc., 9 Ohio St. 406.
[2] McMillan v. Sch. Com., 107 N. C. 609.
[3] County Ct. of Union County v. Robinson, 27 Ark. 116.
[4] Draper v. Cambridge, 20 Ind. 268.
[5] Dallas v. Fosdick, 40 How. (N. Y.) Pr. 249.
[6] Ward v. Flood, 48 Cal. 36.
[7] State v. City of Cincinnati, 19 Ohio, 178.

tablishment of separate schools for each class, equal in every particular, does not contravene the fourteenth amendment to the constitution of the U. S.[1]

§ 32. **Colored schools.**—The act establishing the Ala. University for colored people, 1887, is unconstitutional, as it gives the school fund into the care of the trustees and takes the supervision of the university out of the hands of superintendent of instruction.[2] Acts N. C. 1885, ch. 51, and 1889, ch. 60, providing for separate schools for the Croatan Indians, from which all negroes "to the fourth generation" are to be excluded, is constitutional.[3] Where separate schools are maintained for colored pupils, and the same is unlawful, a petition in *quo warranto* against directors will not be allowed where petition does not show improper exclusion of whites.[4] Under act of 1887, in Ohio separate schools for colored pupils have been abolished, and the regulations must be made without regard to color.[5] It was held, under the Ind. Stat. 1881, courts could not control the rights of school officers to establish separate schools for colored pupils,[6] and mandamus to require trustee to maintain separate school for colored children was refused, the necessity not being shown;[7] and since 1881 a colored scholar could not be required to attend separate colored schools in Pa.[8] A colored pupil cannot be excluded from public school on account of color.[9] The general school committee of Boston had power to establish and maintain separate schools for colored pupils.[10] A resolution of the board of the city of Albany, N. Y., assigning a particular school for colored children, and excluding col-

---

[1] State v. McCann, 21 Ohio St. 198; see also 10 F. R. 735; Lehew v. Brummell, 103 Mo. 546.
[2] Ellsberry v. Seay, 83 Ala. 614.
[3] McMillan v. Sch. Com., 107 N. C. 609.
[4] People v. McFall, 26 Ill. App. 319.
[5] Bd. Ed. v. State, (Ohio) 16 N. E. 373.
[6] State v. Gray, 93 Ind. 303.
[7] State v. Grubb, 85 Ind. 213.
[8] Kame v. Commonwealth, 101 Pa. St. 490.
[9] State v. Union D. S. T., 46 N. J. L. 76.
[10] Roberts v. Boston, 5 Cush. (Mass.) 198.

ored children from schools assigned for white children, is not in violation of the fourteenth amendment of the constitution of the U. S.;[1] and where the officers provide public schools of equal excellence for all children, but do not allow children of colored parents to attend the same schools with children of white parents, the rights of the colored under the constitution of the U. S. are not thereby impaired.[2]

§ 33. **Colored Schools.**—In *Hall v. De Cuir*, 95 U. S. 504, it was held: "Questions of a kindred character have arisen in several of the states, which support these views in a course of reasoning entirely satisfactory and conclusive. Boards of education were created by a law of the state of Ohio, and they were authorized to establish within their respective jurisdictions one or more separate schools for colored children when the whole number by enumeration exceeds twenty, and when such schools will afford them, as far as practicable, the advantages and privileges of a common-school education. Under that law, colored children were not admitted as a matter of right into the schools for white children, which gave rise to contest, in which the attempt was made to set aside the law as unconstitutional; but the supreme court of the state held that it worked no substantial inequality of school privileges between the children of the two classes in the locality of the parties; that equality of rights does not involve the necessity of educating white and colored persons in the same school any more than it does that of educating children of both sexes in the same school, or that different grades of scholars must be kept in the same school; and that any classification which preserves substantially equal school advantages is not prohibited by either the state or federal constitution, nor

---

[1] People v. Easton, 13 Abb. N.Y. Pr. (N. S.) 159. | [2] Bertonmean v. Sch. Drs., 3 Woods C. Ct. 177.

would it contravene the provisions of either. (*State v. McCann et al.*, 21 Ohio St. 198.) Separate primary schools for colored and for white children were maintained in the city of Boston. Children in the state who are unlawfully excluded from public-school instruction may recover damages therefor against the city or town by which such public instruction is supported. It appears that the plaintiff was denied admission to the primary school for white children, and she by her next friend claimed damages for the exclusion; but the supreme court, Shaw, C. J., giving the opinion, held that the law vested the power in the committee to regulate the system of distribution and classification, and that when the power was reasonably exercised their decision must be deemed conclusive. Distinguished counsel insisted that the separation tended to deepen and perpetuate the odious distinction of caste; but the court responded, that they were not able to say that the decision was not founded on just grounds of reason and experience, and in the results of a discriminating and honest judgment. (*Roberts v. City of Boston,* 5 Cush. [Mass.] 198.)

"Age and sex have always been marks of classification in public schools throughout the history of our country, and the supreme court of Nev. well held that the trustees of the public schools in that state might send colored children to one school and white children to another, or they might make any such classification as they should deem best, whether based on age, sex, race, or any other reasonable existent condition. (*State v. Duffy*, 7 Nev. 342.)

"Directors of schools in Iowa have no discretion, under the existing law of the state, to deny a youth of proper age admission to any particular school, on account of nationality, color, or religion. Former statutes of the state invested the directors with such discretion, and it is impliedly conceded that it would be competent for the legislature again to confer that authority. (*Clark v. The Board of Directors*, 24 Iowa, 266.)

"School privileges are usually conferred by statute, and as such are subject to such regulations as the legislature may prescribe. Such statutes generally provide for equal school advantages for all children, classifying the scholars as the legislature in its wisdom may direct or authorize; and the supreme court of N. Y. decided that the legislature of the state may from time to time make such limitations and alterations in that regard as they may see fit. (*Dallas v. Fosdick*, 40 How. [N. Y.] Pr., 249.) Public instruction of the kind is regulated in that state by official boards created for the purpose; and it is settled law there that the board may assign a particular school for colored children, and exclude them from schools assigned for white children, and that such a regulation is not in violation of the fourteenth amendment. (*People v. Gaston*, 13 Abb. [N. Y.] Pr., N. S. 160.)"

34. **Contract; attorney.**—Where attorney was employed by director to defend a suit and it was dismissed, and another suit brought in the circuit court, and then the electors met and appointed a committee to defend, one of which committee was this attorney, a valid contract existed.[1] The Ind. state superintendent of public instruction and state auditor may employ an attorney to collect a desperate claim due the state school fund.[2] Where prudential committee were instructed by vote of district to prosecute for trespasses to property, the district was liable for attorney-fees,[3] and a verbal contract of a school board em-

[1] McCaffrey v. Sch. Dist., 74 Wis. 100.
[2] State v. Sims, 76 Ind. 328.
[3] Kingsbury v. Sch. Dist., 12 Metc. (Mass.) 99.

ploying an attorney is valid,[1] but the prudential committee have no authority, without a vote of the district, to employ counsel in the name of the district to defend a suit against an officer of the district in which the district may be interested.[2] A school district, under act 1821, ch. 117, § 8, Me., may raise money to pay expenses of litigation growing out of the exercise of express powers conferred by the statute.[3] In Iowa, the president of a school district township has no authority to employ counsel, unless in a case brought by or against the district, and an appeal to the county or state superintendent contesting the location of school-house, is not a case.[4] The pendency of a suit, and the employment of an attorney by the prudential committee, without authority, though known to the officers and to the voters, does not show a ratification.[5]

§ 35. **Contracts, notes, etc.**—Notes given by trustees for indebtedness of the district are binding on the district, and on the successors,[6] and plaintiff suing on note made by trustee for price of land, need not allege facts showing that statute had been complied with,[7] and the trustees of a district may become indorsers of a promissory note, and set off the same in an action against them; nor are they under any obligation to show how they came by the note until it is impeached.[8] It is no defense to a note given to school commissioner for school funds that there was an agreement by which the commissioner was to use the money for private speculation.[9] The assent of a majority of the board at a legal meeting is essential to the validity of an order.[10] The directors of a school district have power to borrow

---

[1] Page v. Township Bd., 59 Mo. 264.
[2] Harrington v. Sch. Dist. No. 6, 30 Vt. 155.
[3] Sch. Dist. No. 1 v. Bailey, 12 Me. (3 Fairf.) 254.
[4] Templin v. Tp. of Fremont, 36 Iowa, 411.
[5] Harrington v. Sch. Dist., 30 Vt. 155.
[6] Robbins v. Sch. Dist., 10 Minn. 340.
[7] Craig Sch. Tp. v. Scott, (Ind.) 24 N. E. 585.
[8] Brewster v. Colwell, 9 Wend. (N. Y.) 28.
[9] Ware v. Kelley, 22 Ark. 441.
[10] Herrington v. Sch. Dist. Tp., 47 Iowa, 11; McCortle v. Bates, 29 Ohio St. 419.

money to discharge a debt which has been legitimately created, and may pledge the credit of the district, but they cannot in Iowa make the obligations evidencing such a debt bear a higher rate of interest than six per cent.[1] A note reciting that "inhabitants of Dist. No. 5, in S., promise to pay," etc., and signed by "B., treasurer of Dist. No. 5," was held to be the promise of the district,[2] but a trustee cannot borrow money and give notes in name of school corporation, especially where there is no necessity and party had notice;[3] but advancements by officers for the use of the district in anticipation of taxes may be treated as borrowed money,[4] and advancement for that purpose was held to be an implied pledge of funds for the payment of same.[5]

§ 36. **Contracts, notes, etc.**—A township trustee has no power to borrow money for the school township; but for money borrowed, and actually used in a legitimate way, the township may be held liable.[6] Where no notice was given, a vote to hire money at a district meeting did not impose liability; and a subsequent vote at a meeting legally called, to pay the debts due by the district, was not a ratification.[7] In Ill. the board of school directors have no power to make acceptances of orders or bills of exchange so as to bind the school district and create a right of action thereon against them.[8]

§ 37. **Contract; officer interested.**—Where a committee employ a person to labor for their principal, the person employed may by a suit in his own name recover of their principal the amount due him, though he is one of their own number, employed in good faith by the committee.[9] Proceedings to re-

---

[1] Austin v. Colony, 51 Iowa, 109.
[2] Whitney v. Stow, 111 Mass. 368.
[3] Union v. Crawfordsville Bk., 102 Ind. 464.
[4] Brock v. Bruce, (Vt.) 10 A. 93.
[5] Zartman v. State, (Ind.) 10 N. E. 94.
[6] Crawfordsville Bank v. Union, 75 Ind. 361; Wallis v. Johnson, 75 Ind. 368.
[7] Lander v. Sch. Dist., 33 Me. 239.
[8] Peers v. Bd. Ed., 72 Ill. 508.
[9] Junkins v. Union Sch. Dist., 39 Me. 220.

move a director for refusing to recognize a teaching contract were taken by a township board, one of the members of which was related to a third person who had a contract subject to the same objections; this did not disqualify him from acting on the case before the board.[1] A director will not forfeit his office by making contract with his minor daughter as a teacher;[2] and a contract with one of the school committee to board teacher is valid.[3] A contract by a school board for the purchase for a school-site, of land owned by one of its members, the resolution to purchase which was carried by his vote, all the members acting in good faith, is not void, but voidable merely, and is binding when ratified by a new board acting with full knowledge of all the facts.[4] The Pa. act of Mar. 31, 1860, p. 66 (P. L. 400), providing, "Nor shall any member of any corporation, or any officer or agent thereof, be in any wise interested in any contract for the sale or furnishing of any supplies or materials to be furnished to or for the use of any corporation, municipality or public institution of which he shall be a member or officer, or for which he shall be an agent, nor directly or indirectly interested therein, nor recover any reward or gratuity from any person interested in such contract or sale," cannot be extended to include cases of sales of realty not mentioned therein.[4] A member of the district school board during his membership took a contract from the board for the erection of a school-house, and participated in the proceedings for letting the contract; this was contrary to public policy, and forbidden by law. A school director is prohibited from making personal contract with district, and money paid thereon may be collected

[1] Hamtramck v. Holihan, 46 Mich. 127.
[2] State v. Burchfield, 12 Lea, (Tenn.) 30.
[3] Brown v. Sch. Dist., 55 Vt. 43.
[4] Trainer v. Wolfe, 140 Pa. St. 279.
[5] Pickett v. Sch. Dist. 25 Wis. 551.

from him;[1] and an official making contract for district must not be party to same individually;[2] and where the statute forbade a school officer from being interested in a contract, and a contractor was elected to the office of clerk of district, and the incumbent refused to deliver up the books and office, on the ground that the contractor could not fill both positions and was therefore ineligible, the court refused to install the newly-elected clerk, and sustained the action of the party refusing to give up the office.[3]

§ 38. **Contracts; officers' liability.**—(See also "Officers' Liability.") Where the president of a board promises in their behalf, by a note, to pay a debt contracted in the erection of a school-house, he acts as a public agent, and therefore is personally liable on the note.[4] Where a contract by directors did not expressly show that they were acting on behalf of the district, or intending to make the instrument the contract of the district, the directors were individually liable.[5] In a suit against school directors in their individual capacity on a contract purporting to be signed by defendants in their official capacity, and sufficient in form to bind the district, the averment that it had been determined in a former action, in which defendants were not parties, that they had signed the instrument in their individual capacity, did not aver a cause of action.[6]

§ 39. **Contract, power.**—Under Laws 1858, ch. 52, §§ 1, 8, Iowa, the board of directors may bind the district by a contract after their successors have been elected, but before they have qualified.[7] Contract by two trustees, in Minn., must be authorized at a meeting of the trustees, but use of supplies may amount

---

[1] Sch. Dist. v. Parks, 85 Ill. 338; Hewitt v. Normal Sch. Dist., 94 Ill. 528.
[2] Currie v. Sch. Dist., 35 Minn. 163.
[3] Weston v. Lane, 40 Kas. 480.
[4] Hodges v. Runyan, 30 Mo. 491.
[5] Sharp v. Smith, 32 Ill. App. 336.
[6] Armstrong v. Borland, 35 Iowa, 537.
[7] Dubuque &c. College v. Dubuque, 13 Ia. 555.

to a ratification.[1] One appointed to take charge of a public school may, if necessary, employ a subordinate to keep order outside while the school is in session, especially if one of the school committee approves; and the city will be liable, although the school committee has not acted officially.[2] The board of an independent district may authorize steps to be taken to secure a highway by its school-house, and may bind district for expenses incurred.[3] Where a district committee contract, but not binding the district, and the district votes to accept and pay a certain sum, this binds them to pay a *quantum meruit*, not limited to the sum voted.[4] A legislative change of the board, without altering the limits of the district, does not affect the obligation of a legally created debt thereof.[5] Where a committee were authorized and bought a lot for a site, and gave their individual notes, and the district then rescinded the authority, the district was liable to the officers for the amount paid for it.[6] Those who contract with directors cannot repudiate their contract because their action was unrecorded.[7] Where trustees are authorized by legislature to administer school property and lease it for not more than fifty years, they may lease for that term the 16th section in their township.[8] Where contract and statute gave board power to remove janitor at pleasure, a removal of janitor before expiration of year was authorized.[9]

§ 40. **Contract, power.**—Board, furnished to teacher, under a contract with the prudential committee, constitutes a charge upon the school-money coming to the hands of the committee; and payment by him out of the fund, made after his term had expired, but before demand upon him for the money, extin-

---

[1] Andrews v. Sch. Dist., (Minn.) 33 N. W. 217.
[2] Huse v. Lowell, 10 Allen, (Mass.) 149.
[3] Flint River Ind. Dist. v. Kelley, 55 Iowa, 568.
[4] Kimball v. Sch. Dist., 28 Vt. 8.
[5] Shankland v. Phillips, 3 Tenn. Ch. 556.
[6] Kingman v. 13th Sch. Dist., 2 Cush. (Mass.) 426.
[7] Sch. Dirs. v. McBride, 22 Pa. St. 215.
[8] Garland v. Jackson, 7 La. Ann. 68.
[9] Weidman v. Bd. Ed., (N. Y.) 7 N. Y. S. 309.

guishes the claim against the district for the board.¹ Where the committee notified the contractor that the house would not be accepted unless defects were remedied, and he replied that he should do the work as he pleased, and did not wish their interference until the work was done, no implication can arise from their silence that the defects were waived.² Ind. Rev. Stat., §§ 6006, 6007, as to limiting debts, applies to trustees of school townships.³ A member of a board of education cannot change a contract made by the board, unless he has been authorized,⁴ and the individuals composing the board have no power to act so as to bind the corporation unless at a meeting of the board, and any such contract is void unless regularly approved.⁵ Where two persons are authorized by a board to make a contract in its behalf, a contract signed and sealed by one only, is not evidence against the district.⁶ Contracts made with officers *de facto* are not binding where parties contracting are warned and have notice;⁷ contract made by part of directors at irregular meeting and no notice given to other directors, is not binding.⁸ Under the Minn. Comp. Stat., the trustees of districts cannot take a debt out of the statute of limitations by a new promise.⁹ Where defendant claimed the indebtedness was incurred by a fraudulent agreement between plaintiff and its own agents, it was competent for plaintiff to show that there was a valid consideration.¹⁰ If a district vote to raise money for purposes not authorized, it is a nullity, and whoever presumes to carry it into effect, does so at his peril;¹¹ and the powers of the

---

[1] Barrett v. Sch. Dist. No. 2, 37 N. H. 445.
[2] Hill v. Sch. Dist. No. 2, 17 Me. 316.
[3] Middletown v. Greeson, 106 Ind. 18.
[4] State v. Tiedeman, 69 Mo. 515.
[5] Bd. v. Chitwood, 8 Ind. 504; Ohio v. Treas., 22 Ohio St. 144; McCortles v. Bates, 290 Ohio St. 419; Hazen v. Leiche, 47 Mich. 626.
[6] McLain v. Snyder Tp. Sch. Dist., 12 Pa.St.204.
[7] Genesee Ind. Sch. Dist. v. McDonald, 98 Pa. St. 444; White v. Sch. Dist., (Pa.) 8 A. 443.
[8] Sch. Dist. v. Bennett, 52 Ark. 571; Pa. L. Rod Co. v. Cass Bd. Ed., 20 W. Va. 360.
[9] Sanborn v. Sch. Dist., 12 Minn. 17.
[10] Wormley v. Dist. Tp., 45 Iowa, 666.
[11] Sch. Dist. No. 1 v. Bailey, 12 Me. (3 Fairf.) 254.

building committee are limited to the amount voted by the district.¹

§ 41. **Contract, ratification.**—Where the inhabitants of a district, in a suit for building school-house, repudiated the agreement alleged, denying that it had been accepted by them, though executed by the plaintiff, and it was proved that the district agreed to build the house, raised money for the purpose, chose a committee to superintend the building, and said committee and the inhabitants had seen the work advance, without any objection, the inhabitants of the district were liable to pay what the house was reasonably worth, though not built agreeably to the special agreement.² The vote of electors directing settlement of disputed claim growing out of contract is a ratification though originally the board of directors exceeded their powers;³ and the board of education can legalize and confirm the acts of *de facto* school officers, under a law which is declared invalid.⁴ There is an implied liability on part of district to reimburse a *de facto* committee for boarding teacher and for material furnished, when district did not object, though the district had voted to have the teacher board around,⁵ and school districts like individuals are liable for money had and received;⁶ so where district accepted benefit of contract made by prudential committee *de facto*, it was held there was an implied promise to pay.⁷

§ 42. **Contract, ratification.**—The court says, in *School Town of Milford v. Powner*, Ind., 26 N. W. 485: "The contract of employment is assailed as invalid on the further ground that it never received the concurrent action of the school board as a body, but was acted upon and signed by the trustees sep-

---

1 Wilson v. Sch. Dist., 32 N. H. 118; Harris v. Sch. Dist., 28 N. H. (8 Fost.) 58.
2 Norris v. Sch. Dist., 12 Me. (3 Fairf.) 293.
3 Everts v. Dist. Tp., 77 Iowa, 37.
4 Dubuque &c. Coll. v. Dubuque, 13 Iowa, 555.
5 Rowell v. Tunbridge Sch. Dist., 59 Vt. 658.
6 Trustees v. Trustees, 81 Ill. 470.
7 Rowell v. Sch. Dist., (Vt.) 10 A. 754.

arately and severally. It is undoubtedly true that the individual members of a school board, acting separately, cannot legally employ a teacher, nor can they make any other contract binding upon the corporation. The statute requires that they shall meet within five days after they are elected and organize by electing one of their number as president, one as secretary, and one as treasurer; and they are required to keep a record of their proceedings relative to the schools. The individuals composing the board have no power to act so as to bind the corporation, except when they are convened as a board; and any contract made by them when not thus convened, unless it is afterwards freely approved and confirmed when legally in session, is not valid. (*Board v. Chitwood*, 8 Ind. 504; *Ohio v. Treasurer*, 22 Ohio St. 144; *Hazen v. Lerche*, 47 Mich. 626.) Nor can the members of a board, by any prearrangement or contract entered into when not in session, bind themselves afterward to ratify or confirm any contract or engagement thus entered into. (*McCortle v. Bates*, 29 Ohio St. 419.) There was evidence which tended to show that the plaintiff and one of the trustees signed the contract at a time when the school board was not in session. Afterwards, at a special session of the board, the contract of employment was approved and signed by one of the other members, and the proceedings of the meeting, the employment of the teacher and the approval of the contract were duly entered of record. As applicable to the evidence upon this point, the court stated the law correctly to the jury in a charge in which they were told, in effect, that if the plaintiff and one of the members of the board signed the contract before the meeting on April 26, 1886, and at a called meeting the contract was adopted by the board and signed by another member, it became binding upon the corporation. (*City of Logansport v. Dykeman*, 116 Ind. 15.)"

§ 43. **Corporation.**—Incorporated township for common-school purposes, is a *quasi* public corporation; the legislature may modify or change its powers.[1] By act of 1875, Ark., a district may sue and be sued;[2] but a school district is only a *quasi* corporation, and not included in § 1, art. 12, § 17, art. 2, of constitution of Kansas, in regard to special legislation, and art. 12 applies only to corporations proper in Kansas.[3] The board of education in Ill. may act by agent, and it is not necessary to have seal for the agent to make a contract.[4] The Missouri acts relating to boards of education and school districts do not apply to those incorporated under special acts.[5] School districts and boards of education are not corporations in Ohio within the provisions of const., art. 13, § 1.[6] Changing the name of the district is not a change of corporate character of the district, nor a change in the relations of parties dealing with it.[7] Where districts were established in Mass. under act of 1789, but not by geographical division, they were not made districts by act of 1817.[8] School townships are not municipal corporations in their nature or purpose,[9] and school districts are not strictly municipal corporations, but territorial divisions having many of the attributes of a corporation;[10] they are only *quasi* corporations, and can exercise no powers except those specially conferred by statute.[11] Trustees of school districts are public corporations to be controlled by the legislature.[12]

[1] Bush v. Shipman, 5 Ill. 186.
[2] Sch. Dist. v. Bodenhamer, 43 Ark. 140.
[3] Beach v. Leahy, 11 Kas. 23.
[4] Bd. Ed. v. Greenbaum, 39 Ill. 609.
[5] State v. Vaughn (Mo.) 12 S. W. 507.
[6] State v. Powers, 38 Ohio St. 54.
[7] Robbins v. Sch. Dist., 10 Minn. 340.
[8] Fry v. Sch. Dist., 4 Cush. (Mass.) 250.
[9] People v. Sch. Trs., 78 Ill. 136.
[10] Wharton v. Sch. Dirs., 42 Pa. St. 358.
[11] Rapelye v. Van Sickler, 1 Edm. (N. Y.) Sel. Cas. 175; Sch. Dist. v. Thompson, 5 Minn. 280; Littlewort v. Davis, 50 Miss. 403; Sch. Dist. No. 3 v. Macloon, 4 Wis. 79.
[12] Trs. of Schools v. Tatman, 13 Ill. 27; State v. Hulin, 2 Ore. 306.

§ 44. **Crime.**—Party can be punished for disturbing private school taught in a district school-house.[1] Where indictment avers neglect to maintain school for three years in succession, and there is a verdict of guilty, no certain penalty can be inflicted under Mass. Rev. Stat., ch. 23, § 60, and a motion in arrest of judgment will be sustained.[2] In Conn. it is a crime to disturb any district, public, private or select school while in session, and this applies to a singing-school.[3] In Mass. it is an offense at common law to violently disturb a town meeting.[4] So in Pa., any malicious disturbance of a meeting of school directors, lawfully assembled, is a crime.[5]

§ 45. **District alteration.**—(See also "District Boundary Organization.") Under Ark. Laws, § 75, acts 1887, p. 286, it is not necessary that the petition should be signed by a majority of the electors of each of the districts to be divided.[6] Under notice to district and warning to town meeting for annexation of adjoining district in Conn., where the town meeting refused the change, but on appeal the court decreed that a part only should be annexed, the decree was not error,[7] and a setting aside action of town in dividing school district by appellate court, but making no further order, does not preclude the town from further altering;[8] but a petition by a majority of citizens in district to be affected by change in the boundaries of district, is a condition precedent to formation of new district by county superintendent of Dakota.[9] The act of 1889, Ill., annexing municipalities to others, gives the enlarged city the legal title to the property, and imposes on it the school debt of added

---

[1] State v. Leighton, 35 Me. 195; State v. Yager, 26 Conn. 607.
[2] Commonwealth v. Sheffield, 11 Cush. (Mass.) 178.
[3] State v. Yager, 26 Conn. 607.
[4] Com. v. Hoxey, 16 Mass. 385.
[5] Campbell v. Com., 59 Pa. St. 266.
[6] Hudspeth v. Wallis (Ark.) 15 S. W. 184.
[7] Gravel Hill Sch. Dist. v. Old Sch. Dist., 55 Conn. 244.
[8] Sixteenth Sch. Dist. v. E. Sch. Dist., 54 Conn. 50.
[9] Dartmouth S. Bk. v. Sch. Dist., 6 Dak. 332.

territory,[1] and when municipalities had been annexed to cities before passage of act giving boards of education of cities of 100,000 inhabitants control of public schools, they are under control of same, though not mentioned in the act.[1] A map and a list of tax-payers in the newly-arranged district must be filed in the county clerk's office; this provision of the statute is mandatory in Ill.[2] Under the law of 1877, a petition for a change of a district must aver that the petitioners constitute two-thirds of the legal voters of the territory, and that the district from which they wish to be severed has no bonded debt.[3] When the old district is extinguished, if they fail to apportion its indebtedness and lay it upon the new organizations, the old district will continue in existence to enforce its liabilities, and service upon those who were directors at the time of the change will be good.[3] The legality of alteration cannot be questioned collaterally on an application for judgment for school taxes, but must be tested by *quo warranto* against the directors,[4] and the courts will not interfere in altering districts except in cases of gross injustice.[5] A bill in chancery filed by a creditor against the district into which the debtor district had become consolidated will not lie, the remedy, if any, being at law.[6] Entering the funds distributed to a new school district, in Ill., to the credit of such district by the treasurer of board of trustees, is not condition precedent to the organization of the new district;[7] and where the record shows that the board met for the purpose of appraising and distributing school property and funds consequent upon the formation of a new district, but does not state who made the appraisement, it will be presumed that it was made by the board of trustees.[7]

[1] McGurn v. Bd. Ed. (Ill.) 24 N. E. 529; Cravener v. Bd. Ed., Id. 532.
[2] Potter v. Sch. Trs., 10 Ill. App. 343.
[3] Rudgers v. People, 68 Ill. 154.
[4] People v. Newberry, 87 Ill. 41.
[5] Dirs. v. Trs., 66 Ill. 247; Metz v. Trustee, 66 Ill. 247.
[6] Sch. Dirs. v. Miller, 54 Ill. 338.
[7] Sch. Dirs. v. Sch. Dirs., 73 Ill. 249.

§ 46. **District alteration.**—(Ill.) Where the old districts refuse to pay over the funds to the treasurer of the new, and the board of trustees neglect to compel such payment, the remedy is by a bill in chancery to compel the collection and the application of the fund.[1] The failure to show, in the petition, that the district to be divided has no bonded debt, and that the boundary of the new is not nearer than one mile to a schoolhouse, and that it is signed by all the voters of the new district, and that such district contains not less than five families, is fatal.[2] Until the township trustees shall make a division of the property, each district is bound to pay its debts;[3] and where a district is formed from another the latter may sue in equity to recover as trustee of the former, money or property coming to former.[4] Where directors retain possession of a house on land which has been detached to form a new district, and continue to levy taxes on the detached territory, and the school trustees refuse to sell such house, a court of equity will grant relief from such acts, at the suit of the directors and tax-payers residing in new district.[5]

§ 47. **District alteration.**—(Ind.) If the boundary of a district is changed conformably to a legal petition, the consequent alteration of the adjoining district is valid without petition therefor.[6] Under 1st Rev. Stat., p. 780, § 4, real estate conveyed to a school township, and paid for by it, remains its property, although included in territory afterwards annexed to adjoining city.[7]

§ 48. **District alteration.**—(Iowa.) Certain territory of the independent school district of V. was set apart by resolution of

[1] Sch. Dirs. v. Sch. Dirs., 73 Ill. 249.
[2] Sch. Trs. v. Ball, 71 Ill. 559.
[3] Sch. Dist. v. Miller, 49 Ill. 495.
[4] Sch. Dist. v. Sch. Dist., 16 Ill. App. 651.
[5] Sch. Dirs. v. Sch. Dirs., (Ill.) 28 N. E. 49.
[6] Nutter v. Trs. &c., 4 Blackf. (Ind.) 351.
[7] Reckert v. Peru, 60 Ind. 473.

the electors to "all parties interested desiring to form a new school district," and certain territory of district township of C. was set off by its board of directors for the same purpose; this combined territory applied to the independent district of L. for admission; the district township of C. brought suit to restrain independent district of L. from exercising control over the territory; it was held that the action of electors of independent district of V. was illegal, and that never having been legally detached from independent district of V., the district township of C. could not maintain an action to have it declared part of its territory.[1] In an action by an independent district to compel board of directors of a district township to take action on its proposition to change boundaries, that the independent district is co-extensive with a village does not deprive it of the benefits of the act. (Code, § 1809.)[2] When a part of one district is attached to another, the boards of directors of the two, or arbitrators chosen by them, have power to apportion the assets; and their jurisdiction is exclusive,[3] and it is only upon their failure to agree that the disputes are to be referred to arbitrators.[4] An appeal will lie from their adjudication to the county superintendent, whose decision is binding.[4] The court on arbitration in Iowa on division of assets where district is divided, (Code, §§ 1715, 3416, 3431,) must render same judgment as the award.[5] The boards of directors of independent school districts have no power to change the boundaries; such changes can only be made, if at all, by the county superintendent, under the joint provisions of Code, §§ 1797–1806;[6] and concurrent action of boards of directors of both townships is necessary before an in-

---

[1] Dist. Tp. of Center v. Ind. Dist. Lansing, (Iowa) 47 N. W. 1033.
[2] Ind. Dist. v. Dist. Tp., (Iowa) 47 N. W. 1030.
[3] Dist. Tp. v. Dist. Tp., 45 Iowa, 104.
[4] Ind. Sch. Dist. of Lowell v. Ind. Sch. Dist. of Duser, 45 Iowa, 391.
[5] Little Sch. Dist. Tp. v. Little Sch. Ind. Dist., 60 Iowa, 616.
[6] Eason v. Douglass, 55 Iowa, 390.

dependent district lying within the limits of two district townships can be deprived of its territory.[1] Where no written request was made to call a meeting for an election upon the consolidation of independent district with another, and no call was made at a proper meeting of the board, there could be no legal consolidation, Code, § 1811;[2] and under § 1797, Code, a county superintendent cannot divide district and annex the part to another unless on account of natural obstacles that prevent attendance, and if the order is void a legislative sanction subsequently will not divert the taxes.[3] Before 1866, a transfer from one township was unauthorized, unless it was made because of reason of natural obstacles.[4] The treasurer in refunding an illegal tax under Code, § 870, should apportion the amount between the districts occupying the territory from which it was collected.[5] A portion of township A was annexed to township B, a warrant executed by the A to the B, in consideration that the A should be entitled to receive all the taxes, was valid.[6] The removal of an old school-house to make place for a new one, does not disorganize a district composed of territory in different townships.[7] The apportionment by the directors of assets and liabilities cannot be attacked collaterally.[8] The law does not limit the extent of territory which may be added to a town or city district for school purposes;[9] and where two-thirds of the electors of territory that had been detached from one district and attached to an independent district petition for its restoration, which is refused by the independent district, the remedy is by appeal and not mandamus.[10] Under Code, § 1798, the

---

[1] Ind. Dist. of Fairview v. Durland, 45 Iowa, 53.
[2] State v. Leverton, 53 Iowa, 483.
[3] Ind. Dist. v. Ind. Dist., 62 Iowa, 616.
[4] Troy v. Doyle, 53 Iowa, 667.
[5] Spencer v. Riverton, 56 Iowa, 85.
[6] Wesley v. Algona, 52 Iowa, 153.
[7] State v. McCormick, 37 Iowa, 142.
[8] Ind. Dist. v. Ind. Dist., 45 Iowa, 391; 43 id. 444.
[9] Fort Dodge v. Wahkansa, 15 Iowa, 434.
[10] Barnett v. Ind. Dist., (Iowa) 34 N. W. 780.

boundaries of an independent district might be changed in the same way as where territory had been afterwards attached;[1] and the extension of limits of a town does not necessarily enlarge the district therein.[2]

§ 49. **District alteration.**—(Kas.) Board of education of city of second class may attach adjacent territory in Kansas, and notice to the district affected is not a condition precedent where majority of electors of such territory apply;[3] and apportionment of school property is valid, though not made for seven months after new district was formed.[4] School district admitting liability for property obtained by division of district may be compelled to pay by mandamus;[5] and a petition, stating county superintendent ordered district to pay sum for retaining property on organization of district, held good.[5] It is not necessary to prove that school district had notice of superintendent's action in directing it to pay for property on division of districts.[5] Where there is no provision for compensation, and a district is divided by extension of city limits, and the city claims the building on the ground annexed, without making any compensation therefor, and the officers of the district prevent such control, the original district should retain control of the school-house until some arrangement is made for adjustment of the property rights.[6] Where the territory detached was not organized or placed in any other district for one year, an award made about three years thereafter, that the old district shall pay the new the value of the property retained, is binding.[7]

§ 50. **District alteration.**—(Me.) Where two new districts

[1] Albin v. West B. I. S. D., 58 Iowa, 77.
[2] State v. Ind. Dist., 46 Iowa, 425.
[3] Sch. Dist. v. Board, 16 Kas. 536.
[4] Sch. Dist. v. State, 15 Kas. 43.
[5] Sch. Dist. v. Sch. Dist., 20 Kas. 76.
[6] Bd. Ed. v. Sch. Dist., 45 Kas. 560.
[7] Sch. Dist. v. Sch. Dist., 32 Kas. 123.

are formed from an old one, the title to the school-house is in the district within which it falls;[1] and if a town in dividing a school district includes that which it is not authorized to do by the warrant, a mere stranger cannot therefore avoid the whole proceedings.[1] It is not illegal for a town, in reconstructing its districts, to make its action depend on the wishes of the districts to be affected.[2] Where by a change in the district line the school-house is left out of the district in Me., the district still owns the building, and may authorize an agent to remove the same.[3] Rev. Stat. 1857, ch. 11, § 26, authorizing school districts to unite without the action of the town, is not repealed by the act of 1854, ch. 104, § 1, which provides that towns may determine, etc., so far as to invalidate a union made under the former statute, although after the passage of the latter.[4] A district in Me. cannot be divided by town vote unless selectmen have submitted written statement required by law;[5] and towns cannot form new school districts from adjoining without co-operating and giving due notice to all.[6] A recital in a report of the selectmen and school committee that a division would not be desirable if its inhabitants could agree to it, yet the feeling existing was such as to require the division, is a sufficient "statement of facts;"[7] and a vote passed at an annual meeting as required is not invalidated by the fact that the report had also previously been made at a special town meeting.[7] The vote of a town to discontinue one district and to annex it to others, is not void because of an omission to make any provision about the disposition of the school-house.[8] Under R. S., ch. 11, § 1, requiring the recommendation of the municipal au-

---

[1] Whitmore v. Hogan, 22 Me. 564.
[2] Smyth v. Titcomb, 31 Me. 272.
[3] Whittier v. Sanborn, 38 Me. 32.
[4] Call v. Chadbourne, 46 Me. 206.
[5] Sch. Dist. v. Stearns, 48 Me. 568.
[6] Butterfield v. Inhabitants of Sch. Dist. No. 6, 61 Me. 583.
[7] Webber v. Stover, 62 Me. 512.
[8] Grindle v. Sch. Dist. No. 1, 64 Me. 44.

thorities, it is not necessary that such recommendation should indicate the exact change to be made.[1] Where three districts were added to fourth, a vote to reconsider was legalized by act of legislature;[2] but where district had been annexed by vote of town, it could not be reconsidered except by recommendation of town and school officers.[3] A vote to set off the inhabitants of School District No. 22 with their estates, and annex the same to School District No. 9, as recommended by the municipal officers and supervisors of schools, is sufficiently certain.[2]

§ 51. **District alteration.**—(Mass.) A town in altering a district has no power to destroy the district corporation without its consent, nor so as to impair its contracts;[3] and a town defined an east and a west district by lines, and then assigned certain children to certain schools, and all other inhabitants to the center district of the town; this was invalid.[4] When a town abolishes the old districts, the legal title to the schoolhouses rests in the new districts within whose territory they fall.[5] Where the vote to accept the report of the committee dividing the district filed is recorded, it is not necessary to record the report;[6] and where the town voted at a meeting on the 1st of March to accept report of committee dividing district, and recommitted it to the same committee "for the purpose of setting up the bounds and monuments," and the committee about a week afterward returned to the town clerk a report of their making said four districts into three, "as per vote of the town March 1st," and the clerk forthwith recorded it, said three districts were legally established.[7] Establishing bounds for existing districts by a town is not a districting anew within acts

[1] Grindle v. Sch. Dist. No. 1, 64 Me. 44.
[2] Parker v. Titcomb, 82 Me. 180.
[3] Waldron v. Lee, 5 Pick. (Mass.) 323.
[4] Perry v. Dover, 12 Pick. (Mass.) 206.
[5] Sch.Dist.v.Tapley, 1 Allen (Mass.) 49; Stoneham v. Richardson, 23 Pick. (Mass.) 62.
[6] Howard v. Stevens, 3 Allen (Mass.) 409.
[7] Alden v. Rounseville, 7 Metc. (Mass.) 218.

1849 and 1851.¹ Where town in setting off a person to another district omitted "and his estate," it is invalid.² No town is to be redistricted anew under act 1849, so as to change taxation of land into districts using different school-houses, more than once in ten years.³ Where town was divided into five districts, and in 1853 by selectmen into five new districts, in 1855 there was a vote to abolish the district lines, and in 1856 a vote to divide the town into five districts as in 1852, and then a vote to reconsider this so as to form three of the districts in one, and then a vote to adopt the boundaries made by the selectmen, the three did not then constitute one district.⁴ A town may form new school districts, or alter the limits of or subdivide any of the existing districts, without changing all the districts.⁵ Stat. 1849, ch. 206, and 1851, ch. 303, forbidding the redistricting oftener than once in ten years, do not prevent towns from abolishing all school districts.⁶ A town voting to unite two of its school districts is so "districted anew," in the sense of Gen. Stat., ch. 39, § 25, that a non-resident previously taxed in one of the old cannot be taxed in the new without a new certificate of the assessors.⁷ A statute imposing upon towns the debts of abolished school districts is constitutional;⁸ and Gen. Stat., ch. 39, § 3, and Stat. 1869, ch. 110, 425, abolishing school districts, are not unconstitutional; they do not impair the obligation of contracts.⁹

§ 52. **District alteration.**—(Mich.) The action of board inspectors in Mich. in detaching territory from two districts and adding same to third, is valid where proper notice was given, even though all done at one meeting, and a writ of certiorari

---

¹ Adams v. Crooks, 7 Gray, (Mass.) 411.
² Nye v. Marion, 7 Gray, (Mass.) 244.
³ Gustin v. Sch. Dist., 10 Gray, (Mass.) 85.
⁴ Blankenship v. Hadley, 11 Gray, (Mass.)431.
⁵ Richards v. Dagget, 4 Mass. 534.
⁶ Mendell v. Marion, 82 Mass. (16 Gray) 353.
⁷ Bacon v. Sch. Dist. No. 13, 97 Mass. 421.
⁸ Whitney v. Stow, 111 Mass. 368.
⁹ Rawson v. Spencer, 113 Mass. 40.

will not lie unless the action of the board practically destroys a district.[1] Where ten days' notice has not been given of formation of new district, it cannot be thereafter affirmed by written consent of majority of citizens affected.[2] A return by the board of inspectors that the parties consenting to division are a majority of resident tax-payers, is conclusive evidence;[3] and six years' acquiescence in division of district estops the parties from attacking same.[3] Where a district did not contain more than nine sections, it is legal although it contains five full sections and eight fractional sections.[4] Where the notice for alteration of district shows how it affects contiguous districts, but does not specifically name those affected, it will be valid.[5] The township clerk in Mich. is a school inspector, and his signing of notice for alteration of a district boundary, as clerk of the board of school inspectors, is a compliance with the statute.[5] A school district may enjoin an illegal apportionment of debt,[6] and where the inspectors of the old district apply to the board of supervisors to have the sum apportioned to that district spread upon its taxable property without giving the notice required, the tax is illegal.[6] Proof of notice for meeting of township board of school inspectors must be filed with clerk of board before boundaries of district are to be altered;[7] and a township board has jurisdiction of appeal from decision of school inspectors apportioning liability on division of districts.[8] Township school inspectors cannot enlarge a graded-school district by adding unorganized territory, though they may, with the consent of the trustees, transfer to its jurisdiction primary districts;[9] and where a school district is divided among three other existing

---

[1] Doxey v. Tp. Bd. Sch. Insp., (Mich.) 35 N. W. 170.
[2] Gentle v. Bd. Insp., (Mich.) 40 N. W. 928.
[3] Sch. Dist. v. Union Sch. Dist., (Mich.) 45 N. W. 993.
[4] People v. Gartland, (Mich.) 42 N. W. 687.
[5] Donough v. Hollister, 82 Mich. 309.
[6] Sch. Dist. v. Sch. Dist., 63 Mich. 51.
[7] Coulter v. Sch. Insp., 59 Mich. 391.
[8] Cannon v. Wilcox, 48 Mich. 404.
[9] Simpkins v. Ward, 45 Mich. 559.

districts, the latter cannot be held jointly for a debt of the former district; whatever they are bound to pay must be a several and not a joint obligation.[1] The board of school inspectors had no authority to dissolve the school district numbered 13 established by the act of Feb. 7, 1867.[2] After the incorporation of the city of Saginaw, the officers of the township district embraced in the city claimed to be officers of the School District No. 1 of the city of Saginaw, and brought suit to collect money in this right, etc. Held, the city charter severed the city from the school district of the township, and the city could not recover its proportion of the moneys of the school district or of its other property.[3] Under Laws 1840, p. 215, § 25, the school inspectors of any such district may dissolve one organized district and annex it to another.[4]

§ 53. **District alteration.**—(Minn.) Where certain territory was added to city of Winona, Minn., by statute, it became a part of it for school purposes, and as there was no statutory provision, the addition remained subject to all its liabilities and retained its property, including that which came within the city.[5] A village may not withdraw from district at its election and by its own action.[6] Where districts were divided before the act of 1891 applied, the old district retained all the property and was liable for all the debts;[7] and districts are under control of the legislature, and the property may be transferred from one to another.[8]

§ 54. **District alteration.**—(Mo.) To form a new district from part of two existing, the assent of a majority of each of the three is required.[9] Mo. Sess. Acts of 1868, p. 164, provid-

[1] Halbert v. Sch. Dist., 36 Mich. 421.
[2] Sch. Dist. v. Dean, 17 Mich. 223.
[3] Saginaw v. Sch. Dist., 9 Mich. 541.
[4] People v. Davidson, 2 Dougl. (Mich.) 121.
[5] City Winona v. Sch. Dist., 40 Minn. 13.
[6] State v. Ind. Sch. Dist., 42 Minn. 357.
[7] City Winona v. Sch. Dist., 40 Minn. 13.
[8] Connor v. St. Anthony Bd., 10 Minn. 352.
[9] Sayre v. Tompkins, 23 Mo. 443.

ing for the extension of school districts, applies to both corporated and incorporated towns.¹ Wagner's Stat., p. 1245, § 17, requiring a joint meeting of the township boards of education in order to form a sub-district out of territory in two townships, is not complied with by a meeting of one board and a unanimous consent on paper by the other.² Territory embraced in a school sub-district, outside of and adjoining an incorporated town, may be organized with it for school purposes under the Mo. school law, art. 2, § 1, (Wagn. Stat., 1262.) A previous "mutual agreement" is unnecessary. If after the town sub-district is organized it becomes desirable to have additional territory from the township annexed, it must be done under provisions of § 17.³ Where (Wagn. Stat., ed. 1872, 1267, § 17) a township sub-district becomes merged in adjoining town or city, and the board of the municipality takes control of the school property of annexed district, the municipal board will be liable for contract made previously by sub-district board for a teacher's salary.⁴ The act of 1868, p. 164, § 1, authorizing boards of education to extend the limits of the territory, is constitutional, although not requiring the consent of the districts affected.⁵ Voting down a proposition to organize the city into a separate school district under Gen. Stat. 1865, ch. 47, p. 274, does not prevent its being so organized afterwards.⁶ A resolution adopted by the board of education of a city, attaching territory for school purposes, under Acts 1868, p. 164, § 1, is not inoperative till the clerk of the board certifies to the township clerk and the latter acts;⁷ but the resolution of July 16, 1869, grants no authority to detach territory which has been attached

¹ State v. Heath, 56 Mo. 231.
² Smith v. Tp. Bd. of Ed., 58 Mo. 297.
³ State v. Heiser, 60 Mo. 540.
⁴ Thompson v. Abbott, 61 Mo. 176.
⁵ State v. Miller, 65 Mo. 50.
⁶ Ewing v. Jefferson City Bd. Ed., 72 Mo. 436.
⁷ Henry v. Dulle, 74 Mo. 443.

—5

under the above statute.[1] Under act of 1879 a district cannot vote simply to withdraw from that part outside its county without voting to form a new district or attaching itself to some other;[2] and a county school commissioner can only change the boundaries of district, except as in Rev. St., § 7023.[3] Though Rev. Stat. 1879, § 7031, authorizes the annual meeting to change boundaries, "notice of such change having been posted in at least five public places in each district affected," yet when a new district is formed or other changes made on petition of ten qualified voters, three notices only in each district are sufficient under § 7023, requiring the directors of district affected to post a notice of the desired change in at least three public places in each district, twenty days prior to the annual meeting, and the voters, when assembled, shall decide the question.[4] A notice of the proposed formation of a new district need not give its boundaries, but should refer to the petition and describe the territory to be taken from the district.[4] A notice signed by the clerk of the district in which it is posted is sufficient under Rev. Stat. 1879, § 7067, making it his duty to make copies of election notices, and § 7070, to post notices required to be given of all special meetings.[4] Where officers attempt to carry out void change of district, they will be compelled by mandamus to apportion funds correctly;[5] and where change is made without required vote, it is void;[5] and territory cannot be taken from one and added to another district until voted upon by voters of each district.[5] The statute of 1879, in regard to taxing old district for benefit of new, does not apply to change of boundaries of two old districts.[6]

[1] Henry v. Dulle, 74 Mo. 443.
[2] Shattuck v. Phillips, 78 Mo. 80.
[3] State v. Riley, 85 Mo. 156.
[4] Mason v. Kennedy, 89 Mo. 23, (14 S. W. 514.;
[5] State v. Jnimshaw, (Mo.) 1 S. W. 363.
[6] Sch. Dist. v. Sch. Dist., (Mo.) 7 S. W. 285.

§ 55. **District alteration.**—(Neb.) Under subdivision 3, p. 4, ch. 79, Comp. Stat., for a change in the boundaries of two school districts, it is indispensable that three notices, containing an exact statement of the proposed change and the time when the petition will be presented to the county superintendent, be posted in three public places, one of which places shall be upon the outer door of the school-house, if there be one, in each district affected, at least ten days prior to presenting petition.[1] The affidavit of proof of posting such notices should state where each of the three was posted, and day of posting same; and in a proceeding attacking jurisdiction of the state superintendent, the time and place of posting must appear,[1] and a petition in writing for that purpose is a condition precedent.[2] Ten days' notice must be given of application for division of district.[3] Where consolidated district assumed all the debts of the old districts, a tax was properly levied on new for payment of bonds of one of the old.[3]

§ 56. **District alteration.**—(N. H.) The inhabitants of a town voted to divide the town into school districts, and appointed the selectmen a committee to make such division; their proceedings must be ratified by the town to make them legal;[4] and a division of a town into school districts must be a territorial division.[5] If parts of two towns are by the legislature incorporated into a school district, one of those towns cannot dismember such district.[6] A town may unite two existing districts under an article in the warrant, "to see if the town will alter the boundaries of any of the school districts in the town."[7] Under act of July 4, 1861, towns may be divided into school

[1] Dooley v. Meese, (Neb.) 48 N. W. 143.
[2] State v. Compton, (Neb.) 44 N. W. 660.
[3] Clother v. Maher, 15 Neb. 1.
[4] Sch. Dist. v. Gilman, 3 N. H. 168.
[5] Sch. Dist. v. Aldrich, 13 N. H. 139.
[6] Sch. Dist. v. Smart, 18 N. H. 268.
[7] Converse v. Porter, 45 N. H. 385.

districts, which may be altered by vote of town provided previous written recommendation of the superintendent, school committee and selectmen, etc., is had; this applies where all the districts are altered and the town redistricted; but such recommendation must specify the alterations to be made, and the committee and selectmen cannot delegate their powers.[1] Persons and property annexed to a school district in an adjoining town are subject to school-house taxes in the district in which they are annexed, and not elsewhere.[2] The validity of the action of the selectmen and school committee does not depend upon the correct apportionment of the debts and property of the districts so affected.[3] Independent school districts exercising powers equal to town district were not affected by act 1885.[4] Where debts of district that is abolished are less than value of property, they may be paid by district obtaining the property.[5]

§ 57. **District alteration.**—(N. J.) Under § 41 of the school law, an incorporated school district has no right to alter another district without notice to such district and its consent;[6] and a certificate from the trustees and town superintendents to the county clerk of consent of inhabitants to the abolition of school district, does not satisfy the statute, and will not be required by mandamus, although it has been given, etc.[7] The town superintendent, acting with the trustees of an incorporated district, cannot join thereto another incorporated district,[8] and the tax assessed in both districts will be void.[9] Until the appointment of the trustees the town superintendent has full power to make and alter school districts; but after their ap-

---

[1] Neal v. Lewis, 46 N. H. 276.
[2] Pickering v. Colman, 53 N. H. 424.
[3] Anderson v. Carr, 55 N. H. 452.
[4] Sargent v. Union Sch. Dist., 63 N. H. 528.
[5] Sch. Dist. v. Town of Greenfield, 64 N. H. 84.
[6] State v. Browning, 27 N. J. L. (3 Dutch.) 527; State v. Deshler, 25 N. J. L. (1 Dutch. 177.
[7] State v. Jacobus, 26 N. J. L. (2 Dutch.) 135.
[8] State v. Reeves, 28 N. J. L. (4 Dutch.) 520; State v. Browning, 28 N.J.L. (4 Dutch.) 556.
[9] State v. Reeves, 28 N. J. L. (4 Dutch.) 520.

pointment they must have had full notice.[1] Where the district is to be altered by the town superintendent acting alone or with the trustees with the assent of a majority of the legal voters of the district, and the certificate shows that districts have been abolished by consent of a majority of the legal voters of the districts, and is signed by the superintendent and by two of the three trustees of each district, the proceeding is invalid; and where the board is petitioned to enlarge the district and abolishes the same, it will be invalid.[2]

§ 58. **District alteration.**—(N. Y., &c.) A school commissioner has power to alter or divide a union free-school district, but must give the trustees a week's notice.[3] A school commissioner altered districts 5 and 7 in Town T., and 13 in Towns T. and B., the trustees of 7 and 13 consenting, to take effect immediately as to 7 and 13, and in four months as to 5; two weeks after, he made an order reciting at request of trustee of 5, he met the supervisor and town clerk of T., and then made the order. The town clerk of B. and trustees of 7 and 13 had no notice; the trustee of 5 attended, but without a week's notice; the alteration transferred a party from 5 to 13, and in an action by him against a subsequent trustee of 13 to recover a tax imposed by 13, the orders could not be impeached collaterally.[4] (N. C.) The county commissioner had no right before an election authorized by statute had been held in two districts to establish a graded school, to change and alter the districts, and the assessments imposed thereafter were void.[5] (Ohio.) Where property has been set apart for higher grade by township board for whole township, a division of district could not vest the title

[1] State v. Reeves, 28 N. J. L. (4 Dutch.) 520; State v. Browning, 28 N.J.L. (4 Dutch.) 556.
[2] State v. Barrett, 31 N. J. L. 31.
[3] People v. Hooper, 20 N. Y. Sup. Ct. 639.
[4] Rawson v. Van Riper, 1 Thomp.C.C.N.Y. 370.
[5] McCorme v. Robeson, Co. Clk., 90 N. C. 441.

in the new, although the property may be situated there at that time and the letter of the statute implies that it does.¹

§ 59. **District alteration.**—(O., Pa.) The school act of 1853 merely provides that what had been districts should be sub-districts, with no change in boundaries, so that an old district formed from parts of two adjoining townships still continues as one sub-district.² A township board of education organized under the law of 1853 can, with the consent of the board of education of a town district of the same township, organized under act of Feb. 21, 1849, make transfers or annex adjacent territory to such district.³ (Pa.) A petition under act of 1876, authorizing court of quarter sessions to annex land of residents in one township to another for school purposes, must show that the townships are contiguous.⁴ The law in Pa. is different as to apportionment of real estate and schools, and cash on hand, in the division of districts.⁵ Where a district has been divided, and one again divided, where there is a controversy between the first two as to a division of property and liability, the third cannot intervene in that suit and assert its claim against district it was created from.⁵ The temporary consolidation of schools in a district, when reasonably exercised, will not be interfered with by the courts.⁶ The act of 1854 extinguished all sub-districts which had been formed before its passage.⁷ Where a new school district is carved out of another under act of Apr. 11, 1862, which provides that "the court establishing the same shall determine on hearing whether an undue proportion of the property is within the bounds of the new district," such proportion is to be determined with refer-

¹ Bd. Ed. v. Bd. Ed., (Ohio) 22 N. E. 641.
² Bryant v. Goodwin, 9 Ohio St. 471.
³ Canton &c. School v. Meyer, 9 Ohio St. 580.
⁴ In re Heidler, 122 Pa. St. 653.

⁵ Aleppo Sch. Dist. v. Appeal, 96 Pa. St. 76.
⁶ Heard v. Sch. Dirs., 45 Pa. St. 93.
⁷ Conley v. Sch. Dirs., 32 Pa. St. 194.

ence to the value.¹ Where the school taxes remain uncollected until after the formation of a new school district by the erection of a new from an old township, the new district is entitled to participate in the fund.²

§ 60. **District alteration.**—(R. I., Tenn.) The three villages of G., B. and H. were part of the town of S., and organized as independent districts. When they were set off from S. and annexed to W. they retained their original district organization, the district of G. being known as No. 8, B. as No. 9, and H. as No. 10. At a meeting of the school committee of W. it was voted "that district No. 10, at H., be and it is discontinued; also, that the boundaries of district No. 9 be established so as to include what formerly belonged to both Nos. 9 and 10." Held, that the school committee had power to take this action.³ (Tenn.) In Tenn., under acts 1870 and 1873, the county courts or school directors have no power to alter established school districts.⁴

§ 61. **District alteration.**—(Tex., Utah.) Established school districts of a county shall not be changed unless by consent of majority of valid voters in all the districts affected;⁵ and no method being prescribed for determining the will of the majority, it is left to the discretion of the county commissioners' court;⁶ and under Laws 1884, ch. 25, p. 29, the county commissioners' court can change the boundaries of existing districts, and also divide a district and establish in its territory two or more districts.⁶ To a writ of mandamus to compel appointment of trustees, a return is insufficient which states that the relators are seeking to control the funds of the district in the interest of

---

¹ Williams Tp. v. Williamstown, (Pa. Quart. Sess.) Pa. Co. Ct. R. 65.
² Manchester v. Reserve Tp., 4 Pa. St. 35.
³ Bull v. Sch. Com., 11 R. I. 244.
⁴ Rodemer v. Mitchell (Tenn.) 15 S.W.R.1067.
⁵ Junction City v. Trs. Sch. Dist. (Tex.) 16 S. W. R. 742.
⁶ Porter v. State, 78 Tex. 591, (14 S. W. 794.)

a private college, and that if the funds are apportioned, school could not be maintained in one of the new districts for more than four or five months in a year, whereas they could be maintained eight months before the division.¹ The word "subdivide" used in the Texas statutes in regard to duties of county commissioners' court is used with reference to existing division into counties.² (Utah.) The legislature has the power in Utah to consolidate districts, even if the tax should thereby be made unequal.³

§ 62. **District alteration.**—(Vt.) A town may, by vote, annex a portion of its inhabitants to a district in an adjoining town which shall consent to receive them; but the territory is not itself annexed to the district, as it is in a case where a district is formed from territory belonging to two towns by a concurrent vote,⁴ and the arrangement annexing some of the town's inhabitants to a district is not to be regarded as a compact, but as a mere license, and subject to be revoked;⁴ and the town may, by vote, resume its jurisdiction over its citizens and dissolve their connection with the district without the intervention of a board of three justices of the peace.⁴ Where a town authorized a division without defining the boundaries of the new, it was insufficient to show an organization of the new district, though the district voted to divide; but where a division was made and recorded, and the town afterwards ratified the same, this rendered the division legal and binding upon the inhabitants of the town and district.⁵ A warning "to see if the voters present will vote to set off" the plaintiff and six other persons named "and their real estate from Sch. Dist. No. 5, the same to

---

¹ Porter v. State, 78 Tex. 591, (14 S. W. 794.)
² Reynolds L. & C. Co. v. McCabe, 72 Tex. 57.
³ Lowe v. Hardy, (Utah) 26 Pac. 982.
⁴ Hewett v. Miller, 21 Vt. 402.
⁵ Sawyer v. Williams, 25 Vt. 311.

constitute a new district," was a sufficiently definite description of the real estate proposed to be set off; and the town having voted to "constitute a new school district agreeably to such article in the warning," it was legal.[1] And where a warning was to see if the town will divide a district, and annex a portion of it to one and the remainder to another, the town may set the whole of the district proposed to be divided to either of the other districts named.[1] Districts formed of parts of two or more towns may be dissolved or altered by mutual consent.[2] The control of a town over a farm, and the acquiescence in such acts by the district from which such farm is set off, for a quarter of a century, is a ratification to the separation.[3] A vote of a town to annex one school district to another has the effect to abolish the former and enlarge the latter without the necessity of new organization,[3] but under Rev. Stat., § 557, the union of districts does not merge them until their debts are paid.[4] Where taxes have been levied for the purpose of building school-house and for expenses, and the district is then divided, the district that is set off cannot enjoin the collection of the tax.[5]

§ 63. **District alteration.**—(Wash., &c.) Where district is divided and the building is afterwards burned, and the directors of that district pursuant to an election rebuild with the insurance, they cannot be compelled by mandamus to pay the same to county treasurer for new district.[6] (West Va.) Where a district was divided under act of 1881, and no provision was made for assets and liabilities, the old district was entitled to property situated therein and debts due it, and new district was entitled to the property within its limits, and was not liable to contrib-

---

[1] Moore v. Beattie, 33 Vt. 219.
[2] Jones v. Camp, 34 Vt. 384.
[3] Greenbanks v. Boutwell, 43 Vt. 207.
[4] Needham v. Sch. Dist., (Vt.) 20 A. 198.
[5] Dyer v. Sch. Dist., (Vt.) 17 A. 788.
[6] Elder v. Territory, (Wash.) 19 P. 29.

ute to old one.¹ (Wis.) The notice for alteration of a district must be proved outside of record of the board.² A district included in the towns constituted by the division of a town, becomes a joint district, and requires joint action of the supervisors of the two towns to alter it; and on a division by a joint order of the supervisors, they must determine the sum to be paid by the district retaining the school-house to the other.³ The requirement that such sum shall be determined "at the time of forming such new district," may be performed by the supervisors jointly afterwards,³ but until such determination a levy of a tax on that account will not be compelled.³ Where a portion of a district has been detached, and, with other territory, formed into a free-school district, and the remaining territory also formed into a new district, the latter is alone liable for debts of original district.⁴ By R. S., ch. 19, § 6, on the division of districts either may appeal to state superintendent from an apportionment.⁵ The various districts into which a district is divided may unite in a suit in the name which district had before division to maintain prior rights.⁶

§ 64. **District alteration.**—In the case of *City of Winona v. Sch. Dist.*, 40 Minn. 13, it was decided: "Part of territory of school district, which is annexed to city by statute, becomes part of the city for school as well as for other municipal purposes, and ceases to be a part of the school district. Where part of the territory of one municipal corporation is taken from it and annexed to another, the former corporation retains all its property, including that which happens to fall within the limits of such other corporation, unless some other provision is made by the act authorizing the separation.

¹ Rd. Ed. Barker Dist. v. Bd. Ed., (W. Va.) S. E. 640.
² State v. Graham, 60 Wis. 395.
³ State v. Rice, 35 Wis. 178.
⁴ Briggs v. Sch. Dist. No. 1, 21 Wis. 348.
⁵ Sch. Dist. No. 2 v. Sch. Dist. No. 1, 3 Wis. 333.
⁶ Sch. Dist. No. 3 v. Macloon, 4 Wis. 79.

"We have, then, a case where the legislature has changed the boundaries of two municipalities, (but without abolishing either,) so that corporate property acquired and held by one for public or governmental purposes now falls within the territorial limits of the other, but has made no provision for the division of the property, or apportionment of the debts of the two incorporations. The question is, Under such a state of facts, does the property continue to belong to the incorporation from which the territory has been detached? or, has it become the property of the municipality within whose limit it now falls? The absolute right of the legislature, in all cases not within any constitutional prohibition, to create, alter, divide or abolish all municipal corporations, or *quasi* corporations, and to make such division and apportionment of the corporate property and debts of an old corporation, in case of a division of its territory, as the legislature may deem equitable, is well settled. This doctrine has been fully recognized by this court: *State v. City of Lake City*, 25 Minn. 404. But in the present case the legislature has made no such division or apportionment. The rule generally laid down in both the text-books and the adjudicated cases is, that if a part of the territory of a municipal corporation is separated from it by annexation to another, or by the erection of a new corporation, the old corporation still retains all its property and is responsible for all its debts, unless some other provision is made by the act authorizing the separation.

"In all these cases, beginning with that of *Windham v. Portland*, 4 Mass. 384, the rule is laid down as we have already stated it, Parsons, C. J., in the case just cited, adding: 'Thus it [the old town] would continue seized of all its lands, possessed of all its personal property, entitled to all its rights of action, bound by all its contracts, and subject to all its duties.' (See also *Hampshire v. Franklin*, 16 Mass. 76, 86; and *First Parish in Medford v. Pratt*, 4 Pick. 222.) It is true that in none of these cases did the question arise as to corporate realty situated in the detached territory, but no exception as to such property is even suggested. In *School District v. Richardson*, 23 Pick. 62, although only *obiter*, it is said that the alteration of a school district by increasing or diminishing its size would not destroy its identity or affect its rights of property; that as the identity of the corporation would remain, it would seem that the property would not be divested, although the schoolhouse, by the newly-assigned limits, might fall without the territory of the district.

"In *Union Baptist Society v. Town of Candia*, 2 N. H. 20, the proprietors gave the town of Chester a lot for the use of the ministry. A portion of the town, including this lot, was subsequently incorporated into a separate town by the name of 'Candia.' The town of Candia having realized a sum of money by an assumed lease of the lot, the plaintiff, a religious society incorporated and worshiping in Candia, brought suit for a portion of the interest on the fund. It is true that it may be said that this lot was not strictly public or corporate property, but merely held in trust by the town for pious uses; but in deciding the case the court says the facts do not raise the question whether a town, as a civil corporation, has the sole right to property given 'for the use of the ministry,' or whether each individual, each settled minister or each religious society in the town has a proportionate right to it. 'Because the lot was granted to Chester, and not to Candia, and whether by the grant there vested in Chester an absolute fee, a base fee determinable on the settlement of a minister, a trust for each theological association, or any other imaginable interest, is of no consequence. . . . It is apparent that when Candia was formed from Chester, though this lot fell within its boundaries it was not conveyed to that town, either in its charter or by any vote of Chester. The title to it, therefore, like the title to all other land within its limits, remained unchanged, and the town [of Candia] acquired over that, as over other land, only a corporate jurisdiction.' This was approved in *Southampton v. Fowler*, 52 N. H. 225, 230. *Whittier v. Sanborn*, 38 Me. 32, is directly in point. It was there held that the alteration by a town of the lines of a school district, whereby its school-house is left within the limits of another district, will not defeat or affect its right of property therein. (See also *North Yarmouth v. Skillings*, 45 Me. 133.)

"In the case of *Board of Health v. City of East Saginaw*, 45 Mich. 257, the facts were, that land had been conveyed to the board of health, in trust for cemetery purposes for the township of Buena Vista. Subsequently the city of East Saginaw was incorporated out of a part of the township, including the cemetery. This case, while perhaps like *Union Baptist Society v. Town of Candia*, supra, distinguishable in its facts from the present one, is nevertheless in point, in view of grounds upon which its decision is made to rest and the legal propositions laid down by the court. It was there held that corporate property is not affected at common law by changes which leave the corporate character in existence and do not destroy the corporate identity; that there is no common-law rule by which property can be transferred from one corporation to another without a grant; and that, as there was no statute making any different provision, the property was unaffected by the change in boundaries.

"In *Town of Milwaukee v. City of Milwaukee*, 12 Wis. 102, a portion of the town was annexed to the city, including a tract of land which the town had acquired by purchase. It was held that the act extending the city limits over the land in question did not divest the town of its title. The case does not disclose for what purpose the town acquired or used the land, but it is fair to assume that it was only for some public and municipal purpose. The weight of the decision as an authority in point, however, is weakened by the fact that the court denied the power of the legislature to divest a corporation of its property without the consent of its inhabitants.

"In *Town of Depere v. Town of Bellevue*, 31 Wis. 120, the broad and unqualified proposition was laid down, that if a part of the territory of a town is separated from it by annexation to another, or by the creation of a new corporation, the remaining part of the town, as the former corporation, retains all its property and remains subject to all its obligations, unless some express provision to the contrary is made by the act authorizing the separation. In this case, however, the only question before the court was the right of the old town to compel the new town to contribute toward the payment of corporate debts contracted before the division. We find no decision in conflict with this rule, although there are some *obiter dicta* suggesting the limitation or qualification of it contended for by plaintiff. Thus in *Hartford Bridge Co. v. East Hartford*, 16 Conn. 149, 171, after stating the rule as above, the court adds, 'at least as it regards property which has no fixed location in the new town, as lands, buildings, etc.;' and in *School District v. Tapley*, 1

Allen, 49, the court, referring to the dictum in *School District v. Richardson,* supra, remarks: 'It is at least questionable whether the better practical rule in all cases would not be to regard this species of property [school-houses] in towns as strictly local in its character and uses, and as vesting in the district in which, upon any new division, it might chance to fall.' How far this remark was suggested by the peculiar relations which school districts and school property bore to the towns in that state, it is impossible to say.

"In *Larimer Co. v. Albany Co.,* 92 U. S. 307, 315, the judge delivering the opinion says: 'Old debts she [the original corporation] must pay without any claim for contribution, and the new subdivision has no claim to any portion of the public property, except what falls within her boundaries; and to all that the old corporation has no claim.' The same limitation is repeated in *Mt. Pleasant v. Beckwith,* 100 U. S. 514, 525, and quoted by this court in *State v. City of Lake City,* supra.

"This is all we have been able to find in support of plaintiff's contention. But it is a remarkable fact that these suggestions of a limitation or qualification of the rule are not only purely *obiter,* but the question is not discussed, no reason is assigned, and no authority cited in its support, unless it be the old case of *North Hempstead v. Hempstead,* 2 Wend. 109, which, as we shall see, is not at all in point.

"There is a line of cases, often confounded with, but clearly distinguishable from, that now under consideration, where the old corporation was entirely abolished, and new ones created out of its territory. In such cases it is well settled that the new corporations are to be deemed the successors of the old one, and as such liable for all its debts and entitled to all its property.

And in the absence of any legislative provision on the subject, it is held in such cases that each of the new corporations will take the property which happens to fall within its limits. This result the courts have arrived at from what seem the necessities of the case, in view of the defective legislation on the subject. *School District v. Richardson*, supra, and *School District v. Tapley*, supra, fall under this head. Cases where two corporations have been united or consolidated into one may also be placed in this class. Such is *Robbins v. School District*, 10 Minn. 268 (340, 349.) The case of *North Hempstead v. Hempstead*, supra, also belongs to this class; for, as we understand the statement of facts, the original town of Hempstead had been entirely abolished and two new towns erected out of its territory, called respectively North Hempstead and South Hempstead, the latter afterwards changed to Hempstead; and notwithstanding some loose remarks apparently on both sides of the question we are now considering, the court made the decision of the case largely to turn upon the fact that the two new towns had acquiesced in a practical division of the property (common) for thirty-seven years, and therefore whatever their rights might have been at the date of the division, they were barred by the lapse of time. In *Connor v. Board of Education*, supra, the title of the schoolhouse was held to be in the city of St. Anthony, not by virtue of the act of 1860, extending the city limits, but under the express provisions of the act of 1861.

"The authorities on the question, so far as there are any, are therefore all against the contention of plaintiff, and upon reason and principle we cannot see why any distinction should be made as to property which, on change of boundaries, falls within the limits of another municipality, or why the title should not, like that of all other property, remain unaffected by the change."

§ 65. **District boundary.**—The boundary of a district may be established by its boundaries on a former division of the town into districts,[1] and where school society voted that F. and the occupants of his house shall be set to certain district, this included the farm and a house rebuilt in another place when first was taken down; and acquiescence for many years will estop the owner; and in 1808, school societies of Conn. had power to alter districts.[2] Under Mo. St. of 1879 the county commissioner cannot change, except as shown by the petition and notice.[3] Clerical error in defining boundary made by statute attempting to make union school-district boundary same as city, may be corrected.[4] The Mass. act of 1789, ch. 19, § 2, gives to a town the power to define the limits of school districts by geographical division of the town only.[5] A farm situated in an adjoining town having been annexed to a school district in P., a subsequent act, providing that P. shall constitute but one school district, was construed as meaning that P. (as now existing for school purposes) shall constitute but one school district.[6] Extending the territorial limits of a municipality does not enlarge the school district within it;[7] and courts will not consider whether certain territory included in a district is contiguous thereto, until the action of the officers of the district.[8] Where two districts were organized, embracing certain common territory, it would be included in the district whose organization was first commenced.[9] In Me., where the town

[1] Wilson v. Sch. Dist. No. 4, 32 N. H. 118.
[2] Scoville v. Mattson, 55 Conn. 144.
[3] Sch. Dist. v. Sch. Dist., (Mo.) 7 S. W. 285.
[4] Attorney General v. Hatch, 60 Mich. 229.
[5] Withington v. Eveleth, 7 Pick. (Mass.) 106.
[6] Pickering v. Coleman, 53 N. H. 424.
[7] State v. Ind. Sch. Dist., 46 Iowa, 425.
[8] Ind. Dist. v. Sioux County Supervisors, 51 Iowa, 658.

changes the limits of the district without the recommendation required by law, it is void.[1]

§ 66. District dissolution.—A tax-payer may have sale of property enjoined on dissolution of district, where a majority of the tax-payers do not vote, as required by law.[2]

§ 67. District library.—In the absence of any general and local regulations in regard to libraries, an action cannot be maintained by a tax-payer against the librarian for refusing to allow her children to take out books.[3]

§ 68. District organization.—Where a school society divided itself into five districts, designating them as the eastern, middle, southern, western, and northern, these terms were used as descriptive, and not for fixing their names, and evidence that one had been known by the name of the south district was admissible.[4] Proof that trustees are discharging the duties required by statute is *prima facie* evidence of the organization of the district.[5] On the formation of a town in Ind., it is entitled to the public-school buildings within its limits.[6] In Ill., an omission to file in the county clerk's office a list of the tax-payers and a copy of proceedings as to change of district will not prevent a *de facto* organization;[7] and under the Ill. school law the trustees of schools have no discretion to refuse to form a new district when it embraces at least five families; and when the law is complied with, if they refuse to grant such petition they will be compelled by mandamus;[8] but, in 1874, a new district line cannot be brought nearer than one mile to any school-house.[9] The only way in which the illegality of formation of district can be inquired into is by a *quo warranto*.[9]

[1] Allen v. Archer, 49 Me. 346.
[2] Briggs v. Bordean, (Mich.) 38 N. W. 712.
[3] Kennedy v. Ray, 22 Barb. (N. Y.) 511.
[4] Sch. Dist. v. Blakeslee, 13 Conn. 227.
[5] Swails v. State, 4 Ind. 516.
[6] Sch. Tp. Allen v. Sch. Tp., (Ind.) 10 N. E. 578.
[7] People v. Newberry. 87 Ill. 41.
[8] Trs. of Schools v. People, 76 Ill. 621.
[9] Trumbo v. People, 75 Ill. 561.

Where it does not appear that the trustees, in laying off a township into districts, acted corruptly or oppressively, a court will not interfere;[1] and the legality of the formation of a district cannot be inquired into collaterally.[2] A statute required the petition for a new district to be signed by "two-thirds of all the voters in any territory containing not less than five families": this meant two-thirds of all the voters residing in the territory proposed to be formed into a new district, and not five families residing in the particular territory taken from any one district.[3] In a suit of *quo warranto* against directors of new union district in Ill., formed out of territory in different townships, a plea is bad that does not allege that the petition for formation of the union district showed that it did not contain less than ten families.[4] In Ill., to form a new district from parts of two in different townships, the petition to trustees of each township must show legal necessity, and be signed by two-thirds of all the freeholders and legal voters.[5]

§ 69. **District organization.**—The failure to file a map with the county clerk does not invalidate the new district.[6] Where petition for organization of district lying in several townships is accompanied by the affidavits, mandamus is proper remedy to compel the formation of new district under Ill. Stat., Starr & C., p. 2214, § 34.[7] Under R. S. Iowa, 1860, ch. 88, incorporated cities, towns, and villages of not less than 300 inhabitants may organize as separate districts.[8] A district, formed by giving notice to and taking the votes of only a part of the residents therein, is illegally organized;[9] and under § 1800, Code Iowa as amended, the inhabitants of territory contiguous are not included

---

[1] Thompson v. Beaver, 63 Ill. 353.
[2] Alderamn v. Sch. Dirs., 91 Ill. 179.
[3] Boone v. People, 4 Ill. App. 231.
[4] Carrico v. People, (Ill.) 14 N. E. 68.
[5] Webb v. People, 11 Ill. App. 358.
[6] Sch. Dirs. of Dist. No. 5 v. Sch. Dirs. of Dist. No. 10, 73 Ill. 249.
[7] Trs. Sch. v. People, (Ill.) 13 N. E. 526.
[8] Fort Dodge v. Wahkansa, 15 Iowa, 434.
[9] Fort Dodge v. Dist. Tp., 17 Iowa, 85.

to make the number necessary to create the city into a separate district.[1] Under § 1800, Iowa Code, a village with contiguous territory must contain 200 inhabitants before forming it into an independent district.[2] Under Iowa amendment 1866, ch. 143, §§ 9, 10, the "contiguous territory" need not be confined to the same township in which the city, town, or sub-district is; nor is it restricted to territory in another township forming previously a part of such sub-district,[3] and it is not necessary that the boundaries should be fixed by the concurrent action of the two townships, to form the new independent district.[3] In Iowa independent districts may be created from two or more civil townships, or parts of the same, situated in adjoining counties.[4] Where the board of directors had created a sub-district and then it voted in favor of an independent organization, the fact that a sub-director had not been elected did not invalidate such organization.[5] A statute curing an informality in the election on the question of organizing an independent district, would not have the effect to change or modify the boundaries of such district.[5] Validity of school organization cannot be inquired into, in proceeding by tax-payer to restrain collection of tax,[6] and cannot be attacked except in a direct proceeding prosecuted by a proper officer.[7] The Ky. statute creating Harrodsburg educational district in 1876, does not conflict with common-school provisions of constitution.[8] Where a district is laid out by geographical lines, and then certain individuals and estates are added thereto, this does not violate the rule which requires districts to be established by geographical limits;[9] and where

---

[1] Allen v. Dist. Tp.. (Iowa) 30 N. W. 684.
[2] Allen v. Bertram Dist. Tp., 70 Iowa, 434.
[3] Ind. Sch. Dist. v. Supervisors, 25 Iowa, 305.
[4] Dist of Union v. Dist. of Greene, 41 Iowa, 30.
[5] Ind. Sch. Dist. v. Ind. Sch. Dist. 5, 48 Iowa, 157.
[6] A. T. & S. F. R. R. v. Wilson, 33 Kas. 223.
[7] Voss v. Sch. Dist., 18 Kas. 467; Sch. Dist. v. State, 29 Kas. 57; Stockle v. Silsbee, 41 Mich. 615; Clement v. Everest, 29 Mich. 22.
[8] Bd. Trs. v. Harrodsburg Ed. Dist., (Ky.) 7 S. W. 312.
[9] Alden v. Rounseville, 7 Metc. (Mass.) 218.

the town directed that certain persons named should compose the district (the land occupied by those persons should form the district not being expressed) the limitation of the district was invalid.[1]

§ 70. **District Organization.**—The formation of a village school district, confirmed by the legislature, was held to be legally established,[2] and the act of 1821, ch. 117, Me., made each school district a "body corporate," and included those existing *de facto*.[3] Under Laws of 1850, art. 2, ch. 193, § 2, it will be presumed, in a suit for building a school-house, that the district was legally organized, when for more than a year previous there had been a school, and it was kept in the school-house since it was built, and the expenses have been paid from the town treasury in the usual way, and taxes have been regularly levied.[4] An act of Me., providing that "every school district" shall be presumed to be legally organized, etc., is not conclusive in case of fraud.[5] The exercise of the franchise and privileges of a district by defendants for more than a year is evidence of organization.[6] Legislature may validate action of town that is informally defective,[7] and where a district has existed many years, and received its portion from the county treasury, a tax-payer cannot question the organization, to resist a tax,[8] and a district acting for thirteen years, with acquiescence of everybody, is not liable to have its organization called in question thereafter, in collateral suit.[9] As against a trespasser, the fact that the trustees of a school district have acted for years and had possession of school-house is evidence of their

[1] Withington v. Eveleth, 7 Pick. (Mass.) 106.
[2] Smyth v. Titcomb, 31 Me. 272.
[3] Whitmore v. Hogan, 22 Me. 564.
[4] Collins v. Sch. Dist., 52 Me. 523.
[5] Call v. Chadbourne, 46 Me. 206.
[6] Collins v. Sch. Dist., 52 Me. 523.
[7] Allen v. Archer, 49 Me. 346.
[8] Stuart v. Sch. Dist., 30 Mich. 69; State v. Cent. P. R. R., (Nev.) 25 P. 296.
[9] Stuart v. Sch. Dist., 30 Mich. 69.

incorporation.[1] Continued existence for more than twenty-five years prior to 1808, with acquiescence, the creation by act of legislature will be presumed.[2] After acquiescence for more than fifteen years, the division of the town and the regular organization of such districts will be presumed.[3] The existence of a district may be proved by reputation,[4] and the existence and operation of a school district may be shown by witnesses on the stand when the loss of the records of the district is shown.[5] Where a district has been organized, and has chosen its officers for years, it cannot be organized again as an unorganized district,[6] and a person may contest such organization, even if he was moderator of a meeting under such new organization.[6] There should be some special reason to justify interference by *quo warranto* with the organization of a district, where a speedier remedy is given by appeal.[7] County commissioners forming a district may appeal from order of district court that reverses their action;[8] but error does not lie in Pa. on a refusal of court of quarter sessions to open a decree establishing an independent school district under act of 1855, notwithstanding act of 1857.[9]

§ 71. **District organization.**—In Pa., to form an independent district the commissioners shall give notice of the time and place that they shall inquire into the expediency of establishing it.[10] Record must show proper notice of time and place was given.[11] Where new district in Mo. is petitioned for, only three notices need be posted in each district affected, and they need not describe the entire boundaries of the new.[12] The Mo.

---

[1] Robie v. Sedgwick, 4 Abb. (N. Y.) App. 73.
[2] Bowen v. King, 34 Vt. 156.
[3] Sherwin v. Bugbee, 16 Vt. 439.
[4] State v. Williams, 27 Vt. 755; Barnes v. Barnes, 6 Vt. 388.
[5] Sherwin v. Bugbee, 16 Vt. 439.
[6] Thomas v. Gibson, 11 Vt. 607.
[7] People v. Every, 38 Mich. 405.
[8] Moode v. Cummis, 43 Minn. 312.
[9] Brown v. Ind. Sch. Dist., (Pa.) 16 A. 32.
[10] Ind. Sch. Dist. No. 8, 33 Pa. St. 297.
[11] Frac. S. D. v. Bd. Insp., 63 Mich. 611.
[12] Mason v. Kennedy, 89 Mo. 23.

Rev. Stat., § 7022, in regard to formation of school districts, authorizes creation of districts only from unorganized territory; only three resident tax-payers can call a meeting of the tax-payers.[1] In Mo., the call to organize must come from tax-payers affected, and this is a condition precedent.[1] In Ohio, school district partly in different townships cannot be formed without the consent of a majority of trustees of each township, upon a petition of a majority of the citizens in the contemplated district.[2] A town at annual meeting may add a district to another, and then at a special meeting rescind that action and form a new one out of it;[3] and the action of county superintendent in attempting to organize a new district without authority does not invalidate a lawful meeting of legal voters of the district voting money lawfully.[4] A district, after ceasing to act for ten years, may organize anew, when required so to do by the town, without being by vote of the town set off anew.[5] Geographical limits must be defined by the vote of the town meeting;[6] and the geographical limits of a district must be defined by the inhabitants of the town, at a legal meeting warned for that purpose.[7] If a new district is without boundaries, its existence is suspended until they are designated by law;[8] and the lines of the new district should be reported by a plat.[9] The action on the report must be made at the term after that to which the report is made; a subsequent application to open the confirmation under Pa. act May 20, 1857, does not cure.[9] A city of the second class in Neb., having more than 2,000 inhabitants, including such adjacent territory as may be attached for school purposes, may be formed into one district under Neb.

[1] Perryman v. Bethune, 89 Mo. 158.
[2] State v. Treas. of Tallmadge, 17 Ohio, 32.
[3] Bill v. Dow, 56 Vt. 562.
[4] Baldwin v. Nickerson, (Wy.) 19 P. 439.
[5] Sherwin v. Bugbee, 16 Vt. 439.
[6] Pierce v. Carpenter, 10 Vt. 480; Gray v. Sheldon, 8 Vt. 403.
[7] Sawyer v. Williams, 25 Vt. 311.
[8] Williams v. Crook, 17 Pa. St. 199.
[9] Ind. Sch. Dist. No. 8, 33 Pa. St. 297.

Gen. Stat. 961, § 2, and the boundaries are not restricted to the city limits.[1] Vt. G. S., ch. 22, § 20, does not restrict the formation of a school district by a town, of connected contiguous territory.[2] Independent districts may embrace one or more townships, in Minn.; and Gen. Stat. 1878, ch. 36, § 94, is not controlled by § 17, which restricts the area to thirty-six square miles.[3] Under Mo. (Wagn. Stat. 1262, § 1), any city, town, etc., can organize for school purposes without including in such organization the whole sub-district to which it previously belonged.[4]

§ 72. **District Organization.**—Territory embraced in a school sub-district adjoining an incorporated town, may, under Wagn. Stat. 1262, be organized at the same time with that part within the corporate limits. It is not necessary that the voters within and without the corporate limits shall be in any certain ratio to each other, but a majority of the lawful voters must vote for the organization.[5] An act of the general court, incorporating part of the town known as School District No. 5, with a part of another town, into a school district, does not require that the legal existence of such a district as the one indicated should be proved, if known by that name.[6] A state legislature may pass an act prescribing a mode of organizing schools, and leave it to the people of each locality to determine by vote whether they will organize under the law or not.[7] Under Ohio Laws of 1853 and 1867, the whole of the sub school district which includes the village, continues to be a sub school district of township until the actual appointment of a separate school.[8] A tract containing twenty-eight square miles, of which not more

[1] State v. Bowers, 10 Neb. 12.
[2] Weeks v. Batchelder, 41 Vt. 317.
[3] State v. Sharp, 27 Minn. 38.
[4] State v. Searl, 50 Mo. 268.
[5] State v. Bd. Ed., 64 Mo. 38.
[6] Sch. Dist. v. Smart, 18 N. H. 268.
[7] State v. Wilcox, 45 Mo. 458; Compare King v. Phillips, 1 Lans. (N. Y.) 421.
[8] Clst v. State, 21 Ohio St. 339; Strong v. State, Iowa, 352.

than two are in a town, cannot be incorporated as a town for school purposes only, in Texas.[1] When a new district is formed, it is not, under act of April 7, 1849, recognized as an independent district until the termination of the current school year.[2] Where a town by the legislature was divided by a line, and the new town should organize under the Revised Statutes, the line left about one-thirtieth part of the district in the west town newly created, and the residue in the east town, and the inhabitants of that portion of the district in the east town voted a tax and elected officers, *held*, that the portion of the district was not a legal district.[3]

§ 73. **District, union.**—A union district was composed of parts of three different towns. Under Comp. Stat., ch. 20, § 21, a town in this case could not set one or more of its inhabitants to a district in an adjoining town with the consent of such district, because the parts of the district embraced in two of the towns did not appear ever to have had, or claimed to have, any organization as districts themselves. The district in question being a union district, composed of parts of different towns, one of these parts could not dissolve the district, or act as a district by itself. Acting together as a union district for more than fifteen years was sufficient to raise the presumption, in the absence of evidence as to the formation of the district, that it was legally created; in such a case, the district and one of its towns in which was the school-house, voted to accept into the district those portions of two other towns which had previously acted with and been considered parts of the district. This action could not be regarded as evidence that the existence of the district was not already perfect. Such union district legally formed can only be dissolved by application to the county court under

---

[1] State v. Eldson, (Tex.) 76 Tex. 302.
[2] Williams v. Crook, 17 Pa. St. 199.
[3] Tileston v. Newman, 23 Vt. 421.

the statutes Vt., (Comp. Stat. 150, ch. 20, § 47.) But where a quantity of land in a town, owned by a person residing in another town composing the district, was set off to the district and the towns, and the district for any considerable time acquiesced, all parties were bound. If otherwise, the action of the town would be merely nugatory, and the land would become no part of the district.[1] A village was incorporated including only a portion of district, having the residue in the town; the effect of the act was to create a joint district in the town and village. The town clerk should, upon the order of the school-district board, collect from the tax-payers of that part of the district lying within the town their proportion of the school-district tax.[2] Before the revised statutes N. H., there was no provision for the union of school districts in different towns.[3] A union free-school district in N. Y. may contract with attorney to defend a suit,[4] and trustees of a N. Y. union school district organized under acts 1864 are a body corporate.[5] Union of two or more districts in Me., does not abolish nor create a district.[6] A deed to inhabitants of C. and L. union district, if valid, vests the title in the inhabitants, but a justification under the title of such "inhabitants" is bad unless the names are given. The inhabitants of that portion of territory of C. and L. known as the C. and L. union school district "are not a corporation."[7] Under Ill. law of 1879, § 33, the superintendent cannot reverse the action of the trustees when they have granted the prayer for the dissolution of a union school district, and the circuit court may, on appeal, quash the proceedings had before the superintendent.[8]

[1] Bowen v. King, 34 Vt. 156.
[2] State v. Wolfrom, 25 Wis. 468.
[3] Foster v. Lane, 30 N. H. (10 Fost.) 305; Perkins v. Langmaid, 34 N. H. 315.
[4] Gould v. Bd. Ed., 34 Hun (N. Y.) 16.
[5] Porter v. Robinson, 30 Hun (N. Y.) 209.
[6] Tucker v. Wentworth, 35 Me. 393.
[7] Foster v. Lane, 30 N. H. (10 Fost.) 305.
[8] Badger v. Knapp, 7 Ill. App. 222.

§ 74. **Election.**—(See "Officer"—"Voter.") All tickets having more names than there are vacancies to be filled must be rejected.[1] In Iowa, in voting a tax for a school-house site, vote by ballot is not required, in the absence of a command of the statute;[2] and in the absence of any provision to the contrary, for election of a commissioner of common schools by the judges of a county court, in Ky., a vote may be given *viva voce* or by ballot.[3] In Iowa the requirements of the constitution for ballots do not apply to elections of meetings of the electors of the township for the transaction of business.[4] In Pa. the superintendent of schools cannot decide a question of a contested election.[5] Under P. L. N. J. 225, the presence of a majority of the taxable residents of the district is necessary to vote money at annual meeting, to build school-house, etc.[6] Section 1, Va. Acts, Mich. 5, 1846, entitled "An act for the establishment of a district public-school system," only requires two-thirds of those "legal voters" of the county voting to carry the act into effect in that county.[7] A certificate set forth that "the whole number of directors was 112, of whom 56 voted for S. and 55 for K., one refusing to vote"; there was no election; the number not voting was construed as voting for neither, or for the minority candidate.[8] In Ill. a notice of election in a school district "for the purpose of voting for a school-house site for a school-house for district, etc., and for issuing bonds to erect a school-house," is not invalid for indefiniteness or uncertainty.[9] A vote of the inhabitants of a school district at a meeting not legally called, to raise money for building a school-house, is void.[10] A notice of election "for the purpose of voting for a

---

[1] Contested Election, 6 Phil. (Pa.) 437.
[2] Seaman v. Baughman, (Iowa) 47 N.W. 1091.
[3] Johnson v. De Hart, 9 Bush. (Ky.) 640.
[4] Seaman v. Baughman, (Iowa) 47 N.W. 1091.
[5] Mershon v. Baldridge, 7 Watts (Pa.) 500.
[6] State v. Sch. Dist., (N. J.) 10 A. 191.
[7] Literary Fund v. Dalby, 4 Gratt. (Va.) 523.
[8] Comm. v. Wickersham, 66 Pa. St. 134.
[9] People v. Sisson, 98 Ill. 335.
[10] Haines v. Sch. Dist. No. 6, 41 Me. 246.

school-house site for a school-house for district W., and also for the purpose of voting for or against issuing bonds to erect or purchase a school-house for said district," is not invalid, although the amount of bonds is not named.[1] A notice that election would be held to determine whether a certain tax would be levied for the purpose of maintaining a graded school, is in conformity with Ky. act of 1854.[2] Under Tex. act authorizing special elections for supplementing school fund or building school-houses, the notice is sufficient if it shows that a tax will be imposed for school purposes.[3] A notice of election for tax, posted on three corners of two cross-roads, in Cal., is a posting in three public places;[4] and notice must state time at which election will be held, in conformity with general laws in Cal.[5] A vote to raise a sum to remove and repair school-house is within the statute to raise money "for erecting and repairing" school houses.[6] An election of director at a building rented for school purposes, although the district owned a school-house near by, no one having been prejudiced by the election at that place, was held valid;[7] and it is no objection to the election of trustees, that the meeting was held without the boundaries of the district.[8] The closing of polls prematurely will not defeat unless it works an injustice.[9]

§ 75. **Funds, apportionment.**—In creating Logan out of Weld county, Col., Weld county is entitled to retain the whole school fund belonging to it before the division.[10] It was held that the school trustees of one township were liable to those of another for money of the former, and ordered by the county

---

[1] People v. Sisson, 98 Ill. 335.
[2] Williamstown G. F. Sch. v. Webb, (Ky.) 12 S. W. 298.
[3] Reynolds L. & C. Co. v. McCabe, 72 Tex. 57.
[4] People v. Lansing, 55 Cal. 393.
[5] People v. Searle, 52 Cal. 71, 620.
[6] Bump v. Smith, 11 N. H. 48.
[7] Wakefield v. Patterson, 25 Kas. 709.
[8] Mayer v. Crispell, 28 Barb. (N. Y.) 54.
[9] Holland v. Davies, 36 Ark. 446.
[10] Cook v. Sch. Dist., 12 Col. 453.

board to be paid to the treasurer of the former,[1] and a district carved out of an older one is entitled to a *pro rata* share of the state appropriation for the current year;[2] but where statute makes no provision for apportionment, and the officers follow the statute, mandamus will not issue to compel an equitable division,[3] and an action by a district in Mo., against another carved in part out of the first, for part of school revenues, cannot be maintained.[4] Where a new district is made after apportionment of the fund among the counties on the previous year's enumeration, the new district cannot compel the old district to draw a warrant on the county treasurer for its claim to a proportion of the fund;[5] and where there is no privity between the boards of two districts, one cannot recover from the other taxes erroneously received by it belonging to former.[6] In Me., a district cannot maintain a suit for the money assigned by the town for the schools in that district against their school agent, although he has received it of the town;[7] and where county superintendent has to first apportion, an action cannot be maintained for the amount until so apportioned;[8] and acquiescence will prevent reopening an apportionment and recovery on old claim.[9] The legislature may divide townships and their school funds.[10] In Ind. money from the rent of unsold sixteenth section should be paid into the county treasury; a township trustee has nothing to do with it, except so much of it as may be apportioned to such parts of his township as are within the congressional township,[11] and where part of township is formed into a new one, in Ind., and it brings mandamus to compel the county

---

[1] Trustees v. Trustees, 81 Ill. 470.
[2] Lower A. Sch. Dist. v. Sch. Dist., 91 Pa. St. 182.
[3] State v. Sch. Dist., 90 Mo. 395.
[4] Sch. Dist. v. Sch. Dist., 18 Mo. App. 266.
[5] State v. Sch. Dist., (Mo.) 2 S. W. 420.
[6] Lyme Ed. Bd. v. Sch. Dist. Bd, 44 O. St. 278.
[7] Sch. Dist. v. Brooks, 23 Me. 543.
[8] Sch. Dist. v. Sch. Dist., 17 Neb. 177.
[9] Sch. Dist. v. Tp. Riverside, (Mich.) 34 N. W. 886.
[10] Greenleaf v. Tp. Trs., 22 Ill. 236.
[11] Davis v. Comm'rs, 44 Ind. 38.

auditor to issue a warrant for its share of taxes assessed by original township, the latter is not a necessary party;[1] and the dog-tax fund must be apportioned among the schools of the township, and cannot be used to employ a teacher in a single school district, or used in advance of the general apportionment for the year.[2] Laws 1858, ch. 52, § 32, Iowa, directing division of one-half of the school fund in equal amounts among all the school districts in the county, is unconstitutional and void.[3] Under Vt. Law 1888, ch. 12, § 233, a district cannot sue a town for money paid to other districts by order of selectmen.[4]

§ 76. **Funds, apportionment.**—Where treasurer's books show that he has money belonging to a district that he has not disbursed, to maintain an action on his bond for conversion an apportionment to the district does not have to be proven.[5] The Ky. act of 1874—attempting to empower the commissioner in counties to draw "the bonded surplus of school fund in the state treasury to the credit of his county," etc.—is unconstitutional.[6] The state superintendent may consider payment made to a parish under an erroneous apportionment when he makes a proper apportionment.[7] The Mich. constitution provides that certain revenues shall be applied to "the extinguishment of the state debt"; the debt is to be considered "extinguished" when there is money enough in the state treasury not subject to other claims, to pay it, even though it has not matured and has not been actually paid.[8] Township board cannot apportion money collected for the erection of a school-house in one sub-district, between the two new districts into which the same has been divided since the assessment. The Mo. law,

---

[1] Towle v. State, (Ind.) 10 N. E. 941.
[2] Maloy v. Madget, 47 Ind. 241.
[3] Dist. Tp. v. County Judge, 13 Iowa, 250.
[4] Sch. Dist. v. Town of B., (Vt.) 22 A. 570.
[5] Dist. Tp. v. Esperet, (Iowa) 39 N. W. 809.
[6] Auditor v. Holland, 14 Bush (Ky.) 147.
[7] State v. Fay, 36 La. An. 241.
[8] Aud. Gen. v. State Treasurer, 45 Mich. 161.

§ 25, provides a remedy for inequality of application;[1] and in Neb. a treasurer cannot rightfully demand moneys belonging to his district from the county treasurer, except upon a warrant of the director, countersigned by the moderator;[2] the county treasurer is not authorized to pay out funds to the credit of the county school fund, until they have been duly apportioned by county superintendent.[3] The inmates of Orphans' Home, Carson City, Nev., not having public-school privileges, are not to be counted as part of the children of Ormsby county in making the apportionment under the constitution,[3] and under the statutes, one-tenth of the property tax in Ormsby county in Nev., in 1863, levied for the county purposes, not including building purposes, should be set off for the school fund in lieu of 10 per cent. of county property tax required to be so set off by law, and one-tenth of the tax of 80 cents on $100, levied in 1864 in said county for general county purposes and a contingent fund, should also be set off in like manner.[4] Under Rev. Stat. N. H., ch. 72, the power of the selectmen to apportion school-money among the districts is to be exercised from time to time, as changes in the district may require;[5] money apportioned may be held by trustees for the benefit of the district, even if it is afterward abolished.[6] The act of 1850 — as to incorporated orphan asylums, except in the city of New York — entitles them to share in the distribution of all moneys raised in their respective cities or received by the board of education for school purposes, except moneys which are received from the state for the school fund, the appropriation of which is fixed by art. 9, § 1, of the constitution of 1846.[7]

[1] Rice v. McClelland, 58 Mo. 117.
[2] Donnelly v. Durass, 11 Neb. 283.
[3] State v. Dovey, (Nev.) 12 P. 910.
[4] Trs. Sch. Dist. v. Co. Comm'rs, 1 Nev. 334.
[5] Sch. Dist. v. Sanborn, 25 N. H. (5 Fost.) 34.
[6] Sch. Dist. v. City Concord, (N. H.) 9 A. 630.
[7] St. Patrick's Orphan Asylum v. Bd. Ed., 34 How. (N. Y.) Pr. 227.

§ 77. **Funds, apportionment.**—Laws N. Y. 1864, ch. 555, art. 2, does not confer upon the superintendent of public instruction power to determine an appeal from an apportionment by the board of town auditors under act of 1870. Laws N. Y. 1870, ch. 591, authorized the town of H. to elect a treasurer to receive moneys from the sale of lands, and that so much of the interest as might be deemed necessary for the common schools should be apportioned among the several districts as the public-school moneys of the state were apportioned, and the apportionment certified to the treasurer by the board of town auditors. When the board of town auditors had apportioned the moneys of certain years, mandamus would not lie to compel them to modify their apportionment to conform to the corrections subsequently made by the superintendent of public instruction;[1] and the provision of act of 1848 has reference only to the money raised for the support of schools in and by the city of Brooklyn.[2] Under § 24 of the act to establish the school fund, providing that township tax, levied for the continuation of the schools after the state tax has been exhausted, shall be applied only to the payment of the teachers in the proper townships, the board cannot make distribution in any other proportion than that authorized by statute, although it has not funds to keep a school in each sub-district for seven months without so doing.[3] Mandamus will not lie to compel the payment by treasurer of U. county to M. county of taxes of 1884 collected by U. county; and the board provided for by act 1885 to determine the proportion of net indebtedness to be assessed by M. county had no right to determine the rights of the two

---

[1] People v. Bd. Town Auds., (N. Y.) 27 N. E. 968.
[2] People v. Bd. Ed., 13 Barb. (N. Y.) 400.
[3] Bd. Ed. v. Cheney, 5 Ohio St. 67.

counties to the school taxes for 1884.¹ The state appropriation for schools is based upon the taxable inhabitants of each district, and the amount to be assessed by the directors of a district is based upon the amount of the state appropriation for that year.² On the subdivision of a district, it is the duty of a county judge to apportion its school funds among the new districts formed, under Laws Tex. 1884, ch. 25, p. 46.³ Order of apportionment does not have to be filed in forming a new district.⁴ Mandamus lies to compel the county superintendent to make the proper order for money belonging to any district; and this is so where an act had been passed changing a district to another county, and school-moneys had previously become due the district from the former county.⁵ Under Iowa St. 1885, "credits" in connection with "assets" include houses, sites, furniture and fixtures, school-tax levy, county school tax and cash, less the liabilities of the district.⁶ Where districts were divided before Mich. act 1891, the old district remained liable for all debts and retained title to all the property.⁷

§ 78. **Funds, apportionment.**—A district detached from one county and attached to another, in Ark., (the children of the detached district having been included in the enumeration of the former,) must be included in the apportionment made by the county court.⁸ Counties are owners of the school funds until they are accredited to the several school districts.⁹ The board of education of San Francisco has no power to divert the school-money to any purposes not authorized.¹⁰ The treasurer cannot refuse to pay to one school district the apportionment

---

[1] County of Morrow v. Hendrix, (Oreg.) 12 P. 806.
[2] Alter v. McBride, 7 Pa. St. 147.
[3] Porter v. State, 78 Tex. 591.
[4] State v. Eaton, 11 Wis. 29.
[5] Brown v. Nash, 1 Wy. Ter. 85.
[6] Bd. Pelican v. Bd. Wis., 51 N. W. 871.
[7] City Winona v. Sch. Dist., 13 Mich. 14.
[8] Merritt v. Merritt, (Ark.) 16 S. W. R. 237.
[9] Cooke v. Sch. Dist., 12 Col. 453.
[10] Barry v. Good, 89 Cal. 215.

as part of the primary fund where it is the only district entitled thereto and the superintendent of public instruction makes the apportionment under Mich. St., § 5029, but the township clerk does not.[1] In N. H. a district situated in two or more towns is entitled to its proportion of the money raised;[2] and a district can claim its share of the funds, though no school is kept.[3] An action on a demand belonging to the district must be brought in the name of the district;[4] and a district may maintain a bill in equity against another which retains a tax claimed by the former.[5] The parish treasurer, in La., may demand from the collector the fund due to his parish, and sue to recover it;[6] and one board may recover its apportionment illegally obtained by another board, and when invested the property may be recovered.[7] The superintendent of a new town formed out of a part of an old one is entitled to sue for moneys that may have come into the hands of the treasurer of the latter, and which belong to those parts of districts within the limits of the new town.[8]

§ 79. **Funds, appropriation.**—Where there is an implied appropriation for a certain purpose, funds will not be diverted by mandamus.[9] The Ind. act of Feb. 24, 1871, in relation to the distribution of school funds to the several counties, held to be valid.[10] An action for money had and received is the only proceeding, by one school district against another, for money belonging to the plaintiff and wrongfully in the defendant's possession.[11] Under Mich. C. L., § 3647, a town treasurer can pay school-moneys only to the district assessor, and only on the warrant of the proper officers.[11] In Minn. a district treasurer

---

[1] Molles v. Watson, 60 Mich. 415.
[2] Sch. Dist. v. Twitchell, 63 N. H. 11.
[3] Sch. Dist. v. Morrill, 59 N. H. 367.
[4] Donnelly v. Duras, 11 Neb. 283.
[5] Sch. Dist. v. Dean, 17 Mich. 223.
[6] Hendricks v. Bobo, 12 La. Ann. 620.
[7] East Carroll Sch. Bd. v. Union Sch. Bd., 36 La. Ann. 806.
[8] Cassville v. Morris, 14 Wis. 440.
[9] Zartman v. State, 100 Ind. 360.
[10] Shoemaker v. Smith, 37 Ind. 222; Fulwiler v. Zern, 38 Ind. 208.
[11] Midland Sch. Dist. v. Sch. Dist. No. 5, 40 Mich. 551.

cannot pay a judgment out of moneys applicable only to other specific purposes.[1] The Mo. Constitution of 1875, art. 10, § 19, abrogated the continuing appropriations for the state normal schools made by the act of 1875;[2] and the inhabitants of the school township for the time being cannot dispose of, or in any way impair, the township school fund;[3] and the Neb. State University regents under the charter cannot dispose of the endowment fund or the fund accruing from ⅜ mill tax, in absence of statutory legislation.[4] The town system of N. H. authorizes the annual meeting to direct how the school-money shall be assigned.[5] Payment of a county superintendent's order for the state appropriation for public schools will not be compelled where the money has been applied for school purposes in the preceding year.[6] The common council of a city cannot appropriate money voted by the inhabitants to any other purpose;[7] and where there is no proceeding pending before the superintendent of common schools, he is not authorized to make an order directing the commissioners of a town to retain in their hands, to abide such order as may be thereafter made, the money about to be apportioned, pursuant to law, to a school district for teachers' wages.[8] An act of the legislature directed that the amount of a judgment, recovered against former trustees of a school district, for teachers' wages, should be levied and collected by tax, and the officers of the district had neglected to execute the law; the superintendent of common schools was not authorized to prohibit the school-moneys thereafter apportioned under the general laws of the state, from being paid over to the trustees.[8]

[1] Sch. Dist. v. Roach, 43 Minn. 495.
[2] State v. Holladay, 66 Mo. 385.
[3] Veal v. Charlton, 15 Mo. 412.
[4] State v. Babcock, 17 Neb. 610.
[5] Sch. Dist. v. Prentiss, (N. H.) 19 A. 1090.
[6] State v. Sheridan, 42 N. J. L. 64.
[7] State v. Hammell, 31 N. J. L. 446.
[8] Bennett v. Burch, 1 Den. (N. Y.) 141.

§ 80. **Funds, bonds.**—In a suit in Texas by surety of treasurer of county as assignee of audited school claims against the county, the fact that the treasurer had turned over special school funds to him who is surety on general bond, and that the treasurer had defaulted, will not defeat the suit.[1] La. Acts 1872, abolishing the free-school fund, is unconstitutional, and sale of bonds of said fund thereunder is void.[2] Act of legislature, directing commissioners of school fund to invest same in bonds issued to pay members of legislature, is void.[3]

§ 81. **Funds; constitution.**—The act of Fla. 1885, directing county treasurer to forward school-money to state treasurer, for apportionment by state superintendent, is contrary to Const., art. 8, § 7, which provides for the apportionment and distribution in the counties in proportion to children.[4] Act Ky., April 19, 1886, "to establish a public school in Morganfield, in Union county," the object being, by additional taxation within the district thus created, to have better school accommodations than its annual share of the common-school fund would afford, is not unconstitutional.[5] The act of 1865, Ind., that county auditor's report of amount of school fund when approved by superintendent of public instruction shall be conclusive, is unconstitutional, because it may be the means of not securing all.[6] An act of legislature which in effect makes a donation of a portion of the fund for another purpose than common school, is void.[7] The Ind. school laws of 1852, consolidating the several school funds into a common fund, violates article 8, § 7, of the constitution of the state, and is void.[8] (See also "Sectarian Schools.")

[1] Co. Caldwell v. Crocket, (Tex.) 4 S. W. 607.
[2] Sun Mutual Ins. Co. v. Bd. of Liquidations, 31 La. Ann. 175.
[3] State v. Board, 4 Kas. 261.
[4] State v. Barnes, 22 Fla. 8.
[5] Bd. Trs. Morganfield v. Thomas, (Ky.) 15 S. W. 670.
[6] Howard Co. v. State, (Ind.) 22 N. E. 255.
[7] People v. Allen, 42 N. Y. 404.
[8] State v. Springfield, 6 Ind. 83.

§ 82. **Funds; fines.**—(See also "Funds, Liquor.") In Iowa, the county where a forfeited appearance bond is collectible is entitled to the money for its school fund, under § 3370, Code;[1] and in Dakota, under act of 1875, all fines for offenses committed in the city of Yankton shall be paid into the city treasury to the credit of the board of education.[2] Fines belong to the school districts, and prosecuting officer cannot retain the fees out of them, in Iowa.[3] All such fines in last part of § 5, art. 8, Neb. Const., applies only to those arising under the rules, by-laws, etc., set out in the foregoing part of section.[4] The fines for breaches of penal laws are part of the school fund in Wis.,[5] and this fund belongs to the state, and an action is properly brought in its name for such, in the absence of statute;[5] and the act of 1891, giving two-thirds of a fine to informer, is constitutional; the proceeds for school means the remainder after lawful deductions.[6] The Neb. law of 1877, p. 171, relating to liquor licenses, contravenes § 5, art. 8, Const., and is void;[7] this clause of the constitution, giving license-moneys to the use of "common schools in the respective subdivisions where the same may accrue," passes the same to the school fund of the cities instead of the counties.[7] The county treasurer may maintain a civil action to recover for the school fund of the county, moneys received by towns and cities of the second class for license to sell liquor; this power is implied in his authority to collect.[8] The penalty for failure to forward freight imposed by N. C. Laws 1874–5, ch. 240, is not given to the county school fund by N. C. Const., art. 9, § 5;[9] under Const. N. C., penalties for non-com-

[1] Lucas Co. v. Wilson, 61 Iowa, 141.
[2] Yankton Co. v. Faulk, 1 Dak. 348.
[3] Woodward v. Gregg, 3 Greene (Iowa) 287.
[4] State v. Heins, 14 Neb. 477.
[5] State v. Casey, 5 Wis. 318.
[6] State v. DeLano, (Wis.) 49 N. W. 808.
[7] State v. McConnel, 8 Neb. 28; Hastings v. Thorne, 8 Neb. 160.
[8] City of Tecumseh v. Phillips, 5 Neb. 305; White v. City of Lincoln, 5 Neb. 505.
[9] Katzenstein v. R. & G. R. R. Co., 84 N. C. 688.

pliance with the provision of § 1959 should be paid to the school fund.[1] In Ind. personal effects unclaimed, and found by coroner on dead bodies, belong to common-school fund of county,[2] and the Ind. act of 1844 as to funds from estrays belonging to common-school fund is not repealed by act of 1881.[3] The board of education cannot be substituted as relator, or as party plaintiff, in an action for penalty brought by a private person in the name of the state, the right to sue being vested solely in the state.[4]

§ 83. **Funds, interest.**—The interest of the public moneys in the United States, which by the act of 1836 is appropriated to the use of the common schools, is not a part of the proceeds of the school fund, within the proviso to § 9 of the act of 1827, entitled "An act to provide for the support of common schools."[5]

§ 84. **Funds, investing.**—School boards in Neb. may invest in U. S. three-per-cent. bonds, and the premium paid for same should be paid from permanent school fund; but when so invested they are not to be changed.[6] Mo. Sess. Acts, 1865, p. 16, § 6, providing that the purchase-money arising from the sale of the stock held for school purposes by the state might be paid in the bonds and coupons of the state, is not unconstitutional.[7] Expending the proceeds of the 16th section of lands for the exclusive use of the township in which the land lies, is a sufficient compliance with the act of Congress; nor is a state bound to provide any additional fund for a township receiving the bounty, even though it does for other parts of the state,[8] and the proceeds of the sale in each township becomes a trust

---

[1] State v. R. R., 108 N. C. 24.
[2] State v. Marion Co. Comm'rs, 85 Ind. 489.
[3] Tippecanoe Co. Comm'rs v. State, 92 Ind. 353.
[4] State v. Marietta &c. R. R., 108 N. C. 24.
[5] State v. Jericho, 12 Vt. 127.
[6] *In re* School F., 15 Neb. 684.
[7] State v. Bank of State, 45 Mo. 528.
[8] Springfield v. Quick, 22 How. (Ind.) 56.

fund to be applied to the use of the schools in that township, and not elsewhere.¹

§ 85. **Funds, liquor.** — Where parts of three districts are within the limits of an incorporated village, the moneys received for liquor licenses will be divided equally between them in Neb.;² and where a village is partly in three districts and school-houses of each outside of town, and $1,000 is derived from liquor licenses in the town, each is entitled to equal parts of the money.³

§ 86. **Funds, liquor.** — Under the two acts N. M. 1891, it was held that license-money for liquors should be placed to the credit of school districts and not to that of county;⁴ and in Neb. the money received for liquor licenses issued by county board belongs exclusively to county fund for common schools and not to district in which the liquors are sold.⁵ Where $1,000 was required to be paid in Neb. for liquor license it was held that the whole belonged to the district.⁶

§ 87. **Fund, loan.**—Selling under a school-fund mortgage for a sum materially exceeding the amount due, is a material irregularity.⁷ Laws 1864, ch. 118, § 1, Iowa, reduced the rate of interest on loans after Jan. 1st, 1864, whether before or after, from ten to eight per cent.⁸ The statute provides for loans of the school fund to a certain class of railroad companies; the commissioners of the fund shall draw their warrant if they are satisfied that the work has been done; their determination is a final, judicial decision,⁹ and whether the company is such that their application can be entertained, is a fact upon which their determination is not final;⁹ and in this case the warrant

---

¹ State v. Springfield, 6 Ind. 83.
² State v. White, (Neb.) 45 N. W. 631.
³ State v. Broadboll, (Neb.) 44 N. W. 186.
⁴ Bd. Ed. v. Laforge, (N. M.) 27 P. 616.
⁵ State v. Fenton, (Neb.) 45 N. W. 464.
⁶ State v. Wilcox, 17 Neb. 219.
⁷ Arnold v. Gaff, 58 Ind. 543.
⁸ State v. Hendershott, 21 Iowa, 437.
⁹ Houston etc. R. Co. v. Randolph, 24 Tex. 317.

does not even show that the applicant is an incorporation, and only corporations can receive the aid.[1] Under § 811 of the Revision, Iowa, when the state becomes the purchaser under the foreclosure of a mortgage executed to secure a loan from the school-fund taxes, a purchaser of the same lands from the state acquires a title discharged of all tax liens.[2] By Rev. Stat. Ind., 1881, § 4326, the counties are liable for the public school fund intrusted to them, and the annual interest; by §§ 4390, 5904, it is the duty of the county auditor, when premises mortgaged to secure a loan of such funds fail to sell for sufficient, to bring suit on the notes in the name of the state; the county might pay the deficiency before the auditor brought suit;[3] and where mortgaged lands to secure loans of school funds are sold and the county auditor bids in the land on account of the fund, no deed to the state is required, but the land must be appraised and sold before a suit will lie on the mortgage notes for deficiency.[4]

§ 88. **Funds, loan.**—A surety who signs a note given for a loan of the common-school fund, made by the county auditor, is not released by reason of the loan not being secured by a mortgage of real estate.[5] By Ind. Laws 1833, 89, § 96, it is provided that a school commissioner should not loan to any one applicant a greater amount than $300; a loan for a greater sum than $300 was void, and the mortgage was void.[6] When a county in Ind. has loaned school funds on a mortgage and bought the property in a foreclosure, and at subsequent sale it brings more than debt, the county is entitled to be reimbursed for interest advanced and paid.[7] A *bona fide* purchaser of land incumbered by a mortgage given to secure a loan of school

---

[1] Houston etc. R. Co. v. Randolph, 24 Tex. 317.
[2] Helphery v. Ross, 19 Iowa, 40; Jasper Co. v. Rodgers, 17 Iowa, 254.
[3] Lopp v. Woodward, (Ind.) 27 N. E. 575.
[4] Clark v. State, (Ind.) 10 N. E. 125.
[5] Scotten v. State, 51 Ind. 52.
[6] State v. State Bank, 5 Ind. 353.
[7] Bd. Comm'rs v. State, 122 Ind. 333.

funds, which was never acknowledged or proved, as the statute requires, to admit a mortgage to record, but was nevertheless recorded, is charged with constructive notice of the existence of such mortgage;[1] and a mortgage to secure a loan of school funds upon land on which there is a prior incumbrance, known to the auditor who had charge of the fund, is valid as against the borrower, notwithstanding loans should be made only on unincumbered land.[1] The act of 1861, Ind., which directs a three-weeks notice only, of foreclosure sales, applies to mortgages executed while the act of 1843 was in force.[2] The legislature has the power to direct in what manner the school funds shall be loaned.[3] A declaration on a note given for "school-money," on the school law of 1845, must aver that it was given for school-money, and claim the penalty; otherwise only ordinary interest is recoverable.[4] The act 1865, ch. 537, § 17, Wis., provides that in a certain contingency drainage-money in the town treasury "may be applied under the direction of the board of supervisors"; the money must be paid into the treasuries of the school districts and expended under the direction of the district boards, and not of the supervisors;[5] if the supervisors improperly loan such funds, taking a due-bill therefor, and transfer the due-bill to the school districts, instead of paying the funds into the district treasuries, the districts may maintain an action upon the due-bill against the makers.[5]

§ 89. **Funds, loan.**—Pending a litigation between the board of education of a township and a special school district, as to the custody and control of a fund in the township treasury, the board permitted the treasurer to use the fund in his business on

---

[1] Deming v. State, 23 Ind. 416.
[2] Webb v. Moore, 25 Ind. 4; Jones v. Hopkins, 26 Ind. 450.
[3] Bush v. Shipman, 5 Ill. (4 Scam.) 186.
[4] Sexton v. Sch. Comm'rs, 19 Ill. 51.
[5] Sch. Dists. v. Edwards, 46 Wis. 150.

his agreeing to pay interest thereon; when the treasurer's term expired the loan was renewed and a note with sureties taken. Such loan contravened public policy and the statute; the sureties thereon were not estopped from setting up the illegality of the transaction as a defense; in the absence of statute, the board had no power to ratify a contract made in violation of law.[1] In Ind., under §§ 79, 81, 82, of the act of March 5th, 1855, relating to school-fund mortgages, a county auditor might sell the land under the mortgage, or recover judgment on the debt, or both, or bring an action to recover on the debt and to foreclose the mortgage, but the auditor could not then sell the land under the mortgage, it being merged in foreclosure.[2] Where a county in Ind. loaned the congressional school fund, and on default paid interest, on foreclosure realizing enough to pay all due from the mortgages, the school fund is not entitled to interest paid, but that is for the county.[3]

§ 90. **Fund, loan.**—Under Miss. Acts 1854 and 1856, the board of police or the treasurer have the power to sell land included in the deed of trust from the borrower of the common-school fund to the sureties on the borrower's note; and for such purchase-money and the balance due on the original note may, in renewing the old note, take a new note from the original obligors, with new sureties.[4] In Mo., where additional security is given for prior loan, it relates back to date of original execution of the bond.[5] A mortgage by auditor of county for loan of school funds to himself is not void.[6] Married woman, in Ind., cannot obtain a cancellation of mortgage on her land for loan of school fund, on the ground that it is a debt

---

[1] Hartford Tp. Bd. Ed. v. Thompson, 33 Ohio St. 321.
[2] Ferris v. Cravens, 65 Ind. 262.
[3] Hamilton v. State, (Ind.) 24 N. E. 347.
[4] Gaines v. Faris, 39 Miss. 403.
[5] Co. Montgomery v. Auchley, (Mo.) 4 S. W. 425.
[6] State v. Levi, 99 Ind. 77, (overruling Ware v. State, 74 Ind. 181;) Stockwell v. State, 101 Ind. 1.

of her husband, because the auditor is not a party in interest.[1] In Mo. a payment of a school-fund mortgage to a deputy county clerk, who failed to pay the same into the county treasury, did not release the mortgage;[2] and a mortgage in Mo. to secure a loan of school funds is not invalid by reason of the clause "for the use of a specified section of land," instead of "for the use of the township to which the fund belonged."[3] Ill. statute requiring loans of school funds to be secured by mortgage, does not render an unsecured note void.[4] The riparian commissioners have no power, by a convenant contained in a grant to a railroad company, to discharge a mortgage investment of the school fund, such an act being unconstitutional.[5] A loan of school fund upon other security than that required is a misapplication of the fund for which the trustees are personally liable, but the mortgage or other security is not void;[6] and a mortgage taken by the county for the loan of funds, not under the statute, but good at common law, and containing a power of sale, is valid.[7] The Oreg. act to provide for the loaning of common-school funds, approved Dec. 19, 1865, is constitutional and valid.[8] Where the additional security required in Gross. Ill. Stat. 701, § 60, is demanded and not given, the whole debt matures, and may be foreclosed.[9] Where the statute requires two or more sureties to a note given for a loan, it will be presumed that at least two of the signers are sureties.[10] A person who signs as surety, after delivery, a bond under seal given to secure loan of school-moneys, cannot escape liability by showing that no order requiring additional security was entered

[1] Snodgrass v. Morris, (Ind.) 24 N. E. 151.
[2] Knox Co. v. Goggin, (Mo.) 16 S. W. 684.
[3] Grant v. Huston, (Mo.) 16 S. W. 680.
[4] Edwards v. Trs. of Sch., 30 Ill. App. 528.
[5] American Dock Imp. Co. v. Sch. Trs., 35 N. J. Eq. 181.
[6] Littlewort v. Davis, 50 Miss. 403.
[7] Mann v. Best, 62 Mo. 491.
[8] Kubli v. Martin, 5 Oreg. 436.
[9] Bd. Trs. &c. v. Davidson, 65 Ill. 125.
[10] Trs. of Schs. v. Southard, 31 Ill. App. 359.

of record, without also showing that there was no other consideration.[1]

§ 91. Fund, loan.—The power of a township trustee, under Rev. Stat. Ind., 1881, pp. 4328, 4329, to rent school lands, and to reserve rents payable in money, or improvements on the land, must be strictly construed; and where a tenant has undertaken improvements greater than the aggregate rents for the remainder of the term, an agreement by the trustees to extend the term after its expiration, if the tenant would complete the improvements, is void.[2] Under the Miss. act of Mar. 4, 1846, authority is given to county treasurers to loan out the school fund, not appropriated by the school commissioners.[3] The fact that one who signed a bond after delivery permitted it to remain with the county court without objection for six years, would estop him from setting up want of consideration in an action thereon;[4] such court cannot delegate the power to make loans, or to compromise those already made, without requiring the final approval by the court of the security.[4] In Miss. the trustees of school lands are authorized to loan money only upon personal security; and if a loan is made by them secured by a deed of trust, and lost, they will be liable.[5] In Mo., where a person borrows school-money of a county, and secures the payment by mortgage, the county court may on default of payment of interest, without notice, order the sheriff to sell the land according to the provisions of the mortgage.[6] M., a defaulter to the school fund in the sum of $500, agreed with B., his debtor, that the latter should give his note for $500 to the school fund and execute a mortgage to secure it. M. signed

---

[1] Montgomery Co. v. Auchley, (Mo.) 15 S. W. 626.
[2] Anderson v. Prairie Sch. Tp., (Ind.) 27 N. E. 439.
[3] Murray v. Smith, 28 Miss. 31.
[4] Montgomery Co. v. Auchley, (Mo.) 15 S. W. 626.
[5] Lindsey v. Marshall, 20 Miss. (12 Smed. & M.) 587.
[6] Hurt v. Kelly, 43 Mo. 238.

the note as surety, and it was received by the school fund commissioner and credit given to M., on his liability; the mortgage was never executed; taking the note without the mortgage could not be taken advantage of by the defendants.[1] A sale by the auditor, of lands mortgaged in Ind., is void if made for the payment of a greater sum than actually due;[2] and it makes no difference that the borrower had not filed the treasurer's receipt for interest with the auditor.[3]

§ 92. **Funds, officer.**—Where a school commissioner loans money on real estate to which the mortgagor had no title as shown from the public records, he was at once liable on his bond for the full amount of the loan.[3] Under Mich. C. L., §§ 2272, 7596, district assessor is the sole disbursing officer to be drawn upon by the director for any money of the district in the township treasurer's hands.[4] Under Wagn. (Mo.) Stat., 1246, 1247, the justices of a county court are bound to issue to the township clerk a warrant for the amount of the delinquent list of land taxes due the sub school districts before collection.[5] It is the duty of a school commissioner, on retirement from office, to deliver over to his successor the funds held by him.[6] By receiving money ordered by trustees of a township to be paid to them, the directors of a district are not liable to an action by the directors of another district claiming it; it must be against the trustees.[7] Under the Ill. school act of 1865, the school commissioner may refuse to pay money to a township treasurer who has not filed his bond.[8] In Ill., township collector must pay school tax to township treasurer.[9] In Mo., the county cannot discharge a surety on a bond for the loan of

[1] Bremer Co. v. Barrich, 18 Iowa, 390.
[2] Key v. Ostrander, 29 Ind. 1.
[3] People v. Haines, 10 Ill. 528.
[4] Frac. Sch. Dist. v. Mallary, 23 Mich. 111.
[5] Wallendorf v. Cole Co., 45 Mo. 228.
[6] Hamilton v. Cook Co., 5 Ill. 519.
[7] Sch. Dirs. v. Sch. Dirs., 36 Ill. 140.
[8] Pace v. People, 47 Ill. 321.
[9] People v. Yeazel, 84 Ill. 539.

money upon his giving his note with personal security.[1] The Supt. Pub. Inst. Ky. had no right after the auditing of school commissioner's claim by county judge to reject it because it did not show that the commissioner had visited the schools.[2] Where by statute school commissioners are given exclusive power over the school fund and all money due that fund is made payable to their order, they may sue for money due the fund;[2] and it is no objection that the defendant might have been sued on his official bond in the name of the state, or that the money due was raised by an illegal tax.[3]

§ 93. **Funds, use.**—The Straight University is not a public institution of learning, and therefore the constitutional prohibition to appropriation made in its favor must prevail.[4] The Wis. law, 1869, giving surplus drainage-money to schools, means "to be expended by the school officers of the district."[5] Where public lands were sold for Cornell University, and proceeds invested in four-per-cents, bought at a premium, the university was entitled only to net income.[6] County treasurer in Mo. is proper party in injunction suit to prevent illegal use of school fund.[7] Where the officials of a district have failed for years to account for funds received to pay debts for bounties to recruits, and there was no money in the treasury, the school board were authorized to levy a tax to pay matured obligations.[8] The legislature may delegate the power of taxation to the taxable inhabitants for raising a fund for the support of schools;[9] and the power to authorize local taxation for erection of school buildings is not unconstitutional.[10] The power of townships in N. J.

[1] Montgomery Co. v. Auchley, (Mo.) 15 S. W. 626.
[2] Pickett v. Harrod, (Ky.) 5 S. W. 473.
[3] O'Neal v. Sch. Comm'rs, 27 Md. 227.
[4] State v. Graham, 25 La. Ann. 440.
[5] Sch. Dist. v. Edwards, 46 Wis. 150.
[6] People v. Davenport, 30 Hun (N. Y.) 177.
[7] Black v. Cornell, 30 Mo. App. 64.
[8] St. Clair Sch. Bd's Appeal, 74 Pa. St. 252.
[9] Burgess v. Pue, 2 Gill. (Md.) 11; Steward v. Jefferson, 3 Harr. (Del.) 335.
[10] Newman v. Thompson, 4 S. W. 341; Bd. v. Harrodsburg Ed., 7 S. W. 312; Fitzpatrick v. Bd., 7 S. W. R. 896; Sch. Dist. v. Webb, 12 S. W. R. 298; Bd. Trs. v. Thomas, 15 S. W. 670.

to raise money for schools was restricted by act of 1846 to an amount not exceeding double that received from the state.[1] Where sub-districts lie in two counties, the taxes for contingent and teachers' fund belong to the district township to which the territory was attached, in Iowa.[2] The act of Va., authorizing payment of moneys due the literary fund to be made in coupons, is illegal, and act of 1884, providing that all taxes for school fund shall be paid in lawful money of the United States, is constitutional.[3] The excess over $50 from dog license under Ind. act of 1881, received by a city, goes to the township in which the city is, and the city cannot claim any of it for school purposes.[4] The act directing the purchase of "Collins's Historical Sketches of Kentucky" is unconstitutional in appropriating part of the school fund to that purpose.[5]

§ 94. **Funds, use.**—Where the territorial laws C. L., §§ 1840, 1845, authorized the board of education to designate private institutions where instruction should be given, and the tuition paid by the territory, and a contract was made accordingly, which contract required three months' notice to cancel, it was held that the constitution of the state subsequently adopted prohibiting appropriation to any sectarian institution, terminated the contract; and such provision did not contravene the U. S. constitution prohibiting the impairing of obligations of contract.[6] Miss. Acts 1878, p. 123, allowing pupils in private schools to receive *pro rata* share of the common-school fund, but not requiring freedom from sectarian control, or supervision of any state or county superintendent, or that the conductors exclude no pupils, is unconstitutional.[7]

---

[1] State v. Kingsland, 23 N. J. (3 Zab.) 85.
[2] Honey Creek v. Floete, 59 Iowa, 109.
[3] McGahey v. State, (Va.) 135 U. S.
[4] South Bend v. Jaquith, 90 Ind. 495.
[5] Collins v. Henderson, 11 Bush (Ky.) 74.
[6] Synod of Dakota v. State, (S. D.) 50 N. W. 632.
[7] Otken v. Lankin, 56 Miss. 758.

§ 95. **Fund, use.**—Under N. Y. Laws 1850, ch. 261, orphan asylums incorporated since its passage are entitled to share in money raised by tax in school districts, as well as in that raised by the state; but where a mandamus is asked, to compel the trustees of a district to pay to such asylum its share, and no money has been raised by the district for the asylum, and all the money has been appropriated to specific purposes, and the asylum school has not been taught by a duly authorized teacher, a mandamus ought not to issue.[1] The provision of § 8 of the Ind. law of 1865, prohibiting expenditure of certain school revenues in advance of apportionment, applies only to the school revenue for tuition, which belongs to the state and is by it apportioned.[2] Although a district may have voted a tax for erecting a school-house, the fund is beyond the control of its officers until its expenditure is authorized by a vote of the district.[3] Under the Pa. law of 1854, § 33, school-district taxes for building purposes cannot be diverted to ordinary purposes.[4] Under the authority of the board of school directors of a parish, the treasurer may make valid sale of the warrants of the state which represent that portion of the interest on the free-school fund due to said parish.[5] The power given by the Ky. constitution to the legislature to control the school fund cannot be diverted to the county courts.[6] By the act "imposing an additional tax of fifteen cents for the purpose of increasing the common-school fund," any sum produced thereby can only be applied in aid of the common schools.[7] In Ill., directors of schools may levy a special tax for school purposes without a vote of the people, but cannot use funds raised for one object

[1] St. Thomas Orphan Asylum v. Gowacki, 2 Thomp. & C. (N. Y.) 436.
[2] Harney v. Woden, 30 Ind. 178.
[3] Sch. Dist. v. Stough, 4 Neb. 357.
[4] German Tp. Sch. Dist. v. Langston, 74 Pa. St. 454.
[5] Concordia Sch. Dirs. v. Hernandez, 31 La. Ann. 158.
[6] And. v. Holland, 14 Bush (Ky.) 147.
[7] Collins v. Henderson, 11 Bush (Ky.) 74.

for another.¹ The Ky. act of 1872, appropriating common-school funds to V. Academy, is unconstitutional.² Special legislation which does not aid the general system, or relieve against hardships of its provisions or the defaults of officers, is calculated to destroy the system of common schools, and is unconstitutional.³

§ 96. **Funds, etc.**—In order to entitle the plaintiff to recover the penalty of 20 per cent. interest under the act of 1835, it must be claimed in the declaration, in a suit on a note given for loan of school funds.³ The Miss. acts of 1854, ch. 345, and of 1856, ch. 27, are directory in requiring deeds of trust on real estate to secure the repayment of the loans of the common-school fund, but they do not make void a note given for such loan, not secured by a deed of trust.⁴ In the absence of specific appropriation of 1891, Conn., § 2228, providing for 'annual division of income of school fund," amounts to an appropriation.⁵

§ 97. **Grammar and high schools.**—In Mass. it is not competent for a town to establish a grammar school for the benefit of one part of the town to the exclusion of the other.⁶ The Ky. act of 1884, authorizing the establishment of graded schools and application thereto of the districts *pro rata*, is not unconstitutional.⁷ In Ind. a majority of the whole number of trustees establishing a joint graded school may transact all the business.⁸ The act of March 12, 1858, Iowa, for the establishment of high schools in the counties, is unconstitutional and void.⁹ In Wis., where a joint high school was divided and one

---

¹ Pennington v. Coe, 57 Ill. 118.
² Halbert v. Sparks, 9 Bush (Ky.) 259.
³ Russell v. Hamilton, 3 Ill. (2 Scam.) 56; Hamilton v. Wright, 2 Ill. (1 Scam.) 582.
⁴ Gaines v. Faris, 39 Miss. 403.
⁵ State v. Staub, (Conn.) 23 A. 924.

⁶ Commonwealth v. Dedham, 16 Mass. 141.
⁷ Williamstown G. F. S. v. Webb, (Ky.) 12 S. W. 298.
⁸ Hanover Sch. Tp. v. Gant, 125 Ind. 557.
⁹ High Sch. v. Clayton, 9 Iowa, 175.

—8

of the districts failed to levy its portion of taxes, the remedy is by mandamus;[1] and that a course of study adopted is different from that contemplated by law, is not a ground for enjoining a legal tax for maintaining the school.[2] Where a high school was vested in township board, the formation of that territory into an incorporated village did not transfer the property or control of the high school to the board of education of the village.[3] The Ill. Rev. Stat., 957, § 35, for the creation and maintenance of high schools for a township on a vote of the people, is not unconstitutional.[4] A court will not interfere with establishment of high school when officers do not exceed their powers;[5] and taxes for high school were sustained in Mich.[6]

§ 98. **Judgment.**—In 1864, a school district was indebted to the petitioners. In 1866, it was united with other districts, and ceased to hold district meetings, in 1870; the petitioners recovered judgment upon their claim; the judgment was valid, and a mandamus would issue commanding vacancies in the district offices to be filled;[7] but in Mich. it was held after School District No. 5 of a town had been united to District No. 2 and a judgment was obtained against No. 5, that under 1 Com. Laws, § 2335, the new district was alone liable for the debts of the two former districts, and the judgment was therefore void.[8] A judgment against a school district cannot be impeached collaterally;[9] if judgment is rendered against a school district having no corporate funds, the remedy in the absence of statute is in equity.[10] If the members of a school district are individually liable for the debts thereof, under the school acts prior to 1851,

---

[1] Joint High Sch. v. Town of Green Grove, 77 Wis. 532.
[2] Richards v. Raymond, 92 Ill. 612.
[3] Bd. Ed. v. Bd. Ed., 41 Ohio St. 680.
[4] Richards v. Raymond, 92 Ill. 612.
[5] Wiley v. Sch. Comm'r, 51 Md. 401.
[6] Stuart v. Dist., 30 Mich. 69.
[7] Clark v. Nichols, 52 N. H. 298.
[8] Brewer v. Palmer, 13 Mich. 104.
[9] McLoud v. Selby, 10 Conn. 190.
[10] Kenyon v. Clarke, 2 R. I. 67.

R. I., their goods and chattels, or bodies, if to be found, must be levied upon before resorting to their real estate.[1] Under act of 1836, where there is a judgment against school district and it becomes dormant, it will have to be revived before execution can issue.[2] An order that a judgment for services as a teacher shall, after a return of no property found, be paid out of school funds of the delinquent township in the county treasury, does not improperly divert those funds; and "teachers of common schools," means in the free common schools of the state established by law.[3] The trustees of a district are not a corporation, so as to be liable to an action subjecting school property to execution.[4] In Mass. an execution against the inhabitants of a school district may be levied on the property of an individual member of the district; and may be so levied in the first instance, even if there is corporate property of the district, which can be taken and applied towards satisfaction of such execution.[5] One who has a judgment against a district township upon an order on the school-house fund, and to whom the directors have issued an order upon the treasurer for payment, in compliance with the Iowa Code, § 1787, is not entitled to payment out of the general fund to the exclusion of the holders of other orders on the school-house fund who have not obtained judgments. He may levy upon the property of the district, if any, to compel by mandamus the levy of a special tax, if the district has not levied the limit.[6] In Ill. a district treasurer cannot be compelled by mandamus to pay a judgment against the district, when there has been no order of directors or court for the payment of same.[7]

[1] Kenyon v. Clarke, 2 R. I. 67.
[2] Sch. Dist. v. O'Donnell, (Pa.) 19 A. 358.
[3] Trs. v. Simpson, 11 Ind. 520.
[4] Allen v. Trs. of Sch. Dist., 23 Mo. 418.
[5] Gaskill v. Dudley, 6 Metc. (Mass.) 546.
[6] Chase v. Morrison, 40 Iowa, 620.
[7] Watts v. McLean, 28 Ill. App. 537.

§ 99. **Legislature, powers.**—The rights of inhabitants of school districts, which depend upon the corporate existence of the district, are liable to be taken away by the legislature.[1] And the legislature has the general supervisory power over the public-school system, and may from time to time alter or change it by general laws not conflicting with the constitution of the state.

§ 100. **Mandamus.**—Mandamus to compel payment of debt can only be compelled after it has been reduced to judgment;[2] but this is an appropriate remedy to compel the county commissioners to pay over the amount of taxes levied for school purposes.[3] Mandamus will not lie against the treasurer of the old district to compel payment of funds to the new of such funds beyond his control;[4] and where district was divided into three townships, and one was to pay debts of original, the holder of an order could not compel the two to contribute.[5] The treasurer of the board of school inspectors is the proper custodian of the township library money; and the town treasurer is bound to pay it over; and mandamus will lie to enforce this duty.[6]

§ 101. **Mechanics' lien.**—In Ill. a general execution cannot issue against school directors.[7] The property of a school district is exempt from levy, and it is probable that no mechanics' lien can be maintained against it;[8] but in Conn. the private property of the inhabitants may be taken to satisfy a judgment against such district.[9] The "Board of Education of the State of Illinois" is a corporation, and its property is subject to a mechanics' lien;[10] and a lien was allowed against

---

[1] Farnum's Petition, 51 N. H. 376; Connor v. St. A. Bd., 10 Minn. 352.
[2] Sch. Dist. v. Bodenhamer, 43 Ark. 140.
[3] Bd. Co. Sch. Comm'rs v. Gantt, (Md.) 21 A. 548.
[4] People v. Hodge, 4 Neb. 265.
[5] People v. Bd., 41 Mich. 547.
[6] McPharlin v. Mahoney, 30 Mich. 100.
[7] Watson v. Abry, 9 Ill. App. 280.
[8] Leonard v. City Brooklyn, 71 N. Y. 498; Loring v. Small, 50 Iowa, 251; Charnack v. Dist. Tp. Colfax, 51 Iowa, 70; Bd. Ed. v. Maidenburger, 78 Ill. 58; Quinn v. Allen, 85 Ill. 39; Fluty v. Sch. Dist., 29 Ark. 97.
[9] McLoud v. Selby, 10 Conn. 390.
[10] Bd. Ed. v. Greenebaum, 39 Ill. 609.

school-house in Kas.;[1] but in *Brinkerhoff v. Bd. Ed.*, 37 How. Pr. 520, a mechanics' lien was refused and could not be enforced against a school-house, and so held in many cases;[2] and ordinarily will not lie against school-house in absence of statute authorizing same.[3] Whether execution can issue against school-house on mechanics' lien, is not decided.[4]

§ 102. **Meeting, etc.**—Where time of annual meeting is fixed it cannot be adjourned;[5] but an annual meeting may adjourn to next day in order to complete its business, and may appropriate money to pay for building a school-house.[6] It is not necessary that the meetings of a school district in Ky., to adopt the school system, should be fixed by the county court.[7] In order for the selectmen in Me. to call a meeting under R. S., ch. 11, a vacancy in office of agent of the district or refusal to act, must be shown, and a return on the notice may be amended.[8] A meeting called to see if the district will vote not to defend a suit for labor and materials in building a school-house, is not a meeting "for raising money for building or repairing a school-house," under Pamp. Laws, ch. 222, § 2.[9] Plaintiff offered evidence to show that at a subsequent meeting of the district prior authority was revoked. It was competent for the counsel claiming to have the authority to show that the vote of revocation was passed by illegal votes.[9] Where a meeting voted that the school-house should be sold at auction, and a new one built on the same site, the contract therefor to be given to the lowest bidder, it was a legal vote, and authorized the trustees to raise by tax the amount to be paid the contractor, deducting the pro-

---

[1] Wilson v. Sch. Dist., 17 Kas. 104.
[2] Phillips' Mech. Lien, 255, 610, 611, 60 Mo. 23; State v. Tiedeman, 69 Mo. 306; Wilson v. Cummins, 7 Watts, 197; Williams v. Controller, 18 Pa. St. 275; Foster v. Fowler. 60 Pa. St. 27; Poillon v. Mayor, 47 N. Y. 666; Shattel v. Woodward, 17 Ind. 225; Charnock v. Dist. Tp., 51 Iowa, 70; Mayerhofer v. Bd. Ed., 89 Cal. 110.
[3] Hovey v. Town, (R. I.) 20 A. 205.
[4] Wilson v. Sch. Dist., 17 Kas. 104.
[5] State v. Cones, 15 Neb. 444.
[6] Maher v. State, (Neb.) 49 N. W. 436.
[7] Chiles v. Todd, 4 B. Mon. (Ky.) 126.
[8] Starbird v. Sch. Dist., 51 Me. 101.
[9] Davis v. Sch. Dist., 43 N. H. 381.

ceeds of the old house.[1] A school district in its annual meeting may pay equitable claims.[2] Under the Minn. Comp. Stat., it is not necessary that the time for next annual meeting be designated at the preceding annual meeting;[3] and the directions to contract for erection or lease of a school-house must come from a district meeting in Minn.[4] In Minn. the powers of a special meeting are the same as those of annual meeting;[5] and ratification of act of trustees by district meeting renders the district liable, and this cannot be rescinded. In Vt., when collector of taxes for a school district was elected at annual meeting held at a time other than last Tuesday in March, he cannot justify under a tax warrant.[6] Where a district had adopted the Somersworth act, and had not chosen a committee, it was the duty of the selectmen to appoint a committee, and in case of their refusal to do so, a peremptory mandamus should issue.[7] The N. Y. laws authorizing building of school-house and issue of bonds, whenever the majority of all the inhabitants, etc., means the majority of those voting.[8]

§ 103. **Meeting, notice.**—Where notice of annual district meeting is given by two of the district directors it will be held sufficient, in Ark.[9] The record in a matter where there had been no notice in the warning, is of value only as to those matters upon which the district might lawfully act;[10] and under a call for district meeting to obtain information on assessment, a committee cannot be authorized to employ counsel to litigate at expense of district.[11] Where the warning stated that the object was to be "to take into consideration the expediency of

[1] Ackerman v. Vail, 4 Den. (N. Y.) 297.
[2] Stockdale v. Wayland Sch. Dist., 47 Mich. 226.
[3] Sanborn v. Sch. Dist., 12 Minn. 17.
[4] Robbins v. Sch. Dist., 10 Minn. 268.
[5] Sanborn v. Sch. Dist., 12 Minn. 17.
[6] Willard v. Pike, (Vt.) 9 A. 907.
[7] Butler v. Selectmen, 19 N. H. 553.
[8] Smith v. Proctor, 53 Hun (N. Y.) 143.
[9] Holland v. Davies, 36 Ark. 446.
[10] Wilson v. Watersville Sch. Dist., 44 Conn. 157.
[11] Wright v. North Sch. Dist., 53 Conn. 576.

raising money for the use of schooling for the year ensuing," held, it was sufficient to authorize the laying of a tax for that purpose.[1] Where, in 1839, a meeting was warned by posting a notice on two public sign-posts only, held, that by the act of 1823 (tit. 88, ch. 2, § 2), Conn., under which this meeting was warned, the notification was sufficient, notwithstanding a vote of the society 1822, that the notice should be on all the public sign-posts.[1] All that is requisite in the form of notice of a meeting for a special purpose, is, that it should be so that the inhabitants may understand the purpose.[2] Where the notice stated the purpose of the meeting, to decide whether the inhabitants would direct a suit to be commenced for the damage then lately done to the school-house and its furniture, and appoint agents to conduct a suit if necessary; it was sufficient, although it did not specify the nature or amount of the damage, or when or by whom it was done;[2] and where a notice of an election specifies several purposes in such a way as that no doubt is left as to its meaning, it will be sufficient.[3] Where the law does not prescribe what notice shall be given, reasonable notice only is required, and such notice will be presumed if the board meets and all members are present.[4] No notice is required for a regular meeting.[5] A meeting called to consider whether it would re-establish the school-district system and choose the officers required in such an event, and a vote taken at that meeting to so re-establish, is sufficient, under the Mass. act of 1870 (ch. 196), where the district was abolished by the act 1869 (ch. 110).[6] At a meeting called "to choose a district committee and to act on other business that may be thought

[1] Bartlett v. Kinsley, 15 Conn. 327.
[2] Sch. Dist. v. Blakeslee, 13 Conn. 227.
[3] Merrit v. Farris, 22 Ill. 303.
[4] People v. Frost, 32 Ill. App. 242.

[5] Aikman v. Sch. Dist., 27 Kas. 129; Hazen v. Lerche, 47 Mich. 626; Sch. Dist. v. Jennings, 10 Ill. App. 643; Ballard v. Davis, 31 Miss. 533; Downing v. Ruger, 21 Wend. 178; Sch. Dist. v. Bennett, 52 Ark. 511.
[6] Perkins v. Crocker, 109 Mass. 123.

necessary," it was voted that future meetings should be warned by the clerk of the district; and at a future meeting so warned a sum was voted, which was afterwards assessed; the vote at the first meeting was invalid, there being no article in the warrant concerning the calling of future meetings, and the assessment was illegal.[1] A return on a warning that "he had warned all the legal voters" in the district "to meet at the time and place, and for the purposes within mentioned," was defective in not specifying how or when notice was given.[2]

§ 104. **Meeting, notice.**—Where the warrant for calling the meeting shows the purpose of acting on the articles named in the application for calling the same, the articles are as much a part of the warrant as if embodied in the same.[3] Where the warrant for a town meeting was, "To act on anything in relation to the limits of school districts, that the town may see cause," and a petition from the inhabitants of the four school districts was presented and referred to the selectmen, who made a report, at an adjourned meeting, recommending that said four districts be made into three only, and their report was recommitted to them, "to divide said districts," the warrant for a subsequent meeting included, "To hear all reports of committees and act thereon," "To act on anything in relation to the limits of school districts, or relating to individuals or parts of districts, who may wish to be set off from one district to another," these were sufficient to authorize the last meeting to accept the report of the selectmen making three districts out of said four, and to establish them.[4] Where the clerk issued a warrant not under seal for annual meeting at time and in manner required by the by-law, as per order of the prudential

[1] Little v. Merrill, 10 Pick. (Mass.) 543.
[2] Perry v. Dover, 12 Pick. (Mass.) 206.
[3] George v. Mendon, 6 Metc. (Mass.) 497.
[4] Alden v. Rounseville, 7 Metc. (Mass.) 218.

committee, and returned on warrant in pursuance of the above warrant, "I have warned the legal voters of the district" "as prescribed by the by-laws, to attend and act upon the business therein named," the warrant and warning were valid.[1] A clerk, directed by vote as to how he should give notice for future meetings, has no power to call a meeting except when directed by proper authority;[2] and where a clerk was empowered to warn annual meeting he was not authorized to call other meetings;[3] and the manner prescribed by district for warning future meetings must be pursued;[4] and a district meeting cannot act excepting upon articles stated in the warrant.[5]

§ 105. **Meeting, notice.**—A vote to raise money at a meeting not properly called is illegal.[6] A meeting of a district called by the school agent, without the written application of three or more legal voters, is not in conformity with the statute.[7] The act 1850, ch. 193, Me., provides two modes in which meetings of school districts may be legally called. Since 1856, no opportunity for conflicting meetings has existed.[7] It is not necessary to the validity of a warrant from the selectmen, that the application should be recorded, or produced, or recited in the warrant.[8]

§ 106. **Meeting, notice.**—Where there was no school-house in the district, a return upon the warrant that he had notified, etc., "by posting up four copies of this warrant, one on the sign-post at the confluence of the A and B roads, one on the corner of the blacksmith shop, one on the Methodist meeting-house, and one in the postoffice, all of which places are in said district," was sufficient, under ch. 17, § 24, Me.[8] A district

---

[1] Kingsbury v. Sch. Dist., 12 Metc. (Mass.) 99.
[2] Stone v. Sch. Dist., 8 Cush. (Mass.) 592.
[3] Sch. Dist. v. Atherton, 12 Metc. (Mass.) 105.
[4] Hayward v. Thirteenth Sch. Dist., 2 Cush. (Mass.) 419.
[5] Holbrook v. Faulkner, 55 N. H. 311.
[6] Rideout v. Sch. Dist., 1 Allen (Mass.) 232.
[7] Sch. Dist. No. 5 v. Lord, 44 Me. 374.
[8] Soper v. Sch. Dist. No. 9, 26 Me. 193.

meeting may be called by the selectmen of the town, in Me., on the written application of three voters residing in the district, although not described as such in the application;¹ notice of district meetings is sufficient, if posted on the 16th of the month, the meeting to be held on the 24th.¹ Under act 1834, Me., where notices were posted "one at the school-house and one at the grist-mill, both in said district," this was a compliance with the statute.¹ Where a town has directed the mode of calling the meetings of school districts, it is necessary to show that such directions have been pursued.² A notice "for the purpose of hearing the inhabitants of said district on the subject of their disagreement, respecting a suitable place to be selected for the erection of a school-house in said district, and of deciding where such school-house shall be located, and lay out the same," is insufficient where application had been made to determine damages caused by appropriation of lot, under Me. R. S., ch. 11, § 57.³ Under Mich. law of 1867, § 16, (requiring ten days' notice of the meetings of boards of school inspectors,) no business not specified in the notice can be transacted.⁴ Under ch. 36, § 38, Gen. St. Minn., where the notice failed to recite on its face that the signers were freeholders, it is not void for the want of such recital.⁵ A resolution for the call of a meeting of the legal voters of the district of S. A. for the purpose of determining upon the erection of a school-house or school-houses, and the purchase of a site or sites therefor, and the amount of money to be raised for that purpose, etc., was sufficiently specific under the act of 1860, Minn.⁶ It may not be necessary that all three of the school officers must unite in a contract, to

---

¹ Fletcher v. Lincolnville, 20 Me. 439.
² Moor v. Newfield, 4 Me. (4 Greenl.) 44.
³ Leavitt v. Eastman, 77 Me. 117.
⁴ Passage v. Sch. Insp., 19 Mich. 330; Andress v. Same, id. 332.
⁵ Sturm v. Sch. Dist., 45 Minn. 88.
⁶ State v. St. Anthony, 10 Minn. 433.

make it binding upon the district, yet all of them should be duly notified, and afforded an opportunity to be present at all meetings at which any business is transacted for the district,[1] and official certificate of posting notice of election by director was held to be proof of due notice;[2] so an appearance before the selectmen and committee acting on a change in district may waive notice.[3]

§ 107. **Meeting, notice.**—Where the prudential committee on application of voters refuse to call a meeting, but within ten days afterwards call a meeting for the same purpose, but for a more distant day, this is such a refusal to call a meeting as, under Rev. Stat., ch. 70, N. H., will authorize the selectmen to call it; and the selectmen's warrant, dated before the lapse of ten days, but posted after, is valid.[4] In N. H. a notice of seven days is required for annual school-district meeting;[5] where there is a prudential committee duly appointed and qualified, the selectmen have no authority to warn a district meeting;[6] and an article in the warrant for a district meeting, to be held before the law of July 9, 1855, to "raise money" to build a school-house, will not authorize a vote to borrow money for that purpose, though passed at an adjourned meeting held after said law took effect;[7] and where proper officers neglect to call meeting for election of officers, in N. H., a justice may do so, and the warrant need not recite their failure.[8] Where money is voted to be raised by taxation, at a special meeting, the previous action of the trustees in calling the meeting under act 1867, § 39, subdiv. 11, N. J., should appear in the certificate of

---

[1] People v. Peters, 4 Neb. 254.
[2] State v. Sch. Dist., (Neb.) 33 N. W. 266.
[3] Andover v. Carr, 55 N. H. 452.
[4] Dennison v. Sch. Dist., 17 N. H. 492.
[5] Chapin v. Sch. Dist., 30 N. H. (10 Fost.) 25; Harris v. Sch. Dist., 8 Id. 8.
[6] Giles v. Sch. Dist., 31 N. H. (11 Fost.) 304.
[7] Weare v. Sawyer, 44 N. H. 198.
[8] Pickering v. De Rochemont, (N.H.) 23 A. 68.

the clerk to the assessor;[1] and special meetings of the voters must be called by the board of trustees regularly convened.[2] The notices should set forth the objects of the meeting; the resolutions adopted at the meeting should conform to the notice, and should show the objects for which the tax is voted; and the certificate of the trustees to the assessor should show all the prerequisites of taxation have been complied with.[3] A defective precept for meeting to elect officers cannot be taken advantage of to charge such officers as trespassers for official acts;[4] and in N. Y. it was held that the annual meeting is valid without notice if the time and place are fixed at the next preceding annual meeting, and the clerk acts in good faith;[5] and notice of special meeting to appropriate money to build a school-house gives power to consider the plans for the same, but not unless notice of purpose to build is given.[6] In Pa. an order to commissioners to view for an independent school district must direct ten days' special notice to be given to the directors of the district from which the new one is to be taken; putting up handbills is not such notice.[7] Condemnation proceedings were not illegal because the record did not show how the notices were posted, nor at what hour held, but did recite, "duly notified," and the notice showed the hour.[8]

§ 108. **Meeting, notice.**—A notice of special meeting, stating object to be "to take action in regard to the collection of the tax already assessed," will authorize the election of a collector;[9] posting one on school-house, another on building formerly used as a grain building, and the third against wall facing the road, held to be posting in public places;[9] a notice by

---
[1] State v. Hurff, 38 N. J. L. 310.
[2] State v. Sch. Trs., 43 N. J. L. 358.
[3] State v. Browning, 28 N. J. L. (4 Dutch.) 556.
[4] Ring v. Grout, 7 Wend. (N. Y.) 341.
[5] Marchant v. Langworthy, 6 Hill (N. Y.) 646.
[6] People v. Bd. Ed., (N. Y.) 1 N. Y. S. 593.
[7] Clearfield Ind. Sch. Dist., 79 Pa. St. 419.
[8] Howland v. Sch. Dist., (R. I.) 8 A. 337.
[9] Seabury v. Holland, (R. L.) 8 A. 341.

trustee for district meeting, in R. I., six days before the meeting, stating time, place and purpose is sufficient;[1] and notice of annual meeting in R. I., stating one of the objects to be "to decide what amount of money shall be raised by tax," is not invalid for not stating the use to which the money is to be applied;[2] but the notice of a special meeting, stating the "laying of a tax to meet the expenses of repairs," will not warrant raising, in addition, premium paid for insurance;[3] it was held that it is necessary that the warrant for a meeting of school district should be recorded by the district clerk;[4] and if it does not appear from the record of the warning, that the hour was specified in the warning, it cannot be supplied by parol evidence that it was, nor that all the legal voters in the district were present at such meeting, and voted upon the question of raising the tax;[4] but it has since been held the Vt. statute does not require a warning of a school-district meeting to be dated, and if the record shows no date, the date may be shown by parol; and it may be shown by parol when the warrant was posted up;[5] if a meeting of a district is duly warned by the clerk, without any application to him in writing for that purpose, and is held pursuant to the warning, it is legal and valid, but if such application in writing should have been made, the court would presume that it was made;[6] where a statute requires seven days' notice, a notice dated on the 1st day of the month, for a meeting to be held on the 7th, is insufficient, and the warrant for such meeting must also specify the business to be done;[7] and in computing time for notice, either the day on which the notice was posted, or the day on which the meeting was held, will be

[1] Howland v. Sch. Dist., 15 R. I. 184.
[2] Seabury v. Holland, (R. I.) 8 A. 341.
[3] Holt's Appeal, 5 R. I. 603.
[4] Sherwin v. Bugbee, 17 Vt. 337.
[5] Bealey v. Dickenson, 48 Vt. 599.
[6] Mason v. Sch. Dist., 20 Vt. 487.
[7] Hunt v. Sch. Dist., 14 Vt. 300.

counted;[1] where one article in the warning for a town meeting was, "To see if the town will make alterations in school districts when met," this was sufficient to warrant a vote taking a certain farm from one district and placing it in another;[2] a warning "To see if the town will vote to divide School District No. 9, in said town," was sufficient to make a division of that district.[3]

§ 109. **Meeting, notice.**—It was decided in *Sturm v. School District*, 45 Minn. 88 (Vanderburgh, J.): "A notice of a school meeting, over the signatures of five or more freeholders, qualified electors of the district, issued in a proper case under Gen. St. 1878, ch. 36, § 38, but which notice failed to recite on its face the fact that the signers were such freeholders, is not void for the want of such recital.—The first error assigned is that the notice calling the special school meeting, at which it was voted to remove the school-house in the school district mentioned in the pleadings, was defective in not stating 'who and what the signers are.' The point intended to be made is, that it does not appear upon the face of the notice that the signers are freeholders or householders, and qualified electors in the district. The answer which the court allowed to be interposed on opening the judgment herein shows that the persons named, or more than five of them, were in fact qualified electors and freeholders in the district, as the statute requires, (Gen. St. 1878, ch. 36, § 38,) and that the notices were duly posted as required by law, after the refusal of the district clerk to give notice of the meeting in pursuance of a petition or request so to do, signed by the requisite number of freeholders, and which petition recited that the signers were qualified electors, freeholders and householders in the district. The statute does not require

---

[1] Mason v. Sch. Dist., 20 Vt. 487.
[2] Ovitt v. Chase, 37 Vt. 196.
[3] Weeks v. Batchelder, 41 Vt. 317.

that the notice shall recite the legal qualifications of the persons signing it, although it is the usual and proper practice. But where the proceedings are attacked for want of jurisdiction, it is sufficient that the persons signing are so qualified; and this is a fact which may be easily ascertained by the officers of the district, or other persons interested, before or at the meeting, and before the subjects embraced in the notice are acted on. It is the fact, and not the recital, which gives the notice legal validity in this respect. (*Willis v. Sproule*, 13 Kas. 257; *Austin v. Allen*, 6 Wis. 134; *Washington Ice Co. v. Lay*, 103 Ind. 48.)"

§ 110. **Meeting, etc.**—Act Ill. 1889, p. 296, art. 5, § 19, providing that no official business shall be transacted by school directors, except at a regular or special meeting, does not invalidate official actions at a meeting at which all the directors are present, though such meeting is neither regular nor specially called;[1] the N. H. statute does not require the moderator of a district meeting to be elected by ballot, or to be sworn;[2] proceedings for raising a sum by special tax were held void for want of specification in the vote of the purpose for which the money was raised, and for want of power in the clerk to apportion the sum to be raised;[3] electors of independent districts in Iowa are given same powers of obtaining highways necessary for school, and voting tax, as at annual meeting of district township. (Acts 9th, G. A.)[4]

§ 111. **Normal, etc.**—The Mo. Constitution having vested all legislative power, not prohibited by the federal constitution, in the general assembly, the establishing of normal schools, it is fair to presume, was intended to be left with the legislature. Normal schools are public schools.[5] The es-

---

[1] Lawrence v. Trainer. (Ill.) 27 N. E. 197.
[2] Mitchell v. Brown, 18 N. H. 315.
[3] State v. Greenleaf, 34 N. J. L. 441.
[4] McShane v. Bd. Sch. Dirs., 76 Iowa, 333.
[5] Briggs v. Johnson Co., 4 Dill. 148.

tablishment of Va. normal school for females, is authorized, but the appropriation and handling of the funds provided for to be paid out of the public free school is unconstitutional.[1] In Kas. the principal and interest from sales of state normal school land is to be paid into the state treasury; the interest cannot be drawn out of the treasury except by act of legislature passed two years prior thereto.[2] Neb. state university regents cannot dispose of the endowment fund or that arising from the ⅝-mill tax, in absence of statute;[3] and the Mo. Constitution abrogated the continuing appropriations made by act of 1875.[4] In N. Y. it was held that the state superintendent has general supervision of the normal schools.[5] A statute directing that normal schools be sustained out of a fund which the legislature could not divert for that purpose, does not render the whole act void; and an act diverting common-school funds to normal-school purposes is invalid.[6]

§ 112. **Officer, etc.**—Under R. I. Gen. St., ch. 47, § 5, and the act of 1867, the school committee can appoint the superintendent of schools of Woonsocket, only when the council fails to elect;[7] the power to appoint a superintendent of schools in a union school district is an incident to that control which the district board has over the schools of the districts;[8] under the act of 1864, 825, § 12, the power of appointment and removal of principals and vice-principals in the common schools in the city of New York, is vested in the board of education;[9] where a director refuses to give up the books and papers of his office to claimant, his remedy is under How. St. Mich., ch. 295, providing for proceedings to compel delivery of books and

---

[1] State Female N. S. v. Auditors, 79 Va. 233.
[2] State v. Stover, 47 Kas. 119.
[3] State v. Babcock, 17 Neb. 610.
[4] State v. Holladay, 66 Mo. 385.
[5] People v. Hyde, 89 N. Y. App. 11.
[6] Gordon v. Comm'rs, 47 N. Y. 608.
[7] Verry v. Woonsocket Sch. Com., 12 R. I. 578.
[8] Stewart v. Sch. Dist., 30 Mich. 69.
[9] People v. Bd. Ed., 2 Abb. (N. Y.) Pr. N. S. 177; 32 How. Pr. 167.

papers by public officers to their successors.[1] In Ind., special bond must be given by county superintendents within thirty days from date of issuing of proclamation of governor announcing the making of a contract for furnishing school-books; superintendents must file their bond within thirty days after election if elected after the act; where bond is not given, party is entitled to notice and hearing before removal from office.[2] On a bond to disburse the "funds," a treasurer's bondsmen were held liable for drafts and certificates of deposit which the treasurer failed to turn over to his successor.[3] Where the board of education of a district elected a treasurer, required a bond with security, and it was received and acted upon by the parties, this was a sufficient approval, without any indorsement on the bond or any entry on their records.[4] The Pa. Const. 1874, prohibited special law incorporating cities, or special law changing school districts, or regulating the affairs of officers. The city of Wilkesbarre elected school controllers under the unconstitutional act of 1889, and at the same time elected six directors under act of 1854. These latter constituted the authorized school board.[5] If the clerk of the district fail to attend the meetings, the board may appoint a clerk *pro tem.*, and the entries of the clerk *pro tem.* are competent evidence of the proceedings of the meetings.[6] The clerk of district in N. Y. under the act of 1814 need not take the oath of office within fifteen days if he qualifies before any official act is done, and the collector may also be clerk of the district.[7]

§ 113. **Officer's compensation.**—The act of March 5, 1887, Nev., did not repeal act of Feb. 23, 1887, requiring district

---

[1] Culver v. Armstrong, (Mich.) 43 N. W. 776.
[2] Knox Co. v. Johnson, (Ind.) 24 N. E. 148.
[3] Reed v. Bd. Ed., 39 Ohio St. 635.
[4] Bartlett v. Bd. Ed., 59 Ill. 264; Green v. Wardell, 17 Ill. 278.
[5] Com. v. Reynolds, 137 Pa. St. 389.
[6] Hutchinson v. Pratt, 11 Vt. 402; State v. McKee, (Oreg.) 25 P. 292.
[7] Howland v. Luce, 16 Johns. (N. Y.) 135.

attorney to serve as *ex officio* superintendent of school without further compensation.[1] Where the district refuses to vote a tax to pay expenses of school officer, and he appeals but does not serve notice of appeal in time, it should be dismissed.[2] In Pa., the city treasurer acting as school treasurer as required, can draw salaries for both offices.[3] By the Ky. act of 1884, changing the commissioners to county superintendents, the commissioners were to be paid as before out of the school fund until their successors were elected and qualified.[4] The county superintendent cannot recover compensation for examining teachers at any other time than is provided in Iowa Code, § 1766.[5] When the treasurer of a district did not claim compensation for his services, in an action upon his official bond for misuse of funds nothing should be allowed for his services.[6] The provision of Ill. Rev. St., ch. 122, § 45, that the county collector shall pay over to the township treasurer "the full amount" of the school tax, means the amount less his commission allowed by ch. 53, § 21.[7] The superintendent of public instruction, Iowa, has power to approve of so much of the compensation allowed to a school fund commissioner by the clerk, sheriff and attorney, as he shall deem reasonable.[8] Where a county auditor in Ind. performs duties in the management of the school funds, he is entitled to compensation.[9] Under § 107, of the Ind. school law, the treasurer is entitled to the commission upon taxes levied by the townships for building schoolhouses, etc., authorized by § 12 of the same act.[10] Under the Ky. common-school law the commissioner is not entitled to

[1] State v. County Comm'rs, (Nev.) 23 P. 935.
[2] *In re* Merrill, 8 N. Y. S. 737.
[3] City Scranton v. Simpson, 25 W. N. C. 517; 19 A. 359; McCauley v. Sch. Dist., 25 W. N. C. 519; (Pa.) 19 A. 410.
[4] Pickett v. Harrod, (Ky.) 5 S. W. 473.
[5] Farrell v. Webster Co., 49 Iowa, 245.
[6] Ind. Sch. Dist. v. McDonald, 30 Iowa, 564.
[7] People v. Wiltshire, 92 Ill. 260.
[8] Jones v. Benton, 4 Greene (Iowa) 40.
[9] Wright v. McGinnis, 37 Ind. 421.
[10] Myrick v. Montgomery Co., 33 Ind. 383.

fees for each district visited, but only for each district reported;[1] and where an officer receives money as pay when he is not entitled to the same, it will be applied as a payment to the proper items.[2] Per diem includes fraction of day.[3] A member of the school committee of the city of Manchester, N. H., is, in the absence of any fixed or agreed sum, entitled to reasonable compensation.[4]

§ 114. **Officers, compensation.**—In Iowa, the salaries of secretary and treasurer of board of directors are a part of the necessary expenses for which the contingent fund is appropriated.[5] Under Tenn. Acts 1873, ch. 25, § 8, the county court may regulate the pay of the county superintendent of public instruction; and the decision of the court is final.[6] An account verified by county superintendent for services is *prima facie* case in his favor.[7] A superintendent was entitled to his salary, where the county board had not yet, under Wis. Laws 1874, ch. 342, divided the county into superintendent districts, but had treated such superintendent (who had been duly elected) as an officer *de facto* and *de jure*.[8] Under the Ill. Stat., July 1st, 1872, a county superintendent of public schools had not authority to hold a teachers' institute, at the charge of his county, unless the institute had been provided for by the county board.[9] Where superintendent sues for salary, it is error to exclude evidence that the board knew of his rendering services and accepted them.[10] The Wis. R. S., §§ 703, 704, in relation to counties having more than 15,000 inhabitants according to last census, and fixing salary of county superintendents by reference

[1] (Pickett v. Harrod, 5 S. W. R., overruled.) Pickett v. Adams, 15 S. W. R. 865; 16 S. W. R. 132.
[2] Pickett v. Adams, 16 S. W. R. 132.
[3] Smith v. Comm'rs, 10 Col. 17.
[4] Manchester v. Potter, 30 N. H. (10 Fost.) 409.
[5] Yaggy v. Dist. Tp. Monroe, (Iowa) 45 N. W. 553.
[6] Haile v. Young, 6 Lea (Tenn.) 501.
[7] Smith v. Comm'rs, 10 Col. 17.
[8] Clarke v. Milwaukee Co., 53 Wis. 65.
[9] Murray v. Bd. Sup. Clay Co., 81 Ill. 597.
[10] Davis v. Sch. Dist., (Mich.) 45 N. W. 989.

to inhabitants, means "inhabitants" as shown by last census.[1] In a suit against county commissioners for salary as county superintendent, pending proceedings to obtain the office, the county was not liable;[2] and in Kas., salary of county superintendent is determined from number of school children in the county, excepting cities;[3] in Cal., it is fixed by the supervisors.[4] County superintendents under Ind. R. S., 1881, are not entitled to special compensation for making statistical reports.[5] Acceptance of less than legal amount of salary without protest will not bar an action for remainder.[6] In Ill. a school treasurer is not entitled to any compensation above that fixed by the board of trustees before his appointment, for the performance of any duty imposed on him by law.[7] The collector of school tax in Ga. could retain his commission from tax.[8] In Mich. the director of a school district cannot recover pay for his services.[9] The Ohio Law of 1853, § 41, (S. C. 1360,) authorizing county commissioners to allow the auditor for services, is not repealed by act of 1861, (58 O. L., 7.)[10] Where money was appropriated by directors for bounties, and additional funds raised by subscriptions, and paid to a committee appointed by citizens, the district was not liable for the expenses of the committee.[11]

§ 115. **Officers, contract, etc.**—Where a school commissioner contracts by a writing showing on its face that he acts in his official character, although he does not add his official designation to his signature, he is not bound personally.[12] A board of directors empowered by statute, without any limitation, to employ a superintendent of schools, may contract for a term

---

[1] Geraghty v. Ashland Co., (Wis.) 50 N.W. 892.
[2] Wright v. Comm'rs, 21 Kas. 478.
[3] Comm'rs v. McCleary, 13 Kas. 149.
[4] Peachy v. Redmond, 59 Cal. 326, 548.
[5] Yeager v. Gibson Co., 95 Ind. 427.
[6] O'Herrin v. Milwaukee Co., 67 Wis. 142.
[7] Lovingston v. Sch. Tr., 99 Ill. 564.
[8] Mayor v. Bd. Ed., 87 Ga. 22.
[9] Hinman v. Sch. Dist., 4 Mich. 168.
[10] Gallup v. Lorain Co., 20 Ohio St. 324.
[11] Hartman v. Mt. Joy Sch. Dist., 68 Pa. St. 440
[12] Lyon v. Adamson, 7 Iowa, 509.

beginning after some members of the board go out of office.¹
A school director interested in the sale of a piece of property
may be enjoined from voting in favor of the district purchasing
it.² A contract made by two members of a committee of three
authorized to build a school-house will bind the district, especially when ratified by user.³ In Wis. a director must present
his claims to the board or at the district meeting, before suing
thereon.⁴ Where committee is authorized at meeting to either
build a new school-house or repair the old one, they may do
either.⁵ School directors cannot borrow money or give their
note for a site unless a vote first authorized the same, under
Ill. act, Scates' Comp. 445.⁶ The appointment of school directors by county court of Ark. will be presumed regular, and
warrants drawn by them for teachers' salaries will be valid.⁷
Indictment against school officer for neglect to perform act required must state that the conditions precedent (naming them)
had been performed.⁸ Where moderator of district was appointed by the assessor and director, on the supposition that
there was a vacancy, his official acts are valid;⁹ and a school
director appointed, and performing all the duties of the office,
is a *de facto* officer, and the district was bound by his acts, including a contract with a teacher signed during that time.¹⁰
When contest is against appointee of superintendent, the question as to whether he qualified cannot be inquired into if he
acted as such and has been ever since.¹¹ Where directors were
elected and acted, and their successors also acted for years,
none but the state can question their right to act because of

¹ Gates v. Sch. Dist., 53 Ark. 468.
² Appeal Witmer, (Pa.) 15 A. 428.
³ Fisher v. Sch. Dist., 4 Cush. (Mass.) 494.
⁴ Forbes v. Sch. Dist., 10 Wis. 117.
⁵ Morse v. Sch. Dist., 3 Allen (Mass.) 307.
⁶ Sch. Dirs. v. Miller, 54 Ill. 339.
⁷ Pierce v. Edington, 38 Ark. 150.
⁸ State v. Demerith, (N. H.) 9 A. 99; State v. Corbett, (N. H.) 9 A. 629.
⁹ Talmadge Sch. Dist. v. Town Trs., 61 Mich. 373.
¹⁰ Sch. Dist. v. Cowee, 9 Neb. 53.
¹¹ State v. Horton, 19 Nev. 199.

irregularities in organization of the district.¹ Where contract is with parties not officers *de jure*, no recovery can be had upon the same.² School trustees continue to be officers *de jure*, as well as *de facto*, after the expiration of their term of office if no successors to them are elected.³

§ 116. **Officer, district.**—Pub. Acts Conn. 1889, ch. 125, providing that the secretary of the state board of education shall *ex officio* be a member of the school committee of every town and school district in which is situated a school whose teachers are appointed by the state board of education, is not unconstitutional; in the absence of constitutional limitation, the legislature may make any provision as to the composition and appointment of school committees.⁴ Residents of a new school district who have children of school age may maintain mandamus to compel the county judge to appoint trustees for such district according to the statute.⁵

§ 117. **Officer, election.**—In the election of school examiner in Mich. by the chairmen of boards of school inspectors, only a plurality of the votes cast is necessary to an election.⁶ Where officers should have been elected by ballot and are unanimously elected *viva voce* and are acting and qualified, they will not be removed by *quo warranto*.⁷ In Pa., the continuing members of a school board are not judges of the legality of any election of directors.⁸ The Ark. statute requiring officers elected to take the oath and file it in office of clerk of county court does not make it the duty of that court to canvass the votes for directors.⁹ The absence of a proclamation will not invalidate a municipal election for school directors if the

---

¹ Franklin Ave. etc. v. Roscoe etc., 75 Mo. 408.
² White v. Sch. Dist., (Pa.) 8 A. 443.
³ Town Milford v. Powner, 126 Ind. 528.
⁴ State v. Hine, 59 Conn. 50.
⁵ Porter v. State, 78 Tex. 591.

⁶ People v. Stone, (Mich.) 44 N. W. 333.
⁷ People v. Gartland, (Mich.) 42 N. W. 687.
⁸ Bouton v. Royce, 10 Phil. (Pa.) 559.
⁹ Sch. Dist. v. Bennett, 52 Ark. 511.

election was general.¹ In Mass., where the records of a town meeting showed an election of a prudential and an examining committee, only the latter was construed to mean a school committee.² Where, in Oct. 1853, a school district, not within any incorporated city or village, under the act of June 18, 1853, elected trustees, and on the second Tuesday of Oct. 1858, the plaintiffs were duly elected under the act of April 12, 1858, the latter act repealed the former.³ In Iowa, where an independent district having six directors is, at a date of a certain election, reduced to less than 500, only one director can be elected.⁴ Where a sub-director took the proper oath, but failed to attend a meeting of the board of sub-directors on third Monday in March, the board had no authority to declare a vacancy.⁵ A vote by township trustee for himself for county superintendent is void and contrary to public policy;⁶ but where a board of township trustees elected one of their own number a member of the board of school trustees of the same town, whereupon he resigned as town trustee, and qualified as school trustee, his election as school trustee was valid.⁷

§ 118. **Officer, election.**—The board of education of a city, under Acts Mich. 1877, p. 440, cannot go behind the statements of election made by their canvassers of any of their members.⁸ Where statute of Nev. provides for an election in May each year for school trustees where there are two or more school districts in same election precinct, this does not authorize separate May election in a precinct comprising only a portion of several districts.⁹ The Miss. act providing for election of county superintendents in a part only of the counties of the

---

¹ Commonwealth v. Reynolds, 8 Pa. Co. Ct. R. 568.
² Hartwell v. Littleton, 13 Pick. (Mass.) 229.
³ Briggs v. Outwater, 30 Barb. (N. Y.) 501.
⁴ State v. Simpkins, 77 Iowa, 676.
⁵ Bennett v. Colfax, 53 Iowa, 687.
⁶ Hornung v. State, 116 Ind. 458.
⁷ State v. Meyer, 60 Ind. 288.
⁸ People v. Bd. Ed., 38 Mich. 95.
⁹ State v. Hanson, 20 Nev. 401.

state is not unconstitutional.¹ Act S. D. 1891, ch. 9, § 7, making it the duty of municipal corporations to hold an election at which a new board of education shall be chosen, leaves the time for holding it to be determined by the municipality; and the manner of conducting such election is the same as other municipal elections, except so far as the act provides otherwise;² and this act, providing for the election of a new board, does not oust from office the members of the old board until the new board is elected and qualified.² If the clerk, who has been irregularly elected, holding the office *de facto*, regularly calls an annual meeting of the district, the officers elected then are legally elected.³ Where Wis. act of incorporation provided for the annual election, and a subsequent general law provided for the election of directors every three years, the latter did not apply to the district in question.⁴ In S. C., upon the establishment of a new county, a school commissioner was elected a year before the assembly elections, and accepted a commission "to continue in force until the next general election"; he could not hold office after his successor, elected at such general election, had qualified.⁵ Where the constitution provides for the annual election of only one school inspector, and a statute provides for the election of two, the constitutionality of the statute will not be passed upon in a proceeding to review the action of the board in altering a district, where the action of the board was unanimous.⁶ Under Mich. act 1885, "majority" to elect trustees and "other officers" means moderator, director, and assessor; if none receives a majority vote, the old officers hold over.⁷ The plaintiffs suing as trustees of a school district, their

---

[1] Wynn v. State, (Miss.) 7 So. 353.
[2] *In re* Construction, (S. D.) 48 N. W. 812.
[3] Woodcock v. Bolster, 35 Vt. 632.
[4] State v. Perkins, 13 Wis. 411.
[5] Pettigrew v. Bell, (S. C.) 12 S. E. 1023.
[6] Donough v. Hollister, 82 Mich. 309.
[7] Cleveland v. Amy, (Mich.) 50 N. W. 293.

affidavits and bonds were sufficient evidence.¹ On certiorari, to reverse a tax, the legal existence of the corporation cannot be tried collaterally.²

§ 119. **Officer, liability.**—Where a commissioner collects a school fund he cannot avoid liability therefor by claiming that the funds do not belong to his office.³ Under Ill. Rev. Stat., ch. 122, § 77, for a misappropriation of school funds by school directors, a court of equity will not interfere; there is a remedy at law.⁴ In an action on treasurer's bond for loaning school fund on insufficient security, it is error to permit witnesses to testify that they never heard any dissatisfaction expressed in regard to the loan.⁵ If a township trustee, relying entirely upon the judgment of the board of directors, and against his own judgment, loans school fund on insufficient security, whereby a loss occurs, his official bond is liable therefor.⁵ The final report made by a school township treasurer, and the entries in his books made by him in such capacity, are conclusive evidence against him and his sureties as to the amount due, in an action on his bond.⁶ Where a township collector pays school moneys belonging to a certain school district to any person other than the treasurer of the proper township, he will be guilty of a breach of his bond, and liable to nominal damages, although the district loses nothing.⁷ If school directors exercise powers and functions not conferred upon them, they are responsible for all losses that may occur;⁸ they may borrow money for certain enumerated purposes, and their treasurer is the only proper custodian; should they place it in the hands of anyone else, it is at their own risk.⁸

[1] Eads v. Wooldridge, 27 Mo. 251.
[2] State v. Donahay, 30 N. J. L. 404.
[3] State v. May, 22 Ark. 445.
[4] Moore v. Fessenbeck, 88 Ill. 422.
[5] Bd. Trs. v. Baker, 34 Ill. App. 620.
[6] Longan v. Taylor, 13 Ill. App. 263, affirmed in 22 N. E. 745.
[7] People v. Yeazel, 84 Ill. 539.
[8] Adams v. State, 82 Ill. 132.

§ 120. **Officer, liability.**—Where the treasurer neglects to present a note against decedent for allowance against his estate, where it does not appear but that the sureties are solvent or that the debt is lost, no more than nominal damages can be recovered of the treasurer.[1] Under Ill. Law of 1857, §§ 45, 46, and 62, in actions for school taxes, the judgment on a collector's bond should find the amounts respectively due to each district.[2] Even though the school fund of a township may not be entitled to certain sums paid to its treasurer, yet the treasurer collecting the same is liable therefor to the board of trustees.[3] In a proceeding for mandamus against school trustees, if costs are awarded, it should be against them as trustees, and not personally.[4] School directors who had directed the township treasurer to receive, in lieu of money due the district, certain coupons upon the district bonds, are estopped from tendering back the coupons and demanding payment of the money.[5] If a school treasurer releases a mortgage given, due the school fund of his township, without an order of the board of trustees, entered upon their journal, and subscribed by their president and clerk, he will be liable upon his official bond for any loss.[6] A clerk of school board should not be taxed with costs personally when the record is quashed.[7]

§ 121. **Officer, liability.**—In an action against township treasurer of Ill. for not taking mortgage security in loaning school funds, it is no defense that board of education authorized it.[8] Where, in an action on the bond of a school trustee for a shortage in the funds, it appears that he paid money out of the special school fund, on account of the common-school fund, he

---

[1] McHenry v. Sch. Trs., 68 Ill. 140.
[2] Tappan v. People, 67 Ill. 339.
[3] Lovington v. Sch. Trs., 99 Ill. 564.
[4] Boone v. People, 4 Ill. App. 231.
[5] Humiston v. Sch. Trs., 7 Ill. App. 122.
[6] Bd. Trs. v. Mesenheimer, 78 Ill. 22.
[7] Trustees v. Shepherd, (Ill.) 28 N. E. 1073.
[8] Bd. Trs. v. Baker, 24 Ill. App. 231.

should be given credit on the amount thus paid.¹ An agent of the surplus revenue is bound to pay the interest received by him to the school commissioner, without demand.² An indictment against a school commissioner, for failing to make a report to the county auditor of moneys received and disbursed by him, should contain an averment that money had been received by the defendant, which he was bound to report.³ Under the Ind. act of 1833, the sureties on a commissioner's bond are liable for his acts only during the term of three years.⁴ A school commissioner may be indicted for a breach of duty; but the indictment, to be valid, must show the condition of his bond to be broken.⁵ School trustees are not liable for acts of another trustee in improper use of money where they did not coöperate.⁶ In an action against the treasurer of the city's school trustees, to recover for interest received by him on the funds in his hands, the interest received by him being interest accrued upon warrants issued in his favor by the county auditor on the county treasurer, for the funds themselves, and paid by the latter out of those funds, the defendant was liable.⁷ Under Ind. R. S. 1876, p. 781, § 7, when judgment is recovered against a township trustee on his bond, for default in his duties relating to schools and school revenues, ten per cent. damages upon the amount must be included in the judgment.⁸ The liability of the treasurer of a school district is absolute for all funds which come into his hands in his official capacity;⁹ and where a treasurer has settled and been discharged, the fact that his books are confused does not of itself create any liability.¹⁰ A prudential committee-man, chosen by the district, is not liable to the district

---

¹ Finney v. State, 126 Ind. 577.
² Mullikin v. State, 7 Blackf. (Ind.) 77.
³ Lathrop v. State, 6 Blackf. (Ind.) 502.
⁴ Tuley v. State, 1 Ind. 500.
⁵ Lathrop v. State, 6 Blackf. (Ind.) 502.
⁶ State v. Julian, 93 Ind. 292.
⁷ Hadley v. State, 66 Ind. 271.
⁸ Goldsberry v. State, 69 Ind. 430.
⁹ Bluff Creek v. Hardenbrook, 40 Iowa, 130.
¹⁰ Parish Sch. B. v. Packwood, (La.) 7 So. 537.

for money received by him from town treasury, raised by the
town, appropriated to the district, and placed to the credit of
district by town treasurer;[1] and a clerk *de facto* of a school district is not liable for certifying to the assessor that, at a legal
and duly organized meeting, it was voted to raise a certain sum
of money, on the ground of illegality in the meeting at which
he was elected clerk, or informalities and irregularities in calling and conducting the second meeting.[2]

§ 122. **Officer, liability.**—In an action for moneys unexpended in the hands of a school agent he cannot claim that
he was not sworn, nor retain a balance for services, which was
to be appropriated to certain purposes and belonged to the district.[3] A school district cannot maintain assumpsit against the
town treasurer for school-moneys, upon proof merely that such
moneys have come to his hands; there must be proof of some
default on his part;[4] but a township treasurer may not receive
for school-moneys anything which the law has not authorized
to be so received, and, if he does so and receipts for the taxes,
he must make good the amount.[5] A school-district clerk drawing a warrant in favor of a teacher for his wages, known to
him to be not licensed, is liable for penalty, under Minn. Stat.
1887.[6] A director or freeholder may bring an action against
trustee for penalty imposed for not providing school when
funds and school were voted for by district.[7] Where a statute
imposes a liability on an officer for funds coming into his hands
and requires him to pay and account for same without conditions, or limiting his liability, the obligors on his bond are
liable for the funds, even when the same have been lost or

[1] Sch. Dist. v. Randall, 7 Cush. (Mass.) 478.
[2] Allen v. Metcalf, 17 Pick. (Mass.) 208.
[3] Sch. Dist. v. Deshon, 51 Me. 454.
[4] 67 Me. 239.
[5] People v. Wright, 34 Mich. 371.
[6] Sch. Dist. v. Thelander, 31 Minn. 333.
[7] Soule v. Thelander, 31 Minn. 297.

stolen without any fault on his part;[1] and the discharge from liability, by the vote of the district and by the board of education, of a treasurer, for funds stolen from him, will not avail him or his sureties.[2] County superintendent is not liable in damages for manner in changing district and boundary where one-third of legal voters petition therefor.[3] In an action against a treasurer, it was no defense that he had made out his account, which the district had accepted, or that he deposited the money to his own credit in a bank, and directed that it be paid over to the holders of matured district bonds, but before this was done the bank failed.[4] The selectmen are not liable for indictment for failing to remove a school-house to a new site, designated by report of a committee, if the new site was not the property of the school district.[5] Under N. J. Nix. Dig. 735, §§ 9, 10, it is the duty of the trustees to make out a list of the children capable of attending school; the trustees were not civilly responsible for error or fraud therein, and the truth of the list could not be collaterally questioned.[6] A special meeting of the voters of a district may vote a tax although such has been refused at the annual meeting; and a judgment on appeal remitting the tax will protect the collector, but not for his refusal to collect taxes which have not been appealed.[7] To make district liable on note it must appear the debt was legal obligation;[8] and a note promising "as trustees of, &c.," but

---

[1] U. S. v. Prescott, 3 How. 578; U. S. v. Dashiel, 4 Wall. 182; Boyden v. U. S., 13 Wall. 17; Inhabitants v. Hazzard, 12 Cush. 112; Inhabitants v. McEachron, 33 N. J. L. 339; Com. v. Comly, 3 Pa. St. 372; State v. Harper, 6 Ohio St. 607; Dist. Tp. v. Morton, 37 Iowa, 550; Thompson v. Bd., 30 Ill. 99; Halbert v. State, 22 Ind. 125; Morbeck v. State, 28 Ind. 86; Ward v. Sch. Dist., 10 Neb. 293; Wilson v. Wichita Co., 67 Tex. 647; State v. Nevin, 19 Nev. 162; State v. Moore, 74 Mo. 413; State v. Powell, 67 Mo. 395; Com. v. Lineberger, 3 Mont. 231; Bd. Ed. v. Jewell, 44 Minn. 427; Com. v. Jones, 18 Minn. 119; Co. Com. v. Gilbert, 19 Minn. 214; Redwood Co. v. Tower, 28 Minn. 45.

[2] Bd. Ed. v. Jewell, 44 Minn. 427.
[3] Sch. Dist. v. Wheeler, 25 Neb. 199; Cowles v. Sch. Dist., (Neb.) 37 N. W. 493.
[4] Ward v. Sch. Dist., 10 Neb. 293.
[5] State v. Bailey, 21 N. H. (1 Fost.) 185.
[6] Tp. of Morris v. Carey, 27 N. J. L. (3 Dutch.) 377.
[7] State v. Lewis, 35 N. J. L. 170.
[8] Sch. Dist. v. Thompson, 5 Minn. 221.

signed individually, does not render the signers individually liable;[1] but where they promise as individuals and sign officially it is an individual liability,[2] and where they step outside official duties they must show authority.[3]

§ 123. **Officer, liability.**—The members of a board of trustees of the common schools of the city of New York are not liable in an action against them personally for the negligence of workmen employed by them;[4] and in an action against a trustee for the neglect of the duties of his office, a declaration in very general terms is sufficient.[5] The trustees of union free schools (N. Y. Laws 1864, ch. 555, tit. 9) are individually liable for personal injuries sustained by a teacher in falling through a floor which has become defective through their default and neglect;[6] and the board of education of the city of New York is liable in its corporate capacity for personal injuries caused by its neglect.[7] The board of education created under N. Y. Laws 1864, ch. 555, as to union free-school districts, are not individually liable for a neglect to perform a duty imposed on the corporation; the liability rests upon the corporate body.[8] It seems, however, that a member charged by the board as its agent, distinct from its corporate relation, with a specific duty, is individually liable for his neglect thereof;[9] but a judgment against all the members jointly, for a personal injury caused by one's neglect as agent or servant, is error.[9] School directors who vote for a misapplication of the public funds in payment of a teacher, are personally liable to the township;[10] and the treasurer, who was also a school director, and voted in favor of such payment, cannot shield himself under the warrant of the

---

[1] Sanborn v. Neal, 4 Minn. 83.
[2] Fowler v. Atkinson, 6 Minn. 412; Bingham v. Stewart, 13 Minn. 406.
[3] Sch. Dist. v. Thompson, 5 Minn. 221.
[4] Donovan v. McAlpin, 46 N. Y. Super. Ct. 111.
[5] Fitch v. Miller, 13 Wend. (N. Y.) 66.
[6] Bassett v. Fish, 19 N. Y. Supreme Ct. 209.
[7] Donovan v. N. Y. Bd. Ed., 44 N. Y. S. Ct. 53.
[8] (Reversing s. c., 12 Hun, N. Y., 209) Bassett v. Fish, 75 N. Y. 303.
[9] Bassett v. Fish, 75 N. Y. 303.
[10] Dickinson v. Linn, 36 Pa. St. 431.

board.¹ When school directors neglect to keep the schools open as long as is prescribed by law, they may be removed, but are not liable to indictment.² A certified settlement by the proper officers of the account of the treasurer of a school district, is conclusive if not appealed from.³ Five years' acquiescence on the settlement of collector's account by the township auditors, precludes the board from objecting to the record thereof as *prima facie* evidence; the auditors having destroyed his vouchers.⁴ The penalty for non-performance of duties of office, under the act of N. Y. 1819, does not extend to any particular act, but to general non-performance of the duties of office.⁵ Where a town in Mass. does not provide for care of its school-houses, the school committee employing a suitable person to cut down a tree in the school-yard are not liable for damages from his negligence.⁶ School districts in Pa. are not liable for negligence of their employés;⁷ and for trespasses committed by school officers they are personally liable and not the district;⁸ but school officers in Minn. are not liable for negligence in making repairs.⁹

§ 124. **Officers, power.**—The board of education of the city and county of San Francisco cannot delegate their power of visitation and inspection to other officers appointed by them, and they cannot employ inspecting teachers to visit, inspect, advise, and instruct.¹⁰ Error in appointing a building committee to contract is cured by discharging committee, and the district board acting instead.¹¹ By law, state of Ind. is divided into three classes of distinct municipal corporations, for school

---

¹ Dickinson v. Linn, 36 Pa. St. 431.
² McElhiney v. Commonwealth, 22 Pa. St. 365.
³ Porter v. Sch. Dirs., 18 Pa. St. 144.
⁴ Scott v. Strawn, 85 Pa. St. 471.
⁵ Spafford v. Hood, 6 Cow. (N. Y.) 478.
⁶ McKenna v. Kimball, (Mass.) 14 N. E. 789.
⁷ Ford v. Sch. Dist., (Pa.) 15 A. 812.
⁸ Sch. Dist. v. Williams, 38 Ark. 454.
⁹ Bank v. Brainerd Sch. Dist., 51 N. W. 814.
¹⁰ Barry v. Goad, (Cal.) 26 P. 785.
¹¹ Maher v. State, (Neb.) 49 N. W. 436.

purposes, to wit, "each civil township and each incorporated town or city in the several counties," and within the territorial limits of each of these school corporations each is entitled to the control of its school revenue; and the school trustees of a town within the limits of a township were entitled to the school funds of the township that belonged to such town.[1] Where by act Ga. 1889, pp. 1305, 1306, election notice to determine whether a local school should be established was published once a week for four weeks, and the last publication was inadvertently omitted, the omission may be treated as a mere irregularity if more than two-thirds of the qualified voters actually voted.[2] The failure of school trustees, granting a petition for the formation of a new district, to file a map and to order an election of school directors, will not invalidate the formation of the new district.[3] Where school trustees are compelled by mandamus to grant petition for formation of a new school district, the legality of such school cannot be collaterally attacked.[3] An assessor can be compelled by mandamus to pay sum appropriated by school district, at its annual meeting, to moderator for money paid by him for district.[4] The courts may compel school directors to perform their duties, or restrain them when they transcend their powers; but they cannot interfere in matters of discretion.[5] The board of education of San Francisco may maintain ejectment for a school lot;[6] but school directors can exercise only such powers as are expressly granted;[7] but if district has no school-house, and needs one, the trustees should secure a room.[8] When a trustee of school funds is such by color of title, his acts are valid as regards third persons; much

[1] Johnson v. Smith, 64 Ind. 275.
[2] Irvin v. Gregory, 86 Ga. 605.
[3] Sch. Dir. v. Sch. Dir., (Ill.) 26 N. E. 49.
[4] Phillips v. Sch. Dist., (Mich.) 44 N. W. 429.
[5] Wharton v. Sch. Dirs., 42 Pa. St. 358.
[6] Bd. Ed. v. Donahue, 53 Cal. 190.
[7] Sch. Dir. v. Fogleman, 76 Ill. 189.
[8] Gould v. E. E. Sch. Dist., 7 Minn. 145.

more when he is fully in office, except as to giving bond and taking the oath.[1] Two of the board of trustees, in Ill., concurring, may perform any act which the board is authorized to do, and their acts will be valid until vacated by direct proceedings;[2] but in N. Y. two trustees of a school district cannot act in the performance of their duties, except when all three are present, whether the third one refuses to act, or not.[3]

§ 125. **Officer, powers.**—Act Ill. 1889, p. 296, art. 5, § 19, does not invalidate official actions taken by board of directors at a meeting at which all the directors are present, though such meeting is not a regular one, nor one specially called in a statutory manner.[4] In Oreg. the oldest director in office shall preside as chairman of the meetings of the district; this means the one who has held office longest.[5] A district in Mass. may choose one member of a prudential committee and then adjourn and choose the remainder at adjourned meeting, and a majority of the prudential committee may act for the whole when minority refuses.[6] In Mich., the board of township school inspectors while engaged in altering the boundaries of a district, may adjourn their meeting to another time and place.[7] In a sub-district in Iowa, containing but five pupils, the board could direct that no school should be taught during the winter in their district, and provide for the attendance of their pupils elsewhere.[8] The Revision of 1860, § 2133, Iowa, allowing an appeal to the county superintendent, does not clothe the latter officer with judicial powers.[9] Under the Const. Iowa, the educational board have the primary power to provide for all public

---

[1] Rhodes v. McDonald, 24 Miss. 418.
[2] Trs. v. Allen, 21 Ill. 120; Schofield v. Watkins, 22 Ill. 66.
[3] Whitford v. Scott, 14 How. (N. Y.) Pr. 302; Lee v. Parry, 4 Den. (N. Y.) 125; Keeler v. Frost, 22 Barb. (N. Y.) 400.
[4] Lawrence v. Trainer, (Ill.) 27 N. E. 197.
[5] State v. McKee, (Oreg.) 25 P. 292.
[6] Kingsbury v. Sch. Dist., 12 Metc. (Mass.) 99.
[7] Donough v. Hollister, 82 Mich. 309.
[8] Potter v. Fredericksburg, 40 Iowa, 369.
[9] Sch. Dist. v. Pratt, 17 Iowa, 16.

—10

instruction;[1] and though the legislature can annul acts of the board they cannot originate measures, and they cannot act until the board of education is organized;[1] and the act of Mch. 12, 1858, so far as it provides for a system of public education, is void.[1] Under Iowa Code, tit. 12, ch. 9, a sub-director cannot interfere with the use of apparatus in schools of his sub-district.[2] The duties of school-district board can only be performed by joint action of officers.[3] If a board of education refuses to do an act required to be done at a particular time, and the board could be compelled to perform it, the board may afterwards, on its own motion, do the act.[4] Under Md. Acts 1872 and 1874, the state board of education have a visitatorial power of the most comprehensive character, and such power is, in its nature, summary and exclusive.[5] Section 37, of act of April 6th, 1863, Cal., to provide for the maintenance and supervision of common schools, is not repealed as to San Mateo county, by § 9, of act of Feb. 6, 1864, nor by § 12, of act Mch. 24, 1864.[6] Trustees, in cases beyond their authority and duties, must show their authority;[7] and the action of county board in Minn. in forming districts is legislative and not judicial, and cannot be reviewed on certiorari.[8] A party acting as prudential committee in a school district will be presumed to have been authorized.[9] A trustee for good cause may discontinue a school in Ind. where there are only four scholars and other schools are convenient.[10]

§ 126. **Officer, qualification.**—School commissioner of the city of New York must be at the time a resident of the ward for which he is chosen; and a removal from the ward for which

---

[1] Dist. Tp. v. Dubuque, 7 Iowa, 262.
[2] Dist. Tp. v. Meyers, (Iowa) 49 N. W. 1042.
[3] State v. Sch. Dist., (Neb.) 33 N. W. 480.
[4] Corrothers v. Clinton D. Bd. Ed., 16 W. Va. 5-7.
[5] Wiley v. Allegany Co. Comm'rs, 51 Md. 401.
[6] People v. San Francisco &c. R. R. Co., 28 Cal. 254.
[7] Sch. Dist. v. Thompson, 5 Minn. 280.
[8] Moode v. Stearns Co., (Minn.) 45 N. W. 435.
[9] State v. Williams, 27 Vt. 755.
[10] Tufts v. State, 119 Ind. 232.

he was chosen vacates the office.¹ Pa. act 1867, providing that service as a county, city or borough superintendent is a sufficient test of qualification on re-election, does not preclude other objections when the person is unfit to hold the office.² Pa. act providing that persons residing on certain lands in the township of N. are attached to the borough of S. for school purposes, and shall be entitled to the right to vote for and serve as school directors in said borough, is not contrary to constitution providing that electors shall reside in their election district.³ In N. Y. the same person may be appointed district clerk and collector of the district at the same time;⁴ and in N. H. the offices of selectman and school committee may be held at same time by the same person.⁵ The assessment by a sole prudential committee of a district, who is ineligible for that office, is invalid.⁶ The appointment of district collector under N. Y. L. 1864 should be made in writing, as required by the statute;⁷ but a parol appointment of the collector by a sole trustee of the district, his giving bond and the approval by the trustee, and the delivery of the tax warrant to him, constitute him an officer *de facto;*⁷ but the government may try the right to the office by *quo warranto;* his title may also be questioned where he is sued for an act which he can only justify as an officer.⁷ Section 27, act of April 17, 1873, requiring an applicant, before appointment as county superintendent, to submit with his application a certificate from the board of examiners, is constitutional, and an appointment without such certificate is invalid;⁸ but it has been held that the statute of Miss. which provides that superintendent of education must have a first-grade certifi-

¹ People v. Bd. Ed., 1 Den. (N. Y.) 647.
² Com. v. Wickersham, 90 Pa. St. 311.
³ Colvin v. Beaver, 94 Pa. St. 388.
⁴ Howland v. Luce, 16 Johns. (N. Y.) 135.
⁵ Andover v. Carr, 55 N. H. 452.
⁶ Woodcock v. Bolster, 35 Vt. 632.
⁷ Hamlin v. Dingman, 41 How. (N. Y.) Pr. 132.
⁸ Burnham v. Sumner, 50 Miss. 517.

cate is unconstitutional, and that anyone an elector is eligible.[1] Laws Mo. 1887, p. 273, § 5, which provides no person shall be eligible for a director "who shall not have paid a school tax within said city for two consecutive years immediately preceding his election," means a tax assessed on property in which the school director has an interest subject to taxation at the date of assessment or date of payment, paid at any time within two consecutive calendar years next preceding the year of the director's election.[2]

§ 127. **Officer, Qualification.**—A payment by a copartnership of a tax in part for school purposes against its personal property by one who is a member of the copartnership at the time; the payment of taxes on land by one having a tenancy by the curtsey initiate therein, out of his own means; and the payment of delinquent taxes on land purchased by the payor, though the payment was made for the express purpose of qualifying for the office, constitute a payment of taxes;[2] but the payment of delinquent taxes on land by a stranger for the purpose of qualifying for that office, or the payment of taxes for the current year instead of those for the two years immediately preceding the election, or the payment of a merchant's license which does not appear to be for the benefit of the schools, are not such payments of taxes as will qualify.[2] And superintendent employed by board trustees in Mich. is not required to have teacher's certificate.[3] Clerk of district in Mass., once duly sworn into office, afterward chosen clerk but not sworn again, may act as clerk under R. S., ch. 23, § 27.[4] The failure of a moderator of a school district in Neb. to take oath of office does not vacate the office; school-district officers are not required to take

---

[1] Wynn v. State, (Miss.) 7 So. 353.
[2] State v. Macklin, 41 Mo. App. 335.
[3] Davis v. Sch. Dist., 45 Mich. 989.
[4] Sch. Dist. v. Atherton, 12 Metc. (Mass.) 105.

oath of office;[1] and school director in Vt. is not required to be sworn.[2]

§ 128. **Officer, qualification.**—In Ark. it is necessary for the school director to qualify within ten days by subscribing the oath of office, and filing the same with the clerk, and until he thus qualifies, his predecessor is entitled to exercise the powers of the office, under Mansf. Dig., p. 6205;[3] under Kas. Stat., ¶¶ 5594, 5607, the failure of a district treasurer to give bond for nearly a year, where he was elected his own successor, did not create a vacancy;[4] but in a similar case the sureties on his original bond were liable for succeeding term.[5] Where director accepts the office, no notice to him is then necessary, and if he fails to file oath within ten days, the term of his predecessor will continue, in Ark.[9] An oath attached to the certificate is same as indorsement on, and indorsement on face is as good as indorsement on back of certificate.[10] The oath of office of school director cannot be administered by an election judge.[11] Where assessor and moderator are prevented from qualifying by a conspiracy, and tender their bonds and acceptance to proper party, their acts are valid.[11] An assessor cannot withhold the funds in his hands when the same are properly demanded by his successor, a fortnight after the latter has been regularly elected, and has accepted and qualified, upon any claim that he is entitled to be first personally notified, officially, of such election and acceptance;[18] and the oath of office taken by the clerk of a district will be presumed, when found on the records of the district to have been placed there properly, in the absence of other proof.[13]

[1] Frans v. Young, (Neb.) 46 N. W. 528.
[2] Brock v. Bruce, 58 Vt. 261.
[3] Sch. Dist. v. Bennett, 52 Ark. 511.
[4] Horneman v. Harlan, (Kas.) 29 P. 177.
[5] Riddle v. Sch. Dist., 15 Kas. 168.
[9] Sch. Dist. v. Bennett, 52 Ark. 511.
[10] State v. Horton, 19 Nev. 199.
[11] Culver v. Armstrong, (Mich.) 43 N. W. 776.
[12] Mason v. Frac. Sch. Dist., 34 Mich. 228.
[13] Tozier v. Sch. Dist. No. 2, 39 Me. 556.

§ 129. **Officer, removal.**—Where defendant in *quo warranto* files a disclaimer to office, the case is not to be dismissed, but a judgment rendered prohibiting him from interfering with the office.[1] Where there are two parties claiming to be the committee of school district, the remedy is by *quo warranto*.[2] In Pa. the power of the quarter sessions to remove school directors from office is limited by the act of May 8, 1854, § 9.[3] The school committee of a town cannot remove the clerk of the board, unless for cause, and after due notice, and opportunity is given him to defend himself;[4] but the clerk may waive formal notice, and the vote removing him will be valid.[4] The superintendent of Paris, Ky., city schools may be removed at any time by the board, without the approval of county superintendent, the school being carried on by special statute.[5] Proceedings by a township board to remove a director cannot properly be taken until the action of proper authorities by complaint of some definite violation of duty, (Mich. Comp. L., § 3695); but they may be waived.[6] The willful refusal of a school director to sign a contract made with a teacher, or to accept and file it, or draw orders for the teacher's pay while it is pending, or to furnish necessary supplies, may be considered in proceedings for his removal.[6] The township board is exclusive judge of the facts, under Mich. Comp. L., § 3695, to remove a school director, and its proceedings can only be reviewed by the courts on questions of law.[7] In Ill. supervisors may remove superintendent neglecting duty through intoxication, without giving him a hearing.[8] The directors having exercised their discretion in locating the schools, there was no authority

[1] Atty. Gen. v. Johnson, (N. H.) 7 A. 381.
[2] Hinckley v. Breen, 55 Conn. 119.
[3] Heard v. Sch. Dirs., 45 Pa. St. 93.
[4] Willard's Appeals, 4 R. I. 595, 597.
[5] Adams v. Thomas, (Ky.) 12 S. W. 940.
[6] Geddes v. Thomastown, 46 Mich. 316.
[7] Hamtranck Tp. Bd. v. Holihan, 46 Mich. 127.
[8] People v. Mays, 17 Ill. App. 361; People v. Mays, 117 Ill. 257.

for the court to remove them, under act Pa. May 8, 1854, except on evidence showing want of good faith in their acts;[1] and the court will not interfere to remove school directors, under act Pa. May 8, 1854, 9, for failure to provide a "suitable schoolhouse " (§ 23) where the houses provided are cheap, unsightly, unfit for permanent use, and hard to keep in repair, but not uncomfortable or unsafe;[2] but a refusal to consider a request by two citizens, made for themselves and on behalf of their neighbors, for enlarged school accommodations, in a case where the same is clearly required, is cause for the removal of the board;[3] the superintendent of common schools has the power of removing any county superintendent for neglect of duty, incompetency, or immorality; but there must be first a charge, notice, and opportunity of defense.[4] Where township board did not meet to agree on notice to remove school director, the proceedings for removal are not thereby invalidated in Mich.[5] Where directors were removed for not appointing teachers, the failure to agree as to the salary is no excuse.[6]

§ 131. **Officers, tax.**—The curative act of 1886 cures the irregularities in the election for officers and for taxing under Ky. act 1884, "imposing certain duties on board trustees certain district."[7] The legality of the existence of the district can be tried by an information against the district itself; or by an action of trespass against the members of the committee for any compulsory acts under its authority; or by resisting the payment of taxes laid by it, but not by *quo warranto* against an officer.[8]

§ 132. **Officer, term.**—The term of a truant-officer, appointed

---

[1] Price v. Barrett Tp. Sch. Dirs., 9 Pa. Co. Ct. R. 395.
[2] Ohio Tp. Sch. Dirs., 9 Pa. Co. Ct. R. 392.
[3] Connoquenessing Sch. Dirs., 9 Pa. Co. Ct. R. 425.
[4] Field v. Commonwealth, 32 Pa. St. 478.
[5] Wenzel v. Dorr, 49 Mich. 25.
[6] Appeal Sch. Dist., (Pa.) 15 A. 548.
[7] (Ky.) 7 S. W. 896.
[8] State v. North, 42 Conn. 79.

under Mass. Gen. Stat., ch. 42, § 5, expires at the end of the municipal year.[1] When a school district, at an annual meeting, has appointed one to act as prudential committee, it cannot during the year appoint another in his place, or add more to the number of the committee;[2] school-district officers, elected at annual meeting of district, will hold their offices until successors are elected, at another annual meeting.[3] The members of the board of education of Port Huron, Mich., hold office for specific terms, and are not city officers removable by the common council.[3] Miss. Const., art. 8, § 5, limits the terms of office of county superintendents of education to two years, and makes no provision for their holding over until their successors are appointed and qualified; and the term cannot be extended by legislature;[4] but in Vt., the officers of a school district hold their office until their successors are appointed.[5] Where party ineligible is elected county superintendent there is no election and the incumbent holds over, in Ky.;[6] and where a school trustee has been appointed to fill a vacancy, under Ind. act 1875, he is entitled under constitution to hold office until the qualification of his successor;[7] the successive annual elections for a school trustee should be held at the first regular meeting of the council in June; but a valid election might be had subsequently;[7] and a district trustee elected under § 39 of the act of 1849, Ind., continues in office until a successor is elected by the qualified voters.[8] The Nev. act authorizing trustees to be elected and one to hold for five years when there are five trustees, is unconstitutional.[9]

§ 133. **Officer, term.**—Where statute required division of

---

[1] Hase v. Lowell, 10 Allen (Mass.) 149.
[2] Chandler v. Bradish, 23 Vt. 416.
[3] People v. Port Huron Bd. Ed., 39 Mich. 635.
[4] Burnham v. Sumner, 50 Miss. 517.
[5] Walker v. Miner, 32 Vt. 769.
[6] Howard v. Cornett, (Ky.) 1 S. W. 1.
[7] Sackett v. State, 74 Ind. 486.
[8] Stewart v. State, 4 Ind. 396.
[9] State v. Harris, 19 Nev. 222.

school committee into three classes, the terms of which were one, two and three years, and there was a division of seven into classes of three, two and two, and where the term of two expired and another retired, and the council elected three, the first two held three years and the last only one.[1] The act of Va., in regard to county superintendents, declaring the office vacant July 1, 1886, and that all terms of four years should begin on that day, is unconstitutional and void.[2] In N. Y., where the term of attendance agents expired, they cannot claim that their successors are irregularly elected.[3] In Ark., statute providing that director elected shall within ten days file acceptance of office with predecessor, subscribe oath of office and file it with county clerk, and enter at once on his duties, is not affected by statute requiring officers of election to return the result to county clerk ten days before the meeting of county court, and director's term begins as soon as he has qualified.[4] Where, upon the establishment of a new county, a commissioner was elected a year before the assembly elections, and accepted a commission "to continue in force until the next general election," he could not hold office after his successor, elected at such general election, had qualified; under Const. S. C., a school commissioner is a state officer, and his election is governed by art. 14, § 10.[5] The commissioner was a candidate, and did not contest the election before the state board of canvassers; he was bound by its decisions.[5] Under act 1887, Ark., the term of office of the director so elected begins as soon as he has qualified as required by the terms of the act.[6] The superintendent of public instruction in Mo. continues in office

[1] State v. Lane, (R. I.) 18 A. 1035.
[2] Pendleton v. Miller, 82 Va. 390.
[3] People v. Bd. Ed., (N. Y.) 1 N. Y. S. 742.
[4] Sch. Dist. v. Bennett, 52 Ark. 511.
[5] Pettigrew v. Bell, (S. C.) 12 S. E. 1023.
[6] Sch. Dist. v. Bennett, (Ark.) 13 S. W. 132.

until his successor is duly appointed and qualified.[1] The board of education in Storey county, Nev., did not continue to hold office under art. 17, § 13, of the constitution, until 1867, as the legislature abolished said board prior to 1867,[2] and the president of said board was not entitled to exercise the office of superintendent of public schools after said board was abolished.[2] By the act of June 18, 1853, N. Y., and the act of April 12, 1852, the terms of "all school-district officers" theretofore elected shall expire on the second Tuesday of Oct. 1858.[3] The provision of the Ark. act 1875, as to time of appointing county examiner, is directory and not mandatory.[4]

§ 135. **Officer, treasurer.**—The treasurer of city board of education cannot excuse non-performance of duty as required by the records, by contradicting the records.[5] A settlement and discharge is conclusive unless procured by fraud.[6] The Ga. school law of 1870 repeals Code, § 378, making the ordinaries the treasurer of the boards of education of their respective counties.[7]

§ 136. **Officer, vacancy.**—The failure of a school-district officer, in Neb., to file a written acceptance of the office after the election, does not create a vacancy in the office, especially where there is acquiescence for more than a year.[8] A district prudential committee vacates his office by removal from town;[9] and if a trustee of common schools in the city and county of New York removes from the county, his office becomes vacant;[10] and where the clerk of a school district in Mass. removed from an adjoining district, but within the same town, and another

---

[1] State v. Thompson, 38 Mo. 192.
[2] State v. Tilford, 1 Nev. 240.
[3] Briggs v. Outwater, 30 Barb. (N. Y.) 501.
[4] Neal v. Burrows, 34 Ark. 491.
[5] Port Huron Bd. Ed. v. Runnels, 57 Mich. 46.
[6] Parish Bd. v. Packwood, (La.) 7 So. 537.
[7] Clarke v. Levy, 45 Ga. 498.
[8] Frans v. Young, (Neb.) 46 N. W. 528.
[9] Giles v. Sch. Dist., 31 N. H. (11 Fost.) 304.
[10] Gildersleeve v. B. Ed., 17 Abb. (N.Y.) Pr. 201.

was chosen in his stead, but not sworn, the first continued competent to act as clerk;[1] but a trustee's office is not vacated by an unaccepted resignation.[2] Vacancy in board of trustees (N. J. act 1854) may be filled by inhabitants; this does not exclude other modes of filling the same.[3] A resolution of a special meeting, appointing a trustee in the place of one who had been chosen a few days before, stated that the one first chosen "had refused to serve," in trespass against the trustee for causing a district tax to be collected; the second appointment will be presumed valid.[4] Where the annual district meeting is not held before Apr. 20th, in N. H., the offices become vacant and the selectmen may appoint.[5] A school examiner in Mich. appointed to fill a vacancy holds only for the unexpired term;[6] and failure to take oath of office by city school trustees in Va., in certain time, vacates the office, and others may be appointed.[7] The power of removing trustees of school districts was vested in school trustee electoral board in Va., in 1877.[8] Failure to elect prudential committee does not create a vacancy, but those in office at the time of annual meeting hold over.[9]

§ 137. **Officers, vacancy.**—Where school board organized and adjourned and there being no quorum, the only member present adjourned for several times; where the minutes did not show that the meeting for organization adjourned to that for business, the absence of the members from two consecutive meetings did not vacate their office, in Pa.[10] Where a school board cannot accomplish a permanent organization because no one of the members can obtain a majority of votes for president,

---

[1] Williams v. Lunenburg, 21 Pick. (Mass.) 75.
[2] Townsend v. Sch. Trs., 41 N. J. L. 312.
[3] State v. Patterson, 32 N. J. L. 177.
[4] Randall v. Smith, 1 Den. (N. Y.) 214.
[5] Att'y Gen. v. Burnham, 61 N. H. 594.
[6] People v. Stone, (Mich.) 44 N. W. 333.
[7] Childrey v. Rady, 77 Va. 518.
[8] McTeer v. Caldwell, 77 Va. 596.
[9] Rowell v. Sch. Dist., (Vt.) 10 A. 754.
[10] Genesee Ind. S. D. v. McDonald, 98 Pa. St. 444.

the proper court is justified in declaring their seats vacant, and appointing others in their stead.[1] A board of school directors can appoint to fill a vacancy until the next annual election[2] in Pa., and by acts 1838 and 1840, the remaining school directors have the power to declare the seat of the director vacant, in the county of Philadelphia, as in others, but in Penn township this power and duty are expressly vested in the remaining directors, respectively, of each of its election districts of North and South Penn. Under the school law of 1854, directors' meetings are either stated, including the annual meeting when fixed, or special, adjourned meetings to take place in either case; but the former only are regular meetings, for non-attendance at any two of which in succession, except in case of sickness or absence, the seat of a director may be declared vacant by the other directors.[4] Where a board of directors, at an adjourned meeting (there being no quorum at the regular meeting), declared the seat of one of their number vacant, who had not attended a "special" meeting called by the president, or the last regular or adjourned meeting; the first meeting being "special" was not "regular," and as the third meeting was but a continuance of the second, which, though styled "regular," did not appear to have been a "stated" meeting, the action of the school board in declaring the seat of the absent member vacant, was illegal, because he had not been absent at two regular meetings in succession.[4] The prudential committee of a school district refusing to do a particular act does not create a vacancy in the office, but creating a new district, including him within its limits, vacates the office.[5] The officers of a school district do not become

[1] Bouton v. Royce, 10 Phila. (Pa.) 559.
[2] Com. v. Thomas, 10 Phila. (Pa.) 600.
[3] Felton v. Commonwealth, 8 Watts & S. (Pa.) 267.
[4] Zulich v. Bowman, 42 Pa. St. 83.
[5] Stevens v. Kent, 26 Vt. 503.

vacant in Vt. merely by the failure of the district to maintain a school, (Gen. Stat., ch. 22, § 40,) nor until the selectmen have duly made new appointments.[1]

§ 138. **Parochial school; sectarian school; religious, etc.**—It has been held unconstitutional to use the school-money to buy a state history for each district;[2] and an act which attempts to devote a part of the school fund to a private school is unconstitutional.[3] In the case of *County of Cook v. Industrial School*, where girls were committed to Chicago Industrial School for Girls, and the bills for board, tuition, maintenance and care were presented against the county, and resisted on the ground that the Chicago Industrial School was a sectarian school, the opinion by Scott, J., was: "In *State v. Hallock*, 16 Nev. 373, it was held that the Nevada Orphan Asylum was a sectarian institution, and that the payment of a claim made by it against the state would be a violation of the state constitution;" and, "It is recorded in the national constitution that 'Congress shall make no law respecting an establishment of religion.'" An eminent law-writer says: "Those things which are not lawful under any of the American constitutions may be stated thus: . . . 2d, compulsory support, by taxation or otherwise, of religious instruction; not only is no one denomination to be favored at the expense of the rest, but all support of religious instruction must be entirely voluntary. (Cooley Const. Lim., 5th ed., 580.)"[4] The schools kept by the Roman Catholic Orphan Asylum Society of the city of Brooklyn are not "common schools" within the meaning of the constitution.[5] An act of legislature constituting as a district a private school-

---

[1] Woodcock v. Bolster, 35 Vt. 632.
[2] Collins v. Henderson, 11 Bush (Ky.) 74.
[3] Atkin v. Lamkin, 56 Miss. 764; Gordon v. Cornes, 47 N. Y. 616; State v. Springfield, 6 Ind. 86; Bd. Ed. v. Brooklyn, 13 Barb. 409; People v. Allen, 42 N. Y. 404; Hulbert v. Sparks, 9 Bush (Ky.) 260.
[4] County of Cook v. Industrial School, 125 Ill. 540.
[5] People v. Bd. Ed., 13 Barb. (N. Y.) 400.

house and place of worship erected with money bequeathed for that purpose, and constituting trustees with power of taxation for the support of the school, is unconstitutional;[1] and a city orphan asylum for poor orphans only is not a free public school of the state;[2] and public money cannot be subscribed to aid a private sectarian college.[3]

§ 139. **Parochial, sectarian, religious, &c.**—The statutes in relation to the institution and patronage of a public school in Frederick county, Md., were intended as a part of the general public-school system, and to invest that school with all the rights belonging to the schools previously established in other counties.[4] In Mo., children under six years of age are not entitled to free tuition in public schools; the constitution provides public-school system for scholars between six and twenty years of age.[5] The act of Va., Dec. 1884, giving "Hall's Free School" trustees, funds from school quota, is unconstitutional; this school is not part of free-school system;[6] and under Ohio constitution, the laws for organizing and regulating public schools must be of uniform operation throughout the state.[7] The constitution of all the states in some way prohibits the use of the common-school fund for the support of sectarian institutions. State Normal of N. Y. is not a "public school" so as to enable scholars to claim free scholarship in Cornell University.[8] The inmates of the German Protestant Orphan Asylum of Cincinnati are not children, wards, or apprentices of actual residents in the district of the asylum, and are not entitled to the public-school privileges of that district.[9] Statutes of Wis., authorizing sending specified classes of chil-

---

[1] People v. McAdams, 82 Ill. 356.
[2] *In re* Malone, 21 S. C. 435.
[3] A. T. & S. F. R. R. Co. v. Atchison, 47 Ks. 712.
[4] Thomas v. Visitors Frederick County Sch., 7 Gill. & J. (Md.) 369.
[5] Roach v. St. Louis Sch. Bd., 77 Mo. 484.
[6] Hall's Free S. v. Home, 80 Va. 470.
[7] State v. Powers, 38 Ohio St. 54.
[8] People v. Crissey, 45 Hun (N. Y.) 19.
[9] State v. Sch. Dirs., 10 Ohio St. 448.

dren to public industrial schools, do not involve any interference with the relation of parent and child, nor any imprisonment that may not be imposed.¹ The school law providing for the education of every individual between the ages of five and twenty-one years, is not unconstitutional.²

§ 140. **Parochial, sectarian, religious, etc.**—Where the territorial law authorized the board of education to designate private institution where instruction should be given, and the tuition paid by the territory, and a contract was made accordingly, which contract required three months' notice to cancel, it was held that the constitution of the state subsequently adopted prohibiting apropriation to any sectarian institution, terminated the contract, and such provision did not contravene the U. S. constitution prohibiting the impairing of obligations of contracts.³ A public institution of learning would be one which is controlled by the state through its agents, and in which the state would have a paramount interest and right of property, and which would depend upon the state for its existence.⁴ Although the Illinois Industrial University at Urbana is a body corporate, yet the state appoints its trustees, and may sell and dispose of the property of the institution, or amend or repeal the charter.⁵ Paying rent for use of church for school purposes is not contrary to Ill. constitution.⁶ The Ky. act of 1872, appropriating common-school funds to V. academy, is unconstitutional.⁷ "Not only is no one denomination to be favored at the expense of the rest, but all support of religious instruction must be entirely voluntary; it is not within the sphere of government to coerce it;"⁸ except in N. H., the constitution of

---

¹ Milwaukee Industrial Sch. v. Supervisors, 40 Wis. 328.
² Commonwealth v. Hartman, 17 Pa. St. 118.
³ Synod of Dakota v. State, (S. D.) 50 N. W. 632.
⁴ State v. Graham, 25 La. Ann. 440.
⁵ Trustees Ill. Ind. U. v. Champaign Co., 76 Ill. 184.
⁶ Millard v. Ed. Bd., 19 Ill. App. 48.
⁷ Halbert v. Sparks, 9 Bush (Ky.) 259.
⁸ Cooley Const. Lim., 576.

which permits the legislature to authorize towns, parishes, bodies corporate, or religious societies within the state to make adequate provisions at their own expense, for the support and maintenance of public Protestant teachers of piety, religion and morality, but not to tax other denominations for their support.

§ 141. **Parochial, sectarian, religious, etc.**—In the case of *County of McLean v. Humphreys*, 104 Ill. (Free.) 378, it was decided that "There is nothing in the various provisions of the act of May 28, 1879, entitled 'An act to aid industrial schools for girls,' which authorizes or contemplates the organization of these schools for sectarian purposes, within the meaning of § 3, art. 8, of the constitution, prohibiting any appropriation or pay from any public fund, or anything in aid of any church or sectarian purpose, by any public corporation; but on the contrary, it is expressly prohibited in the last section of the act.

"If, notwithstanding this inhibition in the act, such a school should be prostituted to any church or sectarian purposes, the law affords ample means for a speedy correction of such an abuse of the act.

"Constitution not to be so construed as to deprive the legislature of the power of protecting dependent and unfortunate infants. It is the unquestioned right and imperative duty of every enlightened government, in its character of *parens patriæ* to protect and provide for the comfort and well-being of such of its citizens as, by reason of infancy, defective understanding, or other misfortune or infirmity, are unable to take care of themselves, and all constitutional limitations must be so construed and understood as not to interfere with the proper and legitimate exercise of this important governmental function.

"The act does not infringe constitutional guaranty of personal liberty. The act of 1879, in relation to industrial schools for dependent infant females, is not obnoxious to the objection that it infringes upon the constitutional guaranty of the personal liberty of the citizen."

§ 142. **Parochial, sectarian, religious, etc.**—"It may be said that § 3 of article 8 of the Ill. constitution is an inhibition upon the power of appellees to appropriate any public funds for the support of a public school or any school under the domination or control of any church or sectarian denomination, and that § 3 of the Bill of Rights provides that 'the free exercise and enjoyment of religious profession and worship without discrimination shall forever be guaranteed,' etc. Indeed, these sections are cited in appellant's brief, but there is no question of construction of the constitutional provisions raised, or any necessity for an interpretation apparent." (*Millard v. Board*, 116 Ill. 23.)

§ 143. **Parochial, sectarian, religious, etc.**—In the case of *Milwaukee Industrial School v. Supervisors of Milwaukee County*, 40 Wis. 328, it was decided that "The power conferred in terms by § 5, ch. 325 of 1875, upon certain officers, for the commitment of minors to industrial schools, is judicial, and cannot be exercised by mayors of cities, (3 Wis. 805); and probably not by judges of courts of record at chambers, (39 Wis., 35); but any defect of jurisdiction in these will not affect the authority of courts under the act. . . .

"The statute (which goes on the total failure of the parent to provide for the child) is not invalid on the ground that it invades any natural rights of parent and child.

"The commitment of the child to an industrial school, as authorized by the statute, is not an imprisonment. . . .

"In the second place, the statute, certainly so far as it is involved here, does not go on failure in the measure of support or education by the parent, on some nice fault-finding with the course of the parent with the child, as the court appeared to think that the Illinois statute did, in *People v. Turner*, 55 Ill. 280. It goes on the total failure of the parent to provide for the child. And it is difficult to comprehend the right of a parent to complain, that the discharge by the state of his own duty to his child, which he has wholly failed to perform, is an imprisonment of the child as against his parental right in it. . . .

"We cannot think that it was intended to foreclose the right of a parent, when competent, to resume the custody and care of his child. In this respect there is a significant difference between it and the statute before the court in *People v. Turner*. That statute provided for process against the parent or guardian of the child, making them parties to the proceeding, and apparently bound by it. The statute before us carefully avoids that difficulty, and operates, so to speak, upon the child *in personam*, without citing the parent or guardian, without any color of intent to bind the parent or guardian by the proceeding or by the commitment. It appears to us quite obvious, upon familiar principles, that the parent or guardian is not precluded by the commitment from asserting any right to the custody and care of the child which he may be afterwards able to establish. When a parent or other proper guardian should be able to show that the disability or default on which the child's commitment proceeded was accidental or temporary, and no longer exists, and that he is, in the language of § 5, ch. 112, R. S., not otherwise unsuitable for the custody of the child, his right to the custody should prevail over the commitment to which he was not a party. In such a case, if the officers of school should refuse to surrender a child, no court would hesitate to restore the child to the care of the parent or guardian. The commitment during minority binds the child only, not the parent or guardian when competent to fulfill toward the child the duties assumed by the state. It is conclusive as between the school and the child, but not as between the school and the parent or guardian. The statute is a humane one, and should not be bent to a construction inconsistent with one of the dearest rights of humanity. It is our duty to give it a construction, if we can, to give it effect; and we find no difficulty in giving it this construction, which seems to us to have been in the mind of the legislature when it was framed. . . .

"The case of *People v. Turner* appears to turn on the question of compulsory education — a very different question from that here. We are not prepared to say that we might not decide a similar case, under a similar statute, in the same way."

§ 144. **Parochial, sectarian, religious, etc.**—In *Millard v. The Board of Education*, 121 Ill. 297, it was decided that "Renting building for school purposes, as, a church building, when it becomes necessary for a board of education to procure a building in which to conduct a public school: They are authorized by law to lease a suitable building for that purpose, and it matters not that such building had been used for a church by some religious body. Procuring a building without a vote of the people: Where a proposition to raise money to build a school-house at a site selected is defeated by a vote of the people, the board of education or directors, being required to provide a school for at least six months in each year, may lawfully rent any suitable building or room in which such school may be kept, without any vote for that purpose. The free schools of this state are not established to aid any sectarian denomination, or assist in disseminating any sectarian doctrine, and no board of education or school directors have any authority to use the public funds for any such purpose. The statute has not prescribed any religious belief as a qualification of a teacher in the public schools, and therefore the school authorities may select a teacher who belongs to any church or to no church, as they may think best. A bill to enjoin a board of education from the use of school funds for sectarian purposes, alleged that the children of Catholic parents, and the teachers, who were Catholics, were required to attend at a Catholic church, the basement of which was used for the school, at eight o'clock in the morning on school-days, and hear mass read by the priest, and then repair to the school-room and engage in the study of the church catechism for half an hour before the opening of the school, and at the close of the school at noon the 'Angelus' prayer was read by the teachers and pupils, but failed to show that the board were in any manner connected with such exercises and requirements: *Held*, That the bill did not show any ground of equitable relief, it not appearing that complainant had any children who were required, against his wishes, to attend or receive any religious instruction."

§ 145. **Parochial, sectarian, religious, etc.**—In the case of *State v. Dist. Bd.*, 76 Wis. 177, it was decided: "In a petition by residents and tax-payers of a city for a writ of mandamus to compel the discontinuance of the practice of reading the Bible in the public schools therein, averments that the residents of said city, who are taxed for the support of said schools, are equally entitled to the benefits thereof, by having their children instructed therein according to law, and that the reading complained of is contrary to the rights of conscience, and in violation of law, and is sectarian instruction and in violation of § 3, art. 10, Const., are held sufficiently broad to cover any valid objection which may be made to such reading. Averments in the return to the alternative writ that the reading of the Bible in schools is not sectarian instruction, and that the school board has a lawful right to permit, but none to prevent, such reading,—being mere legal conclusions, are not admitted by a demurrer. Nor does the demurrer admit an averment in such return that there is no material difference between the King James version of the Bible, used in the schools, and the Douay version,—such averment being against common knowledge, and therefor not well pleaded. The courts will take judicial notice of the contents of the Bible, that the religious world is divided into numerous sects, and of the general doctrines maintained by each sect. The whole Bible, without exception, having been designated as a text-book for use in a school, and it being claimed by the school board that the whole contents thereof may lawfully be read in such school if the teacher so elect, the Bible will be regarded as a whole in determining whether such reading is sectarian instruction; and it is immaterial that the only portions thereof thus far read in such school are not sectarian. ⟨The use of any version of the Bible as a text-book in the public schools, and the stated reading thereof in such schools by the teachers, without restriction, though unaccompanied by any comment, has 'a tendency to inculcate sectarian ideas,' within the meaning of § 3, ch. 251, Laws of 1883, and is 'sectarian instruction,' within the meaning of § 3, art. 10, Const.⟩ But text-books founded upon the fundamental teachings of the Bible, or which contain extracts therefrom, and such portions of the Bible as are not sectarian, may be used in the secular instruction of the pupils and to inculcate good morals. ⟨The fact that the children of the petitioners are at liberty to withdraw from the school-room during the reading of the Bible does not remove the ground of complaint. The constitutional prohibition of sectarian instruction being unambiguous, the rules as to interpretation in the light of surrounding circumstances when it was framed and adopted, and as to the authority of contemporaneous exposition, are not controlling. Considered in the light of prior and contemporaneous history, the provisions of our constitution herein cited were manifestly intended to prohibit practices then permitted by other constitutions. The stated reading of the Bible as a text-book in the public schools may be 'worship,' and the school-house thereby become, for the time being, a 'place of worship,' within the meaning of § 18, art. 1, Const.; and to such use of the schoolhouse the tax-payers, who are compelled to aid in its erection and in the maintenance of the school, have a legal right to object. Children of poor parents, who are by law practically obliged to attend the public schools, would, if such reading were permitted, be compelled to attend a place of worship, contrary to said § 18. Such reading being religious instruction, the money drawn from the state treasury for the support of a school in which the Bible is so read, is for the benefit of a 'religious seminary,' within the meaning of said section. By the adoption of the state constitution and the admission of the state into the Union, the third of the articles of compact in the ordinance of 1787 ceased to be longer in force."

§ 146. **Parochial, sectarian, religious, etc.**—In the case of *County of Cook v. Industrial School*, 125 Ill. 540, it was decided that: "A school is sectarian, and comes within constitutional provision 'that public funds shall not be paid out in aid of any sectarian purpose, or in aid of any school, etc., controlled by any church,' where such school is a corporation organized as an industrial school for girls, but does not lease or own any building, although its charter contemplates that it shall have a situs, nor otherwise comply with the provisions of its act of incorporation, but places all girls nominally committed to it under the sole charge, care, and control of two institutions controlled by a church, where they are taught, maintained and clothed by them alone, and in which institutions the inmates, although not obliged to receive instructions in the Romish faith, are yet taught no other faith or creed; and in such case a suit to recover for tuition and clothing furnished girls so placed cannot be maintained against the county.

"To show that a school is controlled by a church, evidence is admissible that a judge of the superior court went to the place where an industrial school was alleged to be carried on, and was refused admittance unless he should first obtain a permit from a bishop or member of the Romish church, it appearing that such judge was authorized to commit girls to an industrial school, and that books containing copies of the warrants of commitments were required to be kept therein.

"If an industrial school that has availed itself of the provisions of the statute of Ill. providing for the payment of moneys to such schools is guilty of the misuse or non-use of its powers, and brings suit against a county upon a contract which the latter can lawfully make, perhaps a defense cannot be maintained solely upon the ground that the school is violating its charter; the proper proceeding to test that question may be *quo warranto*. But if the contract sued on is a contract to pay money out of the public funds in aid of a sectarian purpose, it is absolutely void under the constitution.

"Constitution controls in preference to statute where the statute directs a county board to pay money to an industrial school, and the constitution, in a self-executing provision, directs the county board not to pay money to such school when controlled by a church.

"Appeal lies to supreme court where validity of a statute or construction of the constitution is involved; and motion to dismiss appeal for want of jurisdiction will be overruled where such question of proper construction is directly raised on face of record.

"The constitution of Ill. declares against the use of public funds to aid sectarian schools, independently of the question whether there is or is not a consideration furnished in return for the funds so used.

"In *State v. Hallock*, 16 Nev. 373, it was held that the Nevada Orphan Asylum was a sectarian institution, and that the payment of a claim made by it against the state would be a violation of the following provision in the state constitution: 'No public funds of any kind or character whatever, state, county, or municipal, shall be used for sectarian purposes.'

"In this connection it may be proper to notice one of the errors assigned on the ground of the exclusion of evidence. Defendant, for the purpose of showing that the Chicago Industrial School itself was controlled by the Catholic church, offered to prove that one of the judges of the superior court of Cook county went to the House of the Good Shepherd, and was refused admittance, and was told that 'if he wished to be admitted he must get a permit from the Roman Catholic bishop, or some gentleman member of the Catholic church in good standing.'

"The doctrine here contended for is an exceedingly dangerous one. In county of *McLean v. Humphreys*, 104 Ill. 378, it is intimated by this court that the state is under obligations to protect and educate such classes of female infants as were declared to be dependent girls by § 3 of the act of May 28, 1879, as that section stood before it was amended on June 26, 1885. Under this view, the industrial schools which teach and care for such girls are performing, as substitutes for the state, a duty which the state itself is bound to perform. If they are entitled to be paid out of the public funds, even though they are under the control of sectarian denominations, simply because they relieve the state of a burden which it would otherwise be itself required to bear, then there is nothing to prevent all public education from becoming subjected, by hasty and unwise legislation, to sectarian influences. By § 1 of article 8 of the constitution it is made the duty of the state to provide a thorough and efficient system of free schools. If statutes are passed, under which the management of these schools shall get into the hands of sectarian institutions, then, under the theory contended for, the prohibition of the constitution will be powerless to prevent the money of the tax-payers from being used to support such institutions, inasmuch as they will render a service to the state by performing for it its duty of educating the children of the people. It is an untenable position, that public funds may be paid out to help support sectarian schools, provided only such schools shall render a *quid pro quo* for the payment made to them. The constitution declares against the use of public funds to aid sectarian schools, independently of the question whether there is or is not a consideration furnished in return for the funds so used.

"There is nothing in the doctrine here announced which conflicts with the case of *Millard v. Board of Education*, 121 Ill. 297. There the proceeding was by an individual tax-payer against a board of education, and a majority of the court sustained the act of the board, which had no school-house, in temporarily leasing the basement of a Catholic church, for the purpose of holding one of the public schools therein. But the board did not part with the control of the school. The scholars were taught by teachers whom the board appointed, and under a system of instruction which the board prescribed.

"Nor do the reasons here given for sustaining the jurisdiction of the court in this case conflict with the other case of *Millard v. Board of Education*, 116 Ill. 23. There the opinion expressly states that no question of the validity of a statute or of the construction of the constitution was raised. But here the question of the proper construction of a constitutional provision is directly raised upon the face of the record."

§ 147. **Parochial, sectarian, religious, etc.**—In the celebrated case of *Cincinnati Board of Education v. Minor*, 23 Ohio St. 211, which has been looked upon as the leading case prohibiting the Bible from schools on the ground of being sectarian in its tendency, the chief question presented, tried and decided in that case was: The constitution of Ohio declared that religion, morality and knowledge were essential to good government, and required the legislature to encourage schools for that reason; and it was insisted that this clause of the constitution required to that extent religious instruction. The court held that it authorized the legislature to do certain things, and the legislature never acted under said clause; and that the board of education having excluded the Bible, the court had no power to interfere with the powers exercised by the board of education; or, as they decide it in the syllabus of the case:

"The constitution of the state does not enjoin or require religious instruction or the reading of religious books in the public schools of the state.

"The legislature having placed the management of the public schools under the exclusive control of directors, trustees, and boards of education, the courts have no rightful authority to interfere by directing what instruction shall be given or what books shall be read therein."

§ 148. **Parochial school—religious—Bible.**—The school committee of a town have the legal power to pass a rule requiring a school to be opened by reading from the Bible.[1] Where the legislature has placed the management of the public schools under the exclusive control of directors, trustees, and boards of education, the judicial power will not direct what instruction shall be given, or what books shall be read therein.[2] Permitting some pupils to withdraw during reading of Bible is not uniformity of treatment. Reading of the Bible is held in this case to be sectarian instruction, and against the constitution of Wis. Reading of the Bible is also held in same case to be religious instruction;[3] but in Me. a rule requiring the reading of a particular version was held to be legal;[4] and an expulsion from school for refusing to conform to rule in regard to reading of Bible was sustained.[5]

§ 149. **Pupil, admission.**—The decision of state superintendent that a child is entitled to attend in a certain district will be upheld where he is living there and working for his board,

---

[1] Speller v. Wolburn, 12 Allen (Mass.) 127.
[2] Bd. Ed. Cincinnati v. Minor, 23 Ohio St. 211.
[3] State v. Dist. Bd., (Wis.) 44 N. W. 967.
[4] Donahoe v. Richards, 38 Me. 376.
[5] McCormick v. Burt, 95 Ill. 266.

and did not come there to attend school, and his mother teaches in another city, is not able to support him, and has no home.[1] To obtain admission when pupil is wrongfully excluded by principal in N. Y. city ward school, he must appeal to board trustees of ward, then to board education; and where he had graduated from primary and there was no room to seat him he cannot compel readmission.[2] The board of education in Ill. can refuse to admit pupils in a sub-district, boarding there when the schools there are crowded and there are schools in same district in another sub-district where the parents of such pupil reside.[3] The power of directors to enlarge building, and the fact that education is compulsory, does not prevent directors temporarily excluding for want of room.[4] Legal school age means scholars under twenty-one years, in Mass.;[5] and the Miss. act 1866, as to admission of outside pupils on payment of tuition means such proportion of all tuition in that school as number of outside scholars bears to whole number.[6]

§ 150. **Pupil, admission.**—In the case of *State v. White*, 82 Ind. 278, it was held: "The trustees and faculty of a public university may not refuse admission or exclude students because they are members of a Greek-letter fraternity or other secret college society. . . . This right of admission may not be enforced when there is not sufficient room in the university, and may be postponed until the applicant has made some proficiency in merely preliminary studies; but it is a right which the trustees are not authorized to materially abridge, and which they cannot as an abstract proposition rightfully deny. (*Cory v. Carter*, 48 Ind. 327; *State v. Duffy*, 7 Nev. 342;

[1] State v. Thayer, 74 Wis. 48.
[2] People v. Bd. Ed., (N. Y.) 4 N. Y. S. 102.
[3] People v. Bd. Ed., 26 Ill. App. 476.
[4] People v. McFall, 26 Ill. App. 319.
[5] Needham v. Wellesley, 139 Mass. 372.
[6] State v. Hamilton, (Miss.) 10 So. 57.

Chase v. Stephenson, 71 Ill. 383; *School Trustees v. People*, 87 id. 303; *Rulison v. Post*, 79 Ill. 567; *People v. Board, etc.*, 18 Mich. 400; *Foltz v. Hoge*, 54 Cal. 28; *Ward v. Flood*, 48 id. 36.) . . . Every student, upon his admission to an institution of learning, impliedly promises to submit and be governed by all the necessary and proper rules and regulations which have been or may thereafter be adopted for the government of the institution; and the exaction of any pledge or condition which requires him to promise more than that operates as a practical abridgment of his right of admission, and involves the exercise of a power greater than has been conferred upon either trustees or the faculty of Purdue University. . . . Our conclusion is, that so much of regulation No. 3, adopted by the faculty, as may be construed to impose disabilities on persons already members of the Greek fraternities, and as requires a written pledge as a condition of admission, is both *ultra vires* and palpably unreasonable, and hence inoperative and void, and that the pledge tendered to Hawley was one which the faculty had no legal right to demand as a condition of his admission."

§ 151. **Pupil, Chinese.**—It was decided in Cal., that a Chinese child could not be excluded, and in 1885 statute was passed allowing the establishment of separate schools.[1]

§ 152. **Pupil's discharge, dismissal, and expulsion.**—School authorities cannot expel pupil for attending a social party contrary to rules of school;[2] but in an action for damages for expelling under such rule, as there was no malice on the part of the directors, they were not liable in damages;[3] and a

---

[1] Tape v. Hurley, 66 Cal. 473.
[2] State v. Osborne, 24 Mo. App. 309; Dritt v. Snodgrass, 66 Mo. 286; State v. Osborne, 32 Mo. App. 536.
[3] Dritt v. Snodgrass, 66 Mo. 286.

pupil cannot be discharged for failing to comply with regulation that each scholar shall bring into the school-room a stick of wood for the fire;[1] but when pupil is dismissed by teacher without sanction of committee or without authority, he cannot maintain an action against the city without first appealing to the school authorities;[2] and where directors make a rule in good faith that pupil absent certain time without excuse shall be expelled from school, they are not liable in damages in the absence of malice.[3] So it was held that public officers who err in the discharge of their duties, are not by reason thereof liable in damages.[4] In Iowa, boards of school directors may provide by-rules, that pupils may be suspended from the schools in case they shall be absent or tardy, except for sickness or other unavoidable cause, a certain number of times within a fixed period;[5] and a school board has power to make a rule suspending any pupil absent, without satisfactory excuse, six half-days in four consecutive weeks.[6] The general school committee of a town may exclude from school a pupil of immoral character.[7] Where statute authorizes board to suspend or expel pupils guilty of gross misdemeanor or persistent disobedience, this does not justify suspending for accidents or negligence.[8] A rule, prescribed by a board of education, that a pupil failing to come prepared with a required exercise, or with a reasonable excuse, shall be suspended, is a reasonable rule, such as the board has authority to adopt, and the teacher to enforce.[9] A requirement by a teacher of a district school that the scholars in grammar shall write English composition, and a refusal to comply with, in the absence of a request from the parents that

---

[1] State v. Fond du Lac E. B., 63 Wis. 234.
[2] Davis v. Boston, 133 Mass. 103.
[3] Churchill v. Fewkes, 13 Ill. App. 520.
[4] Donahoe v. Richards, 38 Me. 376.
[5] Burdick v. Babcock, 31 Iowa, 562.
[6] King v. Jefferson Sch. Bd., 71 Mo. 628.
[7] Sherman v. Charlestown, 8 Cush. (Mass.) 160.
[8] Holman v. Sch. Trs., (Mich.) 43 N. W. 996.
[9] Sewell v. Bd. Ed., 29 Ohio St. 89.

he be excused therefrom, will justify the exclusion of a scholar from the school.[1]

§ 153. **Pupil—discharge, dismissal, expulsion.**—It was held that pupils may be suspended from high school department of graded school for failure to provide themselves with a certain music book and practice, even where the child's parent considers such study unnecessary. (But see Text-Book section).[2] The remedy for deprivation of the privilege of attending school is, under Mass. Gen. Stat., ch. 41, § 11, by an action against the city or town and not against the school committee.[3] A member of a district-school committee, at the school-house just before the opening of the school, being addressed by one of the scholars in a profane and insulting manner, ordered him to leave the room, and on his refusing put him out by force; he was justified in that act;[4] an ejection from the room for profanity was not necessarily an expulsion from the school, and it was not so intended; and as it could not have that effect, in an action for an assault for the forcible ejection of the plaintiff from the room the committee would not be chargeable with the loss of his school privileges;[4] and when a pupil has been suspended and uses gross profanity and vulgarity to the board on being called before it, he forfeits his right, if any, to reinstatement, until reparation is tendered.[5] In a suit for damages from the suspension of a pupil, no recovery can be had without allegation and proof that the action of the directors was wanton or malicious.[6] The prudential committee of a school district may suspend children for absence contrary to the rules thereof, though such absence is pursuant to the command of their

[1] Guernsey v. Pitkin, 32 Vt. 224.
[2] State v. Webber, 108 Ind. 31.
[3] Learock v. Putnam, 111 Mass. 499.
[4] Peck v. Smith, 41 Conn. 442.
[5] Bd. Ed. v. Helston, 32 Ill. App. 300.
[6] McCormick v. Burt, 95 Ill. 263.

Roman Catholic parents, and by direction of their priest, for the purpose of attending religious services on Corpus Christi day.[1] The teacher has the power to suspend a pupil in a proper case, unless he has been deprived of that power by the affirmative action of the school board or board of education.[2] In action of trespass for unlawful expulsion of pupil, the defendants, teacher and prudential committee, cannot justify under plea of general issue, and as to which expelled, the teacher or prudential committee, it is a question for the jury.[3] In Ohio it was held that the father may maintain an action against the teacher of a school and the local directors of the sub-district, for damages for wrongfully expelling his child;[4] but the contrary doctrine was held in N. Y., that such action can only be brought in the name of the child, and what is recovered must be for her benefit;[5] and in Me., a child could not recover damages, in an action against the school committee by whose orders the pupil was dismissed for failing to read from the Bible.[6] The board of education may require a pupil to inform it of the name of another pupil who has been guilty of a breach of the rules, if he acknowledges that it is known to him, and, on his refusal, may suspend him;[7] but the suspension does not extend beyond the current school year.[7] A board of directors has no power to suspend except for breach of discipline, or an offense against good morals;[8] and when the rights of a citizen are involved, the courts may determine whether authority of a school officer was lawfully exercised.[8]

§ 154. **Pupil, punishment.**—A teacher is not liable for punishment of pupil if it is not clearly excessive in the judgment

---

[1] Ferriter v. Tyler, 48 Vt. 444.
[2] State v. Burton, 45 Wis. 150.
[3] Mack v. Kelsey, (Vt.) 17 A. 780.
[4] Roe v. Deming, 21 Ohio St. 666.
[5] Stephenson v. Hall, 14 Barb. (N. Y.) 222.
[6] Donahoe v. Richards, 38 Me. 376.
[7] Bd. Ed. v. Holston, 32 Ill. App. 300.
[8] Perkins v. Ind. Sch. Dist., 56 Iowa, 476.

of reasonable men; an instruction that it is lawful punishment if not so clearly excessive that "all hands would at once say it was excessive," is error.[1] If one over twenty-one years of age voluntarily attends a town school, and is received as a scholar by the instructor, he is under the same restrictions and liabilities as if within the age of twenty-one years.[2] If teacher acts in good faith without malice, he is not liable for error of judgment;[3] and a teacher may prohibit and punish scholars for quarreling and swearing on the way home, though not provided for by directors' rules.[4] The Tex. statute authorizes moderate correction, and where a teacher struck a pupil with a switch of reasonable size about nine times on the legs, showing no severe abrasions, it was held to be lawful;[5] and the authority of teacher is not limited to school-room, and moderate correction is allowed.[6] Where an ordinary whipping was inflicted on a boy of nine years of age for fighting away from school and not during school hours, it was held that the teacher was not guilty of an assault.[7] The Wis. statutes give the school board in each district power to suspend any pupil from its privileges for non-compliance with the reasonable rules established by the board or by the teacher with its consent.[8] A school teacher, in regard to a pupil intrusted to his care by a parent or guardian, stands *in loco parentis*, and is responsible in the same manner.[9] While a teacher may not punish a pupil for misconduct committed after the dismissal of school for the day, and the return of the pupil to his home, yet he may at school punish him for any misbehavior, though committed out of school, which has a direct and immediate tendency to injure the school and to sub-

[1] Patterson v. Nutter, 78 Me. 509.
[2] State v. Mizner, 45 Iowa, 248; Stevens v. Fassett, 27 Me. 266.
[3] Heritage v. Dodge, (N. H.) 9 A. 722.
[4] Duskins v. Gore, 85 Mo. 485.
[5] Hulton v. State, (Tex.) 5 S. W. 122.
[6] Balding v. State, (Tex.) 4 S. W. 122.
[7] Hulton v. State, 23 Tex. App. 386.
[8] Morrow v. Wood, 35 Wis. 59.
[9] Commonwealth v. Seed, 5 Pa. L. J. R. 78.

vert the master's authority.¹ The chastisement of a scholar must not be excessive or cruel;² and if there is any reasonable doubt as to the punishment being excessive, the teacher should have the benefit of the doubt.³

§ 155. **Pupil, punishment.** — Where a scholar or other person in school hours, refuses to leave the desk of the instructor on the request of the master, for that purpose he may immediately use such force and remove him as is necessary to accomplish the object, without the direction or knowledge of the superintending school committee.⁴ The teacher has a right to moderately chastise a pupil for refusing to give an excuse for absence without leave.⁵ A teacher has right to require obedience to reasonable rules, and to inflict punishment for disobedience; in the absence of rules by the school board, the teacher may make all necessary rules. The teacher should be governed by the age, size and physical condition of pupil;⁶ and he may whip a pupil in a reasonable manner.⁶ Where teacher on consulting with trustee on account of insubordination of pupil, gives the pupil the choice of chastisement or expulsion, and he chooses the former, and it is administered and quite painful but there is no undue severity or improper motive on part of teacher, a conviction for assault and battery was not justified.⁷ If a parent acts in good faith, prompted by pure parental love, without passion, inflicts no permanent injury on the child, he should not be punished merely because a jury reviewing the case, deem it unwise to proceed so far;⁸ and the right of the parent may be delegated to the teacher.⁹ The law

---

¹ Lander v. Seaver, 32 Vt. 114.
² Anderson v. State, 3 Head. (Tenn.) 455.
³ Lander v. Seaver, 32 Vt. 114.
⁴ Stevens v. Fassett, 27 Me. 266.
⁵ Danenhoffer v. State, 69 Ind. 295.
⁶ Sheehan v. Sturges, 53 Conn. 481.
⁷ Vanvactor v. State, (Ind.) 15 N. E. 341.

⁸ 1 Bish. Cr. Law, (7th ed.,) § 882; Schouler's Dom. Rel., (4th ed.,) § 244; 1 Black Com. 556; 1 Greenl. Ev., § 97; 2 Addison on Torts, (Wood's ed.,) § 840; Danenhoffer v. State, 69 Ind. 295; Com. v. Randall, 4 Gray, (Mass.) 36; State v. Burton, 45 Wis. 150.
⁹ 2 Kent. Com., § 203.

will not hold a teacher responsible unless the punishment occasion permanent injury to the child, or be merely to gratify their own evil passions; the teacher must be governed, when chastisement is proper, as to the mode and severity of the punishment, by the nature of the offense, the age, size, and apparent powers of endurance of the pupil. It is for the jury to decide whether the punishment is excessive.[1] The qualification that the teacher must not act from malice, will protect pupils from brutality, whilst the teacher is protected from liability for mere errors of judgment.[2] Infliction of moderate correction, with a sound discretion, is the extent of authority of school master.[3] A school master is regarded as standing in place of the parent, and may administer in case of misconduct, reasonable and proper punishment to a pupil, having regard to the character of the offense, the sex, age, size, and physical strength of the offender; and he is liable criminally for any abuse of his authority, if prompted by malice or other improper motive, if unreasonably severe, if inflicted with an improper instrument, or if resulting in permanent injury to the pupil.[4]

§ 156. **Pupil, punishment.**—The teacher must not use unreasonable instruments for correction or impose immoderate amount; if he does he will be criminally liable.[5] A teacher cannot lawfully disfigure a pupil, or perpetrate on his person any other permanent injury. As said by Gaston, J., in *State v. Pendergrass*, 2 Dev. & Bat. Law, 365, 31 Amer. Dec. 416, a case generally approved by the weight of American authority: "It may be laid down as a general rule, that teachers exceed the limit of their authority when they cause lasting mischief,

---

[1] 1 Whart. Cr. Law, (9th ed.,) § 632.
[2] Lander v. Seaver, 32 Vt. 114; State v. Alford, 68 N. C. 322.
[3] Kent's Com., 203-206.
[4] Boyd v. State. 88 Ala. 169.
[5] Boyd v. State, 88 Ala. 169; Schouler Dom. Rel., (4th ed.,) § 244.

but act within the limits of it when they inflict temporary pain." Reasonable correction must not exceed the bounds of due moderation, either in the measure of it, or in the instrument used; if the teacher exceeds this he is criminally liable, and if death ensues from the brutal injuries inflicted, he may be liable not only for assault and battery, but to the penalties of manslaughter or even murder, according to the circumstances of the case.[1] Where teacher after chastising pupil severely in school-room followed him into the yard, struck him with a stick, put his hands in his pocket as if to draw a knife, when the pupil only protested, and after apologizing for language imputed, asked to withdraw, and the teacher hit him in the face three times with his fist, and then hit him over the head with the butt end of a switch, from which the eye was closed for several days, and the teacher remarked in the presence of the school that he could whip any man in China Grove beat, he was convicted and fined.[2] When the punishment is unreasonable and from wicked motives under the influence of an unsocial heart, damages should be given; for error of opinion he ought to be excused, but for malice of heart he must not be shielded from the just claims of the child; malice may be proved from the circumstances attending the punishment.[3] Where a child, as directed by the father, refused to prosecute certain studies required by the teacher, and the teacher punished the child, and the father prosecuted the teacher for assault upon the child, the father was held not liable for malicious prosecution of that case;[4] and a teacher cannot punish a pupil for refusing to do that which a parent has asked the pupil to be excused from doing. The

---

[1] 1 Archbold's Cr. Prac., 218; 1 Bish. Cr. Law, (7th ed.,) §§ 881-2.
[2] Boyd v. State, 88 Ala. 169.
[3] Reeves Dom. Rel., (4th ed.,) 357-358.
[4] Morrow v. Wood, 35 Wis. 59.

teacher may refuse to permit a pupil to attend if the pupil does not conform to the rules.¹ To render a teacher liable to criminal prosecution he must have been actuated by bad, malevolent motives, using the legal authority for the gratification of a mind bent on mischief in inflicting punishment;² but a school master is not relieved from liability by acting in good faith and without malice, honestly thinking the punishment necessary, when it was clearly excessive and unnecessary.³ Where a school master punishes, the instrument must be suitable, and be administered with moderation, or he will be guilty of assault and battery.⁴ In a prosecution for an assault on pupil, and the court left it to the jury to say whether the punishment was excessive, and refused to instruct "that he was criminally liable only when acting from malice or passion, or inflicted excessive punishment," there was no error;⁵ and an instruction that for punishment to be illegal it must be so excessive as to excite instant condemnation of all men, is too favorable for the teacher and is erroneous.⁶ A rule requiring pay for school property wantonly or carelessly destroyed, should not be enforced by corporal punishment.⁷

§ 157. **Pupil, punishment.**—In the case of *State v. Pendergrass*, 2 Dev. & Batt. (N. C.), 365, it was held: "The law has not undertaken to prescribe stated punishments for particular offenses, but has contented itself with the general grant of the power of moderate correction, and has confided the gradation of punishments, within the limits of this grant, to the discretion of the teacher. The line which separates moderate correction from immoderate punishment can only be ascer-

---

¹ State v. Mizner, 50 Iowa, 145.
² Commonwealth v. Seed, 5 Pa. L. J. R. 78.
³ Lander v. Seaver, 32 Vt. 114.
⁴ Cooper v. McJunkin, 4 Ind. 290.
⁵ Commonwealth v. Randall, 4 Gray, (Mass.) 36.
⁶ Patterson v. Nutter, (Me.) 7 A. 273.
⁷ State v. Vanderbilt, (Ind.) 18 N. E. 266.

tained by reference to general principles. The welfare of the child is the main purpose for which pain is permitted to be inflicted. Any punishment, therefore, which may seriously endanger life, limbs, or health, or shall disfigure the child, or cause any other permanent injury, may be pronounced in itself immoderate, as not only being unnecessary for, but inconsistent with, the purpose for which correction is authorized; but any correction, however severe, which produces temporary pain only, and no permanent ill, cannot be so pronounced, since it may have been necessary for the reformation of the child, and does not injuriously affect its future welfare. . . .

"We hold, therefore, that it may be laid down as a general rule, that teachers exceed the limits of their authority when they cause lasting mischief, but act within the limits of it when they inflict temporary pain. . . .

"But the master may be punishable when he does not transcend the powers granted, if he grossly abuses them. If he use his authority as a cover for malice, and under pretense of administering correction gratify his own bad passions, the mask of the judge shall be taken off, and he will stand amenable to justice as an individual not invested with judicial power."

§ 158. **Pupil, punishment.**—In the following instances, the exercise of power has been sustained: Suspending pupil for refusing to disclose the name of offending pupil;[1] for tardiness;[2] for failure to use text-books;[3] for absence;[4] for misconduct;[5] suspension of pupil by officer;[5] suspension of pupil by teacher,

---

[1] Bd. v. Helston, 32 Ill. App. 300.
[2] Russell v. Linnfield, 116 Mass. 366; Bendick v. Babcock, 31 Iowa, 562.
[3] Spiller v. Woburn, 12 Allen, (Mass.) 127; McCormick v. Burt, 95 Ill. 266; Donahoe v. Richards, 38 Me. 379; Kidder v. Chellis, 59 N. H. 473; Guernsey v. Pitkin, 32 Vt. 226; Sewell v. Bd. Ed., 29 Ohio St. 89.
[4] Ferriter v. Tyler, 48 Vt. 444; King v. Jefferson City Sch. Bd., 71 Mo. 628; Churchill v. Fewkes, 13 Brad. (Ill.) 520.
[5] Stevens v. Fassett, 27 Me. 266; Larock v. Putnam, 111 Mass. 499; Hodgkins v. Rockport, 105 Mass. 476; State v. Williams, 27 Vt. 755.

where the officer opposed the teacher;[1] expelling for immorality;[2] corporal punishment for misconduct;[3] the teacher refusing to teach pupil, has been held not liable for damages;[4] suspending teacher for immorality was sustained.[5]

§ 159. **Pupil, punishment.**—In the following instances, the exercise of authority has not been sustained: For barring out tardy pupil;[6] for suspending pupil for failure to use text-books required;[7] for suspending for attending a party;[8] for reflecting on the director by newspaper article;[9] for suspending for not paying for broken window;[10] for suspending for using tobacco, the director being opposed to teacher;[11] for manslaughter of slave.[12] Corporal punishment: For failing to use text-book;[13] for not paying for broken window;[14] for misconduct;[15] for accidentally adding aloud.[16]

§ 160. **Pupil, punishment.**—In *Lander v. Seaver*, 32 Vt. 114, which is the leading case on the question as to the right to punish pupil for insulting teacher in presence of other pupils after the pupil has returned home, it was decided: "School master has power to punish pupil for all acts of the latter which are detrimental to the good order and best interest of the school, whether such acts are committed in school hours, or after the pupil has returned home, or while he is engaged in the service of his parent.

"School master is liable in damages for an excessive punish-

---

[1] Scott v. Sch. Dist., 46 Vt. 452.
[2] Sherman v. Inhabitants, 8 Cush. (Mass.) 163.
[3] State v. Pendergrass, 2 Dev. & Batt. (N. C.) 365; Sheehan v. Sturgis, 53 Conn. 481; Dannehoffer v. State, 69 Ind. 295; State v. Mizner, 45 Iowa, 248; Davis v. Boston, 133 Mass. 103; Patterson v. Nutter, 78 Me. 509; Deskins v. Gore, 85 Mo. 485.
[4] Spear v. Cummings, 24 Pick. (Mass.) 224.
[5] McClellan v. Bd., 15 Mo. App. 362.
[6] Thompson v. Beaver, 63 Ill. 356.
[7] Trustees v. People, 87 Ill. 303; Morrow v. Wood, 35 Wis. 59; Rulison v. Post, 79 Ill. 567.
[8] Dritt v. Snodgrass, 66 Mo. 286.
[9] Murphy v. Directors, 30 Iowa, 429.
[10] Perkins v. Directors, 56 Iowa, 476.
[11] Parker v. Sch. Dist., 5 Lea (Tenn.) 525.
[12] State v. Harris, 63 N. C. 7.
[13] State v. Mizner, 50 Iowa, 145.
[14] State v. Vanderbilt, (Ind.) 18 N. E. 266
[15] Com. v. Randall, 4 Gray (Mass.) 36; Boyd v. State, 88 Ala. 169; Cooper v. McJunkin, 4 Ind. 290; Hathaway v. Rice, 19 Vt. 102.
[16] Anderson v. State, 3 Head (Tenn.) 455.

ment of a pupil, even though he acted in good faith and without malice in inflicting it, and considered it necessary, and not excessive; but in case of doubt, he is entitled to the benefit of it.

"Where excessive punishment of pupil is charged against a school master, evidence that the ordinary management of the latter was mild and moderate is not admissible.

"If evidence that school master acted maliciously in administering the punishment should be given by those prosecuting him, evidence that the school master was ordinarily mild and moderate would be admissible.

"It is question for jury to determine whether the instrument used by school master to inflict punishment upon the pupil is a proper one for such purpose.

"To rebut presumption or proof of malice in punishing pupil, it is competent for the school master to prove that the instrument used by him in punishing the pupil was such as was generally used for such purposes by other teachers in the vicinity.

"It is competent for school master, who is defending himself in an action of trespass for assault and battery upon a pupil, to prove that at a former trial of the same case the plaintiff made no claim that the punishment inflicted was excessive, and that then plaintiff only claimed that the master had no right to inflict the punishment, because the offense of the pupil was not committed in school hours.

"By Court, Aldis, J.: The defendant was a teacher in a public school in Burlington; the plaintiff, his pupil. The first question presented is: Has a school master the right to punish his pupil for acts of misbehavior committed after the school has been dismissed, and the pupil has returned home and is engaged in his father's service?

"I. It is conceded that his right to punish extends to school hours, and there seems to be no reasonable doubt that the supervision and control of the master over the scholar extend from the time he leaves home to go to school till he returns from school. Most parents would expect and desire that teachers would take care that their children, in going to and returning from school, should not loiter, or seek evil company, or frequent vicious places of resort. But in this case, as appears from the bill of exceptions, the offense was committed an hour and a half after the school was dismissed, and after the boy had returned home, and while he was engaged in his father's service. When the child has returned home, or to his parent's control, then the parental authority is resumed and the control of the teacher ceases, and then, for all ordinary acts of misbehavior, the parent alone has the power to punish. It is claimed, however, that in this case 'the boy, while in the presence of other pupils of the same school, used toward the master and in his hearing contemptuous language, with a design to insult him, and which had a direct and immediate tendency to bring the authority of the master over his pupils into contempt and lessen his hold upon them and his control over the school.' This, under the charge of the court, must have been found by the jury.

"This misbehavior, it is especially to be observed, has a direct and immediate tendency to injure the school, to subvert the master's authority, and to beget disorder and insubordination. It is not misbehavior generally, or towards other persons, or even towards the master in matters in no way connected with or affecting the school; for as to such misconduct, committed by the child after his return home from school, we think the parents, and they alone, have the power of punishment.

"But where the offense has a direct and immediate tendency to injure the school and bring the master's authority into contempt, as in this case, when done in the presence of other scholars and of the master, and with a design to insult him, we think he has the right to punish the scholar for such acts if he comes again to school.

"The misbehavior must not have merely a remote and indirect tendency to injure the school. All improper conduct or language may perhaps have, by influence and example, a remote tendency of that kind; but the tendency of the acts so done out of the teacher's supervision for which he may punish must be direct and immediate in their bearing upon the welfare of the school, or the authority of the master and the respect due him. Cases may readily be supposed which lie very near the line, and it will often be difficult to distinguish between the acts which have such an immediate and those which have such a remote tendency; hence, each case must be determined by its peculiar circumstances.

"Acts done to deface or injure the school-room, to destroy the books of scholars, or the books or apparatus for instruction, or the instruments of punishment of the master; language used to other scholars to stir up disorder and insubordination, or to heap odium and disgrace upon the master; writings and pictures placed so as to suggest evil and corrupt language, images and thoughts to the youth who must frequent the school — all such or similar acts tend directly to impair the usefulness of the school, the welfare of the scholars, and the authority of the master. By common consent, and by the universal custom in our New England schools, the master has always been deemed to have the right to punish such offenses. Such power is essential to the preservation of order, decency, decorum and good government in schools. Upon this point the charge of the court was substantially correct.

"II. The court charged the jury that although the punishment inflicted on the plaintiff was excessive in severity and disproportioned to the offense, still if the master in administering it acted with proper motives, in good faith, and in his judgment for the best interests of the school, he would not be liable; that the school master acts in a judicial capacity, and that the infliction of excessive punishment, when prompted by good intentions and not by malice or wicked motives or an evil mind, is, merely an honest error of opinion, and does not make him liable to the pupil for damages. The plaintiff claims that this was erroneous.

"1. It is claimed on behalf of the defendant that the school master is a public officer, that in his government of the school he is invested with public authority, with discretionary powers, and acts in a judicial capacity, and so is not liable for errors of judgment. His authority has been likened to that of public officers, such as listers in the case of *Fuller v. Gould*, 20 Vt. 643; the postmaster-general in *Kendall v. Stokes*, 3 How. 87; the mayor of New York in *Wilson v. Mayor, etc.*, 1 Denio 595, (43 Am. Dec. 719); or a commander in the navy, as in *Wilkes v. Dinsman*, 7 How. 89.

"We think the school master does not belong to the class of public officers vested with such judicial and discretionary powers. He is included rather in the domestic relation of master and servant, and his powers and duties are usually treated of as belonging to that class. In some sense he may be said to act by public authority, and to be a public officer, but we do not find him spoken of anywhere as acting in a judicial capacity, except in the passage from Reeves's Domestic Relations, which was read to the jury. In no proper sense can he be deemed a public officer exercising, by virtue of his office, discretionary and *quasi* judicial powers.

"2. It is also said that he stands *in loco parentis*, and is invested with all the authority and immunity of the parent. Such would seem to be the doctrine of the passage cited from Judge Reeves's work.

"The parent, unquestionably, is answerable only for malice or wicked motives or an evil heart in punishing his child. This great, and to some extent irresponsible, power of control and correction is invested in the parent by nature and necessity. It springs from the natural relation of parent and child. It is felt rather as a duty than a power. From the intimacy and nature of the relation, and the necessary character of family government, the law suffers no intrusion upon the authority of the parent, and the privacy of domestic life, unless in extreme cases of cruelty and injustice. This parental power is little liable to abuse, for it is continually restrained by natural affection, the tenderness which the parent feels for his offspring, an affection ever on the alert, and acting rather by instinct than reasoning.

"The school master has no such natural restraint. Hence he may not safely be trusted with all a parent's authority, for he does not act from the instinct of parental affection. He should be guided and restrained by judgment and wise discretion, and hence is responsible for their reasonable exercise. The limit upon the parental authority transferred to the master is well expressed by Judge Blackstone. He says: 'The master is *in loco parentis*, and has such a portion of the power of the parent committed to his charge as may be necessary to answer the purposes for which he is employed.' An English annotator, in a note to the passage, very properly adds: 'This power must be temperately exercised, and no school master should feel himself at liberty to administer chastisement co-extensive with the parent.'

"Judge Swift, in his Digest, in a very admirable summary of the powers and duties of the school master, remarks that if the punishment is immoderate, so that the child sustains a material injury, the master is liable in damages. In a recent case in Massachusetts — *Commonwealth v. Randall*, 4 Gray, 36 — the defendant asked the judge to instruct the jury that the school master is liable only when he acts *malo animo*, from vindictive feelings, or under the violent impulses of passion or malevolence, and that he is not liable for errors of opinion or mistakes of judgment, provided he is governed by an honest purpose of heart to promote by the discipline employed the highest welfare of the school and the best interest of the scholar. In the case at bar the court charged substantially according to that request; but in the case reported in Gray the court refused so to charge, and did charge that if the jury found that the punishment was excessive and improper, then the master might properly be found guilty. The charge was held to be correct, upon the hearing of the defendant's exceptions in the supreme court. In the case of *Hathaway v. Rice*, 19 Vt. 102, we think the principle involved in the decision establishes the same doctrine.

"Suits of this character have frequently arisen in this state, and the rulings of our courts at *nisi prius*, have, we think, been quite uniform on this point. The law, as we deem it to exist, is this: A school master has the right to inflict reasonable corporal punishment. He must exercise reasonable judgment and discretion in determining when to punish, and to what extent. In determining upon what is a reasonable punishment, various considerations must be regarded: the nature of the offense, the apparent motive and disposition of the offender, the influence of his example and conduct upon others, and the sex, age, size, and strength of the pupil to be punished. Among reasonable persons, much difference prevails as to the circumstances which will justify the infliction of punishment, and the extent to which it may properly be administered. On account of this difference of opinion, and the difficulty which exists in determining what is a reasonable punishment, and the advantage which the master has by being on the spot to know all the circumstances, the manner, look, tone, gestures, and language of the offender (which are not always easily described), and thus to form a correct opinion as to the necessity and extent of the punishment, considerable allowance should be made to the teacher by way of protecting him in the exercise of his discretion. Especially should he have this indulgence when he appears to have acted from good motives, and not from anger or malice. Hence the teacher is not to be held liable on the ground of excess of punishment unless the punishment is clearly excessive, and would be held so in the general judgment of reasonable men. If the punishment be thus clearly excessive, then the master should be held liable for such excess, though he acted from good motives in inflicting the punishment; and in his own judgment considered it necessary, and not excessive. But if there is any reasonable doubt whether the punishment was excessive, the master should have the benefit of the doubt. Upon this point there was error in the charge.

"III. The court admitted evidence to show that the general character of the defendant, as a master, in governing his school was mild and moderate.

"As the court put the case to the jury upon the question of the defendant's malice in inflicting the punishment, this evidence, in that view, might be admissible as tending to disprove such intent. It might, perhaps, be properly said, that the nature of such an action, turning upon that point, involved the character of the defendant. But as we have already decided that the question of excessive punishment is not affected by the motive or intent of the master, we are of the opinion that this evidence of general good character is not admissible upon that issue. Good character does not tend to prove that the assault and battery were or were not committed, or that the punishment was or was not excessive. But when evidence is given tending to show that the master acted maliciously or wantonly, from an evil heart, and the plaintiff claims to recover damages on that ground, there, we think, the evidence would be admissible (1 Greenl. Ev., § 54, and notes) to rebut such intent. But it should be strictly limited to that purpose. In other respects, we find no error in the charge.

"IV. Whether a rawhide was a proper instrument of punishment, was left to the jury, with very suitable instructions. The evidence to show that the rawhide was used in other schools in the vicinity was properly admitted to rebut the charge of malice, by showing that he did not resort to an unusual instrument of punishment. The testimony to show that the plaintiff did not claim an excess of punishment on the first trial was proper, as tending to prove that that claim on the then pending trial was not well founded. Judgment reversed."

§ 161. **Pupil, residence.**—School directors have power to send pupils to schools of adjoining district, but such power should be carefully exercised;[1] the abuse of this discretion by the directors will be official misconduct; but unless such abuse is clearly shown, courts will not interfere.[1] Towns and cities in Mass. have no right to receive children into their schools whose parents or guardians reside in another state; and they cannot sue the parents for such tuition, even on an express contract.[2] In Mo., children who are not orphans nor apprentices, and whose parents are non-residents of the district, should not attend in that district.[3] Residents of government reservations for navy yards, forts, and arsenals, where there is no other reservation of jurisdiction to the state than that of a right to serve criminal and civil processes on such lands, are not entitled to the benefits of the common schools, for their children, in the towns in which the lands are situated.[4] Where a father bound out his children as apprentices in a district where he did not reside, for the purpose of schooling his children there, without the consent of the district, they were trespassers, and liable to an action by the district for attending school.[5] In N. H. the children supported at a county poor-farm have the right to attend the public school in that district.[6] Under G. S. Conn., §§ 2102, 2118, requiring attendance at school, a child whose parents are non-residents, and who lives with others with her parents' consent, with whom she

[1] Freeman v. Sch. Dirs., 37 Pa. St. 385.
[2] Haverhill v. Gale, 103 Mass. 104; Wheeler v. Burrow, 18 Ind. 14.
[3] Binde v. Klinge, 30 Mo. App. 285.
[4] Opinion judges, 1 Metc. (Mass.) 580.
[5] Sch. Dist. v. Bragdon, 23 N. H. (3 Fost.) 507.
[6] Sch. Dist. v. Pollard, 55 N. H. 503.

and her parents expect her to live permanently, has a right to attend the school of the district in which she resides.[1]

§ 162. **Pupil, residence.**—In *Lamar v. Micou*, 112 U. S. 452, 5 Sup. Ct. Rep. 221, Justice Gray says, in the opinion: "An infant cannot change his own domicile. As infants have the domicile of their father, he may change their domicile by changing his own; and after his death, the mother, while she remains a widow, may likewise, by changing her domicile, change the domicile of the infants, the domicile of the children in either case following the independent domicile of their parent."[2] "Generally speaking, domicile and residence mean the same thing."[3] Under the Comp. Stat. Mont., pp. 1886, 1907, where the census returns, as residents of one district, children whose fathers reside and who attend school in other districts, it is proper for the superintendent to transfer them to the latter districts, and apportion the money accordingly.[4] Ky. act 1888, § 16, authorizes the trustees to admit children residing outside of the district, "upon such terms and conditions, and upon payment of such charges, as the said board may deem right."[5] To recover payment for instruction given to non-residents' children, there must have been a previous arrangement between the directors of the respective districts, as directed by the Pa. school law of 1854; regular official action, evidenced by official minutes, is required by the statute.[6] In Acts Ga. 1889, pp. 1305, 1306, a provision that the local board may admit pupils not residents of the town on such terms as the board may prescribe, does not allow the board to prescribe terms which would cast upon the town or its inhabitants any

---

[1] Yale v. West Md. Sch. Dist., 59 Conn. 489.
[2] Sch. Dir. v. James, 2 Watts & S. 568; Story Confl. Laws, 46.
[3] Kennedy v. Ryall, 67 N. Y. 379.
[4] Sch. Dist. v. Patterson, (Mont.) 24 P. 698.
[5] Rogers Trs., (Ky.) 13 S. W. 587.
[6] Cascade v. Lewis, 43 Pa. St. 318.

part of the expense of educating non-resident pupils;[1] the main purpose being to establish and maintain a system of public schools in the town, an unconstitutional requirement therein, which exacts an incidental fee annually of all pupils, thereby including resident as well as non-resident pupils, will not vitiate the whole statute;[2] but non-resident cannot be admitted to the exclusion of resident.[3] The school inspectors of Peoria, Ill., may divide the city into districts, and may exercise the same discretion in establishing rules for the admission of pupils.[4] As an appeal lies from the decision of the township trustee upon the application of an inhabitant to be transferred for school purposes to another township, mandamus will not lie against the trustee.[5] Special act for Carlisle (Ky.) schools permits children non-resident of the district to attend by paying charges fixed by board of trustees.[6]

§ 163. **Pupil's tuition.**—A. made a conveyance of real estate to the city of Buffalo, reciting that it was made "with a view of aiding in the establishment of an institution where the children of those who are unable or unwilling to provide for their education may receive the same free of expense," and "for the use, maintenance, and support of a free school, and for no other purpose." The word "free" did not mean free in respect to the universal admissibility of the children of all classes of inhabitants of districts.[7] Where commissioners in Ala. neglect to employ teachers or appropriate money for tuition of children if they attend within the limits of township, the tuition-money may be recovered from any one of them by any legal voter, to defray it.[8] Under Const. Ga., (Code,

---

[1] Irvin v. Gregory, (Ga.) 13 S. E. 120.
[2] Irvin v. Gregory, (Ga.) 13 S. E. 605; 86 Ga. 605.
[3] Irvin v. Gregory, 9 A. 695.
[4] Grove v. Sch. Insp., 20 Ill. 532.
[5] Folge v. Gregg, 96 Ind. 345.
[6] Rogers v. Trs. Graded Sch., (Ky.) 13 S. W. 587.
[7] Le Couteulx v. Buffalo, 33 N. Y. 333.
[8] Burnes v. Minter, 12 Ala. 316.

p. 5304,) a municipal public school cannot exact incidental fees from resident scholars.[1] Under Iowa Code, § 1793, where the directors of the district in which the children reside, upon being notified of their attendance elsewhere, decide not to pay their tuition, no other demand is necessary, and the account may then be filed with the auditor.[2]

§ 164. **Record, etc.**—Parol evidence is competent to prove that a board of education had approved the bond of their treasurer, although no entry was made on the minutes of the proceedings of the board.[3] Record of district meeting which fails to state the hour, but refers to notice which does, is sufficient.[4] Where the record of the proceedings of the school board is defective, it may be explained or supplied by parol testimony,[5] and where certain parts of the minute book of a board of school directors were read in evidence by one party, and the counsel read and commented to the jury upon other parts of the book not given in evidence, to which objection was made, the court properly directed the jury to confine their attention to such parts of the minute book as were read in evidence.[6] Where the records showed a vote to adjourn to another place, and action had at such place, it will be presumed that the adjournment was to meet forthwith, in absence of record otherwise.[7] The records should prove all matters themselves that should be upon the record.[8] Failure to keep proper records will not render subsequent officers liable therefor, nor render prior proceedings void;[9] and the minutes by clerk *pro tempore* entered of record after he became clerk in fact, were held valid.[10]

[1] Irvin v. Gregory, 86 Ga. 605.
[2] Horton v. Ocheyedan, 49 Iowa, 231.
[3] Bartlett v. Bd. Ed., 59 Ill. 364.
[4] Howland v. Sch. Dist., 15 R. I. 184.
[5] Gearhart v. Dixon, 1 Pa. St. 224.
[6] Manchester v. Reserve Tp., 4 Pa. St. 35.
[7] Converse v. Porter, 45 N. H. 385.
[8] Sherwin v. Bugbee, 17 Vt. 337; Bartlett v. Kinsley, 15 Conn. 327.
[9] Higgins v. Reed, 8 Clarke, (Iowa) 298.
[10] Bartlett v. Kinsley, 15 Conn. 327.

§ 165. **Record.**—Where it did not appear that there was an election of a prudential committee and another record was introduced, which the clerk of the district testified contained a true record of the meeting, and in which the election of such a committee was entered, and both records were made by the clerk soon after the meeting, from loose memoranda put on paper at the time of the meeting, the election of the committee was duly proved.[1] Where the clerk *pro tem.* took memoranda for minutes, and made up his record after he had qualified as clerk, about two months later, the record was sustained, and in this case the records were not made up before his oath of office was administered;[2] a delay of one hour and five minutes is not an unreasonable delay, though meetings should be held on time.[3] Where it appears from the records that the meeting was held on the day appointed, the presumption of law is, that it was held in a suitable time in the day, and in pursuance of the warning.[3] Any fact which should be a matter of record should be proved by the record.[4] In Iowa, the proceedings of a school district will not be void, nor will officers subsequently elected become liable, for the reason that their predecessors have failed to keep the records properly.[5] The intention of a corporation can be ascertained only by the language of its recorded acts; and neither the private views nor the public declarations of individual members can be inquired into.[6]

§ 166. **Record.**—To show that additional territory had been added, the record showing the clerk of the district had received from the town clerk a document prescribing new boundaries for the district, (town meetings having power to prescribe

---
[1] Williams v. Lunenburg, 21 Pick. (Mass.) 75.
[2] Bartlett v. Kinsley, 15 Conn. 327.
[3] Sch. Dist. v. Blakeslee, 13 Conn. 227.
[4] Sherwin v. Bugbee, 17 Vt. 337.
[5] Higgins v. Reed, 8 Clarke, (Iowa) 298.
[6] Bartlett v. Kinsley, 15 Conn. 327.

new boundaries to school districts,) was evidence.[1] An amendment of the records of a school district should not be made, on trial of a cause, shaping it to meet a decision of the court.[2] The records of a school district are evidence of its votes for such district, in a suit to which it is a party.[3] By-laws of board of education are repealed by subsequent statute that conflicts therewith.[4] In Mich. parol evidence is inadmissible to prove a resolution of the district board, fixing the rate of tuition of non-resident pupils.[5] A clerk of a district cannot amend his records after his successor is qualified.[6]

§ 167. **Rules and regulations.**—(Ill.) A rule barring the doors of school-houses against little children coming from a great distance, in the winter, for being a few minutes tardy, is unreasonable and unlawful, and, in its practical operation, is little less than wanton cruelty.[7] The officers may prescribe necessary rules for classification of pupils, as to studies they are following, and promotion, but cannot expel for refusing to study a required branch that could be omitted without interfering with the classes where the parent demands that it be omitted;[8] and where trustees refused to admit pupil to high school unless he complied with rules as to course of studies, the request by parent as to excusing him from grammar recitals should have been complied with;[8] where book-keeping was not one of the branches required by law but the board were authorized to have higher branches taught than those enumerated, and where a scholar refused to pursue that study and was ejected forcibly from the building, she was awarded damages;[9] a rule suspending pupils for absence six half-days without a valid ex-

---

[1] Richardson v. Sheldon, 1 Pinn. (Wis.T.) 625.
[2] Hadley v. Chamberlain, 11 Vt. 618.
[3] Sch. Dist. v. Blakeslee, 13 Conn. 227.
[4] People v. Van Sicsen, 43 Hun (N. Y.) 537.
[5] Thompson v. Sch. Dist. No. 6, 25 Mich. 483.
[6] Sch. Dir. v. Atherton, 12 Metc. (Mass.) 105.
[7] Thompson v. Beaver, 63 Ill. 350.
[8] Trustees v. People, 87 Ill. 303.
[9] Rulison v. Post, 79 Ill. 567.

cuse was held to be a reasonable rule.[1] (Ind.) A student is required to submit to any proper rule necessary for the good government of the institution.[2] (Iowa.) If it is necessary for the good of the school that the pupil should study certain branches that the parent objects to his pursuing, the teacher has no power to enforce the rule of study by beating the pupil, but may expel or suspend.[3] Expelling a boy from school because he accidentally broke a window playing ball and did not pay for it as required by a rule of board of directors, was not upheld by the courts.[4] Where a pupil was suspended for being tardy, it was held that rule was for the government of the school, and was proper and reasonable and within the power of the officers to enforce.[5] (Me.) Expelling a Catholic scholar for not complying with a rule which required the use of the Bible in the school, was sustained, and the court held that it was a proper text-book, and not sectarian, and that the committee had the power to adopt and enforce it, the action was by the scholar; and that the conscience of the father was not interfered with.[6] (Mass.) Regulations forbidding attendance of immoral or licentious persons can be enforced, although the conduct of the persons may be proper while at school.[7] Where a pupil refused to obey the rule made by the committee, that the school should be opened with prayer and reading from the Bible, and that during prayer the pupils should bow their heads, but might be excused at request of parent, and a pupil was expelled for refusing and his parent refused to request his being excused, his expulsion was sustained by the courts.[8] A parent sued a city for damages for the expulsion of his child, and the

---

[1] Churchill v. Fewkes, 13 Brad. R. 520.
[2] State v. White, 82 Ind. 286.
[3] State v. Mizner, 50 Iowa, 152.
[4] Perkins v. Directors, 56 Iowa, 479.
[5] Bendick v. Babcock, 31 Iowa, 562.
[6] Donahoe v. Richards, 38 Me. 379.
[7] Sherman v. Charlestown, 8 Cush. 160.
[8] Spitler v. Woburn, 12 Allen, 127.

committee had the sole power of expulsion, but had never acted, (the teacher had suspended the pupil for refusing to take a whipping for disobedience): the court held he should have first applied to the committee to see if they sustained the teacher, and failing to prove this he did not show his child had been expelled.[1] Where the board fails to record the rules it will not render them void.[2] Suspending pupil for violating rules as to tardiness, was sustained, and the court held that this was a reasonable exercise of power by the teacher.[3] (Mo.) Rules beyond the power of board to make will not be enforced.[4] A rule suspending pupils absent six half-days in four consecutive weeks without satisfactory excuse was sustained.[4] (N. H.) A teacher not having a license required one of the scholars to declaim, and on refusing obedience to the rule which was made by the teacher was ejected from the building, although the parent had requested the omission of that branch. The teacher was sustained, the court in that case refusing to follow the Wis. authority.[5] (Ohio.) Where a pupil was suspended for failing to observe a rule adopted by the board of education prescribing rhetoric, the court held the rule to be reasonable, and his suspension until he should comply with it or give a reasonable excuse, was proper.[6] (Pa.) A rule prohibiting an expelled student from attending public exhibitions given at the normal schools of the state is tyrannical, and cannot be enforced if the party conducts himself properly at the exhibition.[7] (Tenn.) A teacher suspending a pupil for using tobacco in violation of rule adopted by the teacher, the directors objecting to that rule and discharged the teacher, the court up-

---

[1] Davis v. Boston, 133 Mass. 103.
[2] Russell v. Lynnfield, 116 Mass. 365.
[3] Russell v. Lynnfield, 116 Mass. 366.
[4] King v. Jeff. City Sch. Bd., 71 Mo. 628.
[5] Kidder v. Chellis, 59 N. H. 473.
[6] Sewell v. Bd., 29 Ohio St. 89.
[7] Hughes v. Goodell, (Pa.) 3 Pitts R. 264.

held the board, they having the power to suspend scholars by law, the teacher in Tenn. only having power of temporary suspension.[1] (Vt.) Where Catholic parents requested permission for their children to be absent on Catholic holidays, the rule of the committee suspending for absence was sustained;[2] where teacher required pupil to write English composition, and suspended for not complying, the rule and power to enforce were sustained.[3] (Wis.) Where parent asked teacher to excuse pupil from study of geography and teacher punished the child for complying with request of parent and refusing to pursue that study, the court held she exceeded the authority given her by law and the assault on the child was unjustifiable.[4]

§ 168. **Site, addition, and appeal.**—The authorities may acquire lands adjoining the school-house lot, when necessary for an extension which has been duly voted.[5] The Ind. statute authorizes appeals from proceedings by trustees to condemn school-house site, but in proceedings to condemn the decision of the trustees cannot be attacked.[6] In N. H., on appeal to county commissioners as to location of school-house, their decision is conclusive as to location for five years.[7] In Iowa, where the state superintendent on appeal grants petition to district directors for removal of school-house, his decision is final, and mandamus will lie to compel the removal.[8] The decision of the commissioner, on appeal, is final. After confirmation by supreme court, another site cannot be chosen except by new proceedings.[9] The jurisdiction of county commissioners to hear petition from voters in district appealing from location of school-house, extends to towns in which the district system has been abolished, in N. H.[10]

---

[1] Parker v. Sch. Dist., 5 Lea (Tenn.) 525.
[2] Ferriter v. Tyler, 48 Vt. 444.
[3] Guernsey v. Pitkin, 32 Vt. 226.
[4] Morrow v. Wood, 25 Wis. 59.
[5] Couzens v. Sch. Dist., 67 Me. 280.
[6] Braden v. McNutt, (Ind.) 16 N. E. 170.
[7] Stickney v. Town Oxford, (N. H.) 10 A. 117.
[8] Newby v. Free, (Iowa) 34 N. W. 168.
[9] Cottrell's Appeal, 10 R. I. 615.
[10] Adams v. State, (N. H.) 18 A. 321.

§ 169. **Site, condemnation.**—An unqualified refusal to sell land selected by a committee as the location of a school-house, would be a sufficient refusal to justify the selectmen in setting off the land;[1] and objections to the persons appointed, if known, must be made before the hearing.[1] Seven days' notice in writing is necessary to condemn, when district fails to agree and selectmen locate the site under R. S., ch. 23, § 30, and act 1848, Mass.[2] The Pa. act 1867, providing for the taking of land for school-house sites, is constitutional.[3] Where building committee of selectmen choose a site, and on refusal to sell, a meeting was called to authorize the selectmen to select a lot, and it was voted that they are authorized to select a school-house lot from the land of H. heretofore selected by the town, this was not sufficient designation under act 1848, Mass.[4] In R. I. the appointment of persons to value, or a tender of price for site of school-house before a vote of the district, is ineffectual to pass title, but location does not precede vote;[5] and the tender of price of land selected, if the owner lives out of the state, may sometimes be made to the party in possession.[6] A petition to the county commissioners by the owner of land taken for a school-house, for increase of damages, estops him from an action for occupation of the lot on the ground of irregularities in condemnation;[7] and when the district has properly designated the lot, and applied to the owner to sell the same, and he has refused, the selectmen may appraise the damages at the time they lay out the lot, in Me.[8] The township, in N. H., should be made a party in an action to establish location of school-house.[9]

§ 170. **Site, contract.**—A contract made by the trustee on

---

[1] True v. Melvin, 43 N. H. 503.
[2] Sch. Dist. v. Copeland, 2 Gray (Mass.) 414.
[3] Long v. Fuller, 68 Pa. St. 170.
[4] Harris v. Marblehead, 10 Gray (Mass.) 40.
[5] Howland v. Sch. Dist., 15 R. I. 184.
[6] Gibbons v. East Granville, 4 Allen (Mass.) 508.
[7] Jordon v. Haskell, 63 Me. 193.
[8] Couzens v. Sch. Dist., 67 Me. 280.
[9] Loverin v. Sch. Dist., 64 N. H. 109.

the authority of a school district, to accept a conveyance of land to be used as a site for a public school, that the district should build and keep in repair the division fence, is valid, though made before any tax to build or repair the fence had been voted.[1] A statutory prohibition against board of education buying schoolsite does not prohibit a lease of temporary site.[2] In N. H. a location made by a committee is not conclusive; the proper notice of a location to be given of a hearing before a committee, to individuals and to the district, is the same as for the service of process; and a selectman cannot act in the appointment of a committee, where his brother is a party.[3]

§ 171. **Site, conveyance.**—The grant made by the town of Ipswich, in 1650, in trust for the use of a school in that town, conveyed a fee, although it contained no words of limitation.[4] Where a site is bought with the restriction that no building should be erected to stand in front of the line of the school-house and another building, and the deed contained the restriction that no erections should be made upon said land between the school-house and the highway, there was no variance to bar a recovery for the price;[5] and one restriction, imposed by the plaintiffs in their proposal, was, that the land should be kept open; in the deed it was expressed that the land should remain as a public common, and in the declaration the restriction was expressed as in the deed. This difference constituted no objection to the plaintiff's recovery.[6] A conveyance of land to a town for the purpose of having a school-house erected and a school taught therein, for the benefit of the youth of the town, for a term specified, imports a sufficient consideration;[7] and an

[1] Albright v. Riker, 22 Hun (N. Y.) 367.
[2] Millard v. Bd. Ed., 19 Ill. App. 48.
[3] True v. Melvin, 43 N. H. 503.
[4] Feoffees Sch. v. Andrews, 8 Metc.(Mass.)584.
[5] Dix v. Sch. Dist., 22 Vt. 309.
[6] Dix v. Sch. Dist. No. 2 in Wilmington, 22 Vt. 309.
[7] Castleton v. Langdon, 19 Vt. 210.

action of trespass *quare clausum*, may be maintained in the name of the town;[1] and if the town erects upon the land a school-house, in which a school should be kept for a reasonable portion of the time, it will not forfeit a part of the land, although it should use that portion of it not wanted for the accommodation of the school-house, for purposes not connected with the main object in view, as if it should lease it for cultivation, or a building for a fire engine, or hay-scales should be put upon it, or it should be used as a passage-way, or be used for the purpose of accommodating teams, or a corner of a meeting-house were allowed to rest upon it, without dissent, or a room in the same building occupied as a school-house, should be finished and used by the town for the purpose of holding town and other public meeting; such conveyances are are always construed liberally.[1]

§ 172. **Site, election.**—Under the N. J. act of 1888, authorizing vote by the district to purchase land and build school-house, the trustees must first designate what lands are to be purchased, and this is to be approved by the voters, and the notice for the meeting must describe the lands.[2] Wagner's (Mo.) Stat. 1244, § 12, construed not to permit the directors to fix the site at their own discretion.[3] A school district voted to repair its school-house and to buy lands enough to straighten the line west of the school-house this was a sufficient location to give the county commissioners jurisdiction of a petition to change the location.[4] By Comp. Stat. Vt., ch. 20, § 38, the majority vote of the school district has the right to locate a school-house.[5] Under R. I. Pub. St., ch. 56, § 5, the selection

---

[1] Castleton v. Langdon, 19 Vt. 210.
[2] State v. Trs., (N. J.) 18 A. 683.
[3] Seibert v. Botts, 57 Mo. 430.
[4] Holbrook v. Faulkner, 55 N. H. 311.
[5] Bean v. Prud. Comm., 38 Vt. 177.

of a school-house site is not a condition precedent to vote to build, and a vote to build on that lot is not a condition precedent to condemnation.[1] Under the vote of a district, requesting the selectmen to fix the location of their school-house, the action of the selectmen is not compulsory on the members of the district.[2] The board of trustees in Dak. has no power to acquire a school-house site, except as designated by the voters of the district at a district meeting, and warrants issued therefor are void.[3] Section 17 of the act of 1856, Conn., to "provide suitable school-rooms," does not qualify the law which requires a vote of two-thirds to establish or change the site of a school-house.[4] Where more than one-third of the voters of a school district object, by their votes, to the place selected for the location of the school, the clerk of the district is required, by Me. Rev. Stat., ch. 11, § 32, to make a record of such fact.[5] In N. Y. the site must be designated by the inhabitants in a district meeting, and such power cannot be delegated to trustees.[6] The N. J. act of 1880 requires majority vote of taxable residents of district to buy land for school-house, or build, and § 86 of school law is repealed by implication.[7] Extra rooms cannot be rented and used by board of directors without a vote of the district, in Missouri.[8]

§ 173. **Site, injunction.**—The removal of school-house to another site before proper steps required have been taken, will be enjoined at the suit of a tax-payer whose taxes will be increased thereby;[9] but a private person cannot prevent removal of school-house unless he shows special damage to himself;[10] and school district will not be enjoined from erecting school-

[1] Howland v. Sch. Dist., (R. I.) 8 A. 337.
[2] Tozier v. Sch. Dist. No. 2, 39 Me. 556.
[3] Farmers Bk. v. Sch. Dist., 6 Dak. 255.
[4] Colt v. Roberts, 28 Conn. 330.
[5] Norton v. Perry, 65 Me. 183.
[6] Benjamin v. Hull, 17 Wend. (N. Y.) 437.
[7] Point P. L. Co. v. Sch. Dist., 47 N. J. L. 235.
[8] Black v. Cornell, 30 Mo. App. 641.
[9] Graves v. Jasper Tp., (S. D.) 50 N. W. 904.
[10] Parody v. Sch. Dist., 15 Neb. 514.

house on a certain site, at instance of person not affected;[1] and a resident tax-payer cannot sue the directors for illegal location and purchase of school-site without first making demand on proper parties to sue, and his remedy against an illegal location is by appeal rather than injunction.[2] Discretion allowed officers will not be controlled though it may be exercised unwisely;[3] but where vote of electors is required before changing site or building of new site, an attempt to act without vote should be enjoined.[4]

§ 174. **Site, notice.**—A committee to locate may be appointed without notice to other parties.[5] The certificate of the officers of a town, of their determination where a school-house is to be placed, is, after the application, notice to all parties, and a hearing, as required by the Me. Rev. Stat., ch. 11, § 32, and conclusive.[6]

§ 175. **Site, officers.**—When location of a school-house by selectmen is returned to the town clerk for record, no subsequent neglect of the town clerk to make a due record will affect the validity of such location;[7] and where a site has been chosen, irregularities of the clerk or omissions in describing the site selected will not invalidate.[8] Under the school act of Ohio, Mch. 14, 1853, the township board of education has the power to designate the particular places where school-houses in sub-districts should be built; and the powers of the local directors of a sub-district are to be exercised in subordination to the township board of education.[9]

§ 176. **Site, place.**—The trustees of a district were liable in trespass for assessing and trying to collect a tax voted to raise

[1] Nixon v. Sch. Dist., 32 Kas. 510.
[2] Ind. Sch. D. v. Gookin, (Iowa) 34 N. W. 174.
[3] Witherop v. Titusville Sch. Bd., 7 Pa. Co. Ct. Rep. 45.
[4] Buchanan v. Hannibal Sch. D., 25 Mo. App. 85.
[5] True v. Melvin, 43 N. H. 503.
[6] Morton v. Perry, 65 Me. 183.
[7] Converse v. Porter, 45 N. H. 385.
[8] Merritt v. Farries, 22 Ill. 303.
[9] Hughes v. Bd. Ed., 13 Ohio St. 336.

money to purchase a site and build a school-house on a site of different location, where the previous consent of the commissioners of common schools had not been obtained to change the site.[1] The trustees of the town of Poplar Plains, under act Ky. of Feb. 28, 1860, and pursuant to vote of the town, sold a lot and school-house, the title to which was in the trustees, and invested the proceeds in the purchase of a seminary lot and buildings just outside the corporate limits of the town; they were not required to make the reinvestment in property within the corporate limits of the town, and after acquiescence for several years, the trustees were not personally liable.[2] If a location is void, by reason of its insufficient and defective description, the district must proceed anew.[3] The municipal officers in Me. have ten days within which to give their certificate to the clerk of the district of their location of the place; they may change their certificate, and agree if their certificate is not recorded, if their determination is duly filed within ten days.[3] The school inspectors of Peoria have power to maintain a school in a house beyond the city limits for children living within them.[4]

§ 177. **Site, sale.**—Under Pa. act of 1836, whether property is any longer required for school purposes is a question within the discretion of the school directors.[5] The N. H. law of 1871, providing for relocation of school-houses, is not unconstitutional.[6]

§ 178. **Site, tax.**—One cannot resist a school tax on the ground that the title to the land purchased for the school building is defective, if there is no ouster of possession.[7] In N. Y. a tax to build may be collected before the site of the school

---

[1] Baker v. Freeman, 9 Wend. (N. Y.) 36.
[2] Samuels v. Trs., 4 Bush (Ky.) 259.
[3] Norton v. Perry, 65 Me. 183.
[4] Grove v. Sch. Insp., 20 Ill. 532.
[5] McCullough v. Sch. Dirs., 11 Pa. St. 476.
[6] Farmers' Petition, 51 N. H. 376.
[7] People v. Sisson, 98 Ill. 335.

building is located;[1] but in Me. a tax for the erection of a school-house upon a lot not legally designated was deemed to be for an illegal purpose.[2] By act Pa. May 8, 1854, § 33, the board of directors of a school district may levy a special tax for purchasing ground and erecting school buildings thereon; and this power is given to boards of controllers in cities and boroughs where the school property is vested in them, and in other cases to the board of directors.[3]

§ 179. **Site, title.**—A school may be taught in rented building instead of school-house, where the directors deem it advisable.[4] The designation, "is included within the bounds of the survey directed to be run by § 1 of act of 1812, as well as within the limits of the town of St. Louis as it stood incorporated June 13, 1812," is valid, though it does not state that the land thus set apart "is or ever was, in whole or in part, a town lot, out-lot, or common field-lot, adjoining or belonging to said town."[5] Where the equitable title is in the school-district board, a contract for the legal title is valid.[6] A writ of mandamus cannot issue to compel a township trustee to locate and build a school-house on land that does not belong to the township, notwithstanding the county examiner, on an appeal from decision of trustee, has required him to erect a school-house on said land.[7] In an action by one of a building committee against the district, for money paid out by him for the district under the direction of the building committee, the fact that a perfect title to the land had not been secured was no defense to the action; and a ratification of the acts of the committee in expending more money than they were authorized to expend

---

[1] Colton v. Beardsley, 38 Barb. (N. Y.) 29.
[2] Marble v. McKenney, 60 Me. 332.
[3] Blair v. Boggs Tp. Sch. Dist., 31 Pa. St. 274.
[4] Scripture v. Burns, 59 Iowa, 70.
[5] Kissell v. St. Louis Pub. Sch., 16 Mo. 553.
[6] Connor v. Bd. Ed., 10 Minn. 439.
[7] Koontz v. State, 44 Ind. 323.

would avail as between the parties, although such ratification was since the commencement of the suit.[1] A payment or tender of the damages after the school-house is built on land of private person without his consent, and after the owner of the land sues in an action of trespass, qu. cl. fr. affords no justification.[2] A location of a site is not void for inadvertently overlapping part of a public way;[3] but a board of education cannot appropriate a public square of a city for a school-house;[4] and directors authorized to purchase land and build a schoolhouse thereon, by vote of district, cannot erect the building on land held in trust for county.[5]

§ 180. **Site, trust.**—A reservation, by a vendor, of certain land for a school-house, was held to be a trust for the benefit of the neighborhood; and the sale as his individual property, was enjoined.[6] Where land was conveyed to school trustees on condition that it should revert to the grantor, if it should cease to be used for school purposes, and a school-house was erected thereon and after being used for seven years for a school, the failure for one year to eject an intruder does not work a forfeiture;[7] and a school-district corporation will not lose its title, in N. Y., to land by non-user for a time less than twenty years.[8]

§ 181. **Statute, constitution.**—The Pa. act of 1873 for the city of A., in so far as it assumes to empower the mayor, etc., to levy a tax and issue bonds, and to exempt the city from county taxation for public schools, contains matter not in the title, and is unconstitutional;[9] and this section is by the subsequent "act to amend," etc., "the several acts granting

---

[1] Davis v. Sch. Dist., 44 N. H. 398.
[2] Storer v. Hobbs, 52 Me. 144.
[3] Jordan v. Heskell, 63 Me. 189.
[4] 51 Cal. 620.
[5] Appeal of Tarbell, 129 Pa. St. 146.
[6] Hamner v. Sharp, 11 Heisk. (Tenn.) 701.
[7] Barber v. Sch. Tr., 51 Ill. 396.
[8] Roble v. Sedgwick, 35 Barb. (N. Y.) 319.
[9] Bd. Pub. Ed. Americus v. Barlow, 74 Pa. St. 232.

corporate authority to the city of A., repealed through inconsistency.[1] The repealing clause of § 1 of Ohio act of 1852, for the organization of cities and incorporated villages, did not abrogate the school systems nor special laws then existing.[2]

§ 182. **Suits, district.**—Individuals cannot as such defend actions against districts;[3] and a school district in Conn. is liable to be sued;[4] but in 1859, school districts were not corporations, and liable to be sued as such, in Iowa.[5] The petition in a suit by a district need not set out the manner of its organization.[6] When right of appeal exists, the circuit court (Ill.) will not review by *certiorari* the record of trustees in redistricting.[7] Where judgment in an action against a school district is obtained by fraud of plaintiff and one of the trustees, the court may set aside the same, and allow an answer to be filed.[8] Justices of peace, in Kas., have not jurisdiction of suit against school district, when amount exceeds $100.[9] A director, in Wis., can recover from the district the expenses in defending a suit against the district;[10] but boards of education cannot use district funds to defend individual lawsuits occurring by reason of the members charging that bidders on work had cheated the district.[11] The school directors of a district should sue in their official capacity for the district.[12] School directors in occupancy of a school-house may maintain trespass for breaking and entering the same, although the legal title is vested in the trustees of the school.[13] A district may submit differences between it and its treasurer to arbitrators.[14]

§ 183. **Suit, parties.**—The school trustees and not the

---

[1] Bd. Ed. Americus v. Barlow, 74 Pa. St. 232.
[2] Blanchard v. Bissell, 11 Ohio St. 96.
[3] Lane v. Sch. Dist., 10 Metc. (Mass.) 462.
[4] McLoud v. Selby, 10 Conn. 390.
[5] Runyan v. Sch. Dist., 12 Iowa, 184.
[6] Fort Dodge v. Wahkansa, 15 Iowa, 434.
[7] Trustees v. Shepherd, (Ill.) 28 N. E. 1073.
[8] Sturm v. Sch. D., 45 Minn. 88; 47 N. W. 469.
[9] Jones v. Sch. Dist., 8 Kas. 362.
[10] Fobes v. Sch. Dist., 10 Wis. 117.
[11] Hotchkiss v. Plunkett, 60 Conn. 229.
[12] Kingsley v. Sch. Dirs., 2 Pa. St. 28.
[13] Alderman v. Sch. Dirs., 91 Ill. 179.
[14] Walnut Dist. v. Rankin, 70 Iowa, 65.

school directors should sue to compel conveyance in an action for specific performance.[1] Where a suit is instituted in the individual names of school directors for a matter in which they are only interested officially, the title of the cause should be amended by striking out the individual names of the directors, and substituting their corporate name.[2] A suit may be maintained in the name of the successor of a school commissioner, upon a note made to the latter under the Ill. act Feb. 26, 1841.[3] An action to recover for materials and services in the erection of a school-house, under the employment of the school trustees of a city, should be brought, not against such trustees, but against the school corporation, by the name and style of "The School City of ———," filling the blank with the name of the city.[4] A suit to set aside a contract for the building of a school-house and to enjoin the doing of the work on the ground of fraud on the part of the township trustee in making the contract, is properly brought in the name of the state for the use of the township, in Ind.[5]

§ 184. **Suit, party.**—Under the Ky. act of 1871, requiring the commissioner to collect and pay over to the "trustees" of the districts in proportion to the amount they are entitled to, for the use and benefit of the teachers thereof, on his default the trustees of each district in the county have a separate cause of action against him and his sureties, for the teachers' benefit.[6] School districts may appoint and instruct agents to prosecute and defend, or to withdraw defenses and confess judgment;[7] but a school district, in N. H., cannot sue in assumpsit the prudential committee of the district, to recover the balance of the

---

[1] Wilson v. Sch. Dirs., 81 Ill. 181.
[2] Shoudy v. Sch. Dirs., 32 Ill. 290.
[3] Manlove v. McHatton, 5 Ill. (4 Scan.) 95.
[4] Sims v. McClure, 52 Ind. 267.
[5] State v. Earhart, 27 Ind. 119.
[6] Hammond v. Crawford, 9 Bush (Ky.) 75.
[7] Denniston v. Sch. Dist., 17 N. H. 492.

school-money raised by the town, assigned by the selectmen and paid to the committee.[1] The trustees of the schools of the township may sue in equity in matters affecting lands held by state for township common schools;[2] and a suit may be instituted by the state on the relation of the board of commissioners for the recovery of congressional school funds.[3] In a suit on a bond of an ex-school commissioner for not paying over the funds in his hands, the successor of such ex-school commissioners should be the relator.[4] In Ind., under act of 1838, the treasurer of a district could not sue in his own name for money due to the district.[5] The county auditor is a proper relator in a suit to collect money loaned by the county auditor, belonging to school fund.[6] A suit for teachers' wages must be brought against the district by its corporate name and not against the trustees as such.[7] The school commissioners of the townships of Ala. may sue as such, and the suit may be styled school commissioners of the township, giving number and range.[8] One commissioner, as such, cannot recover from another the money belonging to the school fund, in his hands;[9] but any legal voters of the township, in Ala., may sue school commissioner for funds in his hands which he fails to pay over as directed by law.[9] The board of education of Troy cannot aid the payee, the chamberlain, in collecting a draft drawn by the board for school expenses, and not countersigned by the comptroller nor audited by the common council.[10]

§ 185. **Suit, party.**—The director of a district, under Neb. G. S. 968, may bring an action for the price of bonds sold by

[1] Sch. Dist. v. Esty, 16 N. H. 146.
[2] Moore v. Sch. Trs., 19 Ill. 83.
[3] Groves v. State, 9 Ind. 200.
[4] State v. Grant, 7 Blackf. (Ind.) 71; Wright v. State, 7 Blackf. (Ind.) 63.
[5] Crawford v. Dean, 6 Blackf. (Ind.) 181.
[6] Scotten v. State, 51 Ind. 52.
[7] Sproul v. Smith, 40 N. J. L. 314.
[8] Sch. Comm'rs v. Dean, 2 Stew. & P. (Ala.) 190.
[9] Burns v. Minter, 12 Ala. 316.
[10] Johnson v. Troy, 19 Hun (N. Y.) 204.

that district.[1] In 1858, in Oreg., a suit to enforce the obligation of a note and mortgage given for a loan of school funds should be brought in the name of county treasurer.[2] A suit to recover a fund belonging to the county school board must be brought in its corporate name, in Va.[3] School board cannot, after a verdict, object to the regularity of the proceeding on account of appearance, by consent of the board, to the action.[4] The provisions of Wis. Laws 1869, ch. 182, make a town board organized under its provisions the legal successor of the previous board, and authorize it to sue for moneys due to the former board.[5] The district board have no authority to take the defense of a suit from the assessor; the control of suits is not among the powers of duties confided by the statutes to the district board, in Mich. (C. L. 1871, § 3613.)[6] In Miss. the county superintendents succeeded, under the new constitution and the laws of 1870, to the rights and powers of the former boards of trustees, and should sue for moneys due to such trustees for lands sold by them.[7] Under N. H. R. S., chs. 70, 73, a school district may sue a prudential committee after its term of office for neglecting to appropriate to the support of schools money received by him belonging to that district.[8] Some of the inhabitants of a district may, in behalf of themselves and others, sue to test the constitutionality of the law creating the district, and the legality of the proceedings of its officers under it;[9] but one tax-payer cannot sue in behalf of himself and the others to restrain the sale of their real estate for the purpose of collecting a delinquent tax assessed to pay certain judgments against the district, on the ground that the judgments were obtained on

---

[1] Bowen v. Sch. Dist., 10 Neb. 265.
[2] Alexander v. Knox, 6 Sawyer C. Ct. 54.
[3] Stewart v. Thornton, 75 Va. 215.
[4] Thompson v. Sch. Dist., 71 Mo. 495.
[5] Sch. Dirs. Sigel v. Coe, 40 Wis. 103.
[6] Sch. Dist. v. Wing, 30 Mich. 351.
[7] Simmons v. Holmes, 49 Miss. 134.
[8] Sch. Dist. v. Sherburne, 48 N. H. 52.
[9] Bull v. Read, 13 Gratt. (Va.) 78.

illegal and void school orders, etc. Each tax-payer must bring his several action;[1] and the owners of the several judgments sought to be declared void should all be made defendants.[1]

§ 186. **Suit, party.**—Prudential committees of themselves cannot sue; and the vote of a district to stop an action does not render it liable for prior expenses in prosecuting it without authority.[2] The answer by clerk and director of school district was held to be the answer of district.[3] In Vt. the district alone, and not inhabitants, can bring action of trespass *quare clausum fregit*.[4] Where a suit was brought against a school district for money borrowed by them to raise money for the township to pay bounties, the record might be amended by substituting the township.[5] An incorporated town, sued as a school corporation, may be designated either in the title of the action as a school corporation, or in the complaint by an allegation of that fact.[6] A complaint cannot be brought against the trustee of a civil township to compel him, as such, to erect a school-house within its territorial limits; it must be against the trustee of the school township.[7] The board of trustees of the normal school at Oskaloosa, Iowa, organized under act of Jan. 15, 1849, was not a body capable of suing or of being sued.[8] In an action on a school order of a district township which has been subsequently reorganized into independent districts, the court may render judgment against the several independent districts, and issue a mandamus commanding the directors to assemble and apportion the same among the several judgment debtors;[9] but either of the districts may maintain an action against the others for contribution if the apportionment is erro-

[1] Newcomb v. Horton, 18 Wis. 566.
[2] Burgess v. Sch. Dist., 100 Mass. 132.
[3] Sch. Dist. v. Carson, 10 Kas. 238.
[4] Chaplin v. Hill, 24 Vt. 528.
[5] Heidelberg v. Horst, 62 Pa. St. 301.
[6] Noblesville v. McFarland, 57 Ind. 335.
[7] Hornby v. State, 69 Ind. 102.
[8] Drake v. Bd. Trs., 11 Iowa, 54.
[9] Asbury Ind. Sch. Dist. v. Dubuque Co. Dist. Ct., 48 Iowa, 182.

neous.[1] The president of the board of directors of a school district, in absence of statute otherwise, has authority to receive service of process in a suit against the school district.[2] An action prosecuted by superintendent of education for La. must be prosecuted by attorney general or district attorney, or it should be dismissed.[3] The board of trustees of schools under Ill. Laws 1865, § 39, can alone maintain an action for a trespass thereon, although not themselves in actual occupancy.[4]

§ 187. **Superintendent public instruction.**—Advice of state superintendent is no defense for unlawful act of trustee depositing money in bank.[5] The law of Wis., giving state superintendent jurisdiction of appeal from division of districts on decision of town boards is valid;[6] and he may make such rules for hearing of cause before him as to him may seem proper, defining the manner of presenting the case, and requiring written briefs and refusing oral argument, when the statute does not otherwise direct;[6] and the state superintendent of Ind. has jurisdiction of appeal on location of site under laws of 1855.[7] The decisions of a state superintendent are entitled to much weight;[8] and his decision on appeal annulling certificate of teacher for cause is valid and final.[9] The state superintendent in La. may consider payments erroneously made when he makes a proper apportionment.[10] The state superintendent of N. Y. cannot determine appeal from apportionment by board of town auditors, (under acts 1864 and 1870.)[11] Where a trustee had brought a proceeding to compel the managers of a normal school to pay certain moneys to teacher employed by the trus-

[1] Kennedy v. Derby Grange Ind. Sch. Dist., 48 Iowa, 189.
[2] Carr v. Sch. Dist., 42 Mo. App. 154.
[3] Fay v. Jumel, 35 La. Ann. 368.
[4] Barber v. Sch. Trs., 51 Ill. 396.
[5] Inglis v. State, 61 Ind. 212.
[6] State v. Whitford, 54 Wis. 150.
[7] State v. Custer, 11 Ind. 210.
[8] State v. Burton, 45 Wis. 150.
[9] People v. Collins, 34 How. (N. Y.) 336.
[10] State v. Fay, 36 La. Ann. 241.
[11] People v. Bd., 27 (N. Y.) N. E. 968.

tee, the refusal of the trustee to abandon such proceeding when requested by state superintendent, justified his removal by the state superintendent, under L. N. Y. 1864, ch. 555.[1] The territorial superintendent of Utah is appointed by the governor under the organic act.[2] The superintendent of public instruction may correct mistakes in his rulings if rights of other parties do not intervene.[3]

§ 188. **Superintendent public instruction.**—In the case of *People v. Draper*, 18 N. Y. S. 282, it was held: *"Removal of School Trustee—Powers of State Superintendent.*—Where the return of a trustee of a school district to an order made by the state superintendent of public instruction, requiring him to show cause why he should not be removed from his office, admitted that he had neglected and refused to comply with and had violated certain orders of the superintendent, he was properly removed from his office, under Laws 1864, ch. 555, § 18, authorizing such removal in case of the willful disobedience of any decision or order of the superintendent on the part of the trustee. The question whether or not the trustee should discontinue a proceeding which he had brought against the local board of managers of a normal school to compel them to pay over certain public school-moneys they had received, to teachers employed by the trustee, was one upon which the decision of the superintendent was conclusive; and the refusal of the trustee to abandon such proceedings, when directed so to do by the superintendent, constituted willful disobedience, justifying his removal. . . . The return of the defendant is conclusive as to the facts therein set forth. (*People v. Fire Comm'rs*, 73 N. Y. 437.) That return set forth that the relator appeared

[1] People v. Draper, 18 N. Y. S. 282.
[2] Williams v. Clayton, (Utah) 21 P. 398.
[3] Desmond v. Ind. S. D., (Iowa) 32 N. W. 6.

in person and by counsel before the defendant on the return-day of the order hereinbefore referred to, and by the return and by the statement of his counsel admitted that he had violated that and a previous order of the superintendent, and had neglected and refused to comply with the orders of the superintendent; and that he had advised teachers to commence suits against the district for their wages, instead of levying a tax to raise the money to pay them, as the superintendent had ordered him to do. As above stated, the facts stated in the return are conclusive upon the court here; and these facts, being true, abundantly justified the defendant in removing the relator from office. The proceeding was perhaps summary, but the facts were admitted; there was no occasion for proof.

"But it is claimed that there are facts stated in the affidavit upon which the writ was issued which are not denied in the return, and therefore the court may consider them, under the case of *People v. Commissioners Dept. Fire and Buildings*, 106 N. Y. 64, 12 N. E. Rep. 641. The claim of the relator is that the real reason the defendant removed the relator was that he refused to discontinue a proceeding he had brought to compel the local board of managers of the normal school at New Paltz to pay over the public school-moneys they had received to be paid to the teachers employed by the relator. Even if that were so, I see no reason to reverse the order of the superintendent. He had made a decision of that question himself. It was in a matter over which he had jurisdiction. He also there and then made a decision in regard to the matter, and it was in a matter where the statute made his decision conclusive. The conduct of the trustee as to school matters was also subject to his supervision and control. He then and there made an order, which he had a right to make, directing the relator to abandon his proceedings against the local board of managers of the normal school. The relator then and there refused to abandon the proceedings, and expressly announced, by his counsel present with him, his intention of continuing such proceedings. This, I think, constituted a willful disobedience of an order or decision of the superintendent, within the meaning of the statute. 'Willful,' I think, in this statute, means intentional, (*Anderson v. Howe*, 116 N. Y. 336, 22 N. E. Rep. 695;) and the relator certainly intended to disobey the defendant's order. It was not a case of neglect, omission, or misapprehension, but of absolute refusal, and an announcement of an intention of doing directly the reverse of what he was ordered to do. The writ should be quashed, and the determination of the defendant affirmed, with $50 costs and printing disbursements."

§ 189. **Superintendent, county.**—Where the rights of a citizen are involved in matters required to be submitted to the county superintendent on appeal, the court may determine whether the exercise of such authority is lawful.[1] In Neb. the county superintendent must apportion the fund before the county treasurer can pay out credits of the county school fund.[2] The county superintendent may be compelled to perform his duty by mandamus;[3] and in Ind. he must execute a special bond under the text-book law.[4] In Iowa he cannot recover compensation for examining teachers at any other than at the time required by law;[5] and his salary may be regulated in Tenn., under acts 1873, by county court.[6] A vote by township trustee for himself for the office of county superintendent is void, and

[1] Perkins v. Dirs., 56 Iowa, 476.
[2] Donnelly v. Duras, 11 Neb. 283.
[3] Brown v. Nash, 1 Wy. Ter. 85.
[4] Knox Co. v. Johnson, 24 N. E. 148.
[5] Farrell v. Webster Co., 49 Iowa, 245.
[6] Halle v. Young, 6 Lea (Tenn.) 501.

contrary to public policy.[1] The Miss. act providing for election of county superintendents in only a part of the state, is not void.[2] Discretion of, cannot be controlled by courts;[3] but he has only such powers as are given by statute;[4] and when he is dismissed from office and appeals, he cannot act pending appeal.[5] Trustees, in Ind., should appoint superintendent on the day fixed by law, or adjourn from day to day.[6] In that state, to be eligible for county superintendent, he must have been an inhabitant of the county one year prior to appointment.[7] If county judge refuses to permit school commissioner to qualify, he may be compelled to by mandamus.[8] Appeals on school questions in N. J. are to the county superintendent,[9]-but in Ind. no appeal lies from action of trustee contracting or dismissing teacher in city or town;[10] and he cannot compel the erection of a school building on land not owned by township.[11] He is not liable in damages for changing district on proper petition.[12] The election of superintendent by town school committee may be reconsidered before he has been informed of his election.[13] An officer ostensibly a principal, cannot be employed by board directors in Pa., whose duties are same as district superintendent.[14] Under N. J. Rev., p. 1071, a dispute over election of a trustee may be submitted to county superintendent for opinion, but the state superintendent is to try and decide the matter in dispute.[15] The failure of school superintendent to give bond, under Ind. act March 2, 1889, will not *per se* forfeit the office.[16]

§ 190. **Superintendent, county.**—Although the county

---

[1] Hornung v. State, 116 Ind. 458.
[2] Wynn v. State, (Miss.) 7 So. 353.
[3] Brinsmore v. Cottingham, 11 Ky. L. R. 486; Bailey v. Ewart, 52 Iowa, 111.
[4] Ratcliff v. Faris, 6 Neb. 539.
[5] Walls v. Palmer, 64 Ind. 493; Matthews v. Chase, 41 Ind. 357.
[6] State v. Harrison, 67 Ind. 71; Sackett v. State, 74 Ind. 487.
[7] State v. Kilroy, 86 Ind. 118.
[8] Greenup Co. Ct. v. Clifton, 5 Ky. L. R. 241.
[9] State v. Gloucester City, 45 N. J. L. 100.
[10] Crawfordsville v. Hays, 42 Ind. 206.
[11] Koontz v. State, 44 Ind. 323.
[12] Sch. Dist. v. Wheeler. 25 Neb. 199; Cowles v. Sch. Dist., 37 N. W. (Neb.) 493.
[13] Wood v. Cutter, 138 Mass. 149.
[14] Delano Land Co.'s Appeal, 103 Pa. St. 347.
[15] State v. Albertson, (N. J.) 22 A. 1063.
[16] Knox Co. v. Johnson, (Ind.) 24 N. E. 148.

auditor is authorized, in Ind., to cast a vote for county superintendent in case of a tie, yet he cannot vote on a resolution to change vote by ballot to yea-and-nay vote, and cannot vote when half the trustees vote for one and the other half vote blank or for a fictitious person.[1] Where superintendent of public instruction was authorized to remove any county superintendent "whenever in his opinion the interests of public education demanded such removal," no notice need be given or charges made, and a removal by him and appointment of another to fill vacancy will be upheld.[2] The action of the county superintendent in regard to changing boundaries is discretionary, from which an appeal will lie; but his judgment cannot be controlled by mandamus,[3] as courts are not disposed to interfere with the exercise of mere discretionary authority.[4] A school board may employ a superintendent whose term of office does not begin until after some of the members of the board go out of office;[5] and the Ind. statutes do not limit the board of school trustees, in contracting with superintendent, as to the time the board shall continue in office.[6] A county superintendent should keep his accounts itemized.[7] The board of directors of public schools in the city of Olney, Ill., were required to establish and keep up a system of graded schools in the city; by necessary implication from the duties imposed upon it, the board had authority to appoint a superintendent.[8]

§ 191. **Superintendent of schools.**—In the case of *Davis v. School District No. 1, of the City and Township of Niles*, 45 N. W. Rep. (Mich.) 989, it was held, Cahill, J.: "Under

---

[1] State v. Edwards, (Ind.) 16 N. E. 627.
[2] State v. Shaver, 54 Ala. 193.
[3] State v. Clary, 25 Neb. 403.
[4] Smith v. Comm'rs, 10 Col. 17.
[5] Reubelt v. Noblesville, 106 Ind. 480; Wait v. Ray, 67 N. Y. 38; Tappan v. Sch. Dist., 44 Mich. 500; Webster v. Sch. Dist., 16 Wis. 337; Gates v. Sch. Dist., 53 Ark. 470.
[6] Reubelt v. Noblesville, 106 Ind. 478.
[7] Smith v. Comm'rs, 10 Col. 17.
[8] Spring v. Wright, 63 Ill. 90.

How. St. Mich., § 5134, par. 5, authorizing the board of school trustees to employ such officers and servants as may be necessary for the management of the schools and the school property, to fix their compensation and prescribe their duties, one employed as a superintendent, not being a teacher, is not required to have the certificate required by law to qualify one for employment as a teacher. . . . In an action for compensation by one employed by a director as superintendent, it is error to exclude evidence that the board of trustees, which alone has authority to make a contract for such employment, knew of his services in that behalf and acccepted them. . . . The plaintiff sued the defendant, being a graded-school district, to recover for services rendered during the months of April, May, and June, 1887, as superintendent. Paragraph 5 of § 5134 authorizes the board of trustees to employ such officers and servants as may be necessary for the management of the schools and the school property, prescribe their duties, and fix their compensation. Under this provision the person employed is not required to be a teacher, nor to have a certificate as a teacher. We think the plaintiff, if duly employed to render the services he claims to have rendered for the school district, was not disqualified from receiving compensation therefor, by the fact that he had no certificate as a teacher. The doubtful question in the case is as to whether the plaintiff was legally employed to perform the duties for which he seeks compensation. It is clear that he was not, in the first instance, so employed, because such employment is required to be made by the board of trustees, and one of such trustees, acting as director, could not lawfully employ the plaintiff so as to bind the district. But, as this contract of employment was one which the board itself could lawfully make, the question arises as to whether, if the plaintiff actually performed the duties with the knowledge and consent of the board, and the district received the benefit of his services, the law will not imply a promise on the part of the district to pay what such services were reasonably worth. Cases are not wanting which hold that municipal corporations may become liable upon an implied assumpsit. Where a municipal corporation receives money or property of a party under such circumstances that the law, independent of express contract, imposes the obligation upon the corporation to do justice with respect to the same, it has been held that it may be liable to an action. (*Argenti v. San Francisco*, 16 Cal. 255.) In the case just cited, Chief Justice Field says that in reference to services rendered, the case is different. "Their acceptance must be evidenced by ordinance (or express corporate action) to that effect. . . . If not originally au_thorized, no liability can attach upon any ground of implied contract. The acceptance upon which alone the obligation to pay could arise, would be wanting." I do not see why any distinction should be made between services rendered and appropriated by municipal corporations, and any other property so received and appropriated, except that it might be more difficult, in the case of services rendered, to show an actual acceptance and intentional appropriation than in the case of tangible property. But, if the proof showed that the services were actually accepted by the corporation with full knowledge of all the facts, I think the same rule ought to apply to services rendered that would apply to money or other property. It does not appear what the plaintiff could have known as to the services having been performed with the full knowledge and assent of the board of trustees. The offer of proof by him on this subject was rejected, and we think erroneously. For this error, and also for the direction of the court that the jury should return a verdict for the defendant, the judgment must be reversed, and a new trial granted."

§ 192. **Supplies.**—Where township refuses to receive supplies on the ground that they are not needed, an assignee of holder of the certificate cannot recover, although he and the seller act in good faith.[1] A complaint on note given by Ind. school trustee must allege that the consideration was necessary, that the articles were suitable, and that they were received and accepted;[2] and evidence of the usefulness and necessity of school supplies, as to the particular township to which they were furnished, is material in an action for the price.[3] Where there was conflicting evidence as to the delivery of the supplies, and whether they were necessary for the common schools of the township, three of defendant's witnesses testifying that the instruments sold were not useful, a verdict for the defendant will not be disturbed;[3] and a school commissioner and superintendent for the county, and a person who has followed farming in the summer and taught school in the winter in that township, are competent to testify as to the usefulness and necessity of such supplies in the township;[3] and a trustee may refuse to furnish any supplies or teachers when the school is not leased or owned by the school township, notwithstanding orders from county superintendent, and vote of district.[4] To enable board directors to buy supplies authorized by Iowa Code, § 1729, the purchase must be made with cash actually in the treasury at the time and unappropriated.[5] Iowa statute requiring physiology

[1] Boyd v. Mill C. S. Tp., (Ind.) 16 N. E. 511.
[2] Reeve Sch. Tp. v. Dodson, 96 Ind. 497.
[3] Litton v. Wright Sch. Tp., (Ind.) 27 N. E. 339.
[4] State v. Sherman, 90 Ind. 123.
[5] Naggy v. Dist. Tp. Monroe, (Iowa) 45 N. W. 553.

and hygiene to be taught does not authorize board of directors to purchase records, maps, etc., except out of the unappropriated funds, or to contract any debt therefor;[1] and where a contract was made with members of a district board for a certain book, and ratified at a board meeting, and at an annual meeting the board were authorized to place a copy of the book in each sub-district in the township, and afterward the board at a regularly called meeting repealed the ratification of the contract, it appears that it was an individual contract of the members, and the ratification was not binding.[2] Neither the board of directors of a district township, nor the directors of a sub-district, have the power to contract for insurance of school-house, without a vote of the district.[3] The board of directors of a district township cannot contract for lightning-rods for school-houses, without vote of the district,[4] and an order drawn on the treasurer for such purchase is invalid.[5]

§ 193. **Supplies.**—Where the district board of a township, without authority from the electors, purchased maps and other apparatus, the subsequent use and failure to repudiate the contract would not amount to a ratification.[6] In Kas., school-district board cannot bind the district for stereoscope, without vote, and the burden of proof is on plaintiff to establish vote;[7] but a director and clerk of school district purchasing school apparatus without authority, are not personally liable, the parties having notice.[8] A district in Me. has not the power to contract for fuel.[9] School charts were held not to be necessary appendages to the school-house, within Mich. Comp. L. 1871,

---

[1] Naggy v. Dist. Tp. Monroe, (Iowa) 45 N. W. 553.
[2] Western Pub. H. v. Dist. Tp., (Iowa) 50 N. W. 551.
[3] American Ins. Co. v. Willow, 55 Iowa, 606.
[4] Monticello Bank v. Coffin's Grove, 51 Iowa, 350.
[5] Wolf v. Ind. Sch. Dist., 51 Iowa, 432.
[6] Taylor v. Wayne, 25 Iowa, 447.
[7] Sch. Dist. v. Perkins, 21 Kas. 536.
[8] Watson v. Pickard, 25 Kas. 662; Duncan v. Niles, 32 Ill. 532; Mann v. Richardson, 66 Ill. 481; Abeles v. Cochran, 22 Kas. 405.
[9] Estes v. Sch. Dist., 32 Me. 170.

§ 3618;[1] and occasional use in the school cannot operate as a ratification;[1] or impose on the district any obligation to pay for them.[2] A custom of a district to apportion the wood itself to the scholars, and, if there was a deficiency, to sell the right of supplying it to the lowest bidder, was not binding upon the prudential committee, in the absence of any vote of the district on the subject.[3] He might supply the deficiency himself, and charge the price to the district, but could not assess the amount on the scholars or the district without a vote.[3] The use of seats in the school-house is no proof that the district has ratified the purchase, where it does not appear that the board ever presented any account for such seats to the district for allowance.[4] The treasurer need not honor a warrant signed by clerk and district director for fuel, when it is the duty of the board to provide and the board has not acted.[5] The certificate given by independent township trustee for necessary supplies binds the corporation;[6] but evidence of the usefulness and necessity of the supplies, as to the particular township to which they were furnished, is material, and all persons dealing with a trustee are bound to know he can bind his township only by contracts authorized by law.[7]

§ 194. **Supplies.**—In Mich. the trustees of graded school may contract for piano for high-school purposes.[8] An independent school district may provide for teaching of music and the board of directors have authority to contract for the purchase of a musical instrument, to be paid for out of any unappropriated funds of the district;[9] and in an action for the price,

---

[1] Gibson v. Sch. Dist., 36 Mich. 404.
[2] Johnson v. Sch. Dist. No. 1, 67 Mo. 319.
[3] Norton v. Tinmouth Sch. Dist., 37 Vt. 521.
[4] Kane v. Sch. Dist., 52 Wis. 502.
[5] Doyce v. Gill, 59 Wis. 518.
[6] Miller v. White River, 101 Ind. 503.
[7] Litton v. Wright Sch. Tp., (Ind.) 27 N. E. 329.
[8] Knabe v. Bd. Ed., (Mich.) 34 N. W. 568.
[9] Bellsmeyer v. Ind. Dist. Marshalltown, 44 Iowa, 564.

the court will presume that there were unappropriated funds of the district on hand at the time the purchase was made.¹ Purchase of flag is authorized in N. J.² A complaint for furnishing school supplies must show necessity, delivery, and acceptance.³ District will be liable in Mich. for contract by one director for fencing land inclosing school-house site; it is a necessary appendage.⁴ A purchase of a mathematical chart by a district board, where such chart may be considered both an appendage and an apparatus, is not illegal;⁵ and at the annual vote for tax for school appendages the district may ratify acts of board simply irregular in purchasing charts.⁵ The division of the school fund by Iowa statute into teachers', school-house, and contingent, is an appropriation of the latter to statutory purpose of rent, fuel, and repairs, and all other contingent expenses necessary for keeping the school in operation as regards empowering directors under Code, § 1729, to use unappropriated for maps, etc.⁶ School warrants issued by a school board under the provisions of S. D. Laws 1879, ch. 14, § 62, in payment of necessary appendages for a school-house during the time a school is taught, are *prima facie* valid claims against a school district, and in the absence of evidence to the contrary, the law will presume that they were lawfully issued.⁷ Under the Ill. statute, school directors may appropriate to the purchase of libraries and apparatus any surplus funds, after all necessary school expenses are paid, and the form of the orders to be drawn by them on the treasurer of the township, as prescribed by statute, must be followed.⁸

---

¹ Bellsmeyer v. Ind. Dist. Marshalltown, 44 Iowa, 564.
² N. J. L. 1890, ch. 177.
³ Bloomington v. Nat. Sch. F. Co., 107 Ind. 43.
⁴ Creager v. Wright Sch. Dist., 62 Mich. 101.
⁵ Sch. Dist. v. Swayze, 29 Kas. 211.
⁶ Yaggy v. Dist. Tp. Monroe, (Iowa) 45 N. W. 553.
⁷ Edinburgh-Am. L. & M. Co. v. Mitchell, (S. D.) 48 N. W. 131.
⁸ Clark v. Sch. Dirs., 78 Ill. 474.

§ 195. **Supplies.**—*Litten v. Wright School Tp.*, (Ind.) 26 N. E. 567—Elliott, J.: "Our decisions affirm that, to entitle a plaintiff to recover for personal property sold to a township trustee for school purposes, it must be shown that the property was delivered to the school township or its officers: *School Tp. v. Barnes*, 119 Ind. 213; *Bloomington School Tp. v. National etc. Co.*, 107 id. 43; *State v. Hawes*, 112 id. 323; *Boyd v. School Tp.*, 114 id. 210; *Union School Tp. v. First Nat. Bank*, 102 id. 464. A note or other obligation executed by the trustee does not bind the school corporation, for it is only bound where the school supplies are actually furnished: *Union School Tp. v. First Nat. Bank*, supra; *Grimsley v. State*, 116 Ind. 130. The notes or certificates issued by a township trustee do not, under the law declared in the cases referred to, preclude the school township from proving the actual or true value of the property purchased by the trustee. If in fact the property is valueless, nothing can be recovered. The rule which prevails in ordinary cases where parties fix the value of property by the exercise of their own judgment does not apply to the purchase of supplies on credit, for school corporations, for no more than the reasonable value of the property can in any event be recovered: *Boyd v. School Tp.*, 114 Ind. 210. The law intends that, where property is sold on credit to school corporations, they shall be only held for the fair and reasonable value of the property received. Parties who deal with school officers are bound to know the limitations placed upon them by law. It was therefore proper in this case to admit evidence of the value of the property which the plaintiff alleged had been sold to the school township."

§ 196. **Surety.**—Raising money for building is "school

purposes" within law of 1864, and the sureties of treasurer are liable for such money;[1] and the receipt of the treasurer's draft, the delivery of the bond to him, followed (on payment of the draft being refused) by a return of the bond and erasure of the word "paid," will not discharge the sureties.[1] Under N. Y. L. 1864, ch. 565, § 7, treasurer of board of education gave a bond, but not under seal, and entered upon the discharge of the office; the writing was enforceable against the sureties as a bond.[1] The sureties of defaulting school commissioner cannot sue to recover the revenues.[2] The sureties of a public officer are only responsible for his performance of the duties assigned him by law; where the law requires the clerk of the county court to keep the bonds for the loan of school funds, and the county court to renew bonds and to pass upon the sufficiency of the bonds, and if, by an order of the court, these duties are devolved upon the treasurer, the sureties of the treasurer will not be liable therefor.[3] If the court permit the treasurer to use the school funds as a loan, and any loss happen, his sureties will not be responsible.[3] Where a chairman, in N. C., gave his bond in Jan. 1855, and continued in office without any new appointment until April, 1857, (when a successor was appointed,) he and his sureties were held liable on such bond for an unexpended balance of school-money in his hands in 1857.[4]

§ 198. **Surety.**—Upon a change in the contract between the school district and the contractor, a consent thereto by his sureties would not increase their obligations or connect them as parties to the amended contract.[5] While a school district in whose favor a bond to secure a contract had been executed

---

[1] Fairport Sch. Bd. v. Fonda, 77 N. Y. 350.
[2] Pryse v. Hewitt, (Ky.) 1 S. W. 469.
[3] Nolley v. Callaway Co. Ct., 11 Mo. 447.
[4] Chairman Com. Sch. v. Daniels, 6 Jones, N. C. L. 444.
[5] Ind. Sch. Dist. v. Reichard, 39 Iowa, 168.

might have power directly to release the sureties, it had authority to change the contract and thus release the sureties.[1] Sureties of a school township treasurer are liable for money coming to his hands during his former term of office and not paid over to his successor.[2]

§ 199. **Tax—Alabama.**—The Board Mobile School Commissioners is a municipal corporation, and the statute authorizing assessing and collection of taxes is not repealed by repealing section of revenue law of 1868;[3] and the statute of 1856 does not repeal the former statute authorizing collection of tax on auction sales.[4] A board of school commissioners is a municipal corporation, and taxes authorized, assessed and collected for it are for municipal purposes, and are not repealed by § 136 of the revenue law.[5] The delegation of power to tax to trustees of Cullman school district, they being appointed, not being a municipal corporation, is unconstitutional.[6]

§ 200. **Tax—Arkansas.**—The failure of judges of election to state the number of votes cast for or against school tax will not vitiate sale of land for same.[7] The trustees cannot assess amount of levy; it is the duty of the electors to determine the amount; if they do not, the trustees then submit the matter to county court.[8] The county court could not levy tax for school purposes unless voted by district or recommended by trustee; and in 1868 there was no limit to amount that might be voted;[9] but the act of 1871 prohibited levy of over five mills school tax, not being a separate district in city or town.[10] The statute

[1] Ind. Sch. Dist. v. Reichard, 50 Iowa, 98.
[2] Kagay v. Sch. Trs., 68 Ill. 75. See also 59 Ill. 149.
[3] Horton v. Mobile Sch. C., 43 Ala. 598; Clark v. Mobile Sch. C., 36 Ala. 621.
[4] Brooks v. Mobile Sch. C., 31 Ala. 227.
[5] Horton v. Mobile Sch. C., 43 Ala. 598.
[6] Schultes v. Eberly, 82 Ala., 242.
[7] Staley v. Leomans, 53 Ark. 428.
[8] Co. Ct. v. Robinson, 27 Ark. 116.
[9] Murphy v. Harrison, 29 Ark. 340; Worthen v. Badgett, 32 Ark. 496.
[10] Vaughn v. Bowie, 30 Ark. 280.

allowing the board of supervisors to levy the district-school taxes in cities and towns organized in single districts was repealed by constitution of 1874.[1] Under act of 1871, the county court had no power to levy tax for school purposes unless the amount had been voted or the trustee had reported the amount;[2] and county court cannot levy district-school tax except as voted, and if it does the sale and levy will be void.[3] School warrants of trustees are receivable for school taxes of the district in which they were issued.[4] Since 1875 the notice for annual meeting for levying tax must be given by the school directors only.[5] The tax title is inferior to lien of state for unpaid purchase-money for school land.[6]

§ 201. **Tax—California.**—Special tax for school purposes can only be levied upon vote of school district,[7] and substantial compliance with law is sufficient for a levy of school tax,[8] but the tax must be based upon an assessment made by an assessor, elected by the qualified electors of the school district.[9]

§ 202. **Tax—Colorado.**—Exemption of seminary property applies to property in actual use for school purposes.[10] Taxes for school purposes are not a lien on personalty until seizure on the tax-warrant;[11] where school tax is properly certified to county commissioners, mandamus is proper remedy to compel levy.[12] The statute in regard to levy of school tax, certifying same to county commissioners, and the levy thereunder, is not unconstitutional.[13] If a school district is divided, the secretary of district cannot distrain property out of his district.[14]

[1] Cole v. Blackwell, 38 Ark. 271.
[2] Cairo etc. v. Parks, 39 Ark. 131.
[3] Rogers v. Kerr, 42 Ark. 100.
[4] Wallis v. Smith, 29 Ark. 354.
[5] Davies v. Holland, 43 Ark. 425.
[6] Simpson v. Robinson, 37 Ark. 132.
[7] People v. Castro, 39 Cal. 65.
[8] People v. Pratt, 59 Cal. 78.
[9] People v. Sac. etc. R. R. Co., 49 Cal. 415.
[10] Comm'rs v. Col. Seminary, 12 Col. 497.
[11] McKay v. Batchellor, 2 Col. 591.
[12] People v. Comm'rs, 12 Col. 89.
[13] McKay v. Batchellor, 2 Col. 591.

§ 203. **Tax—Connecticut.**—Where a school society voted a tax, the omission of the vote to fix a time for the payment of the tax did not render it invalid, as the tax, being legally imposed, was payable on demand, or within a reasonable time.[1] Since 1821 the lands of a non-resident are taxable where situated.[2] Notice given by the district committee of the time and place of the meeting of equalizing board, pursuant to the provisions of § 10 of act 1839, relating to schools, is sufficient notice within that statute.[3] Where the certificate of a district school committee stated the tax, and when and for what laid, and the recorded vote of the district, open to public inspection, specified the list on which it was laid, such rate-bill was not invalid because it did not show on what list the tax was laid.[3] In an action of trespass against the collector and committee of a school society, evidence to prove that the defendants, and other members of the society, voted for the tax, with the intention of having the proceeds distributed among the several districts in the society, was inadmissible.[4]

§ 204. **Tax—Florida.**—The "itemized estimate" of moneys required to be raised by county tax for school purposes, furnished by the board of public instruction to the board of county commissioners, should contain the estimated expenditures for the school year, the estimated income from the state school tax, state school fund, and other probable sources; and may contain an item for outstanding warrants which were issued by the board of public instruction and are still unpaid.[5] Under Laws 1879, ch. 3100, § 1, the tax assessor of a county cannot be compelled by mandamus to levy a county school tax, merely upon

---

[1] Bartlett v. Kinsley, 15 Conn. 327.
[2] Rowe v. Blakeslee, 11 Conn. 483.
[3] Sanford v. Dick, 15 Conn. 447.
[4] Bartlett v. Kinsley, 15 Conn. 327.
[5] State v. Bd. Co. Comm'rs, 17 Fla. 418.

receiving the statement of the board of public instruction, but only upon the requisition of the board of county commissioners.[1]

§ 205. **Tax—Georgia.**—A majority of the complainants having voted in favor of the approval of a local school law, and all of them having acquiesced in the result of the election until after a school was established and put in operation, an injunction was refused;[2] and acquiescence in election authorizing tax, is a bar to suit restraining collection;[3] the act of 1883, as to Richmond county, did not repeal the act of 1872 giving the board of education the power to raise school funds by taxation.[4] The acts 1889-90-91 are to be construed as one, and the commissioners may lower rate of taxation estimated by school board where it does not affect the amount of money needed by the board.[5]

§ 206. **Tax—Illinois.**—The Ill. statute does not exempt from taxation a private academy conducted for profit;[6] to exempt it as a public school from taxation, such school must be property under the immediate control of the school directors;[7] lands held by Illinois Industrial University's trustees are therefore exempt from taxation;[8] and the validity of school tax cannot be questioned by one who participated in the election and seconded the motion to raise the money.[9] A school tax must be certified to the clerk at the appointed time.[10] Directors of district schools have power to levy taxes for the purpose of supporting a school for six months in the year, without first submitting the question to a vote of the inhabitants, but cannot erect a house costing more than $1,000, nor change a site;[11]

---

[1] Jones v. States, 17 Fla. 411.
[2] Irvin v. Gregory, (Ga.) 13 S. E. 120.
[3] Irvin v. Gregory, 89 Ga. 695.
[4] Montgomery v. Richmond Co. Ed. Bd., 74 Ga. 41.
[5] State v. Co. Comm'rs, (Fla.) 10 So. 14.
[6] Montgomery v. Wyman, 130 Ill. 17.
[7] Pace v. Jefferson Co., 20 Ill. 644.
[8] Trs. Ill. Industrial University v. Champaign Co., 76 Ill. 184.
[9] Thatcher v. People, 98 Ill. 632.
[10] Cowgill v. Long, 15 Ill. 202.
[11] Munson v. Minor, 22 Ill. 594; Merritt v. Farris, 22 Ill. 303; Schofield v. Watkins, 22 Ill. 66.

and the tax will be binding, although persons and property liable to assessment are not included.¹ The county clerk cannot extend school taxes from year to year on his own motion.² The act of 1879, authorizing a levy not to exceed 2 per cent. does not affect board of education of Bloomington, that being under a special act, and therefore excepted out of said act of 1879.³ The levying of a tax to defray the expenses, and the acceptance of school-house built without vote, and teaching school therein, could not legalize the act or bind the taxpayers.⁴ The prohibition in Const., art. 4, § 22, that the general assembly shall not pass any local or special law providing for the "management" of common schools, does not prevent levying of taxes by different officers in a city from those discharging these duties in other localities.⁵ A bill to enjoin a school tax, alleging that the determination to levy was not made by the school directors at a regular or special meeting, nor in their corporate capacity, but as individuals, does not charge that the directors acted in the matter without meeting together.⁶ Where the levy of a tax is proper, and is within the statutory limit, it cannot be enjoined as unnecessarily large, or that the directors proposed to use part for another purpose.⁶ Under act 1889, p. 296, art. 5, p. 17, a tax levy which has been duly signed by the directors and filed with the township treasurer is not invalidated by the failure to record the action of the directors in making the levy.⁶ The school law (Rev. Stat. 1874, p. 957, § 35) authorizes trustees of high schools to levy taxes for the support of such high school.⁷ The legislature

[1] Schofield v. Watkins, 29 Ill. 66.
[2] Weber v. R. R., 108 Ill. 451.
[3] People v. City Bloomington, 130 Ill. 406.
[4] Sch. Dirs. etc. v. Fogleman, 76 Ill. 189.
[5] Speight v. People, 87 Ill. 595.
[6] Lawrence v. Trainer, (Ill.) 27 N. E. 197.
[7] Fisher v. People, 84 Ill. 491.

may legalize irregularities in the assessment of taxes;[1] and acts of directors in levying a tax will not be inquired into for irregularities by a court of equity;[1] but if a tax is attempted for the benefit of the directors acting corruptly, equity will relieve.[1]

§ 207. **Tax—Indiana.**—The law of 1855 does not prevent the township trustees from levying over 25 cents on $100 to discharge debts incurred under the old law.[2] The exercise of a valid power to levy a tax will not be vitiated by an additional vote authorizing such tax in pursuance of an unconstitutional section.[3] The trustees of townships have no power to levy a tax to build a township house, but may for a school-house.[4] The constitution requires public schools to be provided for by general laws, and a law authorizing cities to levy school taxes and support schools, not limited to the object of building houses, is unconstitutional.[5] Township school tax, authorized by 1 Rev. Stat., 454, § 130, is illegal.[6] Under R. S. 1881, § 4460, the school board had no power to levy poll tax.[7]

§ 208. **Tax—Iowa.**—A non-resident tax-payer has the right to see that the school funds are property administered;[8] but after erection of school-house and voting of tax to pay for same, a tax-payer cannot enjoin the collection of the tax for irregularities in contract for construction.[9] A sub-district may levy a tax for school-house in addition to that voted by the township.[10] Land not in B. township, which has not been set off into B. by reason of natural obstacles, under Code, § 1797, cannot be taxed for erecting school-house in B. township.[11] A tax voted for a new building will not be enjoined where it appears that the

---

[1] Schofield v. Watkins, 22 Ill. 66.
[2] Wayne v. Alexander, 10 Ind. 221.
[3] Winters v. State, 9 Ind. 174.
[4] Trs. etc. v. Osborne, 9 Ind. 458; Adamson v. Auditor, 9 Ind. 174.
[5] Lafayette v. Jenners, 10 Ind. 70.
[6] Lima v. Jenks, 90 Ind. 301.
[7] Indianapolis S. C. v. Magner, 84 Ind. 67.
[8] Case v. Blood, (Iowa) 33 N. W. 144.
[9] Casey v. Nutt S. D., 64 Iowa, 659.
[10] Wool v. Farmer, 69 Iowa, 533.
[11] Large v. Washington, 53 Iowa, 663.

building used is old and remote from some of the scholars of the district and they cannot attend.¹ An illegal tax having been refunded entirely from the funds of a portion of the district from which it was collected, that portion may sue the remaining parts for contribution.² A board of supervisors cannot levy a tax to pay a judgment against the school-house fund, after the tax for that fund has reached the limit allowed for the year.³ In a proceeding to compel the board of directors of a district township to levy a tax required by the electors of a sub-district, for the erection of a school-house, the records of the proceedings of the sub-district meeting, signed by the proper officers, is admissible in evidence, though not required to be kept.⁴ A tax levied at a district meeting not held within the time fixed by the act of 1858, ch. 52, § 10, is not cured by act passed by board of education, Dec. 15, 1862;⁵ the directors of the school district have the power to levy tax to increase the teachers' fund when it becomes necessary to do so.⁶ Liability to pay a school tax attaches upon levy of the tax by vote of the district.⁷ Where a tax is levied by a county judge, under § 31 of the act Mch. 12, 1858, for the support of school within the county, the county treasurer may lawfully collect the same.⁸ Where there is a failure to collect a school-house tax during the year in which it is levied, the power and authority conferred by the warrant do not expire with the year, and a lost warrant may be supplied by a new one;⁹ and the officer can show that a warrant was issued and lost, and may protect himself by proving its contents.⁹ A resident in a school district

¹ Seaman v. Baughman, (Iowa) 47 N. W. 1091.
² Spencer v. Reverton, 56 Iowa, 85.
³ Sterling Sch. Furniture Co. v. Harvey, 45 Iowa, 466.
⁴ Rose v. Hindman, 36 Iowa, 160.
⁵ Spencer v. Wheaton, 14 Iowa, 38.
⁶ Snyder v. Wampton, 12 Iowa, 409.
⁷ Toothaker v. Moore, 9 Iowa, 468.
⁸ Co. of Louisa v. Davison, 8 Iowa, 517.
⁹ Higgins v. Reed, 8 Clarke (Iowa) 298.

cannot be assessed in that district for the personal property which is in another district.[1] A vote "that there be an appropriation sufficient to build a house on the line between" two specified sub-districts, with a further vote "that there be $800 levied as school-house tax," amounts to voting a tax for the school-house described in the first vote, and cannot be rescinded by the electors.[2] A levy made later than the time directed by Code, § 1778, was sustained;[3] but Code, § 1738, is mandatory, and a tax cannot be levied by board directors after third Monday in May.[4] The action of supervisors in making a levy under Code, § 1777, depends upon the action of the board of directors, and when that is invalid the whole will be.[4] The Code, § 1807, limiting levy, applies only to districts in which no bonded debt has been created;[5] this section does not limit tax under § 1823, for tax necessary for independent district to pay bonds.[6]

§ 209. **Tax — Kansas.** — Agricultural college is wholly a state institution and exempt from taxation.[7] School-district plat filed, but not attested, is not evidence to show that certain property is included in a certain school district.[8] An apportionment and award after lapse of three years will be held binding;[9] and the general rule is, that on a division of a district the original corporation retains its property until settled for.[10] In a suit by a district to recover taxes paid to another, the validity of such district cannot be questioned.[11]

§ 210. **Tax — Kentucky.** — The legislature could compel the payment of tax for 1885 by residents of district outside of city, cut off from the city by act of 1886; the residents of the

[1] Lemp v. Hastings, 4 Greene (Iowa) 448.
[2] Benjamin v. Malaka. 50 Iowa, 648.
[3] Perrin v. Benson, 49 Iowa, 325.
[4] Standard Coal Co. v. Ind. Dist. etc., (Iowa) 34 N. W. 870.
[5] Richards v. Lyon Co. S., 69 Iowa, 612.
[6] U. S. v. Ind. S. D., 20 F. R. 294.
[7] Bd. Trs. v. Champaign Co., 76 Ill. 184; City Chicago v. People, 80 Ill. 384; Board v. Hamilton, 28 Kas. 376.
[8] A. & N. R. R. v. Maquilkin, 12 Kas. 301.
[9] Sch. D. v. Sch. D., 32 Kas. 123.
[10] Bd. Ed. v. Sch. Dist., 45 Kas. 560.
[11] Sch. Dist. v. Sch. Dist., 45 Kas. 543.

outlying district being given the school privileges of the city for one year, said act being adopted by majority of qualified white voters of the district.¹ Unless the report of the division of counties into school districts by boundaries is filed for record with the county clerk, the trustees cannot enforce the collection of taxes.² System of education in a particular district, under act authorizing tax so that school may be taught the entire year, and the teaching of Latin and Greek in common schools, is not unconstitutional.³ One receiving his share of the benefits of the school system cannot complain that the legislative power, as exercised in the expenditure of the school fund, is unwarranted.⁴ Mere irregularity in the election will not invalidate the levy voted for by majority of voters in a district.⁵ A tax on a town for a school, permitting non-residents of a town to attend free, is void.⁶ Under statutes 1884, and 1886, the trustees of a school district may levy a tax to build a new school-house not to exceed a certain rate, without a vote, when a necessity exists, or they have been notified that the old one has been condemned by the superintendent.⁷ The statute for assessment of railroad for its length through county, city, and town, for the purposes of county, city, town, or "precinct," does not authorize an assessment for school district.⁸ The provision of statutes, ch. 92, art. 1, as to use of part of general tax for school, and art. 12, as to application of railroad tax, do not conflict; each can stand.⁹ The power of states to maintain common schools by taxation, and to control such schools when established, is a

---

¹ Fitzpatrick v. Bd. Trs., (Ky.) 7 S. W. 896.
² Ringo v. Stewart, 4 B. Mon. (Ky.) 206.
³ Newman v. Thompson, (Ky.) 4 S. W. 341.
⁴ Following 8 Cow. (N. Y.) 543; 56 Pa. St. 359; 22 Gratt. (Va.) 857; Marshall v. Donavan, 10 Bush (Ky.) 681.
⁵ Common Sch. D. v. Garvey, 80 Ky. 159.
⁶ Town Belle P. v. Pence, (Ky.) 17 S. W. 197.
⁷ Macklin v. Trs., (Ky.) 11 S. W. 657.
⁸ L. & N. R. R. v. Johnson, (Ky.) 11 S. W. 666.
⁹ Auditor v. Frankfort, 81 Ky. 680.

power not delegated to the U. S. by the constitution, nor prohibited by it to the states.¹ The trustees of common schools may appoint their collector and fill vacancies in the office, and a collector failing to give a bond for nine months may be superseded.²

§ 211. **Tax—Louisiana.**—Commercial college is exempt;³ the exemption for school purposes is not affected by the fact that the principal owner and a teacher occupy same as a residence.³

§ 212. **Tax—Maryland.**—The statute requiring the commissioners of Allegheny county to levy the balance estimated by the board of commissioners of public schools and reported to the commissioners of the county, is not unconstitutional, as not being uniform throughout the state.⁴ Where inhabitants of a district have the power to tax, it will not be held invalid because the records do not show that every provision of the law was complied with, the contrary not being shown;⁵ and such tax may be voted to defray the expenses of a preceding as well as of the current year.⁵ Under the school law, (Code Md., art. 77, p. 22,) and the Code of Public (Local) Laws, art. 2, p. 123, providing that in Anne Arundel county there may be an additional levy, the county commissioners cannot deduct from the school levy, unconditionally made, either the amount of the treasurer's commissions or discounts for prompt payment of taxes, but must pay over the gross levy to the school commissioners.⁶

§ 213. **Tax—Massachusetts.**—The Mt. Hermon school property is exempt, notwithstanding agricultural resources and

¹ Marshall v. Donavan, 10 Bush (Ky.) 682.
² Chiles v. Todd, 4 B. Mon. (Ky.) 126.
³ Blackman v. Houston, (La.) 2 So. 193.
⁴ Comm'rs v. Allegheny, 20 Md. 449.
⁵ Burgess v. Pue, 2 Gill. (Md.) 254.
⁶ Bd. Co. Sch. Comm'rs v. Gnatt, (Md.) 21 A. 548.

products.[1] Under Gen. St., ch. 39, and Stat. 1873, ch. 315, the stock of a national bank, belonging to an inhabitant in a town other than that in which the bank is situated, cannot be taxed for building a school-house in the district.[2] Where tax is assessed by united district, the fact that one district did not assent to action of town uniting it with the other will not invalidate the tax;[3] and a school tax assessed at meeting called by prudential committee, that is appointed by town and school district, is not invalid by reason of the town not voting at the annual meeting if it had the year before, that teachers should be contracted with by prudential committee, pursuant to act of 1839, ch. 137.[3] A district valuation based on town valuation for same year need not describe the real estate and machinery taxed if it shows by the names, figures, and by the town valuation that the property is in the district;[3] and a school district tax on realty and machinery in the district and belonging to an inhabitant of the town, although not of the district, may be assessed to him or to the tenant;[3] an assessment of district tax on a lot, the whole of which is not in the district, is void as to that lot, but this assessment will not affect others of separate descriptions.[3] A district tax cannot be assessed against party who is set off to another district before assessment is complete.[4] Where party resides in one town and carries on a trade in another, he is not liable to be assessed on his stock in trade, for building a school-house in the district where he resides, under R. S., chs. 7 and 23.[5] The district in which the land of non-resident shall be taxed must be located before the school tax is assessed.[6] A legislative enactment authorizing a town tax for

---

1 Mt. Hermon Boys' Sch. v. Town of Gill, (Mass.) 13 N. E. 354.
2 Little v. Little, 131 Mass. 367.
3 Blackstone v. Taft, 4 Gray (Mass.) 250.
4 Jackman v. Sch. D., 5 Gray (Mass.) 413.
5 Bates v. Sch. D., 9 Gray (Mass.) 433.
6 Loud v. Darling, 7 Allen (Mass.) 205.

the support of a free school founded by private benevolence, but under the control of trustees, some of whom are not elected by the people, is unconstitutional.[1] An action to recover illegal tax lies against the district and not against the town or assessors;[2] and it is no defense that the town treasurer advanced the whole amount of the assessed tax before the collection from the plaintiffs of his part.[3] Under R. S., a female high school for purpose of teaching the higher branches than those taught in grammar schools of the town, was a town school, and money for its support was legally raised by tax.[3] An inhabitant removing from district before the money is voted to erect or repair school-house, is not liable for the tax.[4]

§ 214. **Tax—Maine.**—A district cannot be formed so as to possess corporate powers, except by vote of a town.[5] An assessment was sustained, though the clerk did not certify to the assessors the vote of the district;[6] where assessors of a town assess a tax in pursuance of a vote of the district, and the district is not formed by a vote of a town, the assessment is illegal.[7] An action cannot be maintained against a town for the assessment and collection of an illegal school-district tax.[8] If the intention of the voters of a school district to raise a sum of money to build a district school-house is apparent upon their records, it is sufficient to authorize the assessment and collection of the amount.[9] The mere refusal by the inhabitants of a school district to vote any particular sum of money for a given purpose will not confer jurisdiction upon the town as for a disagreement, under the act of 1850, ch. 193, § 12.[10] A tax assessed

[1] Jenkins v. Andover, 103 Mass. 94.
[2] Bacon v. Sch. Dist. No. 13, 97 Mass. 421.
[3] Cushing v. Inhabitants, 10 Metc. (Mass.) 508.
[4] Savary v. Sch. D., 12 Metc. (Mass.) 178.
[5] Tucker v. Wentworth, 35 Me. 393.
[6] Smyth v. Titcomb, 31 Me. 272.
[7] Tucker v. Wentworth, 35 Me. 393.
[8] Trafton v. Alfred, 15 Me. 258.
[9] Soper v. Sch. Dist. No. 9, 28 Me. 193.
[10] Powers v. Sanford, 39 Me. 183.

under a vote to "remove and repair the old school-house" is valid, although the school-house was removed from another district.[1] Tax collector cannot decide that the law is unconstitutional, or refuse to do his duty, and must collect the school taxes as well as the taxes of the town.[2] The statutes exempt the assessors of a town, levying a tax on a school district, from personal liability when they act with faithfulness, and the district is not liable for errors of the town.[3] Where municipal officers may locate site on failure of district to do so within sixty days after vote, they can only expend the amount voted.[4]

§ 215. **Tax—Michigan.**—Where the school board failed to certify to the township clerk in time for the supervisor to spread it on his roll, the assessment may be made the succeeding year, under § 5090.[5] The township public school of Long Rapids includes the territory of Montmorency county, and this applies to taxes.[6] Where an injunction is asked to restrain the collection of a school tax irregularly assessed, the school district is a necessary party;[7] and a tax on only a part of a district is void.[8] Where school moneys are received by treasurer of city board of education, they are at once payable to the proper depository.[9]

§ 216. **Tax—Minnesota.**—The lease of building for school purposes does not give the owner thereof the benefit of exemption from taxation;[10] the act of 1860 requires that voters must determine the number of houses, the sites, and the sum to be raised, before the tax.[11]

§ 217. **Tax—Mississippi.**—A statute authorizing levy by

---

[1] Tozier v. Sch. Dist. No. 2, 39 Me. 556.
[2] Smyth v. Titcomb, 31 Me. 272.
[3] Powers v. Sanford, 39 Me. 183.
[4] Carleton v. Newman, 77 Me. 408.
[5] Wilcox v. Tp. Eagle, (Mich.) 45 N. W. 967.
[6] Johnson v. Cathro, 51 Mich. 80.
[7] Folkerts v. Power, 42 Mich. 283.
[8] Auditor v. McArthur, 49 N. W. 592.
[9] Port Huron Bd. Ed. v. Runnels, 57 Mich. 46.
[10] State v. Bell, 43 Minn. 344.
[11] State v. St. Anthony 10 Minn. 433.

board of supervisors of county for school purposes, but which does not include a town which is a separate school district, is not thereby unconstitutional.[1] In Marion county, the levy was limited to 13 mills, 3 of which are for school purposes, but county levy may be 15 where county owes debts; teachers' warrants are county debts, and to pay them the levy may be increased to 15 mills.[2] A petition for a mandamus to compel the board of supervisors to levy a tax for the erection of school-houses, must define the sub-district where erected.[3] A tax on liquor licenses or privileges is not "money received for license" which must be used for free schools.[4]

§ 218. **Tax—Missouri.**—A building used in part for a school-house and in part for other purposes, is not exempt.[5] The merchant taxes on stock on hand are property taxes, and the merchandise is taxable for school purposes.[6] Where county clerk did not extend school tax, under act 1867, on the assessment books, there can be no recovery on tax bill, under back-tax law.[7] Under Laws 1885, p. 246, the duty of county clerk is merely to extend and apportion the amounts of revenue upon the property assessed for each school district.[8] Where an academy taught higher branches and a small tuition fee was charged when necessary, and poor children were admitted free, and the trustees were authorized to receive all the school moneys due that town and the commons attached, the tax levied under statute authorizing same for academy was legal.[9] Four years' *laches* in attacking irregularity of formation of district will bar relief from taxes levied, where that is the objection.[10] Mandamus will

---

[1] Bordeaux v. Meridian L. & I. Co., (Miss.) 7 So. 296.
[2] Cowart v. Taxworth, (Miss.) 7 So. 350.
[3] Jarvis v. Warren Co., 49 Miss. 603. (Rev. Code, § 2053; Laws 1870, ch. 11, § 32.)
[4] Portwood v. Baskett, 64 Miss. 213.
[5] Wyman v. St. Louis, 17 Mo. 335.
[6] State v. Tracey, (Mo.) 6 S. W. 709.
[7] State v. Harper, 11 Mo. App. 301.
[8] Sch. Dist. v. Wickersham, 34 Mo. App. 337.
[9] State v. Vaughan, (Mo.) 12 S. W. 507.
[10] Stamper v. Roberts, (Mo.) 3 S. W. 214.

—16—

not lie to compel a county court to rescind an order prohibiting the county clerk from assessing and extending a school tax;[1] and county court has no control over the county clerk in that matter.[1] A tax levied under Const. 1875, art. 10, § 11, prior to May 24, 1877, was void, legislation being necessary;[2] and defendant is not estopped because he did not endeavor to restrain the enforcement of the levy.[2] From 1875 to 1877, taxes for school in district could not exceed 40 cents on $100. And under act of 1877, notice is required to make election under the act valid, to increase levy over 40c.[3] It is improper to unite taxes for school purposes and building purposes into one levy.[4] Before a constable can distrain for school tax, he must make a demand upon the person liable.[5] Taxes should be distributed according to law in force when distributed.[6] Taxes for "school purposes" cannot be levied to build house or to pay indebtedness, under R. S. § 6880, there being different qualifications prescribed for voting taxes for different things in statutes.[7] The apportionment of funds derived from taxing railroad bed, to be distributed *pro rata* to districts, is not unconstitutional.[8] Under statute of 1875, railroad taxes are applied to the districts when that township has subscribed to the railroad;[9] tax for building school-houses cannot be levied on property of railroad.[10] Where party paid school tax for 1873 on realty within extended limits of St. Louis, he was entitled, under act of 1874, to have the same credited on school tax bill for 1881, notwithstanding changes in district.[11]

§ 219. **Tax—Nebraska.**—School lands which have been

---

[1] State v. Byers, 67 Mo. 706.
[2] State v. St. L. K. C. R. R. Co., 74 Mo. 163.
[3] State v. R. R., 75 Mo. 526.
[4] State v. R. R., (Mo.) 2 S. W. 275.
[5] (Rev. Code 1855, 1439.) Atkinson v. Amick, 25 Mo. 404.
[6] Sch. Dist. v. Weber, 75 Mo. 558.
[7] State v. R. R., 83 Mo. 395.
[8] *In re* Tax Apportionment, 78 Mo. 596.
[9] Sch. Dist. v. Rhoads, 81 Mo. 473.
[10] State v. R. R., 90 Mo. 166.
[11] State v. Schnecko, 11 Mo. App. 165.

sold on credit, are subject to taxation;[1] a medical college is exempt.[2] Where, a few days before the annual meeting, two and a half townships were added to district, and tax voted, and a few days thereafter a new district was formed out of the added territory, but the tax voted was paid to old district, the new district and those formed out of it could recover that tax back.[3] Boards of education in cities of the first class have only power to report an estimate; the power to levy a tax is with the city council.[4] The certificate of county superintendent to the county clerk, of the amount due from one district to another, is sufficient to authorize a tax on the district indebted.[5] A tax was held to be leviable upon the district as it existed at the time of the levy;[6] and the district into which the two and one-half townships had been organized could sue the former district for the amount collected in the latter's territory.[6]

§ 220. **Tax—New Hampshire.**—Statute authorizing annual town meetings to direct in what manner the school-money shall be assigned to the school districts is constitutional;[7] and a statute authorizing town tax to erect a school building, and authorizing a perpetual lease of the same to an academy corporation for school purposes, without the payment of rent, is constitutional.[8] Where persons not liable to school district tax are assessed, they should make application for an abatement.[9] The statutes 1885 provide for abolishing the division of towns into school districts, and provide for an appraisal of the property of the abolished districts, and a remission to the tax-payers of that district of its value; and a petition for a

---

[1] Hagenbuch v. Reed, 3 Neb. 17.
[2] Omaha M. C. v. Rush, (Neb.) 35 N. W. 222.
[3] Sch. Dist. v. Sch. Dist., 13 Neb. 166.
[4] State v. Mayor etc. of Omaha, 7 Neb. 267.
[5] B. & M. R. R. Co. v. Lancaster Co. Com'rs, 12 Neb. 324.
[6] Sch. Dist. No. 9 v. Sch. Dist. No. 6, 9 Neb. 331.
[7] Sch. Dist. v. Prentiss, (N. H.) 19 A. 1090.
[8] Holt v. Town Antrim, (N. H.) 9 A. 389.
[9] Sch. Dist. v. Oxford, 63 N. H. 277.

new appraisal will be refused.[1] On refusal of district to build or repair school-house, it devolves on the selectmen of the town, who are bound to assess a sufficient tax on the district for this purpose.[2] Assessment of tax to build a school on ground that is private property, cannot be compelled.[3] On Sept. 14, 1872, a district voted a tax to build a school-house; Oct. 26, 1872, the district was changed, so as to include the dwelling and real estate of plaintiff; April, 1873, said tax was then assessed upon the invoice of 1873, which included the plaintiff and his property; the tax was legal.[4] Section 1, act of Dec. 28, 1844, includes assessments made for taxes for erections and repairs of school-houses already completed, as well as those required to be made for taxes raised for building and repairing such house.[5] Where the selectmen of the two towns in which a school district is organized under the provisions of Comp. Stat., 167, § 2, erroneously supposed that the statute required a tax for school-house purposes in such district to be assessed in each town, by their joint action, and the record of the assessment was accordingly made by them as a joint board of assessors, it cannot be amended by striking out the names of the selectmen of one of the two towns, so as to make it an assessment by the selectmen of the other;[6] and a tax assessed for school-house purposes by the boards of selectmen of the towns in which a new district is situated, acting together as a joint board, is illegal; the assessment should be made under the provisions of § 3 of act of June 26, 1845, and not of the act of July 2, 1845.[7] As a justification for assessing a school-house tax, the proceedings of the school district at which it was voted

---

[1] Perry v. Town Fitzwilliam, 64 N. H. 289.
[2] Blake v. Sturtevant, 12 N. H. 567.
[3] Loverin v. Sch. Dist., (N. H.) 14 A. 810.
[4] Fifield v. Sweet, 56 N. H. 432.
[5] Rogers v. Bowen, 42 N. H. 102.
[6] Perkins v. Langmaid, 36 N. H. 501.
[7] Perkins v. Langmaid, 34 N. H. 315.

should be shown by the records of the district.¹ The clause in the statute which requires the selectmen to assess, in thirty days after the clerk of the district shall certify to them the sum, is directory, and the tax will be legal, though not assessed within the thirty days.² If a person removes for a temporary purpose, with an intention of returning, he is still liable to taxation as an inhabitant of the district.³

§ 221. **Tax—New Jersey.**—A vote at a town meeting, to raise "all that the law will allow for schools," is deficient in precision, but it may be made certain, and will not therefore render the assessment void.⁴ A tax voted by the inhabitants of a school district, under laws of 1851, is properly assessed on "all lands liable to be taxed" within the district,⁵ but an assessment by inhabitants of a district, under the law of 1851, will be set aside if it does not appear that ten days' notice was given of the time, place, and purposes of the meeting; the court will presume those who voted were legal voters, unless the contrary appears. A book of minutes kept for trustees by the town superintendent may be received as evidence of their acts.⁵ The act of 1851, regulating public schools, is not in force in the town of Belvidere.⁶ Where there was an illegal tax the court held that ample relief could be afforded the prosecutors by setting aside so much as aggrieved the plaintiffs.⁷ The trustees are not bound to comply with the act of 1851 in assessing the cost of a school-house under the act of 1862.⁸ The title of a trustee to his office cannot be tried in suit resisting a tax.⁹ The board of education of the city of Newark cannot be compelled by man-

---

¹ Rogers v. Bowen, 42 N. H. 102.
² Johnson v. Dole, 3 N. H. 328.
³ Bump v. Smith, 11 N. H. 48.
⁴ State v. Middletown, 24 N. J. L. (4 Zab.) 124; State v. Sickles, 24 N. J. L. (4 Zab.) 125.
⁵ State v. Van Winkle, 25 N. J. L. (1 Dutch.) 73.
⁶ State v. Belvidere, 25 N. J. L. (1 Dutch.) 563.
⁷ State v. Browning, 27 N. J. L. (3 Dutch.) 527.
⁸ State v. Ryerson, 30 N. J. L. 268.
⁹ State v. Donahay, 30 N. J. L. 404.

damus to disburse, as the council may desire, certain moneys appropriated for the schools.[1] On a certiorari to set aside an illegal assessment, the court will not go behind the certificate to inquire whether the trustees were legally elected.[2] When a tax for a school-house is ordered to be assessed under the act of 1851, (Nix. Dig. 739,) the sworn certificate by the trustees to the assessors should show all the conditions precedent have been performed.[3] The notice, resolution, and the certificate, should show that the conditions precedent have been complied with.[4] The certificate of the trustees of a district for the raising of money, is sufficient as to notice if it states that they were posted in at least three public places in the district;[5] the notice and certificate for the meeting to assess a tax by the inhabitants must state the purpose.[6] Nix. Dig. 879, § 80, requires the certificate upon which a school tax is assessed to show how the money ordered to be raised is to be apportioned;[7] the certificate of the district clerk must show that the apportionment was made by authority of the voters, to render the tax valid;[8] and the certificate of meeting directing special taxes to be raised by taxation must show apportionment of specific amount for each purpose, and the oath of clerk attached must verify all the material facts stated.[9] The certificate of the district clerk preliminary to delivery to assessor for assessment on the township of tax, must show that all the conditions precedent, as to time, place and manner, have been complied with.[10] School taxes are to be levied for the fiscal year beginning Sept. 1 succeeding the assessment.[11] A county collector cannot set off funds due from

[1] Newark v. Bd. Ed., 30 N. J. L. 374.
[2] State v. Van Winkle, 25 N. J. L. (1 Dutch.) 73.
[3] Hardcastle v. State, 27 N. J. L. (3 Dutch.) 551; State v. Hardcastle, 26 N. J. L. (2 Dutch.) 143.
[4] State v. Browning, 28 N. J. L. (4 Dutch.) 556.
[5] State v. Donahay, 30 N. J. L. 404.
[6] State v. Garrabrant, 32 N. J. L. 444.
[7] State v. Sullivan, 36 N. J. L. 89.
[8] State v. Duryea, 40 N. J. L. 266.
[9] State v. Padden, 44 N. J. L. 151.
[10] State v. Sch. Dist., (N. J.) 10 A. 191.
[11] State v. Sheridan, 42 N. J. L. 64.

him to town treasurer for school funds, by claim for state or county taxes due from town treasurer to him.¹ On a vote for building school-house a majority of those voting is all that is necessary, and not a majority of all the residents of the district.² Special meetings may be called by trustees to vote for improvements; the term "incidentals" is not specific enough.³ Where resolution to issue bonds for building school-house provides they should be payable in successive years, it is error to issue certificate to levy it all in one year.⁴

§ 222. **Tax — New York.**—Where school owned by religious body is exempt, it is immaterial if deed is in name of pastor, if held for that use, or if top floor is occupied temporarily by teachers in charge as residence, and is not for profit.⁵ It was held, under act of 1882, which provides that school buildings used exclusively as such and owned exclusively by a religious society are exempt from taxation, that a school-house was exempt although the society was not incorporated until after the time for assessing tax.⁵ If the trustees of a district, in apportioning a tax voted at a district meeting among the taxable inhabitants of the district, change the assessment, they should give notice; but the omission does not render them responsible as trespassers.⁶ If the district clerk, in giving notice of a district meeting called by the trustees, prevents some from attending by misrepresentations, the trustees who cause the tax voted at such meeting to be collected are not trespassers unless they are parties to the fraud.⁶ A district meeting voted a tax for building a school-house in October, and voted a tax at a special meeting in the succeeding February; the last-mentioned vote

---

[1] State v. Sheridan, 45 N. J. L. 276.
[2] Crandall v. Trs., 51 N. J. L. 138.
[3] State v. Cole, (N. J.) 18 A. 52.
[4] State v. Clark, (N. J.) 19 A. 462.
[5] Church St. Monica v. City N. Y., 55 N. Y. Sup. Ct. 160.
[6] Randall v. Smith, 1 Den. (N. Y.) 214.

was notwithstanding a legal and valid one.[1] A district-school tax is valid, though it is assessed and the tax list therefor is made out by the trustees after the expiration of one month from the time of holding the district meeting at which it was voted.[2] A district tax was voted, and subsequently the tax repealed; still later, the vote to repeal the tax was itself repealed, and the warrant was then renewed and delivered to the officer; although the last vote revived the tax, a new tax list should have been made out after that vote.[3] It is no objection to a tax for building a school-house, that other districts had not consented to an alteration to which that district had consented; nor that the notice stated the meeting was to be held "for buying or building a school-house," and a tax was voted to buy a house already built; nor that the quantity of land or the site was not more fully designated.[4] Where defendants in trover justified as school-district officers under a warrant for the collection of a school tax, and they were chosen at an annual district meeting held by adjournment voted at the annual district meeting of the preceding year, but no notice was given, the meeting was a legal one.[5] School-district trustees, in justifying under a tax warrant issued by them, are not bound to prove that the district was duly organized.[6] Under a resolution of a school-district meeting, authorizing the trustees to erect a school-house to cost $400, sell the old house and collect the balance by tax, the trustees might collect the balance by warrant.[7] The sum voted for building a school-house must be precise and clear.[8] An assessment "on all the taxable inhabitants of the district, agreeably to the levy on which the town was levied the preceding

---

[1] Randall v. Smith, 1 Den. (N. Y.) 214.
[2] Gale v. Mead, 2 Den. (N. Y.) 160.
[3] Mead v. Gale, 2 Den. (N. Y.) 232.
[4] Williams v. Larkin, 3 Den. (N. Y.) 114.
[5] Marchant v. Langworthy, 3 Den. (N. Y.) 526.
[6] Stevens v. Newcomb, 4 Den. (N. Y.) 437.
[7] Trumbull v. White, 5 Hill (N. Y.) 46.
[8] Robinson v. Dodge, 18 Johns. (N. Y.) 351.

year," the tax list for the "preceding year" must be understood, according to the general law, to mean the year ending on the 1st day of August.[1] The trustees of a district are not authorized by a vote for tax for building a school-house, without specifying the sum to be levied, to issue their warrants.[2] Under the act Apr. 15, 1814, the freeholders and inhabitants at regular meeting must vote a precise and definite sum as a tax for building a school-house.[2] Persons not inhabitants of a town are not liable to be taxed for the support of common schools in that town; and the trustees who issue the warrant, and collector, are trespassers;[3] the trustees issuing an erroneous tax warrant are liable in trespass, but the collector is not.[4] An owner of land not occupied by him, his agent, or servant, but in the actual occupation of a tenant, is not a "taxable inhabitant" within the meaning of the act of 1819.[5] Where the trustees made an erroneous apportionment by making it upon the sum voted and the percentage allowed the collector, they were not liable in trespass, nor for omitting names of some of the inhabitants, if there is no malafides; the remedy is by appeal or by certiorari.[6] A school district collector may levy upon any goods and chattels lawfully in the possession of the person liable to pay the tax, although such person is not the owner.[7] A school-district warrant issued subsequent to the act of 1831, commanding the collector to levy a tax "in the same manner as on executions issued by justice of the peace," is void, and the collector, as well as the trustees, are trespassers.[8] A party cannot object to the validity of a warrant for school tax under which his goods are sold,

[1] Ryder v. Cudderback, 19 Johns. (N. Y.) 412.
[2] Robinson v. Dodge, 18 Johns. (N. Y.) 351.
[3] Snydam v. Keys, 13 Wend. (N. Y.) 444.
[4] Alexander v. Hoyt, 7 Wend. (N. Y.) 89.
[5] Dubois v. Thorne, 8 Wend. (N. Y.) 518.
[6] Easton v. Callender, 11 Wend. (N. Y.) 91.
[7] Keeler v. Chichester, 13 Wend. N. Y.) 629.
[8] Clark v. Hallock, 16 Wend. (N. Y.) 607.

because that, after the delivery of the warrant to the collector, the sum is reduced by one of the trustees.[1] Where the trustees have been sued in trespass and the tax-money recovered back, they cannot relevy the tax.[2] An account of costs, etc., of school officers, under Laws 1847, ch. 172, § 2, need not be submitted to the taxable inhabitants of the district previous to its being laid before the board of supervisors for their action.[3] Where supervisors have jurisdiction of a claim of district school officers for costs and expenses, their determination is conclusive.[4] Under the Rev. Stat., trustees have the power to issue a new warrant for collection from delinquents;[5] and in an action of trover, for property distrained, the plaintiff giving parol evidence of the rate-bills and warrants, cannot object to the defendants relying upon such rate-bills and warrants, as a justification for the trover and conversion, for the reason that the defendants have not produced them.[6] The taxable inhabitants of a school district cannot legally repeal a resolution imposing a tax, after the greater part of the tax has been collected.[6] Where the rate-bill made out by the trustees of a school district for teacher's wages, is erroneous, for a longer time than the teacher taught, the warrant is not void, but appeal may be had to the state superintendent.[7] A district vote is necessary before assessing the uncollected arrearages of a quarter on a subsequent quarter;[8] but the trustees of a school district are not authorized by the act of Mch. 26, 1849, to lay a tax, without submitting their estimates for a district vote.[8] When indigent persons are exempted by the trustees from the payment of teachers' wages, the amount

---

[1] Folsom v. Streeter, 24 Wend. (N. Y.) 266.
[2] Benjamin v. Hull, 17 Wend. (N. Y.) 437.
[3] People v. Trs. Sch. Dist. No. 13, 8 How. (N. Y.) Pr. 125.
[4] People v. Van Leuven, 8 How. (N. Y.) Pr. 358; People v. Greene, 10 Id. 468; People v. Trs. Sch. Dist. No. 13, 8 Id. 125; 6 Id. 332. But see People v. Snyder, 10 Id. 143.
[5] Seaman v. Benson, 4 Barb. (N. Y.) 444.
[6] Smith v. Dillingham, 4 Barb. (N. Y.) 25.
[7] Finch v. Cleveland, 10 Barb. (N. Y.) 290.
[8] Enos v. Hulett, 13 Barb. (N. Y.) 111.

thereof must be assessed on other persons.¹ A. resided on a homestead farm in one district, but improved another lot not adjacent to his farm, in another district; under Laws 1847, ch. 480, § 87, A. was taxable for lot in district where situated.² In Dec. 1857 there was no law authorizing two of the three trustees to apportion school taxes, or to issue a warrant for their collection;³ but where two trustees of a school district issue a tax warrant; the presence of the third trustee will be presumed.⁴ A tax warrant valid on its face, issued by the trustees in pursuance of an order of the supervisors, will justify the collector, though the order is void.⁵ School taxes are to be assessed and levied in the same manner as those for town, county and state purposes.⁶ Under Laws 1864, ch. 555, tit. 7, art. 7, § 69, when the trustees assess property not upon such roll, or change any of the assessment thereon, they are required to give notice of time and place.⁷ A school collector selling property for an unpaid tax of the owner, without posting the notice required, is a trespasser, and the sale is void; the owner, however, can only recover the amount paid by him to regain the property.⁸ The law authorizing vote of tax to supply deficiency for non-collectible tax does not give trustee power to include the unpaid tax in this levy, and if he does the whole is void and the tax-payer may sue the trustee in trespass.⁹ School trustees may maintain action of assumpsit for tax.¹⁰ A county treasurer must pay the delinquent school tax, and a defect in title of new site for school-house, preventing a conveyance, will not excuse non-payment.¹¹ Colored orphan

[1] Enos v. Hulett, 13 Barb. (N. Y.) 111.
[2] Myer v. Crispell, 28 Barb. (N. Y.) 54.
[3] Harding v. Head, 35 Barb. (N. Y.) 35.
[4] Doolittle v. Doolittle, 31 Barb. (N. Y.) 312; McCoy v. Curtice, 9 Wend. (N. Y.) 17.
[5] Doolittle v. Doolittle, 31 Barb. (N. Y.) 312.
[6] Chadwick v. Crapsey, 35 N. Y. 196.
[7] Jewell v. Van Steenburgh, 58 N. Y. 85.
[8] Bedell v. Barnes, 17 Hun (N. Y.) 353.
[9] Haley v. Whitney, 53 Hun (N. Y.) 119.
[10] Torrey v. Willard 55 Hun (N. Y.) 78.
[11] People v. Hegeman, (N. Y.) 4 N. Y. S. 351.

asylum of New York formed under Laws 1838, as place of refuge for colored orphans, is not exempt from taxation as a school-house.[1]

§ 223. **Tax—North Carolina.**—Under the act of 1844, ch. 36, a regular scholar is not bound to work on a road during a holiday or temporary recess occurring within the period of the school session.[2] Act of 1889 authorizing state and county school tax paid by citizens of Greensboro to be paid by county treasurer to city treasurer of Greensboro, and by him applied, is unconstitutional.[3] The constitution requires a majority of the qualified voters of the town to vote in favor of school bonds and tax; an act that authorized the issue on a vote of majority of those voting when they are not the majority of the qualified voters is unconstitutional.[4]

§ 224. **Tax—Ohio.**—Land once taxed for a school-house is not subject to a second tax for the same purpose until the expiration of three years.[5] The mode of making estimates in cities of class of Cincinnati is not affected by territory being added for school purposes.[6] Where board of education had certified the estimate to county auditor, who placed same on the tax list in a reduced form, in a suit to compel placing the estimate certified on the list, brought by tax-payer, the burden was on him to show that the board did not consent to the reduced form.[7] Where a law was claimed to be general, and not of uniform operation throughout the state, and a party attempted to enjoin the collection of tax thereunder, and there was no showing made that he had not been enjoying and accepting the benefits of the law, it is too late to question the law.[8]

[1] Assc'n Co. O. v. City N. Y., 12 N. E. 279.
[2] Estes v. Oxford, 4 Jones (N. C.) L. 474.
[3] City Greensboro v. Hodgin, 106 N. C. 182.
[4] Markham v. Durham G. Sch., (N.C.) 9 S. E. 40.
[5] Baker v. Black, 6 Ohio, 53.
[6] State v. Brewster, 39 Ohio St. 653.
[7] State v. Cappeller, 39 Ohio St. 435.
[8] Clarke v. Bd. Ed., (Ohio) 9 N. E. 790.

§ 225. **Tax—Oregon.**—Taxable property for school taxes is assessed on the same principles as govern general taxes.¹

§ 226. **Tax—Pennsylvania.**—A county poor-house is exempt.² The act of 1866, exempting certain real estate "from taxation for state purposes," did not exempt it for school purposes.³ A supplemental act to act incorporation of Wagner Free Institute of Science, provided for exemption from taxation for cabinet collection, land on which it was erected, and gifts, bequests and endowments, other real estate subsequently conveyed, the rents of which were used for purposes under original charter were not exempt;⁴ the statute 1873 repealed the act granting exemption to Wagner Free Institute so far as the land attached was concerned.⁵ Section 1 of the act of 1835 does not limit the power of the inhabitants of a borough or township to assess for school purposes.⁶ The duplicate and warrant of the school directors justify a collector, after a demand and a refusal, to levy and sell.⁷ Section 4 of the act entitled "An act to consolidate and amend the several acts relative to a general system of education by common schools," is directory as to time; and if the levy is omitted it may be performed within a reasonable time thereafter.⁷ Money payable under articles of agreement, and bearing interest, is taxable for school purposes.⁸ Under the appropriation act of Apr. 11, 1848, the abatement of 25 per cent. was to be limited to the taxes assessed for the school years of 1848 and 1849, and was not to extend to taxes which had been assessed for the school year commencing on the first Monday of June, 1850, but which had been advanced or paid into the treasury before that day.⁹ Excessive tax for

---

¹ Stephens v. Sch. Dist., 6 Oreg. 353.
² Schuylkill v. North Manheim, 42 Pa. St. 21.
³ Conyngham v. Sch. Dist. App., 77 Pa. St. 205.
⁴ Appeal Wagner Free Inst., (Pa.) 11 A. 402.
⁵ Appeal Wagner Free Inst., 132 Pa. St. 612.
⁶ Wilson v. Lewistown, 1 Watts & S. (Pa.) 428.
⁷ Gearhart v. Dixon, 1 Pa. St. 224.
⁸ Vaegtly v. Sch. Dirs., 1 Pa. St. 330.
⁹ Commonwealth v. Fraim, 16 Pa. St. 163.

building that is not needed will be enjoined as to such excess.[1] The statute must be strictly complied with in order to increase indebtedness of district beyond two per cent. of its valuation, under act of 1874. Notice and statement showing indebtedness must be filed.[2] A collector may enforce payment of school taxes by suit, after the expiration of his warrant.[3] The board of school directors may issue a warrant for school taxes, returnable in a shorter period than two years.[3] Property held for non-resident minors is taxable in the county where the guardian resides, under the act of Apr. 22, 1846;[4] but where a minor resides with her father in one district and her guardian in another, in the same county, the property is taxable for the district wherein the minor lives.[4] Under the school law of May 8, 1854, the power of taxation is committed to the school directors, but without any right of appeal.[5] The act of Mch. 25, 1864, § 7, to levy a tax "on all property, etc., subject to taxation for state and county purposes," did not authorize directors to tax property not included in the adjusted valuation of the assessors and commissioners.[6] Where a school board levy a tax, it is to be collected under a warrant issued by the president and countersigned by the secretary;[7] and if signed by two justices of the peace instead of by the president and secretary, it is of no validity.[7] Mandamus was refused to compel central board to appropriate to sub-district for improvements, and add the same as for next year, and certify same to council of Pittsburgh.[8]

§ 227. **Tax—Rhode Island.**—The provision of Gen. Stat., ch. 58, § 13, opening "all the public schools in the state to the

---

[1] Comm'rs Appeal, 103 Pa. St. 356.
[2] Witherop v. Titusville Sch. Bd., 7 Pa. Co. Ct. Rep. 451.
[3] McCracken v. Elder, 34 Pa. St. 239.
[4] West Chester v. Darlington, 38 Pa. St. 157.
[5] Wharton v. Sch. Dirs., 42 Pa. St. 358.
[6] Shirk v. Bucher, 53 Pa. St. 94.
[7] Hilbish v. Hower, 58 Pa. St. 93.
[8] Commonwealth v. Shaw, 96 Pa. St. 268.

children of officers and soldiers," etc., "without any cost, or expense, or taxes, or other charges imposed for purposes of public education," does not exempt the estate of such officer or soldier from taxes levied for school purposes.[1] A school district can raise money by taxation provided the amount shall be approved by the school committee of the town; this need not precede the voting of the tax.[2] Objection that powers of district do not authorize the tax, must be taken by appeal.[3] When assessors are to be appointed, by the school commissioner, under Rev. Stat., ch. 64, § 1, to assess a tax, the school district must have notice.[4]

§ 228. **Tax—South Carolina.**—Under Constitution and Acts 1882 and 1883, the city of Spartanburg became a separate corporation, authorized to issue bonds to build schoolhouses in that city, and the auditor may be compelled to compute the amount and levy the same on the property.[5]

§ 229. **Tax—Tennessee.**—Act of Feb. 28, 1870, conferring upon the board of president and directors of the Cleveland public schools power to levy a school tax, is unconstitutional.[6] Although a county, without special statute, cannot, after levying taxes for general county purposes in amount equal to the state tax, make additional levy, yet a levy of an equal amount for school purposes is valid, under act of 1873.[7] Under act of March 22, 1877, county courts cannot levy a school tax at a higher rate than the state tax, but the illegality goes only to the excess;[8] and it is immaterial that a levy was made in July instead of at the first quarterly term of court.[8]

---

[1] Carpenter v. Hopkinton Sch. Trs., 12 R.I. 574.
[2] Seabury v. Howland, (R. I.) 8 A. 341; Holt's Appeal, 5 R. I. 603.
[3] Seabury v. Howland, (R. I.) 8 A. 341.
[4] Peckham v. Bicknell, 11 R. I. 596.
[5] State v. Bacon, (S. C.) 9 S. E. 765.
[6] Waterhouse v. Cleveland Pub. Sch. Bd., 9 Baxter (Tenn.) 398.
[7] N. C. etc. R. R. Co. v. Franklin Co., 5 Lea (Tenn.) 707.
[8] Bright v. Halloman, 7 Lea (Tenn.) 309.

§ 230. **Tax—Texas.**—Land owned and used by proprietor of private school adjacent thereto, for supplying table with vegetables, is not exempt.[1] Legislature could not grant power to levy taxes for schools except as provided in constitution.[2] Whenever an incorporated town assumes control of its public schools, it may levy a school tax thereafter if voted for by two-thirds of property tax-payers; this does not mean two-thirds of those voting, but two-thirds of the qualified voters that are taxpayers.[2] The act of 1876, appropriating the "dog tax" to the county free schools, is not unconstitutional.[3] Constitution, art. 9, § 3, authorizes the legislature to confer upon district boards of education power to levy the school tax, and also those conferred by act of April 24, 1871.[4] The legislature may delegate the power to district the state for educational purposes.[4] The one-per-cent. school tax, levied under § 5 of the act of April 24, 1871, was not repealed by the act of April 22, 1871, even though the former act may be prior in the true date of its passage.[4] If a board of school directors levy taxes for school purposes for that year, their successors cannot levy a different school tax for that year.[5] The legislature may confer upon boards of school directors power to assess taxes for school purposes.[6] The section of act Aug. 13, 1870, requiring the boards of school directors to levy an *ad valorem* tax not exceeding one per cent., applied to assessments made in 1871.[6] Where act authorized school tax of one-fourth of one per cent., and a city adopted an amendment to its charter allowing one-half of one per cent., and the statute forbade any amendment contrary to constitution and laws, the amendment was invalid.[7] "Shall such an amount be

---

[1] St. Ed. College v. Morris, 17 S. W. 512.
[2] Ft. Worth v. Davis, 57 Tex. 225.
[3] *Ex parte* Cooper, 3 Tex. App. 489.
[4] Kinney v. Zimpleman, 36 Tex. 554.
[5] Oliver v. Carsner, 39 Tex. 396.
[6] State v. Bremond, 38 Tex. 116.
[7] Jodon v. Brenham, 57 Tex. 655.

raised by taxation?" is not the same as "whether or not the city council should be allowed to levy a tax of one-fourth of one per cent.;" and a vote for latter would not authorize levy under law providing for the former.[1]

§ 231. **Tax—Utah.**—Under act of Jan. 18th, 1865, no provision is made for adjusting the amount of the tax to the necessities of the district; no appeal is allowed the tax-payers for the equalization of assessments, and the trustees are neither required to take oath nor to give bond for the faithful performance of their duty, and the law is void, and collection will be restrained;[2] and the act of 1865 for school tax, not providing for equality of tax, or impartial assessment, or faithful disbursement, is void.[3] Extending boundaries of district so as to take in railroad property and tax the same for school-house twenty-five miles distant, by action of county court, is authorized.[3] Where a vote of a levy of one per cent. was voted, the county officials cannot extend the levy for the following year upon that basis, where it would raise three times the amount needed.[4]

§ 232. **Tax—Virginia.**—School taxes must be paid in lawful money of the United States, and not in states' tax receivable coupons.[5]

§ 233. **Tax—Vermont.**—The buildings owned by St. Johnsbury Academy, a private educational institution, including club house and residence of students and faculty, and part rented, is exempt.[6] "Public schools," in laws exempting from taxation, is construed to mean public in sense of colleges and academies.[6] To justify taking property, as collector of a school district, all the conditions precedent must be shown to have

[1] Ft. Worth v. Davis, 57 Tex. 225.
[2] Kerr v. Woolley, 3 Utah, 456.
[3] King v. Utah C. R. R., (Utah) 22 P. 158.
[4] Lowe v. Hardy, (Utah) 26 P. 982.
[5] Greenhow v. Vashorn, 81 Va. 336.
[6] Willard v. Pike, (Vt.) 9 A. 907.

—17

been complied with.¹ A collector of a school-district tax is liable in trespass, if the district proceeded illegally in voting; and this, though his warrant and rate-bill be, on their face, regular.² The limitation to a maximum amount, of the sum to be raised in a school district, imports sufficient certainty.³ Under the act of Nov. 1827 and act 1833, the voters in district could assess a tax for the support of a school upon such scholars only as actually attended the school.³ A committee is justified in assessing individual's real estate situated in the district, for a value proportioned to the value of all his lands on the town list where statute provides no means of separation; a vote to raise such a tax need not specify ratio and amount.⁴ In assessing a school-district tax the committee cannot assess upon lands which are wholly omitted in the grand list, though they know them to be within the district.⁵ If an inhabitant. has no list in the school district, his name need not appear in the rate-bill of a tax laid by such district.⁶ Since the act of 1854 (Laws 1854, 44), authorizing school districts to elect a treasurer, the warrant for school-district tax should require the money to be paid to that officer.⁶ A resident of a school district, on the 1st of April, assessed as owner of personalty, and whose list is designated by the listers as belonging to such district, is liable to pay such district taxes, though he removes from the district.⁷ The prudential committee of the district is alone authorized by law to assess and certify the tax for removing a school-house.⁸ A school district has a right to assess taxes to pay for defending suits against a tax collector, for collecting taxes.⁹ The omission of the officer to enter upon the

¹ Bates v. Hazeltine, 1 Vt. 81.
² Waters v. Daines, 4 Vt. 601.
³ Brown v. Hoadly, 12 Vt. 472.
⁴ Adams v. Hyde, 27 Vt. 221.
⁵ Moss v. Hindes, 29 Vt. 188.
⁶ Bull v. Griffith. 30 Vt. 273.
⁷ Woodward v. French, 31 Vt. 337; Walker v. Miner, 32 Vt. 769.
⁸ Johnson v. Sanderson, 34 Vt. 94.
⁹ Johnson v. Colburn, 36 Vt. 693.

warrant the time when he received the same, does not invalidate;[1] if the warrant was sufficient, no subsequent alteration in it can invalidate the acts done under it;[1] proceedings of prudential committee in assessing taxes, and in making out and delivering a rate-bill to the tax collector of the district, will justify that officer in serving the warrant.[1] Parol evidence was admissible to show the true time when the rate-bill and certificate were made; and clerical error will not vitiate, and parol evidence may explain an altered warrant.[1] A vote of a school district to sustain a school for a definite period is not equivalent to a vote to defray the expenses of that school.[2] Under acts of 1868, No. 38, a district enlarged in 1873 cannot vote, in 1874, that a tax be assessed on the list of 1872.[3] The listers and assessors, being unable to determine the boundaries of a district, set the lands therein to an adjoining district, and the collector of the latter distrained for tax therein; this was held to be illegal.[4] Where selectmen were required to assess annually a school tax previous to Jan. 1, without specifying the list, it should be assessed on the list last completed and in force at time of assessment.[5] That a tax shall not be assessed until the money is required, means that the assessment may be made long enough beforehand to raise the money needed.[6]

§ 234. **Tax—Washington.**—Where the boundaries of a city of 10,000, constituting one district, are enlarged, the funds of the enlarged district are charged with maintenance of the school in the whole district, and the board at its meeting next preceding the annual tax levy shall fix the amount required for school purposes.[7]

[1] Goodwin v. Perkins, 39 Vt. 598.
[2] Adams v. Crowell, 40 Vt. 31.
[3] Hassam v. Edwards, 49 Vt. 7.
[4] Hubbard v. Newton, 52 Vt. 346.
[5] Sprague v. Abbott, 58 Vt. 331.
[6] Brock v. Bruce, (Vt.) 10 A. 93.
[7] City Seattle Sch. D. v. Bd. City Comm'rs, (Wash.) 28 P. 376.

§ 235. **Tax—West Virginia.**—Four months' school voted for means only that year.[1] A sheriff cannot pay over school taxes in his hands to his successor without order of board education.[2]

§ 236. **Tax—Wisconsin.**—Trustees authorized under a special act to vote a tax to be assessed by the trustees, had the power to make a valuation to levy the assessment.[3] A town treasurer paid to the treasurer of a school district in his town the delinquent tax, and for which the town had settled with the county. Subsequently the amount so credited to the town was charged back to and paid by it; the town could not recover the amount from the district if the tax was in fact legal; but this tax having been invalid, and the town treasurer not having knowledge, the town was entitled to recover the amount so paid.[4] Under R. S., § 776, when school taxes are voted by town they may be levied without regard to the fact that the money is to be applied to benefit of specific districts in the town.[5]

§ 237. **Tax exemption.**—In the case of *St. Mary's College v. Crowl, Treasurer, &c.*, 10 Kas. 448, it was held that "Under the laws of this state all property not expressly exempted is subjected to taxation. (Gen. Stat. 1019, ch. 107, § 1.) And no property is exempt because it is used for educational purposes unless it is exclusively so used. (Const., art. 11, § 1.) Property used partially for educational purposes and partially for some other purpose is not exempt. Even property used mainly for educational purposes, but not exclusively, is not exempt. In the present case we shall not discuss separately the taxability of each article or piece of property claimed to be exempt, but shall

[1] Wells v. Lincoln Bd. Ed., 20 W. Va. 157.
[2] Spencer D. Bd. Ed. v. Cain, 28 W. Va. 758.
[3] Richardson v. Sheldon, 1 Pinn. (Wis. T.) 624.
[4] Ripon v. Joint Sch. Dist., 17 Wis. 83.
[5] Griggs v. St. C. Co., 27 F. R. 333.

discuss more especially the taxability of the inclosed arable and cultivated land; for if any portion of the plaintiff's property is exempt from taxation it is certainly that portion. This property was used for at least three purposes: 1st. It was used for the purpose of teaching certain Indians agriculture; 2d. It was used for the purpose of raising food for a large amount of live stock kept on the farm, and food for said Indians, their tutors, etc.; 3d. It was used for the purpose of raising produce to sell. The proceeds of the sales, however, were used to feed and clothe the Indians, to feed and clothe 'the employés in their training,' and to feed and clothe 'the missionaries among them.' We suppose it will be conceded that if the property were used exclusively for the purpose of teaching the Indians agriculture, it would be exempt. But even this may not be certain, for agriculture was hardly considered a branch of education when our constitution was framed. For the purposes of this case it may also be conceded that if the property were used exclusively for teaching the Indians agriculture, and for raising food for them and the professors, and the necessary stock kept on the farm, it would still be exempt. But when it is used to raise food for stock not necessary to be kept on the farm, and to raise produce to sell, no further concessions in favor of its exemption can be made. Such use goes at least one step beyond where concessions can be made in favor of its exemption. It is solely the use of the property which determines whether the property is exempt or not. (*Washburn College v. Shawnee County*, 8 Kas. 344.) It makes no difference who owns the property, nor who uses it. Property used exclusively for educational purposes is exempt, whoever may own it, or whoever may use it. Property not used exclusively for educational purposes, (if otherwise taxable,) is not exempt, whoever may own it, or whoever may use it. And this use must be direct and immediate, and not indirect or remote. (*Cincinnati College v. State*, 19 Ohio, 110.) If a farm be used for the purpose of raising produce to sell and get money to carry on a school, it will not be exempt. The use for educational purposes is in such a case too remote. The immediate or primary object for cultivating the farm in such a case is to obtain the produce; the secondary object is to obtain the money that the produce will bring; and the remote object is to aid and foster the school. The farm itself, in such a case, is not used in teaching anything, or in illustrating or explaining anything, as books, charts, apparatus, etc., are. It is not used as a necessary shelter and protection for the students, their books, apparatus, etc., as a school-house always is. And it is not used as a necessary site for a school-house, as school-house grounds always are. In fact, it answers no direct or immediate educational purpose or necessity. It is no part or portion of the school, and is not used as such. It therefore does not come within the constitutional exemption."

§ 238. **Teacher's certificate.**—There need be no second examination of a teacher upon the granting of a renewal certificate, the original certificate having expired by limitation.[1] In an action against the superintendent of schools for illegally revoking a teacher's certificate, the plaintiff is not compelled to show personal hatred or ill-will; but if the defendant acted rashly, wickedly and wantonly in revoking the certificate, the jury may infer malice;[2] and where a county superintendent maliciously withholds teacher's certificate, he is liable in damages.[3] In an action against citizens for a conspiracy in a

---

[1] Doyle v. Sch. D., 36 Ill. App. 653.
[2] Love v. Moore, 45 Ill. 12.
[3] Elmore v. Overton, 104 Ind. 548.

groundless remonstrance to the school directors against appointing a teacher, his having no certificate would not prevent his recovery of actual damages.[1] The county superintendent canceling a teacher's certificate without concurrence of the local trustees does not deprive him of compensation if he still teaches to the end of the term.[2] A town superintendent of common schools (N. Y.) has no right, under act of 1847, to annul a certificate given by his predecessor until at least ten days' previous notice in writing to the teacher and to the trustees of the district in which he is employed.[3] It is no defense to an action brought by the teacher against the district to recover his wages, that the certificate was granted without any examination having been in fact made by the town superintendent.[4] A certificate of qualification cannot be impeached in an action brought by a teacher for salary due, nor will it be invalidated by the improper introduction of testimony going to show that for the certificate in question he was not in fact examined.[5] Where a teacher had a certificate, but was discharged for incompetency, and he sued for service, and he was asked the question, "What would $3\frac{1}{4}$ pounds of butter cost at $11\frac{1}{2}$ cents a pound?" this question was ruled out, as the certificate was conclusive as to his right to teach.[6]

§ 239. **Teacher's certificate.**—In Vt. the certificate of qualification by town superintendent need not contain any statement as to the teacher's good moral character.[7] Under Ill. Rev. Stat., ch. 122, § 52, the certificate need not state that an examination was had; it is in the nature of a commission, and cannot be attacked collaterally.[8] In Vt., in an action by a teacher

---

[1] Vanarsdale v. Laverty, 69 Pa. St. 103.
[2] Jamison v. Senter, 56 Miss. 194.
[3] Finch v. Cleveland, 10 Barb. (N. Y.) 290.
[4] George v. Sch. Dist. No. 8, 20 Vt. 495.
[5] Doyle v. Sch. D., 36 Ill. App. 653.
[6] Doyle v. Sch. Dist, 36 Ill. App. 654.
[7] Crosby v. Sch. Dist., 35 Vt. 623.
[8] Union Sch. Dist. etc. v. Sterricker, 86 Ill. 595.

against a district for breach of contract, it need not be averred that the plaintiff had procured from the town superintendent a certificate of qualification, as required by Comp. Stat., ch. 20, § 15.[1] In an action by a teacher against a town, proof that he was employed by the agent and the services were rendered as agreed, *prima facie*, entitles the plaintiff to recover; and if the town would avail themselves of the want of the certificates required by the act of 1834, ch. 129, Me., they must show that fact.[2] Although a teacher of a public school may not be entitled to recover her wages without the certificate required by the statute, yet the town alone is entitled to raise that objection; and if money has been paid by the town to the school agent, for the teacher, he will hold it to her use, and cannot object to the want of such certificate.[3] The certificate of a majority of the superintending school committee of a town, produced by the school master to the agent employing him, is a valid certificate, under Rev. Stat., ch. 17, although that majority did not act together in the examination.[4] Under Me. Rev. Stat., ch. 11, § 41, requiring the teacher's certificate to be obtained from the superintending committee of the town "where the school-house of such district is situated, or has been located, or where the school is kept," where the last vote of union district lying partly in F. and partly in C., and having a house in each town, fixed the location of the house in F., and the school was kept in F., the teacher properly obtained the certificate from the committee of F.[5] In a suit for money paid to teacher not having a certificate, it was a good defense that the teacher was entitled to the certificate, which had been withheld by inadvertence;[6] and when

---

[1] Doyan v. Sch. Dist., 35 Vt. 520.
[2] Rolfe v. Cooper, 20 Me. 154.
[3] Dore v. Billings, 26 Me. 56.
[4] Stevens v. Fassett, 27 Me. 266.
[5] Brown v. Chesterville, 63 Me. 241.
[6] Sch. Dist. v. Brown, 55 Vt. 61.

teacher had no certificate for part of the term, the board cannot set off the money paid during that time, in an action for compensation for time when she had a certificate.[1]

§ 240. **Teacher's certificate.**—When board of education in district in Ill., of 2,000 population or more, examine and employ a teacher, he can recover salary though he has not received from county superintendent his certificate, which is required by another statute;[2] a pupil or parent cannot contest the right of teacher for want of proper certificate.[3] Failure to file state normal certificate until after contract for teaching has been made is no defense for services rendered after it is filed.[4] Mandamus will not lie by one consenting, to compel a suit on an assessor's bond for paying a salary of a teacher not qualified legally, but employed as a necessity, and the board employing being satisfied.[5] School committee may employ a teacher when the teacher employed by the prudential committee fails to obtain a certificate and after the lapse of two months they inform the school committee that they will not engage another. (G. S., ch. 39.)[6] The statute is satisfied if the certificate is obtained on the evening of the first day, especially where the delay has been at the request of the superintendent;[7] so if a certificate was made out at the proper time, although by accident it was not put into the teacher's hands;[8] and one who at the time she signs a contract to teach has a certificate from the county superintendent can recover, though at the time of application to the board, and date of contract, she had no certificate.[9] Where a teacher taught school for five weeks before her certificate expired, and six weeks afterwards without obtaining a new certifi-

---

[1] Dodge Co. Sch. Dist. v. Estes, 13 Neb. 52.
[2] Knemster v. Bd. Ed., (Ill.) 24 N. E. 609.
[3] Kidder v. Chellis, 59 N. H. 473.
[4] Smith v. Sch. Dist., (Mich.) 37 N. W. 567.
[5] State v. Risley, (Mich.) 37 N. W. 570.
[6] Sch. Dist. v. Mowry, 9 Allen (Mass.) 94.
[7] Paul v. Sch. Dist., 28 Vt. 575.
[8] Blanchard v. Sch. Dist., 29 Vt. 433.
[9] Sch. Dist. v. Stilley, 36 Ill. App. 133.

cate, held, that she might recover for the services performed both before and after the expiration of the certificate.[1] The plaintiff's minor daughter contracted to teach for eleven weeks, and taught one week without a certificate; then she obtained a certificate and taught another week, with the approbation of the committee, at which time she quit on account of unjustifiable conduct of the committee; the continuing after she had obtained her certificate was equivalent to making a new contract on the same terms as the original; not making the entries in the school register required, at the close of the school, did not prevent recovery.[2]

§ 241. **Teacher's certificate.**—In a suit for services, the objection that the plaintiff had no certificate as required by N. J. Rev., p. 1077, § 33, comes too late if made after the evidence is closed;[3] and the plaintiff's right to recover is not barred by the fact that he was employed by the trustees of a district afterwards consolidated with another district.[3] A school teacher, under the direction of the superintendent, examined after she had begun the school, received an ante-dated certificate; after teaching a few weeks she was dismissed; she could recover her wages.[4] In the absence of evidence that a teacher having a certificate has been discharged for lack of qualifications, if subsequently employed in another ward and in a higher grade she is entitled to pay for her services, whether examined or not.[5] Under Mo. Rev. Code 1855, 1430, § 5, div. 4, although the approval of the commissioner was not indorsed in writing on the certificate, yet where he signified his approval in words and declared the teacher competent, and

---

[1] Holman v. School Dist., 34 Vt. 270.
[2] Scott v. Sch. Dist. No. 2, 46 Vt. 452.
[3] Sproul v. Smith, 40 N. J. L. 314.
[4] Wells v. Sch. Dist., 41 Vt. 353.
[5] Commonwealth v. Lyndall, 2 Brews. (Pa.) 425.

gave his sanction to the previous arrangement of the school, in the presence of the trustees, the trustees could not be held liable for the amount paid the teacher from the time of the expiration of his certificate.[1] Notwithstanding Gen. St. Colo., § 3055, one who is employed by the board to teach when, as they are aware, she has no license, but who shortly afterwards procures one, may maintain an action against the board for compensation.[2] A teacher's certificate from the school commissioner is *prima facie* evidence of qualification, and it devolves upon directors to prove incompetency or neglect of duty when they have dismissed him for either of such causes.[3]

§ 242. **Teacher's certificate.**—A contract by a common-school district to hire a teacher not having a certificate of qualification, is void; and a complaint by the teacher should aver possession of the certificate.[4] A warrant issued to teacher who has not the certificate required by Dak. Stat., is void, and non-negotiable so as to cut off defense, and township is not liable for services rendered.[5] Where teacher failed, on examination, to obtain a renewal of certificate, and kept on teaching as ordered by a director who had no power to bind the district, he could not recover for teaching after failure.[6] The secretary of board of examiners, Mich., has not power, four days after teacher fails to pass at public examination, to grant such teacher a special certificate, and the teacher cannot complain of third party assisting at the public examination unless it is shown that was cause of failure to pass.[7] A contract employing a teacher who has not a certificate as provided for by the school law, is void, and is not susceptible of subsequent ratification; and where,

[1] Barnhart v. Bodenhammer, 31 Mo. 319.
[2] Hotz v. Sch. Dist. No. 9, (Colo. App.) 27 P. 15.
[3] Neville v. Sch. Dirs., 36 Ill. 71.
[4] Ryan v. Dak. Co. Sch. Dist., 27 Minn. 433.
[5] Goose River Bk. v. Willow Lake Sch. Tp., (N. D.) 44 N. W. 1002.
[6] Devoe v. Sch. Dist., (Mich.) 43 N. W. 1062.
[7] Lee v. Sch. Dist., (Mich.) 38 N. W. 867.

after having taught three months, he obtained the certificate, and the directors then made a new contract with him, whereby he was to teach three months at a salary of twice the amount per month he was to receive under the first contract, both contracts were void.[1] To entitle a teacher to recover on a contract to teach, he must prove he had a certificate at time of employment.[2] A trustee of the owners of a building leased to the directors of schools is liable for a trespass, although the school has no funds, and the teacher has not been examined for that year, if such teacher has a certificate, and has been examined on a previous occasion.[3] A school committee is not confined to moral character and literary qualities of a teacher in determining his fitness.[4] In Tenn., the common-school commissioners are indictable for employing a teacher who has no examiner's certificate of his competency, as required by § 1019 of the code.[5]

§ 243. **Teacher's certificate.**—Every teacher is required to obtain a certificate of his qualifications before he opens his school, and circumstances cannot supersede the statute, and it cannot be waived.[6] A certificate granted to a teacher may be anulled by the city superintendent of common schools for the city and county of New York.[7] Where a town superintendent refused a certificate on the ground of moral character, and on appeal having been taken to the state superintendent it was ordered that the town superintendent examine into her literary qualifications, and if satisfied with them, that he license her, by a tender of a certificate of literary qualification, the town superintendent has discharged his duty, moral qualification being, by appeal, left to the state superintendent;[8] and from the refusal

[1] Wells v. People, 71 Ill. 732.
[2] Stevenson v. Sch. Dist., 87 Ill. 255; Jenness v. Sch. Dist., 12 Minn. 448.
[3] Kingsley v. Sch. Dirs., 2 Pa. St. 28.
[4] Sch. Dist. v. Mowry, 9 Allen (Mass.) 94.
[5] Robinson v. State, 2 Coldw. (Tenn.) 181.
[6] Goodrich v. Fairfax, 26 Vt. 115; Baker v. Sch. D., 12 Vt. 192; Welch v. Brown, 30 Vt. 586.
[7] People v. Bd. Ed., 17 Barb. (N. Y.) 299.
[8] People v. Masters, 21 Barb. (N. Y.) 252.

for want of literary qualifications, no appeal lies to the state superintendent.[1] One who has not a certificate of the superintending committee, required by law, cannot recover any compensation for his services.[2] A judgment in favor of the teacher will be restrained by injunction, at a suit of any person interested as a tax-payer within the district, suing in behalf of himself and others; a school district cannot waive the law requiring the school master to produce the certificate of the superintending committee, or to dispense with the certificate;[3] and in an action by a teacher, under the act of 1857, Ill., it must be alleged that the certificate of qualification was exhibited to the directors before his employment;[3] and the same was held under law of 1849.[4] Under Law of Ill., 1849, a teacher must present to the school directors, before the commencement of the school, his certificate.[5] The power given board of education of Galesburg (Ill.) to appoint teachers, does not authorize appointment of teachers not possessing statutory qualifications.[6] In Ill., the law prohibiting paying teachers not having certificates applies only to those districts acting under the general law.[7] In Ill., a school board cannot employ a teacher who has not, at that time, the certificate required by law;[8] and one who renders services as a teacher, without the certificate required by law, cannot recover.[9] Under § 28, Ind. R. S. 1876, p. 780, a contract for the employment of an unlicensed teacher is void, and is not ratified by the subsequent issuance of a license to the teacher.[10] A county superintendent cannot sue to restrain a person from teaching, the treasurer of the town from paying him, and the

[1] People v. Masters, 21 Barb. (N. Y.) 252.
[2] Barr v. Deniston, 19 N. H. 170.
[3] Botkin v. Osborne, 39 Ill. 101.
[4] Smith v. Curry, 16 Ill. 147.
[5] Casey v. Baldridge, 15 Ill. 65.
[6] Galesburg Ed. Bd. v. Arnold, 112 Ill. 11.
[7] Kuenster v. Bd. Ed., 134 Ill. 165.
[8] Sch. Dirs. v. Jennings, 10 Ill. App. 643.
[9] Harrison Tp. v. Conrad, 26 Ind. 337.
[10] Putnam v. Irvington, 69 Ind. 80; Butler v. Haines, 79 Ind. 575.

director from permitting the use of the school-house, because such party has no certificate; but residents of the district might maintain such a bill.¹ A certificate of a majority of the superintending school committee as to the qualifications of a teacher, is to be regarded as *prima facie* evidence that they have performed all their duty;² but if a member has not been notified, a certificate by the majority is void.² A teacher cannot recover pay for teaching without the certificate of the superintending school committee, even though all the members wantonly refuse to examine him.²

§ 244. **Teacher's certificate.**—In the case of *Goose River Bank v. Willow Lake S. Tp.*, 44 N. W. Rep. (N. D.) 1002, it was held: "Every contract relating to the employment of a teacher who does not hold a lawful certificate of qualification, is void by the express terms of the statute, and every warrant issued in payment of services of such teacher is without consideration, and void. School township warrants are not negotiable instruments, in the sense that their negotiation will cut off defenses to them existing against them in the hands of the payee. The officers of a school township cannot estop the township by a representation, express or implied, that the facts to authorize the issue of a lawful warrant exist. Where a contract is expressly prohibited or declared void by statute, retention of the fruits of such contract will not subject a municipality to liability under the contract or on a *quantum meruit*. A person who assists a public officer in depriving the public of the benefits of a statutory protection designed to guard the people against unfit and incompetent teachers has no standing in court, and his assignee will receive no greater consideration. . . .

¹ Perkins v. Wolf, 17 Iowa, 228.
² Jackson v. Hampden, 20 Me. 37.

"There is no force in the position that the defendant having received the benefit of the teacher's service, is liable. Such a doctrine would defeat the policy of the law, which is to give the people of the state the benefit of trained and competent teachers. The law recognizes only one evidence that that policy has been regarded—the certificate of qualification. If the defendant could be made liable by the mere receipt of the benefit of the services rendered, the law prohibiting the employment of teachers without certificates, and declaring void all contracts made in contravention of that provision, would be, in effect, repealed, and the protection of the people against incompetent and unfit teachers, which such statute was enacted to accomplish, would be destroyed. Where a contract is void because of the express declaration of a statute, or because prohibited in terms, the retention by a municipality of the fruits of such a contract will not subject it to liability, either under the contract or upon a *quantum meruit.* (*Dickinson v. City of Poughkeepsie,* 75 N. Y. 65; *McBrien v. City of Grand Rapids,* 22 N. W. Rep. 206; *Thomas v. Richmond,* 12 Wall. 349; *Argenti v. San Francisco,* 16 Cal. 255; *City of Litchfield v. Ballou,* 114 U. S. 190; 5 Sup. Ct. Rep. 820. See also *Tube-works Co. v. City of Chamberlain,* [Dak.] 37 N. W. Rep. 762.) This is particularly true in a case like the one at bar, where no person can teach without the certificate, without being actually or legally in collusion with local officers to defeat a wise and salutary statute, enacted as a barrier against the employment of unqualified teachers. The person who teaches without the certificate has violated the letter and spirit of the law. The wrong done is without remedy. The people who have thus had this barrier torn from about them have no redress. Shall the wrong-doer be compensated for aiding the school township officers in breaking down this barrier, thus depriving the people of the protection of this important law? In this connection the language of the court in *Thomas v. Richmond*, 12 Wall. 349, is very applicable: 'The issuing of bills as a currency by such a corporation, without authority, is not only contrary to positive law, but, being *ultra vires*, is an abuse of the public franchises which have been conferred upon it, and the receiver of the bill, being chargeable with notice of the wrong, is *in pari delicto* with the officers, and should have no remedy, even for money had and received, against the corporation upon which he has aided in inflicting the wrong. The protection of public corporations against such unauthorized acts of their officers and agents is a matter of public policy, in which the whole community is concerned, and those who aid in such transactions must do so at their peril.'

"In *City of Litchfield v. Ballou*, 114 U. S. 190, (5 Sup. Ct. Rep. 820,) the same court said: 'The money received on the bonds having been expended, with other funds raised by taxation, in erecting the water works of the city, to impose the amount thereof as a lien upon these public works would be equally a violation of the constitutional prohibition as to raise against the city an implied assumpsit for money had and received. The holders of the bonds and agents of the city are *particeps criminis* in the act of violating that prohibition, and equity will no more raise a resulting trust in favor of the bondholders than the law will raise an implied assumpsit against a public policy so strongly declared.' The judgment of the district court is affirmed.—All concur."

§ 245. **Teachers' compensation.**—Salaries, under the consolidation act in Cal., are to be paid in the same order as other claims against the San Francisco treasury.[1] A teacher engaged for a specific term, and discharged without cause, can recover compensation; the measure of damages is ordinarily the amount of stipulated wages, but may be reduced by proof of ability to earn from other sources.[2] A rule that the teachers should be liable to discharge at the pleasure of the board is no defense to an action on a contract of hire for a specific term.[2] Where a teacher was dismissed for cause, and he took forcible possession of the school-house and continued to teach, he was not entitled to any compensation from the time of his dismissal.[3] Under the act of 1857, Ga., all accounts for teaching poor children are to be paid *pro rata*;[4] under the act of 1852, Ga., whenever the teachers are not paid in full, the balances due are to be paid out of the taxation for the next year before the accounts of the teachers for that year.[5] The act of 1854, Ga., requires the treasurer of the poor-school fund in the county of M. to pay the teachers for 1851 and 1852 their accounts in full; such act does not impair any contract made under the act of 1852;[5] but promises made by the ordinary, in Ga., under a mistaken construction of said last-mentioned act, create no contract.[6] In Ga. the county board of education cannot try claim for teacher's compensation until the county commissioner has audited account.[6] A teacher kept a regular schedule under Ill. act 1855, certified it himself, and it was certified by one director only, the rest being absent; and it was not presented to the township treasurer before or on the day prescribed; he was not entitled to recover by bill in chancery, but remedy is by mandamus.[7]

[1] Knox v. Woods, 8 Cal. 545.
[2] Sch. Dist. v. Hale, 15 Col. 367.
[3] Pierce v. Beck, 61 Ga. 413.
[4] King v. Barker, 28 Ga. 293.

[5] Johnson v. The Governor, etc., 17 Ga. 179.
[6] Cheney v. Newton, 67 Ga. 477.
[7] Cotton v. Trs., 20 Ill. 607.

A teacher delivered the teacher's schedule to one of the directors, who signed and retained it; he was entitled to recover.[1] Mandamus is not the remedy of a teacher; he should sue the school directors of the district, and upon a recovery enforce the special execution by attachment or mandamus.[2] Under the provision of Ill. Rev. Stat., ch. 122, § 53, it is not lawful for the treasurer to pay the teacher or assignee before the filing of the schedule.[3] Section 41 of Ill. law of 1849, in relation to the distribution of the school fund among teachers on first Saturday of April and October, is mandatory.[4]

§ 246. **Teacher's compensation.**—In an action for salary of a teacher in a township school, the complaint need not allege that the trustee had, at the beginning of the suit, sufficient school revenue for tuition to pay his claim;[5] and it is no defense to action for teacher's wages under a contract, that there is no money on hand.[6] If the treasurer has money belonging to the district, and devoted to payment of teachers' wages, and refuses to pay it over on a proper order and demand, he is personally liable.[7] In Ind. a teacher contracts with reference to the provision of law, that only seventy-five per cent. due him shall be paid before he makes his report.[8] Where sufficient tax had been collected to pay the balance due to a teacher, for which he had an order on the treasurer, and payment was refused, he might recover of the district.[9] On appeal to superintendent of public instruction from district-board directors, a decision that teacher was wrongfully discharged is binding on the district.[10] Trustees failing to collect school funds as required by law, are

---

[1] Adkins v. Mitchell, 67 Ill. 511.
[2] Rodgers v. People, 68 Ill. 154.
[3] Sch. Dirs. etc. v. Greenville Bank, 3 Ill. App. 349.
[4] Thomas v. Trs. Schs., 16 Ill. 163.
[5] Harmony v. Moore, 80 Ind. 276.
[6] Harrison v. McGregor, 96 Ind. 185.
[7] Edson v. Hayden, 18 Wis. 627.
[8] Owen Sch. Tp. v. Hay, 107 Ind. 351.
[9] McCasky v. Sch. Dist. No. 1, 2 Greene (Iowa) 482.
[10] Park v. Pleasant Grove S. D., 65 Iowa, 209.

personally liable to the teacher.[1] The exaction of extra compensation by the teacher, from the parents of children, does not constitute a defense to the payment of the warrant drawn by directors.[2] Section 11 of the act La., which requires that the warrant drawn for the salary of any teacher should be accompanied by a statement of the number of children taught, etc., is directory only.[3] The act of 1855, La., did not fix the amount to be paid to teachers in the public schools; and where there is no contract they can recover on a *quantum meruit*.[3] Under Md. act of 1872, ch. 377, sub. ch. 8, § 3, the principal of a public school is not exempt; and if he fails to make these reports, or to perform the duties of a teacher, he cannot recover the salary agreed to be paid him for his services.[4]

§ 247. **Teacher's compensation.**—A Boston teacher, elected annually and payable quarterly, if dismissed at end of quarter by committee, under acts 1844 and 1854, without misconduct on her part, cannot recover compensation for remainder of time.[5] Teacher cannot recover compensation for his services until he has completed the register required by act of 1849.[6] In Mass., the act of 1838 authorized the school committee to contract for teachers for the town and district schools, and they could bind the town to pay for them;[7] the power given to the school committee to contract with teachers, includes the power to determine their salaries; and the city council have no control except by voting to close a school after it has been kept the length of time required by law.[8] Payment of the teacher's wages by the town to the committee, does not discharge the town's liability to him.[9] Except in graded schools maintained

---

[1] Ferguson v. True, 3 Bush (Ky.) 255.
[2] Miahle v. Fournet, 13 La. Ann. 607.
[3] Offut v. Bourgeois, 16 La. Ann. 163.
[4] Sch. Comm'rs v. Adams, 43 Md. 349.
[5] Knowles v. Boston, 12 Gray (Mass.) 339.
[6] Jewell v. Abington, 2 Allen (Mass.) 592.
[7] Batchelder v. Salem, 4 Cush. (Mass) 599.
[8] Charlestown v. Gardner, 98 Mass. 587.
[9] Clark v. Great Barrington, 11 Pick. (Mass.) 260.

by districts, towns alone are liable for support of schools, and are liable for the teacher's compensation, in Me.[1] A teacher employed by a *de facto* agent may recover compensation for his services, but not for services rendered after notice of dismissal by school committee.[2] There should be no deductions for holidays from the teacher's wages,[3] or for closing school on account of small-pox;[4] and a teacher may sue district for compensation, although mandamus would lie to compel the treasurer to pay the warrant;[5] but issuing an order knowingly to an unlicensed teacher, subjects the officer to penalty in Minn.;[6] though act Miss., Mch. 15, 1884, does not relieve the county from the obligation to pay valid certificates which were not presented under the act, because they had been mislaid.[7] Warrants for the payment of teachers of both white and colored schools of the same district, are properly drawn upon the teachers' fund of said district, in Mo.[8]

§ 248. **Teachers' compensation.**—Where teacher left on being notified that he did not give satisfaction, he cannot recover for the remainder of the term, his leaving being construed as voluntary on his part;[9] but the neglect of parents to send their children to a given school cannot, of itself, affect the right of its teacher to compensation.[10] Where teacher, in Neb., has his certificate to teach in another county indorsed by the superintendent of the district, the school-district treasurer must pay him.[11] The teacher cannot lawfully be paid until he has made a report to the superintending committee, as required by statute;[12] and the school district may maintain an action against such com-

---

[1] Norton v. Soule, 75 Me. 385.
[2] Woodbury v. Knox, 74 Me. 462.
[3] Sch. Dist. v. Gage, 39 Mich. 484; Halloway v. Ogden S. D., 62 Mich. 153.
[4] Dewey v. Alpena Sch. Dist., 43 Mich. 480.
[5] Martin v. Elwood, 35 Minn. 309.
[6] Sch. Dist. v. Washington Co., 31 Minn. 533.
[7] Douglas v. Downing, (Miss.) 9 So. 297.
[8] State v. Thompson, 64 Mo. 26.
[9] Frazier v. Sch. Dist., 24 Mo. App. 250.
[10] Doyle v. Sch. Dist., 36 Ill. App. 653.
[11] State v. Grosvenor, 19 Neb. 494.
[12] Moultonborough v. Tuttle, 26 N. H. (6 Fost.) 470.

mitteeman, to recover back the money paid; the certificate of the superintending committee that a report is made, is not conclusive.¹ A teacher in N. J. is entitled to a mandamus to compel the trustees to pay the salary due him.² A teacher under contract with a *de facto* trustee can recover pay for services.³ Giving a note made to a teacher for wages earned in the employment of the district, is within the scope of power of trustees of a district.⁴ Under the by-laws of the board of education of New York city, mandamus will not lie to the board of education to pay the salary of a teacher alleged to have been wrongfully dismissed; relator's only remedy being to have his name put on the pay-roll, that his salary might be paid in the regular way.⁵ A teacher discharged before the end of the term sued the district trustee in the county court and was non-suited; the non-suit did not bar appeal from trustee to superintendents; an appeal could be taken to the superintendent, under laws of 1864, and the superintendent's decision was final, and the trustee, by submitting the case to the superintendent, without objection, waived a jury;⁶ and the trustee may be directed by the superintendent to issue a tax list and a warrant to collect sufficient to pay the claim, if he has not enough on hand.⁶ A school committee in N. C. are not personally liable on contracts made in the line of their duty, but mandamus is the remedy to compel them to give an order on the county treasurer.⁷

§ 249. **Teachers' compensation.** — The wrongful exclusion of a pupil from a school by a teacher, under the direction of the directors, does not defeat the right to wages.⁸ A township clerk cannot refuse to draw order for wages, on the

---

¹ Moultonborough v. Tuttle, 26 N. H. (6 Fost.) 470.
² Apgar v. Trs., 34 N. J. L. 308.
³ De Wolf v. Watterson, 35 Hun (N. Y.) 111.
⁴ Horton v. Garrison, 23 Barb. (N. Y.) 176.
⁵ People v. Bd. Ed., 15 N. Y. S. 308.
⁶ People v. Eckler, 19 Hun (N. Y.) 609.
⁷ Robinson v. Howard, 84 N. C. 151.
⁸ State v. Blain, 36 Ohio St. 429.

ground that the contract wrongfully stipulated for the exclusion of some pupils;[1] nor because refusal is made by order of the township board of education.[1] The board of education employed the plaintiff to teach a school in the district, which he did for three months without any notification from the local directors to desist; upon a refusal of the township treasurer, by order of the local directors, to pay the order given by the board for his wages, a mandamus would lie.[2] Mandamus is the proper remedy to compel a clerk of a school district to pay over money in his hands applicable to a warrant issued in favor of a teacher, for salary.[3] The board of public education of the city of Philadelphia had no power to appoint a superintendent of music.[4] Under the ordinance of councils, Mch. 4, 1861, Pa., a suit brought against the city by one of the teachers for her salary, before the adoption of scale of salaries, was prematurely brought, and could not be sustained;[5] and the discretion in board of controllers of public schools in Philadelphia, as to salaries of teachers, must be exercised in subordination to the appropriating power of the councils.[5] County commissioners had power to approve an account of a teacher of poor children, under the act of Apr. 4, 1794, in a township which refuses to accept the general school law.[6] Mandamus is the proper remedy for a teacher whose certificate is wrongfully withheld by the controllers.[7] In R. I., the town committee voted to not pay certain teacher's wages; on appeal, the commissioner of public schools decided they should be paid; the commissioner had no authority to draw an order on the treasury, but must certify his decision to the town committee.[8]

---

[1] State v. Blain, 36 Ohio St. 429.
[2] Case v. Wresler, 4 Ohio St. 561.
[3] Howard v. Bamford, 3 Oreg. 565.
[4] Perot v. Philadelphia, 11 Phila. (Pa.) 181.
[5] Phila. v. Johnson, 47 Pa. St. 382.
[6] Parker v. Lancaster Co., 1 Watts & S. (Pa.) 460.
[7] McManters v. Sch. Cont., 7 Phila. (Pa.) 23.
[8] Randall v. Wetherell, 2 R. I. 120.

§ 250. **Teacher's compensation.**—By custom, in N. C., school masters charge by the quarter; the defendant's children continuing over one quarter, he is liable to pay for two entire quarters.¹ The Tenn. act of 1870, as to payment of teachers by the county trustees, is not repealed by the act passed two days later.² Teachers cannot draw pay from public funds unless it is a public school.³ The Tex. act of 1883, allowing auditing of unpaid claims for teachers' services rendered between Sept. 1st, 1873, and Aug. 1st, 1876, is a substitute for the law in force; and where a school voucher was audited, for which a levy has been made, and it was not presented for six months, it was barred — and the act is not unconstitutional.⁴ The act of 1883, Tex., makes it the duty of the counties to pay the claims of the teachers that have been audited, and recovery may be had by assignee of such claim.⁵ After a teacher was dismissed she offered to accept $20, and the district voted to settle with her "if it could be done for $20," but they never communicated to her any acceptance of her proposal; the offer was not binding on the teacher.⁶ In a suit for teacher's salary it is improper to require him upon cross-examination to answer questions propounded, to test his competency, or to show that after his employment a remonstrance was circulated in his district, and signed by divers persons;⁷ and evidence that a majority of the voters in the district were dissatisfied with the plaintiff, and plaintiff and committee contracting knew this at the time the plaintiff was employed as teacher, is inadmissible.⁸ In Vt., a teacher did not forfeit her salary by neglect to answer the inquiries in the school register, and to certify to the correctness of

¹ Keckely v. Cummins, Harp. (S. C.) 267.
² Arrington v. Cotton, 57 Tenn. 316.
³ Ussery v. Laredo, 65 Tex. 406.
⁴ Parker v. Buckner, (Tex.) 2 S. W. 746.
⁵ Co. Caldwell v. Crocket, (Tex.) 4 S. W. 607.
⁶ Richardson v. Sch. Dist., 38 Vt. 602.
⁷ Doyle v. Sch. Dist., 36 Ill. App. 653.
⁸ Mason v. Sch. Dist. No. 14, 20 Vt. 487.

her record of the attendance and deportment of pupils; but she was liable for any loss to district which her neglect has caused.[1]

§ 251. **Teachers, contract.**—Under Me. act 1821, ch. 117, a school committee of three appointed by a district had no authority to hire a school master, that power being vested in the school agent;[2] and under the Ga. act 1881, giving mayor and council of B. power to employ teachers, the citizens cannot employ against will of the officers.[3] Where contract does not provide as to time, but the commissioners of the 16th section, Ala., agree to remunerate him with its "available funds" for one year, the inference is that he is to render service for that time and enter on his work in a reasonable time.[4] The trustee of a school district, disputing the legality of an adjourned school meeting at which his successor was elected, held over, and employed plaintiff as teacher; such acts were valid as those of an officer *de facto*.[5] A contract, in Wis., for teaching the district school for a term extending beyond the time when the term of office of its officers will expire, unless made contrary to a determination of the district at the previous annual meeting, under Rev. St., ch. 23, § 15, is valid, subject to the power of the district at its next annual meeting, or of the same officers or their successors, to end it by determining the length of time a school shall be taught in the district, and by whom.[6] Board of directors at end of their term cannot contract for teacher for ensuing year;[7] and in New Orleans a teacher cannot be employed in public schools for longer term than one year.[8] School directors in Ill. cannot employ teachers for a succeeding year without the annual reorganization of the board;[9] and in N. C. a

---

[1] Crosby v. Sch. Dist., 35 Vt. 623.
[2] Patterson v. Butler, 11 S. E. 399.
[3] Moor v. Newfield, 4 Me. (4 Greenl.) 44.
[4] Comm'rs v. Criswell, 6 Ala. 565.
[5] Barrett v. Sayer, 12 N. Y. S. 170.
[6] Webster v. Sch. Dist., 16 Wis. 316.
[7] Cross v. Sch. Dirs., 24 Ill. App. 191.
[8] Golden v. N. O. Sch. D., 34 La. Ann. 354; Sch. Dirs. v. Hart, 4 Ill. App. 224.
[9] Davis v. Sch. Dirs., 92 Ill. 293.

school committee have no power to employ teacher beyond their term of office.[1] "In the case of *Stevenson v. School Directors*, 87 Ill. 255, the decision was placed upon the ground that the meeting which chose directors determined what should be taught in the schools, and that it was a necessary inference that no contract could be made until it was known what service was to be contracted for."

§ 252. **Teacher, contract.**—An answer which alleges that the persons who signed plaintiff's contract were not duly elected and qualified school trustees, but mere usurpers, is demurrable when pleaded after a general denial, since it is only a special denial.[2] A contract, when signed by the teacher and one of the trustees, when the board was not in session, and afterwards approved at a special session of the board, and there signed by another trustee, is binding.[3] The admission of evidence concerning rumors in regard to the purpose of the board, and their intention not to permit plaintiff to teach, is not reversible error.[3] There is no law that forbids the school board to make a contract for a superintendent, for a term beginning after some members of the board go out of office.[3] A contract cannot be annulled by the subsequent action of the school town in abolishing the department in which teacher was engaged to teach.[4] Where trustees, with the acquiescence of the town, continue to act as such after the expiration of their term, and before their successors are appointed, they are officers *de facto*, and their contract with a teacher is binding.[4] Such contract cannot be assailed by subsequently-elected trustees, when it is not alleged that the teacher was a party to the fraud in effort to forestall them;[4] the

---

[1] Taylor v. Sch. C., 5 Jones (N. C.) L. 98; Stevenson v. Sch. Dirs., 87 Ill. 255.
[2] Town Milford v. Powner, 126 Ind. 528.
[3] Reubelt v. Sch. Town, 106 Ind. 480; Wait v. Ray, 67 N. Y. 38; Tappan v. Sch. Dist., 44 Mich. 500; Webster v. Sch. D., 16 Wis. 317.
[4] Sch. T. Milford v. Zeigler, (Ind.) 27 N. E. 303.

board of school trustees may bind the school town by a contract with a teacher, although the contract is not to be performed before the election of a new board.[1] In N. Y., a contract with teacher made by the sole trustee of a school district, extending beyond the trustee's term of office, was valid;[2] and the power of a school committee to contract with a teacher for a period longer than their own term of office, upheld.[3] The district. school board, Mich., need not wait for the annual meeting of district before hiring teacher for following year, though two of the members of the board go out of office at that time.[4] Assumpsit lies against the trustees of a school district for the wages of a teacher employed under a contract with their predecessors, whether funds are in the defendant's hands or not.[5] Contracts with teachers are binding on the successors of the trustees of the district.[6]

§ 253. **Teacher, contract.**—The provisions in the Mich. primary-school law, whereby the voters and the district board shall have full control of the schools during the entire school year, did not apply to graded schools and cannot affect any contract for teaching, made by the trustees before the year opened.[7] The prudential school committee, chosen in March, cannot interfere with a teacher engaged by the general committee of preceding year, under act of 1846, for that term.[8] A school district was bound by the contract of its prudential committee, although it extended beyond the official year of the committee, and the school district had neither authorized the prudential committee to enter into a contract extending beyond

---

[1] Sch. T. Milford v. Zeigler, (Ind.) 27 N. E. 303; Reubelt v. Sch. T., 106 Ind. 478.
[2] Gills v. Space, 63 Barb. (N. Y.) 177; Waid v. Ray, 67 N. Y. 36.
[3] Wilson v. East Bridgeport Sch. Dist., 36 Conn. 280.
[4] Cleveland v. Amy, (Mich.) 50 N. W. 293.
[5] Williams v. Keech, 4 Hill. (N. Y.) 168.
[6] Silver v. Cummings. 7 Wend. (N. Y.) 181.
[7] Tappn v. Carrollton Sch. D., 44 Mich. 500.
[8] Sch. D. v. Morse, 8 Cush. (Mass.) 191.

the official school year, nor authorized this term of school which he was employed to teach.[1] Under Rev. L. Vt., § 515, a committee elected in March might make contract for the ensuing school year, September to June.[2] Where *de facto* trustee contracts with a teacher, the election of a trustee *de jure* who ignores the contract, will not defeat the teacher's right to compensation for discharge by him.[3] Where statute Ala. enacts, "where but one school is supported, the commissioners shall have power to employ a teacher," etc., a teacher so employed need not allege there is but one school.[4] Mandamus is the remedy to restore a teacher to the position from which he has been removed wrongfully and unlawfully.[5] Two of three directors may contract at a meeting of which the third has had notice, and notice need not be given for regular meeting;[6] and this applies to a school-district committee.[7] A vote directing the committee not to employ a certain teacher, was inadmissible in evidence, where the notice of the district meeting was not sufficient.[8] If the district neglects to act, the committee are authorized to provide rooms and employ teachers at the expense of the district;[9] but if the district acts, the committee must conform to its action.[9]

§ 254. **Teacher, contract.**—That the plaintiff had miscalculated the amount due him, is not admissible evidence of incompetency.[10] Where not waived, a teacher's contract cannot be fulfilled by procuring a substitute, however competent.[11] In order to create a liability, under a contract provided for by the common-school law, the statutory requisitions must be complied

---

[1] Chittenden v. Waterbury, 56 Vt. 551; Mason v. Sch. Dist., 20 Vt. 487; Chaplin v. Hill, 24 Vt. 528; Waterbury v. Harvey, 56 Vt. 556.
[2] Chittenden v. Waterbury, 56 Vt. 551.
[3] O'Neil v. Battle, (Sup.) 15 N. Y. S. 818.
[4] Comm'rs v. Criswell, 6 Ala. 565.
[5] Kennedy v. Bd. Ed., 82 Cal. 483.
[6] Sch. Dist. v. Bennett, 52 Ark. 511.
[7] Wilson v. Waltersville, Sch. Dist., 46 Conn. 400.
[8] Wilson v. Sch. Dist., 44 Conn. 157.
[9] Gilman v. Bassett, 33 Conn. 298.
[10] Doyle v. Sch. Dist., 36 Ill. App. 653.
[11] Sch. Dirs. v. Hudson, 88 Ill. 563.

with.[1] The defendant wrote: "We have had a meeting of all the citizens of the place that are interested in a female school, and all are satisfied with Miss J., and are anxious to employ her, and are resolved to make her this proposition: we will guarantee to her the sum of $400 for one year," etc. The plaintiff accepted the proposition, and taught the school three months and ten days, when the parties separated by consent. The petition was filed for discovery of the names of the trustees and guarantors, and for payment; defendant was not liable; there was no contract shown, and the plaintiff's remedy was at law.[2] A teacher cannot hold a school district in N. H., liable for his wages, under a contract made with him by the prudential committee.[3] In an action to recover subscription in aid of a common-school fund, it is a good defense that the teacher admitted scholars not entitled to by law.[4] Employment of unlicensed teacher by trustee of school district, in N. Y., is illegal.[5] The Pa. statute of 1862, requiring names of all the directors and manner of voting for teacher to be recorded, is mandatory and must be strictly complied with, and cannot be supplied by other evidence.[6] The employment of teacher by committee of District No. 3, Chowan county, N. C., after acts 1883 and 1885, was unauthorized, this district having been put in hands of trustees.[7] Where the president of a board of school directors is authorized to employ teachers with the consent of the board, and one whom he employs by written contract begins teaching, with the knowledge of each member, the consent of the members will be presumed.[8] The trustee of a civil township, in Ind., as such, cannot employ a teacher, an action against such town-

---

[1] Cascade v. Lewis, 43 Pa. St. 318.
[2] Willie v. Price, 5 Rich. (S. C.) Eq. 91.
[3] Stebbins v. Sch. Dist., 16 N. H. 510.
[4] Chalmers v. Stewart, 11 Ohio, 386.
[5] Blandon v. Moses, 29 Hun (N. Y.) 606.
[6] Sch. Dist. v. Mercer, (Pa.) 9 A. 64.
[7] Skinner v. Bateman, (N. C.) 1 S. E. 539.
[8] Hull v. Ind. Dist., (Iowa) 46 N. W. 1053; 48 N. W. 82.

ship cannot be sustained,[1] and a civil township was not liable on a contract made by a township trustee with a common-school teacher.[2]

§ 255. **Teacher, contract.**—In Mich. a teacher cannot be employed by two members of the board without the concurrence of the third, and without any meeting of the board.[3] A contract with teacher, made by two members of the board, in absence of each other, and without knowledge of third, is not binding on district.[4] A contract made by two of three directors of a district, at a time different from the time fixed for regular meetings, and of which the third director had no notice, is not binding.[5] A contract between the president and secretary of board with teacher, is void; Pa. Acts 1862, p. 472, requires concurrence of the board.[6] Where statutory mode of contract is required to be by the board, a contract by individual members of board will not bind, and ratification will not make valid;[7] but the fact that the officers of the district were not together when the contract was signed, does not overcome the presumption that it had been authorized by the board at a meeting, as required by R. S. Wis., § 432.[8] The board of directors cannot waive the fact that the teacher is unfit or incompetent to teach; they should discharge him.[9] Where contract with teacher was for definite time unless discontinued by directors, a discontinuance for diphtheria is to be deducted from the time.[10] Section 28 of 1 Ind. Rev. Stat. 1876, p. 788, applied to the school trustees of cities and incorporated towns, as well as to the trustees of school

[1] Greensboro v. Cook, 58 Ind. 139.
[2] Harrison v. McGregor, 67 Ind. 380.
[3] Hazen v. Lerche, 47 Mich. 626.
[4] Aikman v. Sch. Dist., 27 Kas. 129.
[5] Sch. Dist. v. Bennett, (Ark.) 13 S. W. 132.
[6] Dennison Sch. Dist. v. Padden, 89 Pa. St. 395.
[7] Pa. L. Rod Co. v. Cass Bd. Ed., 20 W. Va. 360.
[8] Dolan v. Joint Sch. Dist., (Wis.) 49 N.W. 96).
[9] Sch. Dist. v. Maury, 53 Ark. 471.
[10] Goodyear v. Sch. Dist., 17 Oreg. 517.

townships.¹ A vote to discontinue the school and to pay her $17.50, "for teaching in sub-district," etc., was no ratification of contract made by sub-director without authority.² A trustee, employed as a teacher by the two others, vacates his office as trustee.³ No recovery can be had on contract to teach school, made with a sub-director, in Iowa, but not approved by the president of the board, unless approval is waived, and contract ratified;⁴ a contract with a teacher becomes binding upon a district township only when made by a sub-director and approved by the president of the board, under Iowa Code, § 1753.⁵

§ 256. **Teacher, contract.**—Contract in book, signed by assessor and director, but not at same time, and moderator consenting, is valid.⁶ Where the resolution is passed at a session of the board of school trustees, it is immaterial that the trustees signed the contract at different times.⁷ Where a township trustee pays teacher out of his own pocket, in good faith, and the school funds are insufficient, he may maintain an action for money so paid.⁸ Where one of the board signed the contract with a teacher, which was afterwards approved at a called meeting and signed by another member, it became binding;⁹ and where an order employing a teacher is passed at a session of the board of school trustees, it is immaterial that the trustees signed the contract at different times.¹⁰ In Iowa the discretion of directors to employ teacher for less than fifteen scholars will not be controlled by mandamus.¹¹ A township obtaining services of a teacher under claim of authority is estopped to deny its liability.¹² Although a contract did not comply with the

---

¹ Putnam v. Irvington, 69 Ind. 80.
² Herrington v. Liston Dist. Tp., 47 Iowa, 11.
³ Furguson v. True, 3 Bush (Ky.) 255.
⁴ Place v. Colfax, 56 Iowa, 573.
⁵ Gambrell v. Lenox, 54 Iowa, 417.
⁶ Holloway v. Ogden, 62 Mich. 153.
⁷ Sch. T. Milford v. Zeigler, (Ind.) 27 N.E. 303.
⁸ Kiefer v. Troy, 102 Ind. 279.
⁹ Logansport v. Dykeman, 116 Ind. 15.
¹⁰ Sch. T. Milford v. Zeigler, (Ind.) 27 N.E. 303.
¹¹ Ananson v. Anderson, 70 Iowa, 102.
¹² Heill v. Dist. Tp., 41 Iowa, 494.

statute requiring it to be in writing, (Iowa School Laws 1872, § 51,) the acceptance of part performance was a ratification, rendering the district liable.[1] While a sub-director is authorized to make contract with teachers, his authority is subject to the rules prescribed by board of directors, in Iowa.[2] A petition on teacher's contract, stating contract and certificate of qualification, is good on demurrer, and an action will lie on the same.[3] A school teacher, without written contract, is entitled to reasonable compensation from the district, in Kas.[4] Contract by district with teacher, reserving right to discharge him at any time he fails to give satisfaction, is valid.[5] Where moderator of district hired her husband to teach for more than a better teacher would charge, she could not be removed as moderator, under primary-school law, for that reason, in Mich.[6] Where two or three officers of a board are related to teacher, and others could have been hired for much less, this is not sufficient fraud to render the contract void.[7]

§ 257. **Teacher, contract.**—Where a contract, signed by the director of their school district, and teacher, and the moderator writes on it, "Approved," subscribing as moderator, it will be valid.[8] Where Minn. statute requires a contract with a teacher to be in writing, and where it is admitted that a majority of the trustees signed, it is proper to instruct the jury that where the necessary trustees signed, it would be a compliance with the law, and to leave the question as to whether there was a contract or not, to the jury;[9] signed by a majority at different times and filed with clerk is *prima facie* binding.[10] Although § 6 of Mo. Law 1865, allows the local directors to employ

[1] Cook v. North McGregor, 40 Iowa, 444.
[2] Potter v. Fredericksburg, 40 Iowa, 369.
[3] Hamrick v. Bd. Ed., 28 Kas. 385.
[4] Jones v. Sch. Dist., 8 Kas. 362.
[5] Sch. Dist. v. Colvin, 10 Kas. 283.
[6] Hazen v. Akron, 48 Mich. 189.
[7] Dolan v. Jt. Sch. Dist., (Wis.) 49 N.W. 960.
[8] Everett v. Sch. Dist., 30 Mich. 249.
[9] McGinness v. Sch. Dist., 39 Minn. 499.
[10] Armstrong v. Sch. Dist., 28 Mo. App. 169.

teachers, a teacher may sue the township board of education for a breach of the contract, under § 7.[1] Contract made by directors in accordance with statute is not to be avoided by district on account of want of funds.[2] Where directors close the school they cannot claim teacher has forfeited his contract by not making his reports during that time.[3] In Neb., a contract with teacher, made by director and treasurer of district, without knowledge of moderator, was valid.[3] A district cannot deprive the prudential committee of the power to provide board for teachers.[4] Where a teacher made a contract with a member of the district board, who paid her for teaching and boarded her, he could only contract on the credit of the school-money of the district and not on the credit of the district.[5] The authority conferred by statute upon local directors, to employ teachers, and certify the amount due them for services, cannot be controlled by any rule of the township board.[6] Where, at special meeting of school board that is called for other purposes, a quorum is present and a unanimous vote is had to employ a teacher, this will be sufficient, under Acts Pa. 1862.[7] In Pa. the board of directors may employ a teacher if not chosen by the inhabitants.[8]

§ 258. **Teacher, contract.**—A contract, in Tenn., for one year at so much per month, from Aug. 16, was held to begin at usual time for opening school and to end with usual time for closing, or when funds gave out.[9] In Tex., it was not intended that the county judge should approve the contracts in the community system, where the trustees make contracts with the teachers;[10] where county judge approves two copies of contracts

---

[1] Puterbaugh v. Tp. Bd. Ed., 53 Mo. 472.
[2] Rudy v. Sch. Dist., 30 Mo. App. 113.
[3] Russell v. State, 13 Neb. 68.
[4] Sch. Dist. v. Currier, 45 N. H. 573.
[5] Wheeler v. Alton Sch. D., (N. H.) 23 A. 89.
[6] State v. Wilcox, 11 Ohio St. 326.
[7] Genesee Ind. S. D. v. McDonald, 98 Pa. St. 444.
[8] Kingsley v. Sch. Dirs., 2 Pa. St. 28.
[9] Morley v. Ponver, 10 Lea (Tenn.) 219.
[10] Caviel v. Coleman, 72 Tex. 550.

and retains the third, he cannot afterward claim that he intended to approve them qualifiedly.[1] Where the school-house was burned, and no house was provided, and teacher was not discharged, etc., an action would lie for her wages for the full term;[2] and a teacher may recover where school-house is destroyed by fire and no other is furnished;[3] but it was held in Mo., that where teacher was hired for four months and the school-house burned down after two months had elapsed, the teacher could not recover compensation for the remainder of the time.[4] In Vt., the vote instructing the committee to hire a female teacher for the district, is advisory merely.[5] Defendant cannot avail itself of its refusal to certify that the register is returned, to defeat plaintiff's right of recovery for her services.[6] R. L. Vt., p. 515, provides that the prudential committee of a school district shall "appoint and agree with a teacher to instruct the school."[6] Where the school committee had left an order for $7.50 at boarding house for her services as teacher, which she took, but returned in two or three hours, saying that she did not accept it, she lost nothing by taking and returning.[7] An infant may contract with a school board to teach a school.[8] A contract by which the board declares, "We reserve the right to close the school at any time if not satisfactory to us," is unauthorized and inoperative.[9] A contract made between a teacher and the school-district clerk, in the name of the district, with the consent of the director or treasurer, is *prima facie* valid.[10]

§ 259. **Teacher, dismissal and discharge.**—After a teacher has been irregularly dismissed, his continuance in the

---

[1] Caviel v. Coleman, 72 Tex. 550.
[2] Cashen v. Sch. Dist., 50 Vt. 30.
[3] Sch. Dirs. v. Crews, 23 Ill. App. 367.
[4] Hall v. Sch Dist., 24 Mo. App. 213.
[5] Sch. Dist. v. Harvey, 56 Vt. 556.
[6] Cobb v. Sch. Dist., (Vt.) 21 A. 957.
[7] Richardson v. Sch. Dist., 38 Vt. 602.
[8] Monaghan v. Sch. Dist. No. 1, 38 Wis. 100; Cashen v. Sch. Dist., 50 Vt. 30.
[9] Tripp v. Sch. Dist., 50 Wis. 651.
[10] Webster v. Sch. Dist., 16 Wis. 316.

school, with the assent of a majority of the trustees, is a waiver of such dismissal.¹ In an action for services, evidence "that the said plaintiff was incompetent to manage the said school; that she was unreasonable in her requirements of the scholars in said school; and was uneven in her treatment of them, and partial and abusive in her treatment of certain ones in said school, and that she failed in all respects as a teacher of said school," was admissible.² An action on the case by a teacher will not lie against the school directors for removing her when they acted within the scope of their authority, unless malice and injury were the impelling motives.³ The certificate of school teacher as to morality is not conclusive, and the power to revoke a certificate does not prohibit or prevent the board of directors from terminating a contract on the ground of incompetency or gross immorality.⁴ "The delicate nature of the duty devolved upon the trustees, to see that unfit or incompetent persons are not put or kept in charge of the children who attend the common schools, forbids the idea of a trial with the formality and strictness that belongs to courts."⁵ The directors of a school district may undoubtedly discharge a school teacher for incompetency or neglect of duty.⁶ The trustees of a public school (N. Y.) may terminate the employment of the teacher at pleasure, and the only remedy is on the contract.⁷ The teachers of the city (of New York) are simply employés of the trustees.⁸ A teacher discharged by directors for incompetency, without a compliance with Iowa Code, § 1734, cannot sue for damages unless he has appealed, as required by § 1829, to the county superintendent.⁹ A teacher (Iowa) contracted to "faith-

¹ Finch v. Cleveland, 10 Barb. (N. Y.) 290.
² Holden v. Sch. Dist., 38 Vt. 529.
³ Burton v. Fulton, 49 Pa. St. 151.
⁴ Sch. Dist. v. Maury, 55 Ark. 47; McCutchen v. Windsor, 55 Mo. 149.
⁵ The People v. Bd. Ed., 3 Hun (N. Y.) 181.
⁶ Neville v. Sch. Dirs., 36 Ill. 71, 73.
⁷ Swartwood v. Walbridge, 57 Hun (N. Y.) 33.
⁸ The People v. Bd. Ed., 3 Hun (N. Y.) 179.
⁹ Kirkpatrick v. Ind. Sch. Dist., 53 Iowa, 585.

fully and impartially govern and instruct the children"; the sub-director had a right to dismiss her for a failure to control the school, even conceding that she was not unfaithful in the discharge of her duties.[1] If a teacher proves incompetent and unable to teach the branches of instruction he has been employed to teach, the trustees are authorized to dismiss him.[2] The trustees, before the time expired, paid the teacher to date, informing her that they no longer needed her services; for such violation of their contract the trustees were not personally and individually liable.[3]

§ 260. **Teacher, dismissal and discharge.**—A contract with teacher may be rescinded when he is charged with outrageous crimes.[4] The act (70 Ohio L. 195) gives local directors of schools authority to dismiss teachers for sufficient cause.[5] A district-school board has power to discharge a teacher for cause, notwithstanding employment for a certain time, (Neb. Gen. Stat. 968, §§ 45, 56.)[6] Permission to teacher for absence can only be given by the directors as a board.[7] Under N. J. Rev., p. 1076, dismissal of a teacher should be done at a meeting whereof all the trustees have had notice.[8] Teacher may be discharged for incompetency or neglect of duty;[9] the law only requires average qualification and ability, and the usual application to the discharge of his duties, to fulfill his contract.[9] The board undertaking to discharge an employé, could properly do so only after taking certain prescribed steps.[10] "Under the common law, the teacher would be subject to discharge if he failed to perform his duty in any material point."[11] In Mo., under

[1] Eastman v. Rapids, 21 Iowa, 590.
[2] Crawfordsville v. Hays, 42 Ind. 200.
[3] Morrison v. McFarland. 51 Ind. 206.
[4] Tingley v. Vaughn, 17 Ill. App. 347.
[5] Dirs. of Sub.-Sch. Dist. No. 7 v. Burton, 26 Ohio St. 421.
[6] Bays v. State, 6 Neb. 167.
[7] State v. Leonard, 3 Tenn. ch. 177.
[8] Townsend v. Sch. Trs., 41 N. J. L. 312.
[9] Neville v. Sch. Dist., 36 Ill. 71.
[10] Kirkpatrick v. Ind. Sch. Dist., 53 Iowa, 587.
[11] Tripp v. Sch. Dist., 50 Wis. 657.

R. S. 1879, § 7083, a teacher is to be removed by county commissioners for incompetency or immorality, and not by board of school directors.[1] Dismissal of teacher, under by-law of board that a majority may dismiss at will, is legal.[2] A teacher may be discharged for refusing to receive back a pupil whom he has suspended, and his action has been overruled by the directors.[3] Where directors may discharge teacher "for incompetency, improper conduct, or inattention to duties," notice must be given and trial had; and a notice that they would try the teacher's "fitness," is insufficient.[4]

§ 261. **Teacher, dismissal and discharge.**—Where the local directors of a subordinate district in good faith dismissed the teacher, because they claimed he had not been employed, they are not liable for damages.[5] A teacher may be removed by board of education, New York city, without cause asserted or notice given.[6] Pa. Acts 1854, authorized school directors to dismiss a teacher for incompetency, negligence and immorality, and where they dismiss for incompetency, in good faith, she could not recover salary on ground that it was without cause.[7] "If they [the board of trustees] were satisfied as to the relator's incompetency, their power to remove cannot be questioned;"[8] but the trustees of a school district have no power to dismiss a teacher holding the proper certificate, without cause, and against his consent, before the expiration of his contract.[9] A contract with teacher, with right of district to dismiss on one month's notice, enforced, and the district board may for incompetency or negligence from which the school suffers dismiss the teacher

---

[1] Arnold v. Sch. Dist., 78 Mo. 226; Armstrong v. Sch. Dist., 19 Mo. App. 462.
[2] McLellan v. St. Louis S. B., 15 Mo. App. 362.
[3] Parker v. Sch. Dist., 5 Lea (Tenn.) 525.
[4] Morley v. Ponver, 10 Lea (Tenn.) 219.
[5] Gregory v. Small, 39 Ohio St. 346.
[6] People v. N. Y. City Bd. Ed., 52 N. Y. Sup. Ct. 520.
[7] McCrea v. Sch. Dist., (Pa. Sup.) 22 A. 1040.
[8] The People v. Bd. Ed., 3 Hun (N. Y.) 185.
[9] Finch v. Cleveland, 10 Barb. (N. Y.) 290.

without any formal trial, and without the concurrence of the county superintendent.[1] In the absence of any direction to the contrary, by the district at a meeting, the board has power to discharge the teacher for just cause, before the expiration of his term.[2] Where other employment is obtained and wages amounting to as much as could be recovered under the first contract, are earned, nominal damages only may be recovered.[3] Where statute authorizes employment by board and removal at pleasure, and contract is made "at $30 per month during the term you shall teach," the board could discharge without giving notice or reasons for the same.[4] Where directors contract with teacher for a certain time, "provided he gives satisfaction," they have the discretion to discharge and are not bound by statutory requirements as causes for discharge;[5] and under a contract "that teacher should leave if the school was not satisfactory," dissatisfaction with her school, and not personal unpopularity, would be a reason for dismissal.[6]

§ 262. **Teacher, dismissal, etc.**—In a suit for school teacher's wages, "discharged for incompetency" is a good defense, even if no record is kept of the proceedings.[7] Under Mansf. Dig. Ark., pp. 6265, 6266, the school directors have power to remove a teacher for incompetency and for immorality; and the fact that the teacher has been duly licensed by the county examiner, and that the latter has failed to revoke the license, is not conclusive on the board as to the competency or morality of the teacher;[8] the fact that the board has tolerated the teacher's misconduct and inefficiency for a time does not operate as a waiver of its right to discharge him therefor.[8] The

---

[1] Armstrong v. Sch. Dist., 28 Kas. 345.
[2] Scott v. Joint Sch. Dist., 51 Wis. 554.
[3] Doyle v. Sch. Dist., 36 Ill. App. 653.
[4] Donavon v. Bd. Ed., (N. Y.) 47 Hun 13.
[5] Sch. Dirs. v. Ewington, 26 Ill. App. 379.
[6] Richardson v. Sch. Dist., 38 Vt. 602.
[7] Sch. Dist. v. McCoy, 30 Kas. 268.
[8] Sch. Dist. Ft. Smith v. Maury, 53 Ark. 471.

superintending school committee had no power to dismiss a teacher, unless for cause mentioned in act of 1821, ch. 117, § 3, and the cause of dismissal must be assigned;[1] in Me. under the act of 1834, ch. 129, § 3, two out of three members of the superintending committee have no power to dismiss a teacher without notice to the third member.[2] Under Ia. Code, p. 1734, a discharge by any other method than that prescribed, is wrongful;[3] and in an action for a wrongful discharge, evidence that there were good grounds for discharge is irrelevant, as that question is not involved.[3] Under Neb. act of 1866, a school board could remove teacher at pleasure, notwithstanding a contract for one year.[4] Under Wagn. (Mo.) Stat. 1243, § 7, the directors had no authority to dismiss a teacher unless for sufficient cause shown; and for forcibly dispossessing him of the school-house and wantonly obstructing him in the discharge of his duty, they would be liable to him in damages.[5] One cannot maintain a bill to have an appointee as school teacher removed in his favor;[6] and the question as to who is a legal teacher cannot be determined in an action to restrain one who assumes to act as such from interfering with the school.[7]

§ 263. **Teacher, dismissal, etc.**—In Cal., where teacher has city certificate and is elected to teach, the board of education cannot dismiss or reduce to lower grade except for causes stated in statute; and where statute that prevents removal of teacher was passed after election of a teacher, it will apply to such teacher.[8] When a teacher is discharged without cause before the close of a term, the district will be liable to him for

---

[1] Searsmont v. Farwell, 3 Me. (3 Greenl.) 450.
[2] Jackson v. Hampden, 16 Me. 184.
[3] Hull v. Ind. Dist. Aplington, (Iowa) 46 N. W. 1053; 48 N. W. 82.
[4] Jones v. Neb., 1 Neb. 176.
[5] McCutchen v. Windsor, 55 Mo. 149.
[6] State v. Leonard, 3 Tenn., ch. 177.
[7] Soldier Dist. Tp. v. Barrett, 47 Iowa, 110.
[8] Kennedy v. Bd. Ed., 82 Cal. 483.

damages.[1] Under Tenn. Acts 1873, ch. 25, § 20, sub-sec. 3, the right to dismiss a teacher already employed under a valid contract can be exercised only after notice and for cause.[2] Principal of normal school established under N. Y. Laws 1866 cannot be removed by superintendent of public instruction without assent of local board.[3] A reduction in rank and pay of a teacher to another and lower grade is same as a discharge; and this cannot be done in New York city by trustees of the ward, except by written approval of majority of district inspectors, and on appeal of board of education.[4] Some authorities hold that a teacher is entitled to a formal trial to determine as to incompetency, negligence, or injury to the district in retaining him.[5] Where a school teacher is discharged without cause, she may recover the amount of her wages according to her contract, unless she could have procured similar employment, the burden of proving which is on the board;[6] and an instruction where teacher had been improperly discharged imposing upon the plaintiff the burden of proving that he had tried and failed to get other employment, should not be given.[7] Regents of agricultural college making contract with teacher, of three months' mutual notice to quit, except in cases of gross misconduct, held liable for salary, when they discharge without notice and without cause;[8] and a teacher wrongfully dismissed is entitled to recover for the balance of the salary contracted for.[9]

§ 264. **Teachers' institutes.**—The duty of N. H. towns to pay for the support of teachers' institutes a sum equal to two per cent. of the amount required by law to be raised for the

---

[1] Scott v. Joint Sch. Dist., 51 Wis. 554.
[2] Morley v. Power, 5 Lea (Tenn.) 691.
[3] People v. Hyde, 89 N. Y. 11.
[4] In re Gleese, 50 N. Y. Super. Ct. 473; 67 How. (N. Y.) Pr. 372.
[5] Murdock v. Phillips Acad., 29 Mass. 244; Searmont v. Farwell, 3 Greenl. (Me.) 450; Morley v. Power, (Sup. Ct. Tenn.) 12 Cen. Law J. 540.
[6] Sch. Dist. v. Stilley, 36 Ill. App. 133.
[7] Doyle v. Sch. Dist., 36 Ill. App. 653.
[8] Bd. Regents v. Mudge, 21 Kas. 223.
[9] Ewing v. Sch. Dirs., 2 Ill. App. 458.

maintenance of the schools is imperative;[1] and mandamus may issue to compel the payment of the money by the selectmen to the school commissioners of the county.[1]

§ 265. **Teacher's liability.**—The teacher is not liable to an action by a parent for refusing to instruct his children.[2] A teacher may use such force as is necessary to take a pistol from his pupil.[3] A rule requiring tardy pupils to wait until opening exercises are over before entering the room is to be enforced with regard to health and physical condition of pupil, and depends upon each particular emergency;[4] whether a rule is reasonable is a question for the court, and a school officer is not personally liable for mere mistake of judgment.[5] Whether mandamus can be issued in any case to the teacher of a public school to compel him to reinstate a suspended pupil, is a question.[6] (See "Pupil," "Punishment," "Rules," etc.)

§ 266. **Term, time.**—In Mo. the power conferred on the annual meeting of school district to determine the length of school year applies to current year, and an annual meeting cannot order three months' school prior to commencement of school year, the school year having been changed by legislature.[7] Under the Iowa Code, § 1727, requiring school in sub-district twenty-four weeks in a year unless the county superintendent excuses, a resolution by directors for less hours is valid, although the superintendent's consent is obtained afterwards.[8]

§ 267. **Text-books, adoption.**—Act 1875, Cal., continuing text-books in use, was repealed by new constitution.[9] Each board of education in Cal. may adopt text-books as to its own

[1] Hall v. Selectmen, etc., 39 N. H. 511.
[2] Spear v. Cummings, 23 Pick. (Mass.) 224.
[3] Metcalf v. State, 21 Tex. App 174.
[4] Fertich v. Michener, (Ind.) 14 N. E. 68.
[5] Fertich v. Michener, (Ind.) 11 N. E. 605.
[6] State v. Burton, 45 Wis. 150.
[7] Matney v. Boydston, 27 Mo. App. 36.
[8] Herrington v. Liston Dist. Tp., 47 Iowa, 11.
[9] People v. Bd., 55 Cal. 331.

jurisdiction.¹ A meeting adopting text-books will be presumed to have been a regular meeting.² Reasonable notice is required, but it may be waived.² The Ind. statute of 1881 does not authorize a trustee to buy text-books for pupils; and the use of the same does not create any liability.³ The Ind. Const. makes it the duty of the legislature "to provide by law for a general and uniform system of common schools," and the standard of text-books and method of obtaining same is for the legislature, and not a matter of local power.⁴ Ch. 160, Md. act of 1865, provides a system for the state, and is operative in Baltimore, and vests in the state board of education the exclusive power and authority of selecting and prescribing the text-books to be used in that city.⁵ In Mass., under the act of 1826, school committees may purchase books and make themselves the creditors of the town.⁶ Minn. Laws 1877, ch. 75, "to provide uniform and cheap text-books for the public schools of Minnesota," is constitutional;⁷ the provisions of said ch. 75, as applicable to the common schools and school districts of the state, are not repealed by ch. 74, except so far as the same is affected by sub. 8, § 18, sub. 7, ch. 74, giving boards of education of independent school districts power to prescribe text-books.⁷ A resolution to adopt text-books, by Nev. state board, may be rescinded before adoption by school districts.⁸

§ 268. **Text-books, change.**—Where proposition to furnish text-books is accepted and time is not mentioned, evidence cannot show that a certain time was intended; and the law prohibiting changes in text-books in six years does not apply to cities; besides, changes could be made by unanimous consent of

¹ People v. Bd., 55 Cal. 331.
² People v. Faust, 32 Ill. App. 242.
³ Honey Creek Sch. Tp. v. Barnes, 119 Ind. 213.
⁴ State v. Haworth, 122 Ind. 462; Same v. Blue, 122 Ind. 600.
⁵ Sch. Comm'rs etc. v. State Bd. Ed., 26 Md. 505.
⁶ Hartwell v. Littleton, 13 Pick. (Mass.) 229.
⁷ Curryer v. Merrill, 25 Minn. 1.
⁸ State v. Nev. Bd. Ed., 18 Nev. 173.

board; and the fact that a contemplated change is contrary to a by-law is no difference where by-law can be changed by two-thirds vote.¹ Under 70 Ohio Laws 209, § 52, where certain text-books were adopted there could be no change for three years without the consent of three-fourths of members of board at a regular meeting, and mandamus would lie to compel use and prevent change.² In suit for mandamus to compel adoption of certain school-books, demand must be first made; plaintiffs must have identity of interests;³ and injunction to protect the interests of the public can only be granted at the instance of a public officer, and where certain patron desires to prevent the use of a certain text-book and compel the use of another, he must show legal adoption of the one desired, and damages from any change.⁴ Use illegally adopted may be enjoined by a private individual where those in use had been legally adopted, and the change would interfere with scholar's use;⁴ but injunction will not be granted to prevent school board adopting another reader, it not being shown that the first was legally adopted.⁴ The Mich. act of 1887 prohibiting change in text-books for five years, applies to city of Detroit, and after adoption and 6,000 copies received by the board, it could not reconsider the resolution adopting.⁵ Certiorari cannot lie to review change of text-books by board education, in Cal.⁶ The state board education in Cal. could not change the books once adopted as a part of a uniform series without giving six months' notice;⁷ and notice to change text-books by the publications in a newspaper as a matter of news, is not sufficient notice.⁷

[1] Ivison v. Bd. Sch. Comm'rs, 39 F. R. 735.
[2] State v. Columbus Bd. Ed., 35 Ohio St. 368.
[3] Dobbs v. Stauffer, 24 Kas. 127.
[4] Sch. Dist. v. Shadduck, 25 Kas. 467.
[5] Jones v. Bd. Ed. Detroit, 50 N. W. 309.
[6] People v. Bd. Ed., 54 Cal. 375.
[7] People v. State Bd. Ed., 49 Cal. 684.

§ 269. **Text-books, free.**—The school board of a city has no power to furnish text-books free unless authorized to do so by legislature.[1]

§ 270. **Text-book, German.**—Act Ind. Mch. 3, 1871, which transfers the control of the public schools of Indianapolis to the board of school commissioners, does not repeal or modify the law regulating the study of German;[2] and it is no reason for refusing to introduce German in a school that there are no funds therefor, when studies not required are pursued at a greater expense.[2] Under Rev. Stat. Ind. 1881, p. 4497, the parents of twenty-five children attending one school in a city may compel the introduction of German into the curriculum of such school, even in the lower grades.[2] The St. Louis board directors may require more than simply the rudiments to be taught.[3] The right, in union school districts of Mich., to levy taxes for high schools and to make free the instruction of children in other languages than the English, was sustained.[4]

§ 271. **Text-books, studies.**—There is nothing, either in state policy, or in constitution, or laws, of Mich., restricting the primary school districts of the state in the branches of knowledge which may be taught, or instruction that may be given, if the voters of the district consent, or to prevent instruction in the classics and living modern languages.[4]

§ 272. **Text-books, pupil.**—There is no implied contract between a teacher and a pupil in the public schools that the former shall teach the latter; so held, where a teacher refused to hear the pupil recite any lesson in any study unless he would procure a copy-book and take lessons in a certain system of pen-

---

[1] Bd. Ed. v. Common Council Detroit, (Mich.) 45 N. W. 585.
[2] Bd. Sch. Comm'rs v. State, (Ind.) 28 N. E. 61.
[3] Roach v. St. Louis S. B., 77 Mo. 484.
[4] Stewart v. Sch. Dist., 30 Mich. 69.

manship.[1] The failure of pupil to study one or more branches in the course, so long as the other branches are kept up, will not justify expulsion.[2] Under Ill. Rev. Stat., p. 962, § 48, empowering the township trustees, as to high schools, to direct what branches of study shall be taught, etc., the right of the parent to select the branches to be studied by the child, is only withdrawn to the extent that its exercise will not interfere with the system prescribed. No particular branch of study is compulsory on those who attend school;[3] so where trustees refused to admit a pupil who passed a satisfactory examination in all the studies except grammar, which his father did not wish him to study, any rule excluding the son from admission as to the other studies, on that ground, was unreasonable, and could not be enforced.[3] In Ill. a pupil cannot be expelled for refusing, by direction of parents, to pursue a branch of study assigned by the directors, but not prescribed by law.[4] The school trustees of a high school may prescribe the courses of study and text-books for the use of the school; the parent, however, has a right to make a reasonable selection from the prescribed studies for his child to pursue; and this selection must be respected by the trustees, as the right of the parent in that regard is superior to that of the trustees and the teacher.[5] A pupil may be excused, by parental objection, from pursuing certain studies.[6] Where a father had directed his child to pursue only certain studies selected from those required by law, and forbade the child to pursue a certain other study, and this was known to the teacher, such teacher was not authorized to inflict corporal punishment

---

[1] Stuckey v. Churchman, 2 Ill. App. 584.
[2] Trs. v. People, 87 Ill. 303; Morrow v. Wood, 35 Wis. 59; Perkins v. Bd., (Iowa) 9 N. W. Rep. 356; Rulison v. Post, 79 Ill. 567; Guernsey v. Pitkin, 32 Vt. 294.
[3] Lake View Sch. Trs. v. People, 87 Ill. 303.
[4] Rulison v. Post, 79 Ill. 567.
[5] State v. School District, (Neb.) 48 N. W. 393.
[6] Morrow v. Wood, 35 Wis. 59.

upon the child for the purpose of compelling it to pursue the study so forbidden by the father.[1]

§ 273. Text-books.—In the case of *Effingham, Maynard & Co. v. Olson*, May 1891, Kas. Sup. Ct., the court held: "The attorney for the defendant, in his brief in this court, claims that no sufficient bond under the statute was ever given. His language is as follows: 'The act providing for a uniform series of text-books (§ 5) prescribes that no text-books shall be prescribed in pursuance of the provisions of this act unless the publisher thereof shall first file with the county superintendent of public instruction a guarantee of its price and quality, and permanence of supply for five years, together with a good and sufficient bond for the faithful compliance with said guarantee, conditioned in such sum as the county text-book board shall determine and approve.' Now this is the allegation in the petition of the relator: 'That they executed a good and sufficient bond in the manner prescribed by law, and that said bond was conditioned that the said plaintiffs would furnish the books in accordance with the said guarantee and proposition.' Now it is absolute that this statute makes the execution of the bond and guarantee a prerequisite to the award; that no award shall be made until after the bond and guarantee are filed with the text-book board—and not only that, but until after its approval, and the amount shall be fixed and the bond approved by the text-book board.

"Now assuming that this was a *de facto* board: All the acts which it undertook to perform, so far as this bond is concerned, were absolutely void under the statute. The evidence shows that a committee was appointed to accept this bond and ap-

[1] Morrow v. Wood, 35 Wis. 59.

prove it, and that no definite amount was fixed except $10,000. That the board adjourned *sine die*, and that after this adjournment, this committee, composed of two members of the board and the county attorney, who was not a member of the board and who had no business there so far as we can learn from the statute, made and fixed the amount of the bond at $4,000, but failed to approve it so far as the bond itself shows, which is attached to the deposition of the defendant. The evidence shows, at least inferentially, that this committee undertook to approve this bond, but the board had adjourned and was '*functus officio*,' and that afterward this bond in its present condition was returned to the county superintendent of public instruction. No action of the board was ever taken approving the bond. Now then, the relators themselves have failed to comply with the plain requirements of the statute, and being in default, have no obligation resting upon them, cannot now ask the order of this court to issue the writ to compel compliance with the conditions of their award. The text-book board had no authority to delegate this power to a committee, not even of its own members. Whatever power or authority this text-book board had, had been conferred by the act itself, and they could take nothing by implication. This writ never issues in doubtful cases. (High's Ex. Legal Remedies, § 9.) And to warrant the court in granting the writ, all the facts must appear so clear that his right to the same cannot be doubted, and it will not be granted to compel the performance of an official act where substantial doubt exists as to the duty of the officer to perform it. (*Ex parte Barnwell*, 8 Rich. N. S. 264.)

"No reply to this portion of the defendant's brief has been made by counsel for the plaintiff. The statute (said § 5) evidently means that no text-book shall be prescribed or awarded until after the proper bond has been given. Of course the board might indicate what books it would prescribe, and then while the board is still in session or before it finally adjourns a proper bond to the satisfaction of the board could be given, and then the award would be made or become final. This was not done in the present case. The minutes of the meeting show that the board fixed the amount of the bonds at $10,000, and no other amount was mentioned, and then the board appointed a committee consisting of the president, secretary and attorney to draw up the bonds; but the board, according to the minutes, did not give authority to such committee to fix the amount of any bond, or to change the amount, or to pro-rate between bonds, or to approve any bond, or the amount thereof, or the security thereon. In fact, according to the minutes, no power was given to this committee except to 'draw up bonds.' The bond in all cases should be drawn up and presented to the board while it is in session or before it finally adjourns; but in this case it was not. The question whether the board could delegate its power to a committee is not fairly presented in this case, and we shall not decide it. Under the evidence in the present case we cannot say that the plaintiff company complied with the statutes in executing the required bond, and therefore we cannot say that it is entitled to a peremptory writ of mandamus to compel the county superintendent to perform an act which he is not required to perform unless such a bond has in fact been given."

§ 274. **Text-books.**—"Judge Cooley says that 'It is held competent for the state to contract with a purchaser to supply all the schools of the state with text-books of a uniform character and price.' (Const. Lim., 5th ed., 225, n. 1.) In *Curryer* *v. Merrill*, 25 Minn. 1, (33 Am. R. 450,) it was held that the state might purchase books and compel the patrons of the school to buy the books from its officers. The question was presented in *Bancroft v. Thayer*, 5 Sawyer, 502, in substantially the same general form as it is here, and it was held that a state may provide by legislation that a designated person shall have the exclusive privilege of furnishing all the text-books needed for the use of the public schools. This decision was made upon the constitution of Oregon, which is very similar to ours, and the right to make such a contract is referred to the police power, the court saying: 'To authorize and provide that, by means of contract or legislative grant, a particular person or persons shall have the exclusive right to do or furnish a particular thing, upon certain conditions, for the use and convenience of the public, has always been a common mode of exercising the police powers of the state.' In *State ex rel. v. State Board of Education*, 18 Nev. 173, the power of the legislature to require the adoption and use of the books of a designated publisher was assumed to exist by court and counsel, and this is true of the case of *People ex rel. v. State Board of Education*, 55 Cal. 331. The court held in *People ex rel. v. State Board of Education*, 49 Cal. 684, that 'the decision of the state board of education as to the textbooks that should be used was final, and must be obeyed by all of the local boards and officers. These authorities, and those to which we have heretofore referred, seem to us to so conclusively settle the question as to leave no room for debate.'"

§ 275. **Text-books.**—In *Jones v. Bd. of Ed. of Detroit*, 50 N. W. Rep. 309, it was held: "Act Mich. 1887, No. 165, § 15, provides that when school boards have adopted text-books they shall not be changed for five years without the consent of a majority of the voters of the district, and that the act shall apply to all schools, including those in cities. *Held*, that the act applies to the city schools of D., though organized under special act Feb. 24, 1869, which conferred on the school board of D. 'full power and authority to make by-laws and ordinances in relation to the regulation of its schools, and the books used therein.' The fact that such special act made no provision for an annual meeting of the voters of D., fails to show the intention of the legislature to not make the general law applicable to the schools organized under the special act.

"As the power to adopt text-books was conferred by act Mich. 1887, No. 165, on school boards, a rule of the school board of the city of D., fixing a time for the reconsideration of a resolution adopting a certain text-book, cannot affect such resolution.

"After the school board of the city of D. had adopted a certain text-book, and 6,000 copies of it were received by the school superintendent and sold to patrons of the school, the board had no right to reconsider the resolution adopting such book. . . .

"The respondent provided by rule that a motion to reconsider shall be in order only at the same or first subsequent meeting; and no resolution shall be acted upon at the meeting at which it is introduced if objected to by any member, but shall lie upon the table, to be taken up as unfinished business at the next or any subsequent meeting. As above shown, action was taken, and the board adjourned; the publishers of the book adopted and the patrons of the school had acted upon it. We think, under these circumstances, the board had no
—20

power to reconsider its action. The power to adopt text-books is conferred by the law, and cannot be affected by any rule of the board fixing a time for the reconsideration of motions and resolutions. (*State v. Board of Education*, 35 Ohio St. 368; *State v. State Board of Education*, 18 Nev. 173, 1 Pac. Rep. 844.) We have not before us a case where the motion to reconsider was carried before the publishers and patrons of the schools had acted upon the faith of the resolution originally adopted, and upon that we express no opinion. The writ must issue as prayed."

§ 276. **Text-books.**—In the case of *State v. Bd. Ed.*, 35 Ohio St. 368, it was held: The city of Columbus, in the state of Ohio, is a school-district of the first class. On the 15th of July, the committee on text-books condemned the Cornell series, which had been adopted more than three years previous, and recommended a part of the Eclectic series. On the 12th of August, at a regular meeting, a proposition was received from D. & P., offering Harper's geographies for the schools. The report was then amended, substituting Harper's geographies for the Eclectic series, and this was adopted, and the board adjourned — there being no motion to reconsider. On the 26th of August, the board, by a vote of six to five, attempted to reconsider its action on the 12th of August, and six of the eleven members claimed that this left the Cornell series as text-books. In an action to compel the board to use Harper's geographies, it was held that the action of the board on the 12th of August was the adoption of Harper's geographies as text-books, and that such text-books could not be changed within three years from that date without three-fourths of the members of the board consentant at a regular meeting; and the action of a mere majority on the 26th of August did not affect the action on the 12th, and the board was compelled by mandamus to allow the use of Harper's geographies.

§ 277. **Text-books.** — In the case of *The State v. State Board of Education*, 18 Nevada, 173, it was held: "The state board of education may, after it has passed a resolution prescribing a certain series of text-books, reconsider its action and rescind such resolution at any time before the adoption of such books by the different school districts. . . .

"We shall concede, for the purposes of this decision, that on the first day of December, 1879, respondent, the board of education prescribed Appleton's Readers as text-books for the public schools of this state, and that, if it did not have power to reconsider its action then had, it is now its duty to cause those readers to be adopted and used in the public schools for the period of four years. *State v. Bd. Ed. of The City of Columbus*, 35 Ohio St. 368, is cited by counsel for relator as being a case on all fours with this, and we are urged to follow the decision there made as authority here. . . . The reason why the Ohio court said the board could not reconsider its former vote or adoption was because the statute prohibited further action for three years after August 12th, the time of adoption. There is no semblance of such prohibition in ours. Here, text-books cannot be changed oftener than once in four years. There, they could not be changed within three years after their adoption, and the action of the board alone constituted an adoption. Under our law it is the board's duty to prescribe and cause to be adopted a text-book in reading. . . . The board's duty is to prescribe and cause to be adopted a uniform series of text-books. The statute makes the last duty as imperative as the first. The complaint made in this case is that the board fails to cause the adoption of text-books by it prescribed. By prescribing a text-book simply, the board's duties are only half done. It must also see that the prescribed book is adopted; and thereafter, for four years, it cannot be changed. This is the sensible view of the statute. The law declares no means by which the board shall cause the adoption of text-books; but, the duty being enjoined, a power is given to use such reasonable means as are necessary for its proper performance. By a judicious exercise of this power the board need not experience much difficulty in performing their entire duty. We find no fault with the Ohio decision under the statute there in force. We only say that, under ours, it is not in point. Counsel for relator refers also to *People v. State Bd. Ed.*, 49 Cal. 684, where it is held that the board could not change text-books once adopted as a part of a uniform series without giving six months' notice as required by law. The question there decided is not involved in this proceeding, but an examination of the statute there referred to shows a marked difference between it and ours. The eighty-eighth section of the Cal. Stat. provided that the state board of education should *prescribe and adopt* a uniform series of text-books, and that any books once adopted in the state series should be continued in use for four years. Indeed, the substance of the statute is that, when the board once adopts a text-book, it shall not thereafter change the same for four years. (See Stat. Cal. 1869, 1870, p. 847.) There, as in Ohio, the board alone adopts the text-books, and thereafter they cannot be changed for the period stated, except in Ohio, by consent of three-fourths of all the members at a regular meeting, while here, after the board prescribes the book, the district must adopt it as directed by the state board; and until both are done, there is no change in text-books in the sense of our statute."

§ 278. **Text-books.**—In the case of *Board of Education of the City of Detroit v. Common Council of Detroit*, N. W. Rep. 45, (Mich. 585,) it was held: ". . . We must therefore determine whether the item for free text-books is legal. It has never been claimed, so far as we are aware, that school boards had the power to furnish free text-books except by virtue of special legislation. That this has been the common understanding is evidenced by the fact that this power has been specially conferred upon some municipal corporations, and the policy of its general adoption has been discussed in the legislature, and bills have been introduced for that purpose. Such a bill was passed in 1889—act No. 147, Pub. Acts 1889. By § 6 of this act it is provided that school districts in cities organized under special charters shall be exempt from the provisions of the act unless the boards are authorized to proceed under it by a majority vote of the qualified electors of such districts. No such vote has ever obtained, and the relator has taken no steps to submit the question to a vote of the electors. Its action, therefore, in providing for free text-books, was absolutely void. But whether the common council properly exercised its power, or not, is in fact immaterial. The writ of mandamus cannot be invoked to assist in the enforcement of a claim which is illegal. The writ must be denied, with costs to the respondent."

§ 279. **Text-books.**—In the case of *Western Publishing House v. Dist. Tp. of Rock*, (Iowa,) 50 N. W. Rep. 551, it was held that "In an action on contract, the complaint showed that plaintiff made a contract with the members of defendant school district board of directors for the sale of eight copies of a certain book published by plaintiff for a price named, and specifying the manner of shipment to the president of the board; that 'the members of the board' agreed to pay for the same; that plaintiff was to take in payment an order on the treasurer of the township; that afterward, at a regular meeting of the board, a vote was passed to ratify the purchase of the books; that afterward, at the regular annual meeting of the electors of the township, the board was authorized to place a copy of the book in each of the sub-districts in the township; that afterward, at a regularly called meeting of the board, a resolution was adopted repealing the ratification of the contract; that the books were shipped in accordance with the order, and were yet in the express office, awaiting the acceptance of defendant. *Held*, that the contract alleged did not purport to be a contract of, or binding on, defendant, or that the alleged purchase was made for the use of defendant, or pursuant to its authority or order.

"Since the contract declared on did not bind defendant, it could not ratify it, as a ratification would create a contract other than the one declared on. . . .

"A consideration of the agreement upon which plaintiff bases its right to recover, discloses the fact that it does not purport to be the contract of the defendant, the school district, and that there is not one word in it indicating the purpose of the directors to bind the district, or the intention of plaintiff to require it to be bound by the agreement. The obligors in the instrument described themselves as directors of the school district; but it does not appear that the goods sold were bought for the use of defendant, or pursuant to its authority or order. It is stipulated in the contract that the goods shall be shipped to the directors, not to defendant or its officers. On the face of the instrument it is plainly shown that the persons who signed the instrument, and who are designated therein as 'directors,' are alone bound by it as obligors. Plaintiff agrees in the instrument to accept in payment an order or warrant issued by defendant, but this stipulation does not bind it to look to defendant for payment, or make the instrument its contract. Upon the face of the instrument the defendant is not bound, and the intention clearly appears to bind the signers individually. The petition does not allege or show that defendant is bound by·the contract, or was intended by the parties to be bound. It specifically alleges that the 'members [of the board of directors] agree to pay for the books.' It alleges that the books were 'ordered by said members of said board of directors for the use and benefit of defendant in its schools.' It is not alleged that the contract was made pursuant to any prior order, request, or authority of defendant; and it is averred that the books 'are now' in the express office, thus showing and averring, negatively, that the goods have never come into possession of defendant, and have never been used in its schools.

"The plaintiff, while inferentially conceding that the contract was made without authority, insists that it was afterwards ratified. But, as the contract did not purport to bind defendant, it could not ratify it. There is no such thing as the ratification of a contract by an obligor made by another, when it does not purport to bind him but binds the other. In such a case the obligor cannot be bound by a ratification. He can only become bound by a new contract assuming or adopting the obligation of the prior one. If it be assumed that the defendant did adopt the contract, (which is not alleged in the petition,) it must appear what the terms of the contract adopting it are, and that they have been performed. But no such showing is made in the petition.

"If the action of the board of directors of March 11th be regarded as the adoption of the individual contract of the directors, it does not appear that plaintiff assented to or accepted it at any time. Nor is it shown that defendant acquired the right under such adoption, by the assent of the plaintiff, to take the property. It is not shown that plaintiff in any way accepted such adoption of the contract so as to bind the defendant. Until that was done, it could withdraw its adoption of the contract, which it did do by the resolution and action of its board of directors in their meeting of March 18, 1889.

"We reach the conclusion that the contract was not intended to bind defendant, and therefore was not ratified by it, and that, if the act claimed to be a ratification may be regarded as a contract of adoption, it was rescinded before it was accepted and plaintiff acquired thereby any rights by reason of such adoption. These considerations lead us to the conclusion that the judgment of the district court ought to be affirmed."

§ 280. **Title, property.**—The legislature may provide for change in trusteeship of property where town succeeds township, etc.[1] A lease during the time the land is occupied for school purposes is not contrary to statute requiring conveyances for school purposes to be in fee or ninety-nine year lease.[2] Where a bequest was being properly administered, there was no necessity to appoint special trustees.[3] In Minn., the title to land of a district is in the district, and not in trustees, and they cannot of themselves make a mortgage without authority.[4] . . .

[1] Allen Sch. Tp. v. Macy Sch. Tp., 109 Ind. 559.
[2] Delhi Sch. Dist. v. Everett, 52 Mich. 314.
[3] Myers v. Sch. Trs., 21 Ill. App. 223.
[4] Sanborn v. Sch. Dist., 12 Minn. 17.

§ 281. **Town corporation.**—Under Sayles' Ann. St. Tex., art. 541, authorizing "towns and villages" to incorporate for school purposes only, a tract of twenty-eight square miles, not more than two of which are a town, cannot be incorporated as a town for school purposes only.[1]

§ 282. **Town-site, constitution.**—A statute granting unclaimed lots to Denver for use of schools is void.[2]

§ 283. **Treasurer.**—(See "Officer, Liability.") Treasurer's books and reports are not conclusive evidence against him.[3] Suit against school treasurer, for moneys not paid over, not error to refuse evidence of his private account book, there being no evidence that the report required each year had not been made.[4] In a suit on school treasurer's bond, it is not a defense to say he had loaned money to a contractor for building school-house, and had an order from the contractor on the board for amount of loan;[5] and where he deposits money of a district in a bank on his own responsibility or without law requiring same, and the bank fails, he must lose and not the district.[6] The action by the school trustees on the bond of the township treasurer, under Ill. Rev. Stat., ch. 122, §§ 40, 55, for neglecting to pay over moneys to his successor, would be permitted whether the apportionment required by § 34 has been made among the several districts or not.[7] An action on school treasurer's bond should be in name of district.[8] School treasurer may qualify after twenty days from election, having sufficient cause for failing to do so within time, in Kas.[9]

§ 284. **Trespass, tax, &c.**—A school district in Minn. is liable in trespass for taking private house for school purposes,

---

[1] State v. Edison, (Tex.) 13 S. W. 263.
[2] City of Denver v. Kent, 1 Col. 336.
[3] Saville v. Sch. Dist., 22 Kas. 529.
[4] Hinton v. Sch. Dist., 12 Kas. 573.
[5] Snyder v. Bd. Ed., 16 Kas. 542.
[6] Sch. Dist. v. Carson, 10 Kas. 238.
[7] Sch. Trs. v. Stokes, 3 Ill. App. 267.
[8] Coffman v. Parker, 11 Kas. 9; Armstrong v. Durland, 11 Kas. 15.
[9] Carpenter v. Titus, 33 Kas. 7.

under Laws 1861.[1] The school authorities may exclude from their grounds anyone who enters to disturb the peace, or interfere with the exercises of the school; beyond that they cannot exclude some from exhibitions to which all the public are invited.[2] Trespass lies against a collector who collects money by distress, under a warrant by the selectmen of the town in which the school district was situated, to collect the money voted to be raised by the district, when its limits had not been defined by a legal vote of the town.[3]

§ 285. **Truant.**—Pub. St. Mass., ch. 48, § 14, provides for the establishment of a county truant school on the requirements of three "towns," and also for the establishment of a union truant school for different counties when required by a stated number of "towns or cities." *Held*, that the word "town," in the first part of § 14, must be construed to include cities;[4] and the Mass. statute requiring county commissioners to establish truant schools when required, is mandatory and not discretionary;[5] and the legislature has the power to establish reformatory and industrial schools, and commit certain classes of vagrant pauper children to them.[6]

§ 286. **Truant school.**—*City of Lynn v. County Commissioners*, 26 N. E. Rep. (Mass.) 409, Knowlton, J., it was held: "Pub. St. Mass., ch. 48, § 14, provides for the establishment of a county truant school on the requirements of three 'towns,' and also for the establishment of a union truant school for different counties when required by a stated number of 'towns or cities,' Pub. St., ch. 3, § 3, cl. 23, provides that the word 'town' may be construed to include cities. The first part of § 14 is derived

---

[1] Gould v. Sub-Dist., 7 Minn. 203.
[2] Hughes v. Goodell, 3 Pittsb. (Pa.) 364.
[3] Johnson v. Dole, 3 N. H. 328.
[4] City Lynn v. Co. Comm'rs, (Mass.) 26 N. E. 409.
[5] City Lynn v. Co. Comm'rs, 148 Mass. 148.
[6] Milwaukee Ind. Sch. Dist. v. Supervisors, 40 Wis. 328.

from St. 1873, ch. 262, § 5, in which the words used were 'cities or towns,' and in the revision the commissioners omitted the word 'cities.' Their first report did not contain the last part of § 14, which was derived from St. 1881, ch. 144, and incorporated in the report by an amendment in which the words 'cities or towns,' were retained as in the original act. *Held*, that the word 'town,' in the first part of § 14, must be construed to include cities.

"By Pub. St., ch. 3, § 3, cl. 23, it is provided that, in the construction of statutes, 'the word town may be construed to include cities.' If this provision is applicable to the word 'towns,' as used in the first part of § 14, of Pub. St., ch. 48, the cities of Lynn and Haverhill are to be counted as having required the county commissioners to establish a truant school, and the votes of Beverly and Danvers to rescind their former votes are immaterial, and a peremptory writ of mandamus must be issued. Reading Pub. St., ch. 48, § 14, as if it were a single enactment, the use of the word towns alone in the first part of the section, and of the words 'cities or towns,' in a similar connection in the last part of the section, creates an ambiguity, and raises a doubt whether a distinction was not intended between the method of requiring the establishment of a county truant school under the first part of the section, and of a union truant school for different counties under the last part of the section. But upon considering the history of the legislation the whole matter becomes clear. The first part of the section is a re-enactment of St. 1873, ch. 262, § 5, in which the words used were 'cities or towns,' and the commissioners, without intending to change the meaning, and evidently with a view to conciseness, omitted the word 'cities' as unnecessary. Their first report to the legislature did not contain the last part of § 14, Pub. St., ch. 48, and this was derived from a subsequent enactment of the legislature, (St. 1881, ch. 144,) and incorporated into their report by an amendment. In this amendment the words 'cities or towns' were retained as found in the original act. We are of opinion that the word 'towns,' in the first part of the section, includes cities, and that if the towns of Beverly and Danvers could effectually rescind their action, after having joined with other towns in requiring the county commissioners to establish a truant school, which we do not intimate, there are still more than three cities and towns continuing in the requirement, and the order must be, peremptory mandamus to issue."

§ 287. **Trust, etc.**—The act of Neb. 1869, donating Capitol square to the city of Omaha, "that the said property shall be used by said city for the purpose of a high school, college, or other institution of learning, and for no other purpose whatever," does not include the mere primary department; "high school" may be defined as a school where the higher branches of a common-school education are taught; the substitution of the board of education for the board of regents of the high school, by act of 1871, did not change the trust.[1] The boards of trustees for common schools in the wards of the city of New York are corporations to the extent of holding property for school purposes.[2] Where land was dedicated by the owner, partly for a burial-place and partly for a school-house lot, in default of the appointment of trustees by the donor the management of that part dedicated to school purposes would devolve upon the school directors.[3] Where there is a dedication of land for a school-site, the former owner, after the lapse of twenty

[1] Whitlock v. State, (Neb.) 47 N. W. 284.
[2] Betts v. Betts, 4 Abb. (N. Y.) N. Cas. 317.
[3] Pott v. Sch. Dirs., 42 Pa. St. 132.

years, was required only to make to the school trustees such a deed as would confirm that dedication.[1] The McIntire fund, given to establish "a school in the town of Zanesville, for the poor children of said town," is not limited to that locality which constituted the town corporate of Zanesville at the decease of the testator, but should be administered for the benefit of poor children in the town of Zanesville, according to the most general and popular sense of the term.[2] Where the donor of a site, after his offer had been accepted by the district and the building commenced, filed a deed limiting the use to white children only, with a forfeiting clause, it was held that the forfeiting clause could not be added.[3] When real estate is conveyed for school purposes expressed in the deed, the directors and trustees will have no right to sell the land and apply the proceeds to school purposes.[4]

§ 288. **Universities, colleges, etc.**—The charter of a state university may be altered, amended or repealed at pleasure;[5] and where a college is founded exclusively by private benefactors, it does not make it a public institution by being chartered;[6] and the state is not authorized to dispose of its lands where it is claimed that a condition has been broken.[7] The Board of Education of Illinois, under act of 1857 for establishment of a normal university, is a private eleemosynary institution, and not a public corporation.[7] In Ind. each county has the right to send two students free to the Indiana University, and to the law department as well as to the others.[8] Under the act of 1650, the property of Harvard College not exceeding £5,000

---

[1] Wilson v. Sch. Dirs., 81 Ill. 181.
[2] Zanesville Canal etc. Co. v. City of Zanesville, 20 Ohio, 483.
[3] Price v. Sch. Dirs., 58 Ill. 452.
[4] Sch. Trs. v. Braner, 71 Ill. 546.
[5] University of Ala. v. Winston, 5 Stew. & P. (Ala.) 25; University v. Maultsby, 8 Ired. (N. C.) Eq. 257.
[6] Dartmouth College v. Woodward, 4 Wheat. 518; Allen v. McKeen, 1 Sumn. 276.
[7] Board v. Bakewell, 10 N. E. 378; Board v. Greenbaum, 39 Ill. 610.
[8] McDonald v. Hagins, 7 Blackf. 525.

should be exempt from taxation; it was to be exempt until its value exceeded £5,000 a year. During that time the lessee of a farm owned by the college is not liable to be taxed for the farm in town or county taxes.[1] A college has no right to a professor's private literary manuscripts, although the college has aided him, by reason of its facilities, in the preparation of said manuscripts.[2] The Cornell University, of N. Y., under its charter, has no power to take or hold property valued more than $3,000,000 in the aggregate;[3] and it is entitled to income of the congressional agricultural fund under the act of 1862; and the trustees are entitled to the income without any deduction.[4] Where a professor has been advertised in a catalogue of a university, is connected with the institution, and has performed services, this proves a contract, although there is no formal resolution regarding it.[5] Where a student complies with all the regulations of the college, passes examination, and pays the fees, the college cannot refuse to permit him to take a final examination.[6] Where a college charter provides that the entire management shall be in a board of trustees, who may make rules and by-laws for the government thereof, and to appoint a faculty, the trustees have certain judicial powers, and they would not be compelled to reinstate a pupil who is dismissed without a hearing, where it is not shown that he had applied for a hearing.[7] Brown University, of R. I., having been established for the purpose of agricultural and mechanical arts, by the state, is entitled to receive money under the act of congress Aug. 30, 1890, making appropriations for the benefit of agricultural and mechanical arts.[8] Where a medical society was

[1] Hardy v. Waltham, 7 Pick. (Mass.) 108.
[2] Peters v. Bourat, 24 Abb. (New Cas.) 1.
[3] In re McGraw Estate, 111 N. Y. 66.
[4] People v. Davenport, 117 N. Y. 541.
[5] Tyler v. Tualtin Academy etc., (Or.) 13 Pac. 329.
[6] People v. Belvue Hospital College, 14 N. Y. S. 490.
[7] Dunn's Case, 9 Pa. Co. Ct. Rep. 417.
[8] In re Agricultural Funds, (R. I.) 21 A. 916.

incorporated with power to organize a college, which it did, and the college afterwards became specially chartered by the legislature, the act of incorporation of the college was void;[1] and where a college is incorporated its trustees may sue by the corporate title, without setting out their individual names.[2]

§ 289. **Universities, colleges, etc.**—In the case of *Elsberry v. Seay*, 83 Ala. Rep. 614, it was held: "The Alabama University for the Colored People, as established by the act approved February 27th, 1887, (Sess. Acts 1886–7, p. 198,) being under the exclusive control and management of a board of trustees appointed and selected as therein provided, and not subject to the supervision of the state superintendent of education, in whom is vested the general supervision of the public schools as established and regulated by constitutional provisions, cannot be regarded as one of these public schools; and the sums appropriated by said act for the purchase of lands, the erection of buildings, and the annual support and maintenance of the university, being 'set apart and appropriated from the school fund for the education of the colored people,' which is an unauthorized perversion of the funds from their only proper use, such appropriations are unconstitutional and void; and the other parts of the enactment being incapable of operation, without the aid of these unconstitutional provisions, the entire act is void.—A bill being filed by citizens and tax-payers to enjoin the further payment of moneys out of the state treasury in aid of the Alabama colored university, on the ground that the act establishing it is unconstitutional, the several trustees of the institution, the governor in his official capacity, the state superintendent of education as one of the trustees, but not officially,

---

[1] State v. Heyward, 3 Rich. (S. C.) 389.

[2] Legrand v. Hampden Sydney College, 5 Munf. (Va.) 324.

and the state treasurer, are all properly joined as defendants. . . .

"The constitutional system of common schools must extend throughout the state, and must afford equal benefit to all the children thereof within the specified years. The general assembly is without authority to establish a system of common schools which does not possess, in its entirety, these distinguishing features. It is more than a presumption, that the term public schools was employed in the constitution in its popular meaning and sense, the system of public schools to which the people of the state had been accustomed, and as they would understand it, in adopting the constitution. As we have said in another case, the system of public schools commanded to be established, organized, and maintained, was intended to operate upon, and in favor of all the children equally, without special local privileges to any. (*Schultes v. Eberly*, 82 Ala. 242.) . . .

"The act in question not only does not purport, but negatives the idea, that the university thereby established should constitute a part of the system of common schools. It establishes a university, with the implied privileges and powers appertaining to such institutions of learning, and as contradistinguished from high schools, and even colleges. It is not subject to the supervision of the superintendent of education, in whom the constitution vests the supervision of the public schools. It provides for the appointment of trustees, who are empowered to elect a faculty, and such officers and agents as they may deem necessary; to discharge any member of the faculty or officer or agent, at their pleasure; to prescribe their duties, and fix their compensation; and generally, to govern and control the faculty and the university, 'so that the students therein may be taught in the best manner possible the things they are to live by, preferring always the English language and the industries, to an education for culture only.' The act authorizes the trustees, in the event no suitable lands or buildings are given for the location of the university, to buy not exceeding forty acres of land, and for the purpose of buying the land and erecting suitable buildings thereon, appropriates the sum of ten thousand dollars, payable on the order of the governor, in amounts and at times specified; and also appropriates for the support and maintenance of the university the sum of seven thousand and five hundred dollars annually, to be paid to the treasurer in equal installments, on the first days of January, April, and October of every year; and further provides that these several sums so appropriated shall be 'set apart and appropriated from the school fund for the education of the colored race.' . . .

"Having reached the conclusion that the university is not a public school in the meaning of § 1 of art. 13 of the constitution, and as the appropriations for its establishment are expressly set apart and appropriated from the school fund for the colored race, we are forced to hold that the seventh and tenth sections of the act are unconstitutional; and as what remains is incapable of full execution according to the legislative intent, the entire act falls."

§ 290. **Universities, colleges, etc.**—In the case of *State v. Babcock*, 17 Neb. 612, it was held: "The question as to their power over the university funds was before this court in *Regents v. McConnell*, 5 Neb. 423. In that case they brought an action against McConnell to recover the 'sum of about $3,500, moneys belonging to the regents' fund, which came into the hands of the defendant as treasurer of the university, under his appointment by the regency.' The opinion was written by Chief Justice Gnatt, who said (page 428): 'Under the act of 1869 the university corporation had no control over or disposition of the endowment fund, and now by the act of February 25, 1875, the legislature has deemed it proper to abolish the office of treasurer of the university, and to make the state treasurer the custodian of the funds appropriated for the support and maintenance of the university, to be disbursed by him upon warrants drawn by the state auditor, in the same manner as funds appropriated for the support of other state institutions not incorporated are disbursed. Hence, by this latter act, the custody and control of these funds are taken from the corporation and placed in the custody of the state treasurer for disbursement, and under the settled rule of law, in respect to public corporations of this kind, the legislature had the undoubted authority to take these funds from the custody of the corporation and divest it of any corporate power over them; and having done so, we think it clear that the regents as such corporation have no authority in law to bring or maintain this action.' The same question was again before the court in *State v. Liedtke*, 9 Neb. 468, the opinion being written by the present chief justice, and it was held in effect that without an appropriation by the legislature 'no such funds or any other funds once in the state treasury can be drawn out,' and because there was no appropriation from the regents' fund, the court refused to compel the auditor to draw a warrant thereon."

§ 291. **Universities, colleges, etc.**—In the case of *Ligget et al. v. Ladd et al.*, (Ore.) 21 Pac. Rep. 133, it was held: "A college was incorporated under articles, one of which stated its

object to be 'to acquire and hold property in trust for the ——
church, and to endow, build up and maintain an institution for
educational purposes, and to confer . . . degrees, etc.,
usual in colleges,' to be controlled by the trustees and their
successors, who were to be chosen by the church: '*Provided*,
That said college shall be a strictly literary institution.' An
act of the legislature gave certain privileges to the college, on
the condition of its teaching agriculture. The college accepted
the proposition, thus virtually becoming the agricultural college
of the state. Land was conveyed to the college, 'to be used
by said college as an agricultural farm in connection and for
the purpose of the agricultural college,' with a conditional limitation over in case the premises should cease to be used for
that purpose. *Held*, that under its charter the college had the
power to take and hold land for collegiate purposes entirely
independent of any benefit to the church, and therefore the
church had no interest whatever in the land mentioned, which
the trustees had full power, so far as the church was concerned,
to convey to the regents of the agricultural college."

§ 292. **Vaccination, constitution.**—"An act to encourage
and provide for a general vaccination in the state of California,"
is constitutional, although the title refers to "general" and
body of act to scholars of public schools.[1]

§ 293. **Voters.**—In Kas. a woman may vote for school-district treasurer,[2] but cannot vote for state superintendent or county
superintendent.[3] In N. J. aliens have no right to vote at a
meeting of district, to alter the district, pursuant to law of 1851.[4]
In N. Y. where a charge for teacher's wages in a district, for
the teaching of a son, was included in the rate-bill against father,

---

[1] Abeel v. Clark, 84 Cal. 226.
[2] Wheeler v. Brady, 15 Kas. 26.
[3] Winans v. Williams, 5 Kas. 227.
[4] State v. Deshler, 25 N. J. L. (1 Dutch.) 177.

and paid by son, a resident of the district, and authorized to vote at town meetings of the town in which such district was situated, such payment qualified the son to vote at the district meetings.¹ In Vt. it is not a necessary qualification of a voter or office-holder in a town or school district, that he be a freeman.² A widow cannot vote at meeting in Vt. where her property was listed to the estate of husband. (R. L., § 2644.)³ Where fraudulent voting is charged at a district meeting, and new vote is taken, and different result declared by the chairman, the last will be sustained.⁴

§ 294. **Warrants.**—In Ind. a school commissioner is not authorized to pay interest collected by him on money of a congressional township, except on a draft of the township trustees;⁵ and if he has paid the money to a person not authorized to receive it, still, if he is ready to pay the trustees' draft when presented, his duty will be discharged.⁵ Payments for repairs on school-house by district officers are presumed to have been authorized by the district.⁶ A township treasurer cannot pay a warrant in excess of the funds in his hands due that township and be allowed a credit for the excess out of the funds belonging to any other township.⁷ A county treasurer may refuse to honor warrants given by officials for salaries when there is want of authority to issue the warrants.⁸ In N. J. the township collector is not responsible for the application of the money paid out on proper orders;⁹ but where officers contract for book, signing and receipting for the same personally, they are individually liable although they issued a warrant for payment.¹⁰ Where sub-contractor obtains an order from the district

---
¹Crawford v. Wilson, 4 Barb. (N. Y.) 504.
²Woodcock v. Bolster, 35 Vt. 632.
³Sch. Dist. v. Town, 22 A. 570.
⁴State v. Hutchins, (Neb.) 50 N. W. 165.
⁵State v. Wright, 8 Blackf. (Ind.) 65.
⁶Brock v. Bruce, (Vt.) 10 A. 93.
⁷State v. Cook, 72 Mo. 496.
⁸State v. Bateman, 96 N. C. 5.
⁹Zimmerman v. Mathe, (N. J.) 7 A. 674.
¹⁰Western P. v. Bachman S. D., 51 N. W. 214.

after contractor abandons the work, and sues on such order, he can show that more than that amount was due the contractor from the district at the time of giving the order.[1] In Kas. it is the duty of a director of a school district to sign the orders when presented to him for his signature. He has no discretion in the matter, and may be compelled to sign a proper warrant for a teacher by mandamus.[2]

§ 295. **Warrant.**—A school order was issued to a teacher in a sub-district; before its payment the several sub-districts of the township were organized into independent districts; an action could not lie against the independent district,[3] but recovery could be had thereon of all the independent districts united, and they should apportion their liabilities.[3] Under Iowa statute, an action can be maintained against a school district upon proper order on its treasurer; and the payee is not restricted to mandamus as his sole remedy.[4] A complaint on a warrant for apparatus need not anticipate the defense.[5] The act authorizing board of trustees University of California to draw money does not require an appropriation or a controller's warrant; they draw money on their warrant indorsed by the governor.[6] School-district orders drawn by the officer and accepted by the treasurer, and indorsed "Not paid, for want of funds," are subject to the same defense against an indorsee as against the payee.[7] The assignee of an order issued in excess of the constitutional limitation is in no better position than the assignor.[8] A school township may execute a valid promissory note for any debt contracted for the benefit of its property; an assignee

---

[1] La Febre v. Bd. Ed. Superior, (Wis.) 51 N. W. 952.
[2] Faulk v. McCarthy, 42 Kas. 695.
[3] Knoxville National Bank v. Washington, 40 Iowa, 612.
[4] Cross v. Dayton, 154 Iowa, 28.
[5] Jefferson School Tp. v. Litton, 116 Ind. 467.
[6] Cal. Uni. v. January, 66 Cal. 507.
[7] Sch. Dist. v. Stough, 4 Neb. 357.
[8] Nat. St. Bk. of Mt. Pleasant v. Ind. Sch. Dist., 39 Iowa, 490.

takes it subject to all defenses.¹ A school order carries notice to every person becoming its holder of its validity, and he must at his peril ascertain what defenses can be interposed.² Where a school-district board contracted for a school-house, and issued orders before any work was done, never having been authorized by a vote, and the house was not erected, the district was not liable to an indorsee.³

§ 296. **Warrants.**—Payment by treasurer of school district of orders drawn by teacher, held to be good offset in a suit on school warrant to teacher, assigned to C., who had notice.⁴ Where duplicate warrants are issued for those lost, the statute of limitation will run from date of original and not of issue of duplicates.⁵ A warrant issued to settle dispute over contract for school-house ground is not without consideration though the ground has been conveyed to others by payee, if the district is in peaceable possession.⁶ Warrant is not binding on district, because never properly allowed, never executed at any regular meeting, and only allowed by one legal member of the board.⁷ In Ill. the board of school directors had no power to make acceptances of orders or bills of exchange, so as to bind the school district and create a right of action thereon against them.⁸ A township trustee has no power to borrow money for the school township; but for money borrowed and actually used in a legitimate way, the township may be held liable.⁹ Orders on the treasurer of a school district, directing him to pay certain judgments, issued under Code Iowa, § 1787, are not evidences of debt independent of the judgments on which they are based;

---

¹ Sheffield Sch. Tp. v. Andrees, 56 Ind. 157.
² Newell v. Sch. Dirs., 68 Ill. 514; Cap. Bk. v. Sch. Dist., (N. D.) 48 N. W. 363.
³ Sch. Dist. v. Stough, 4 Neb. 357.
⁴ Sch. Dist. v. Collins, 16 Kas. 406.
⁵ Sch. Dist. v. Cromer, 52 Ark. 454.
⁶ Everts v. Dist. Tp., 77 Iowa, 37.
⁷ Mincer v. Sch. Dist., 27 Kas. 253.
⁸ Peers v. Bd. Ed., 72 Ill. 508.
⁹ Crawfordsville Bank v. Union, 75 Ind. 361; Wallis v. Johnson, 75 Ind. 368.

and a demurrer to a petition by an assignee, in which it is not averred that the judgments have been paid or canceled, on the ground that it fails to state a cause of action, must be sustained.[1] In Neb. the orders on the school-district treasurer must be signed by the director and countersigned by the moderator;[2] and a warrant must specify the fund out of which it is to be paid or it may be disregarded by the treasurer.[3] The provision of the Ill. statute, that all orders drawn upon the school fund must express the purpose for which they are drawn, is mandatory, and, if invalid, they cannot be rendered valid by any succeeding board paying interest.[4]

§ 297. **Warrants.**—Warrant payable immediately, issued in excess of amount authorized by statute, is invalid; and the district may plead *ultra vires;*[5] but where warrants were issued in excess of the limit for that year, but not in excess of what would be the limit for two annual issues, for purchasing a site and building and supplies, an acceptance, use and ratification by the district and approval of disbursement after the two years had elapsed, will bind the district;[6] but a district was held liable for orders issued for money to pay for building a house to the extent of debt incurred before the limit was reached.[7] In Tex., where claim is allowed by county commissioners' court, but no record made, a mandamus will lie to compel issue of warrant, though the commissioners subsequently and without notice order that no warrants shall issue, for lack of funds.[8] Mandamus lies to compel a school district to pay orders issued by it, even though the district has since been subdivided.[9] Interest upon such orders was denied, there being no authority given to im-

---

[1] Richards v. Ind. Sch. Dist. of Rock Rapids, 46 F. 460.
[2] State v. Bloom, 19 Neb. 562.
[3] State v. Slavin, 11 Wis. 158.
[4] Gilidden v. Hopkins, 47 Ill. 525.
[5] Farmers etc. Bank v. Sch. Dist., 6 Dak. 255.
[6] Capital Bank v. Sch. Dist., 6 Dak. 248.
[7] Austin v. Dist. Tp., 51 Iowa, 102.
[8] Brown v. Reese, (Tex.) 7 S. W. 489.
[9] Turnbull v. Alpena Bd. Ed., 45 Mich. 496.

pose it.[1] When a warrant is drawn by those who are *de facto* directors of the public schools of a particular district, the treasurer cannot claim that the directors were not elected and had not qualified;[2] but warrant made by two, as members of board, not binding, for one was not member either *de jure* or *de facto*, and it was not executed in pursuance of any order made at proper meeting.[3] A board of education acting separately cannot contract a debt or direct the issuance of an order to pay it.[4] The power must be executed in person by each and all;[5] but the record showing authority to issue warrant cannot be impeached by showing that no action was had at that meeting, or that entry was in handwriting of party interested, who was not a secretary, and that he signed the director's name.[6] School-district order is *prima facie* valid.[7] Warrants for past years cannot be paid out of fund specifically raised to carry on school for current year.[8] A petition on order issued by town in Wis., that is a school district, need not state that there is money in the fund to pay the same, the order being on the general school fund in town treasurer's hands.[9] A petition on warrants issued by directors of school district which has been attached to district of defendant is defective unless it shows liability by reason of apportionment of funds.[10] Directors in Ill. may give a warrant on their treasurer for money borrowed for school purposes.[11] Interest at 6 per cent. is recoverable on an Iowa school board order.[12]

§ 298. **Women officers.**—In Minn. a woman can hold the office of county superintendent; this eligibility is conferred by

---

[1] Turnbull v. Alpena Bd. Ed., 45 Mich. 496.
[2] Miahle v. Fournet, 13 La. Ann. 607.
[3] Mincer v. Sch. Dist., 27 Kas. 253.
[4] State v. Treas. Liberty Tp., 22 Ohio St. 144.
[5] Glidden v. Hopkins, 47 Ill. 525.
[6] Everts v. Dist. Tp., 77 Iowa, 37.
[7] Sch. Dist. v. Swayze, 29 Kas. 211.
[8] Foote v. Brown, 60 Miss. 155.
[9] Brown v. Tn. Bd. Sch. Dist., (Wis.) 45 N. W. 678.
[10] Moll v. Sch. Dist., 23 Ill. App. 508.
[11] Folson v. Sch. Dist., 91 Ill. 402.
[12] Austin v. Dist. Tp., 51 Iowa, 102.

the constitution.[1] Women are eligible to office of county superintendent of public instruction in Kansas.[2] In Mass. there is nothing in the constitution which prevents a woman from being a member of the school committee.[3] Mass. Stat. of 1874, ch. 389, made women eligible on the Boston school committee. Under the charter of Boston, (Stat. of 1854,) the city school committee is the judge of the qualifications of its members; its decision that a seat is vacant for want of a legal election and qualification is conclusive, although the sole reason for the decision is that the petitioner is a woman.[4] Where a majority of the board, not counting the female members, voted in favor of changing a boundary, the constitutionality of the act making women eligible to office will not be passed upon.[5]

§ 299. **Women voters.**—Art. 2, § 23, of the Kas. constitution, which provides that "The legislature, in providing for the formation and regulation of schools, shall make no distinction between the rights of males and females," does not confer upon females the right to vote for school officers.[6] The Ill. act 1891, authorizing women to vote for superintendent of schools, is unconstitutional in that regard.[7] "In Minn. the county superintendent's office pertains solely to the management of schools within art. 7, § 8, of constitution. Sec. 8 takes matter of allowing women to vote for offices out from under art. 7, and leaves it to the legislature, subject only to restrictions in § 8, and under this the legislature may make women eligible to a school office."[8]

[1] State v. Gorton, 33 Minn. 345.
[2] Wright v. Noell, 16 Kas. 601.
[3] Opinion of Justices, 115 Mass. 602.
[4] Peabody v. Sch. Comm., 115 Mass. 383.
[5] Donough v. Hollister, 82 Mich. 309.
[6] Winans v. Williams, 5 Kas. 227.
[7] People v. English, (Ill. Sup.) 29 N. E. 678.
[8] State v. Gorton, 33 Minn. 345.

APPENDIX.

SYNOPSES OF SCHOOL LAWS.

ALABAMA.

(Compiled by Hon. JOHN G. HARRIS, State Superintendent.)

System: Superintendent of education, county superintendent, township trustees, county educational board.—**State Superintendent of Education** shall have general supervision; may require reports from county school officers; annually visit each county; encourage education and teachers' and superintendents' institutes; make provision as to instruction on effects of alcohol and narcotics; annually apportion and distribute funds, prepare forms and blanks, furnish county school officers necessary books; keep an accurate account of state school funds; preserve bonds of school officers; institute suits against defaulters; may employ attorneys where required; supervise the collection of poll-tax; exchange reports with other states; may collect books, maps, apparatus, charts, and specimens without expense; compile the laws; provide for teachers' institutes; make report.—**County Superintendent,** one in each county; term two years. The county superintendent may be removed by state superintendent for cause; shall take oath; give bond; compensation, $75 per annum and two per cent. on funds distributed—varies in some counties. County superintendent must have office at county seat, and be present on the first Saturday of each month of school year; take charge of school funds in his county; apportion, distribute and pay out money; examine into school funds of his county, and lands unsold; may bring suit for the use of township, to recover lands, or against trespassers; make annual report before the 1st of November; post at the court-house, semi-annually, an itemized statement of his accounts; may remove township trustee for cause; fill vacancies; must pay teachers quarterly; must report to probate judge. Commissioner's court audits his accounts. County superintendent, failing to make annual report, is liable to forfeiture of pay and office. Superintendent of education fills the vacancy by appointment. Three township trustees for each township or school district are appointed by the county superintendent, subject to the approval of the state superintendent; and in lieu of township superintendent, county superintendent appoints three **Township Trustees.** (They are elected in some counties.) Township trustees have the supervision of the public schools of their township, and have the power to establish, subject to the approval of the county superintendent, such schools as may be required. The trustees shall annually, on the last Monday of October or within seven days thereafter, call a meeting of the parents and guardians of the children of their district to transact business, and then determine the number of schools to be established in the district, locate the same, fix the time, apportion the revenue, transfer children, and such other business as may be necessary; make a report in ten days; ten days' notice of the meeting must be given. Appeal may be had to county superintendent from action of the meeting. Contracts with teachers by the trustees shall be in writing, and must be approved by the county superintendent. They shall visit schools once a year; may remove teacher for cause.—**Teachers**: Three grades certificates, each of which shows the branches in which the holder has been examined and his relative attainments therein. No certificate shall be granted where applicant fails on 70 per cent. of the questions; third-grade certificate, one year; second grade, two years; first grade, three years in the county.—**Educational Board** in the county: County superintendent and two teachers;

examine and license teachers. There are other acts for local schools governed by local statutes.

ARIZONA.

(Compiled by Hon. GEO. W. CHEYNEY, Superintendent of Public Instruction.)

System: Territorial board education, superintendent public instruction, territorial board examiners, county school superintendent, county board examiners, districts, trustees, census marshal, clerk school district.—**District** formed on petition of parents or guardians of ten school census children to county superintendent; one week's notice to be given, posted at three public places, one at the school-house door. County superintendent must transmit petition to board of supervisors with approval or disapproval, and it acts upon the same. One of three trustees elected in school district last Saturday of June in each year.—**Meetings** of district direct by vote the location, change, purchase and sale of site, erection of buildings, attending to suits.—**Trustees** have power to prescribe and enforce rules; control property; to purchase furniture, apparatus and supplies; rent, furnish and repair, and insure property; to build, purchase or sell school-houses when directed by vote; to make conveyances; to employ teachers and employés—no contract to extend beyond 30th of June next ensuing; to expel pupils for misconduct; to exclude children under six years old; to enforce study and text-books prescribed; to appoint librarians; to exclude immoral publications; to provide for non-resident pupils; and visit.—**Teachers:** Territorial board of examiners grant recommendations for life, and educational diploma; grant territorial certificate—first grade four years, second grade three years; revoke certificates for cause, and renew certificates. County board examiners grant county certificates—first grade four years, second grade two years; enforce text-books prescribed, and revoke for cause certificates granted by them, and grant county certificates to holders of life diplomas and normal-school diplomas.—**Text-Books** can be continued in use four years, sixty days' notice of change to be given. Publishers must give good bond. Sectarian books or religious exercises may cause teacher's certificate to be revoked. Pupils may be expelled for profanity, vulgarity and injuring property.—**Superintendent of Instruction** superintends schools; investigates questions; apportions funds; prescribes forms and certificates; appoints county board examiners; makes reports, and has general supervision. County superintendent apportions county money; draws warrants by order of board of trustees for expenses; presides over teachers' institutes; issues (on order of county board) temporary certificates; appoints trustees in case of vacancies; requires building to be repaired; grades the schools; appoints deputies; and endeavors to harmonize boundaries. Teachers' institute to be held once in a year.

ARKANSAS.

System: State superintendent, board commissioners of common-school fund, school districts, county examiners, school directors. Cities and towns may be special districts.—**State Superintendent of Public Instruction** has general supervision of the school system of the state; shall keep an office and record; shall furnish questions for examination of teachers to county examiner; shall hold a teachers' institute annually in each judicial district; prepare blanks; supervise funds; make report; make apportionment; may grant state certificates, valid for life unless revoked; shall prepare and recommend a list of text-books; have a seal of office.—**New District** may be formed on petition to the county court, and must have not less than thirty-five school children. County court may alter district on petition; may appoint one county examiner for each district.

—**Examiner** shall examine and license teachers; he shall hold quarterly sessions and give twenty days' notice. He may revoke license for good cause. Shall issue three grades of certificates: First grade, good in the county where issued two years; second grade, good in the county where issued one year; third grade, good in the county six months. He shall labor to promote the cause of education in the district; make annual report; number the districts; may designate some one to hold teachers' institutes and examine teachers when unable to attend. County judge may remove county examiner for cause.—**District:** Annual meeting, third Saturday in May, at 2 P. M.; may choose a chairman; elect director; designate and so determine the time when school shall be had more than three months; determine the amount of taxes, not to exceed one-half of one per cent.; repeal or modify their proceedings from time to time.—**School Directors** hold office for three years. When a new district is formed, hold office for one, two and three years, respectively. Board of directors have care of the school property, may purchase or lease a site, designated by voters; hold, purchase, or build school-house, sell or exchange school-house when directed by vote. They shall hire licensed teachers, and make a written contract. Shall adopt one series of text-books for their district, and no change shall be made for three years. They shall visit schools, and shall attend to suits, shall draw warrants on the county treasurer; give notice of meeting fifteen days, and notice for annual meeting to fix a school-site, or build or purchase a school-house, and must state these facts in the notice. Directors, at the instance of the teacher, may suspend a pupil for gross immorality, refractory conduct, or insubordination, or infectious disease, for that term. County court may permit non-residents to attend in districts. Directors and county examiners are exempt from working on roads, or serving on juries. Persons teaching without a license are not entitled to compensation from state revenues. Teachers must attend teachers' institutes. No sectarian books allowed.—**State Superintendent** shall hold an annual teachers' institute; has the supervision of public schools; shall prepare examiner's papers; supervise school funds; make annual report of pupils and money. State superintendent and county examiner shall not be interested in any school contract.

CALIFORNIA.

(Compiled by Hon. J. W. ANDERSON, State Superintendent.)

Appeals lie from disagreement of trustees in providing for attendance of non-resident children in district school. Appeals may be taken from dismissal of teacher by board of trustees, and from withholding teacher's salary.—**New Districts** formed on petition of parents or guardians of fifteen census children between the ages of five and seventeen to the superintendent of schools. Notice is given to trustees of district affected, and posted in three public places, one on school-house, for at least one week, and county superintendent must transmit the petition to board of supervisors, with his approval or disapproval, and they act upon the same.—**District Annual Meeting** for election of trustees, first Tuesday of June of each year; ten days' notice to be given. Trustees may call special meeting of district by posting three notices in public places, one on the school-house, for ten days. Notice must specify the purpose, and nothing else can be transacted. These meetings can instruct the board in regard to change and location of site, in regard to sale or purchase of site, in regard to lawsuits and insurance.—**Teachers' Certificates:** State board of education may grant educational diplomas valid for six years, and life diplomas; and may revoke diplomas. State educational diplomas may be issued to teachers who have held a first grade, grammar grade, high school, city or county grade, or city and county certificate, and who shall have been a teacher five years. Life diplomas are issued on the same conditions to persons who have taught ten years. County superintendent may issue temporary certificates good until next meeting of county board of education to persons holding certificates, but can only grant a temporary certificate to such person once. County board of education may grant high-school certificates for six years, grammar certificates for three years, and primary for two years. City or county boards of examiners may grant high-school certificates for six years, city certificates for three years and city certificates for two years, and special certificates.—**Trustees** of district boards of education may make rules for the government of themselves and schools; may control school property; purchase text-books in the state, school furniture, organs and pianos, and apparatus. Incorporated cities having board of education and trustees of districts can purchase only such books and apparatus as have been adopted by the county or city board of education. Trustees may rent, furnish, repair and insure school property; when directed by vote, may build, purchase or sell lots; may make conveyances; may employ teachers and employés, and fix compensation; suspend or expel pupil for misconduct; exclude children under six years; enforce text-books, and course of study; appoint librarian, exclude sectarian or partisan publications; furnish books to those unable to buy; keep a register; appoint a school census marshal; and visit. Pupils may be expelled for willful disobedience, open defiance, habitual profanity and vulgarity, and for cutting, defacing, or injuring school property.—Certain **Textbooks,** published by state, furnished and provided for school children at cost. County board may enforce uniformity of textbooks. County board may grant, without examination, county **Certificates** to the holders of life diplomas, Cal., Nev. and Oreg., State educational diplomas, Cal. Normal School diplomas, San Francisco Normal Class diplomas, Cal. State University diplomas, State Normal School diplomas of other states, high-school and grammar-grade certificates of any county or city in Cal., and may renew certificates.—**State Superintendent** superintends all the schools of the state, makes report, apportions state fund, furnishes blanks, visits, and may convene in session county and city superintendents.

COLORADO.

(Compiled by Hon. NATHAN B. COY, State Superintendent.)

New Districts are organized from old on petition of parents of ten or more children of school age, to county superintendent, who shall give notice and order election. A district is organized from unorganized territory without petition by election of majority of legal voters of the district. Over 1,000 population, first-class district; 350, second-class; under, third-class.—**Annual Meeting**, first Monday in May, at which election for members of board takes place and any lawful business may be determined. Notice to be posted at three public places in district, at least six days previous to election, one on school-house, and in first-class district four weeks in newspaper. Two voters may give notice on failure of secretary.—**School Boards** may employ and discharge teachers, fix tuition fee of non-resident pupil, fix compensation of secretary, fix course of study and text-book. But one kind of text-book is to be used in same department of school, and after adoption no change in less than four years unless price unwarrantably advanced, or mechanical quality lowered, or supply stopped. They may provide for supplies, build, remove, rent, repair, and insure school-house. They may hold property, suspend or expel pupils refusing to obey rules, determine number teachers, furnish books to indigent children, exclude immoral books, make annual report. No high-school building is to be built without a vote. President signs all orders on county treasurer; none to be given except to parties to whom district is lawfully indebted. Teacher not licensed at time of commencing teaching shall forfeit all claim to compensation out of school fund for that term.—**Appeals** from board directors in thirty days to county superintendent, appeals from county superintendent in thirty days to state board of education; but neither can render judgment for money. Officer interested in school contracts liable to imprisonment and fine. **Teacher** who is graduate of state normal may teach by filing in county superintendent's office a copy of his diploma.—**County Superintendents** may grant certificate: first grade two years, second grade one year, third grade six months; and he may revoke for just cause.—**State Superintendent** shall decide all questions touching the construction of the school laws submitted in writing, and this decision is final until set aside by a court having jurisdiction or by legislature; and may give his decisions through an educational periodical. He shall have general supervision of all the county superintendents and public schools, and prepare lists of questions for examination of teachers.

CONNECTICUT.

System: State board, towns, school visitors, board of education, school districts, district committee.—**State Board** may adopt text-books, not to be changed for five years; compulsory education required. Town may direct school visitors, board of education or school committee to purchase text-books or school supplies, to be loaned to the pupils free of charge. The selectmen control the school property.—The **School Visitors** provide text-books, subject to the state board of education, examine teachers, give certificates, and may revoke certificates; the effect of alcohol is required to be taught. Board of education, town committee, and board of school visitors may appoint the superintendent.—**District** may sue and be sued; purchase and hold property; build, purchase, hire and repair school-houses; furnish supplies; maintain libraries, employ teachers, levy taxes. Non-resident scholars may be provided for. School-houses may be used for other purposes, by vote of the district or town.—**District Committee** give notice of meetings; call special meetings; may direct school visitors to employ teachers, provide room, furnish fuel, visit the school; may suspend or expel scholars, and assist school visitors.

DELAWARE.

State superintendent's and assistant superintendent's offices have been abolished; and in lieu a **County Superintendent** is appointed for each county by the governor. They shall be residents of the county. They shall visit each school in the county twice a year, examine into the qualifications of teachers and condition of schools, advise with teachers, suspend or withdraw teacher's certificate on his refusal to comply with reasonable directions, subject to an appeal. The county superintendent shall strive to promote the cause of education. He shall examine teachers at such place as he may appoint. First-grade certificate, good for three years; second grade, 90 per cent. of answers to be correct; third grade, from 90 to 60. School commissioners cannot employ a teacher who does not hold a certificate from the superintendent of the county. Superintendent shall make annual report to the president of the board of education. Secretary of state, the governor of the state, and three superintendents shall constitute the **State Board Education.** They shall hear appeals and finally determine all matters between a superintendent and teacher or an applicant for a certificate, between a superintendent and commissioner, and between a commissioner and teacher. State Board of Education shall determine what **Text-Books** are to be used. Each superintendent shall hold teachers' institute in county. Superintendent shall collect school books undisposed of and dispose of the same and turn the proceeds over to the state treasurer. Pupils are to be instructed on the effect of alcohol and narcotics. **Text-books** to be furnished to pupils free. School commissioner or trustees shall order from the publisher the books which have been adopted by the state board of education on contract prices. State treasurer shall pay the publisher out of the school fund. Text-books for colored schools are ordered by county superintendent. County superintendent shall have the entire management, control, and supervision of the colored schools. Annual school meeting is to be held on the last Saturday of June of each year.

FLORIDA.

(Compiled by the Hon. Albert J. Russell, State Superintendent of Public Instruction.)

System: State board of education, county boards of public instruction, county superintendents, treasurer, and school supervisors.—**County Boards** of public instruction for county appointed by state board of education on the nomination of the state superintendent.—**Supervisors** appointed by county boards of public instruction. Each county is a district.—The **County Superintendent** is elected by the people every four years.— The **County Boards** of public instruction hold titles, locate and maintain schools, appoint supervisors and teachers, provide sites, examine teachers, grant certificates of the second and third class, fix the compensation of the county superintendent, purchase and rent sites, furnish apparatus and supplies, and select text-books. —**Supervisors** take charge of school property, attend to instruction, rent and repair school buildings, fence, fencing supplies, text-books; may suspend or expel pupils.—**Teachers' certificates** from the county boards of public instruction, good in county where issued for one year. The state superintendent of public instruction may grant certificates to graduates of departments of teaching, good in any part of the state during the time given; there are three grades of certificates.—**Teachers** may enforce proper regulations; suspend pupils ten days for cause, giving notice to the trustees and parents. Bible not prohibited. Disputes are to be settled by arbitration. Appeals may be made from one officer to the next superior. Decisions of the state superintendent of public instruction and state board of education are final.

GEORGIA.

(Compiled by Hon. S. D. BRADWELL, State Superintendent.)

System: State board of education, state school commissioner, county school commissioner, county board education, school trustees.—**Sub-Districts** created by county board. Trustees for sub-school districts to be appointed by county board.—**County Board** has power to purchase, sell or rent school-site; to buy, build, repair or rent school-house; to purchase supplies; have care of property; may provide separate schools for white and colored races; determine controversies, appeal being given to state school commissioner from county commissioner. County board appoints county commissioner. County board prescribes text-books; Bible shall not be excluded;

text-books not to be changed for five years except by three-fourths vote of the board; sectarian text-books shall not be used; no teacher shall receive pay from pupil.—**Teacher:** County board grants license—first grade three years, second grade two years, third grade one year. State commissioner may grant permanent license. County commissioner may revoke license for cause; right of appeal to the county board is given. County commissioner shall visit schools, keep records, audit accounts, exercise general supervision, and is purchasing agent. School property is exempt from taxes, not to exceed four acres. Teacher must have license at time of contract, to enable him to draw pay. Private term may be contracted by teachers and patrons, and must be approved by board education.

IDAHO.
(Compiled by Hon. J. E. Harroun, State Superintendent.)

System: State board public instruction, state superintendent, county superintendent, districts, trustees, independent school districts.—**Districts** formed on petition of parents or guardians of ten children to county superintendent. Notice to be posted in three public places. District established on vote of two-thirds voting. Joint district formed from land in two counties. Trustees elected first Monday in June, annually. Notice of meeting to be given, posted in three places, one on school-house, for ten days. Annual meeting may transact any lawful business pertaining to schools.—**Trustees** hold the property, and must furnish necessary supplies and apparatus, and allow claims not to exceed twenty-five per cent. of the school funds. District having $200,000 worth of taxable property may be organized into independent school district on vote of one-fifth of voters. They may contract, sue and be sued, take, hold and convey; shall choose officers of the board of trustees. Two trustees are elected biennially. No officer can receive pay or compensation. Board of trustees make by-laws; employ or discharge teachers and employés; fix compensation and tuition for non-residents; prescribe course of study and text-books, one kind of text-book to be used in same grade, and must not be changed in less than three years unless price is unwarrantably raised, mechanical quality lowered, or supply stopped; may provide furniture and apparatus; rent, repair or insure school-house; build or remove school-house; purchase or sell lots; suspend or expel pupils; exclude children under six years of age; determine the time of teaching; provide books for poor; exclude sectarian publications; protect morals.—**State Superintendent** has general supervision; furnishes blanks and forms.—**County Superintendent** issues teachers' certificates: First grade two years, second grade one year, third grade six months. County superintendent has commission on fund expended. Teachers' institute may be held annually by county superintendent by giving ten days' notice. Bonds may be issued for building schoolhouses, by vote of district.

ILLINOIS.
(Compiled by Hon. HENRY RAAB, State Superintendent.)

System: Superintendent public instruction, county superintendent, township trustee, township treasurer, board directors of district, boards of education of cities and towns.—**State Superintendent** exercises general supervision; can establish rules, hear and determine appeals, grant state certificates to teachers.—**County Superintendent** may sell township lands; register applicants for admission to State Normal University and to the University of Illinois; visit, and exercise supervision over, the schools of the county; conduct teachers' institutes; examine accounts of township treasurers; attend to changes of boundaries on appeal; give notice of election of school directors in certain cases; examine teachers, grant certificates to teachers, require trustees to report, renew and revoke teachers' certificates, and remove school director for cause.—**Township Trustees** hold school property. Supervision and control of school-houses and sites vested in board of directors of the district. Trustees may alter districts by direction of voters, on petition of voters.—**Board of Directors**, three in a district, elected annually, one for three years; notice of election to be given for ten days, in three public places. No director shall be interested in contract. Their duty is, to make report of expenses; employ teachers, to provide revenue, establish schools, to make rules, to visit schools, direct course of study and text-books, and enforce uniformity of text-books—no text-book to be changed oftener than once in four years; may purchase text-books for poor children, to be loaned; may dismiss teacher for incompetency, cruelty, negligence, immorality, or other good cause; may admit non-resident pupils and fix tuition; may suspend or expel pupils guilty of gross disobedience or misconduct, and are not liable therefor; may sell property not needed; grant special holidays; and grant use of school-houses for religious, literary, and other purposes.—**Boards of Education** of cities and villages of 1,000 or more inhabitants have the power of school directors, and may furnish, repair, or improve school-houses, and furnish supplies; examine and employ teachers; establish schools; lease or buy sites, but may not purchase or locate unless by vote of the district; employ superintendent; expel pupils; dismiss or remove teachers; apportion scholars, make rules; and erect buildings.—**Teachers:** Graduates of county normal have first-grade certificates for two years; state superintendent may grant certificates for life and for five years; county superintendent may grant for two years and for one year, and may renew or revoke. No teacher without a certificate is entitled to funds. Township high schools may be established.—**Appeals** from change in boundaries by trustees to county superintendent; in all controversies opinion of county superintendent first had, and appeal to the state superintendent.

INDIANA.

(Compiled by Hon. HARVEY D. VORIES, State Superintendent.)

System: State superintendent, state board of education, county superintendent, school trustees, school directors, general and special state institutions.—**State Board of Education** may make rules and by-laws; grant state certificates for life unless revoked; also, eight years' professional license. County superintendent is appointed by township trustees. He shall examine teachers and license them for six, twelve, twenty-four and thirty-six months, and may revoke license for incompetency, cruelty, immorality, or negligence; and shall report basis of apportionment to county auditor. County board of education shall have charge of all matters in regard to furniture, maps, charts, etc. State board of education may select or procure a series of **text-books,** and when adopted by the board they shall be used by the schools. Township trustees employ teachers, locate schools, build suitable houses, furnish necessary supplies, establish graded schools, have charge over the property belonging to their corporation.—**Cities** of 30,000 or more may have board of school commissioners, who may levy taxes, examine and license teachers, purchase grounds, contract for building, teachers, superintendent, disburse money, regulate instruction and discipline, and issue and sell bonds. Bible shall not be excluded from public schools.—**Teachers:** No teacher can be employed without license, and shall forfeit compensation for time teaching without license. Person insulting teacher in presence of school is liable to fine. School-house may be used for private school by order of trustees; and it may be used for religious or other meetings by direction of voters.—**Appeals** lie from county superintendent to superintendent public instruction, and from trustees to county superintendent. School trustees may furnish books for poor; school-books now adopted are sold by the state.

IOWA.

(Compiled by Hon. J. B. KNOEPFLER, State Superintendent.)

Districts: In law, two forms—district townships and independent districts. The district township, divided into sub-districts, is conterminous with the civil township. A civil township may be one or more independent districts. A city or village may be independent. Most boundaries may be changed by boards. Electors meet in sub-districts first Monday in March. —**Annual Meeting** of electors in all districts on second Monday in March. Special meeting when school-house is destroyed, also in independent districts to vote bonds and divide district. All taxes to build voted by electors. May direct board to have certain branches taught, dispose of property, and direct use of school-houses. Ten days' notice of meetings.—**Boards**: Women eligible to any school office. President chosen third Monday in March; secretary and treasurer, third Monday September. Boards determine amount of teachers' and contingent funds, and fix months of school. May establish graded schools and adopt course of study; have full control over schools, teachers and scholars; locate sites and build school houses; provide extra school for any ten scholars. Must have effects of alcoholic drinks, stimulants and narcotics taught. May maintain an industrial exposition in each school. Must set out shade-trees. May insure property. Receive no compensation. —**Contracts**: Boards must carry into effect vote of electors. For apparatus, must be for cash. All claims must be audited and allowed before order is drawn. Orders not paid draw six per cent. after being indorsed by the treasurer.—**Text-Books**: Counties may vote uniformity, town and village independent districts being exempted. Any district in county not having voted county uniformity may contract for five years, purchase, and sell text-books at cost; or, such district may adopt for three years without contracting or purchasing.—**Teachers' Contracts**: All contracts with teachers must be in writing, be approved by the president and filed with him, and copy filed with secretary. Teachers may be discharged only after full and fair investigation by the board.—**Teachers' Certificates**: Every teacher drawing public money must have a state certificate or diploma, or a certificate from the county superintendent. Such credentials may be revoked, for cause.—**Scholars**: School age, both for enumeration and attendance, five to twenty-one.

Teacher has full control over scholars, unless restricted by a rule of the board. Corporal punishment is not forbidden. The sub-director, with concurrence of the president, may dismiss for gross immorality, or persistent violation of the rules or regulations. Same power is vested in majority of board in independent districts, with concurrence of president.—**County Superintendent** and **Superintendent of Public Instruction:** The county superintendent has general control over schools and teachers in his county. May visit schools. Must visit any school at least once in the term, on request of majority of the board. Must select instructors and hold normal institute. Examines teachers and issues certificates for one year or less. Hears and decides appeals from orders made by boards. Makes a complete annual report. The superintendent of public instruction has general supervision of the county superintendents and the common schools. May meet county superintendents in convention. As far as able, must attend and lecture before teachers' institutes. Must give written opinion in explanation of the school laws. Decides appeals from decisions made by county superintendents on appeal. Appoints county normal institutes and approves of instructors therein. Compiles school laws and decisions. Is president of board of state normal school, president of board of educational examiners, and a regent of the state university. Makes to the governor, biennially, a full statistical report of the condition and progress of the public schools, with plans for their more perfect organization and efficiency.

KANSAS.

(Compiled by Hon. G. W. WINANS, State Superintendent.)

System: State superintendent, county superintendent, school districts, board education cities, school fund commissioners, county examining board, city examining board, state board of education.—**State Superintendent** has charge of educational interests, distributes state school fund, gives opinion to county superintendents, publishes school laws, and visits.—**County**

Superintendent visits, suggests, reports, encourages, keeps record, keeps register, apportions dividend, alters districts on petition, and from such alteration or formation an appeal lies to the county commissioners.—**Districts:** Meeting designates site, votes annual taxes and directs the same to be used to build, hire, or purchase school-house; authorizes contract, sale of school-house and property; and the **District Board** is director, clerk, and treasurer. It has care of property, admits non-resident scholars, hires teachers, and with the county superintendent may dismiss for incompetency, cruelty, negligence, or immorality. District board may suspend pupil for immorality or violation of regulation, for the term. An appeal to the county superintendent, whose decision is final, is given to the pupil. District board shall provide necessary appendages for the school, and may authorize use of building for religious or other purposes.—**County Board Examiners**, county superintendent and two persons appointed by the county commissioners. They may issue certificate to teachers: first grade three years, second grade two years, and third grade one year. Temporary certificates may be granted by the county superintendent. Board education of cities of the first and second class appoint examining committee, employ teachers, hold property, and may elect superintendent; and cities of third class are governed as districts and union districts. County high school may be established in counties of 6,000 population. School districts and boards of education in a county may adopt uniform series of **Text-Books**; and text-book board may be elected to select and prescribe text-books to be used in county. No sectarian books shall be used, but Bible may be read. Persons willfully refusing to admit children into common schools of the district, when entitled, forfeit $100 a month.—**State Board of Education** consists of the state superintendent, chancellor of State University, president of State Agricultural College, and president of the State Normal School. The state board prepare questions for examination of teachers. They may issue diplomas, countersigned by the state superintendent, good for life; or certificate of high qualification for three or five years, valid in any county, city, town or school district in the state.

KENTUCKY.

(Compiled by Hon. ED. PORTER THOMPSON, State Superintendent.)

School Districts may not be larger than sixteen square miles, and are seldom so large; and in the country contain from 45 to 100 pupils; governed by three trustees, who may meet at any time. District lines may be altered by the county superintendent on due notice.—**Trustees** may levy a tax to build and furnish a house; employ a teacher, and agree on the price and length of term—not less than five months, except in special cases; must visit parents in the interest of their schools; must visit school once a month; make report annually of children in their district to county superintendent; must report school as taught, month by month; must supplement teacher's report, &c., &c. All money raised by taxes for the schools goes into the hands of the county superintendent, and he pays the same on the order of the trustees. Money paid by the state is assigned to each district by the state officer and paid to county superintendent for the benefit of said district, and paid to teacher of same by county superintendent monthly, on order of the trustees.—The **State Board of Education** adopts a number of school-books on each subject required to be taught, from which the county superintendent is authorized to select one on each subject for his county, which may not be changed for five years; at end of the five years, he readopts or changes for others on the state list.—**Teachers** contract with the trustees of each school district for one session. Contract must be in writing.—The **State Board** formulates questions on each subject required to be taught. These are sent to a county board—of which the county superintendent is one—in July, August, September, November and January of each year, and county board conducts the examination and estimates the value of answers which are written, and grants first, second, and third-class certificates on an average of 85, 75, and 65 per cent. of correct answers, good for four years, two years, and one year, respectively, but only in the county in which issued.—**Pupils** are white and colored from six to twenty years old—separate schools for each.—**Teacher** is *in loco parentis;* chooses his own mode of punishment, and is responsible in damages for abuse; makes his own rules, subject to statute.—**State and County Superintendents** are elected by popular vote for four years. They superintend the distribution of state funds to districts, which has amounted to $2.25 to each pupil for some years. They are to see that properly qualified teachers only are employed, suitable school-houses are provided, and only suitable text-books are used, and in every way possible promote popular education. County superintendent makes several annual reports to state superintendent showing condition of the schools. These the state superintendent compiles and publishes biennially for the legislature, with such recommendations as he deems important.

LOUISIANA.

(Compiled by Hon. W. H. JACK, State Superintendent.)

The legislature is commanded "to establish throughout the state free public schools for the education of all the children between the ages of six and eighteen years, and to provide for their maintenance and support by taxation or otherwise. And the money so raised (except the poll tax) is to be distributed to each parish in proportion to the number of children between the ages of six and eighteen years."—The **State Superintendent** is made the chief director of the department of education. He is expressly charged with the duty of seeing that the school system is carried into effect properly, and he is vested with sufficient power and authority to direct and control the subordinate branches of his department in matters of administration. His office is constitutional and elective, and his term of service is for four years. In case of vacancy, the governor appoints his successor, subject to the confirmation of the senate at the next meeting of the general assembly. He is charged with the general supervision of the various boards of education and of all the common, high and normal schools of the state, including the deaf and dumb and blind institutes, and is required to visit annually each parish or school district in the state. It devolves on him to make the quarterly apportionments of the school funds, receive the annual reports of the parish superintendents and parish treasurers, keep records of the proceedings of the state board and of his official acts, file all papers pertaining to the department, decide controversies and disputes between directors, between parish superintendents and the local boards, and between superintendents and teachers, subject to appeal in fifteen days to the state board. He is required to give advice, explanations, construction and information to the district officers, superintendents, and citizens, relative to the common-school law, and generally on all questions pertaining to the cause of public education. He is required to report to the general assembly, at its biennial session, the amount and condition of the public school fund, the sources from which derived, and the disposition of the same, as well as the amounts collected and disbursed for schools from local taxation and other sources, with abstracts of the reports of the parish superintendents and of the parish treasurers incorporated therein, with such suggestions and recommendations as to the public school system as he may deem proper. All papers from his office under his seal and certificate are as admissible in evidence as would be the originals. The several members of the state board of education and the various parish boards, with their superintendents and treasurers, comprise the other officers belonging to the educational department. The **State Board** appoints, for each rural parish in the state, not less than five nor more than nine duly qualified citizens, as **School Directors** for such parish, who are accordingly commissioned by the governor for a term of four years. This board is specially charged with the duty of preparing rules, by-laws and regulations for the guidance and government of the common schools, to be enforced by the parish superintendents and parish board, and they are furthermore required to give directions as to the branches of study to be taught. One of their main duties is to select and adopt a series of **Text-Books** to be used in all the public schools for a period of four years, with the view and to the end of securing uniformity in this respect, in all the schools; and to contract with publishers therefor on certain terms and conditions. They are moreover, when assembled, a *quasi* court of appeal to review the decisions of the state superintendent in cases properly brought before them. A record of their proceedings is kept by the state superintendent, and preserved in the archives of his office. The state boards and parish boards are severally "bodies corporate," with powers to sue and be sued, and to exercise other powers common to such bodies. **The Parish Boards,** with their officers, are placed in immediate charge of the public schools, and in the nature of things their powers and responsibilities are great, and their duties are delicate and difficult. They elect a president from their own number, and appoint or elect a parish superintendent. Their more prominent duties may be thus stated: They determine the location of school-houses; number of schools to be taught; number of teachers to be employed and their salaries; the proportion of funds to the several school districts; and they establish graded schools, also central or high schools with the sanction of the state board when the site and buildings are donated. Moreover, they divide the parish into school districts in manner best suited to the interest of the schools, receive land by purchase or donation for the purpose of erecting school-houses, and make all necessary contracts for the erection or repair of such houses. The parish superintendent, in point of active duty, is the principal local officer. He is *ex officio* secretary of the board, and as such keeps a record of their proceedings and of his own official acts. It is made his duty to visit every school in the parish at least once in every year of his term. In conjunction with the president of the board, and another member appointed for that purpose, he selects the public-school teachers, and with the aid of two competent persons appointed by the board he examines applicants for schools and pronounces upon their qualifications. The grades are regulated and determined by the character of studies pursued in the particular school, and certificates are issued to the teachers of those schools accordingly, as follows: A **Teacher** found competent to teach spelling, reading, primary mental arithmetic, rudiments of practical arithmetic through fractions and simple interest, elementary geography, primary grammar lessons, and laws of health, receives a third-grade certificate, and is paid a salary graduated accordingly; one found qualified to teach arithmetic, geography, English grammar and composition, United States history, elements of natural philosophy, and elements of physiology, is entitled to a second-class certificate and a proportionately higher salary; and one pronounced competent by the examiners to teach elocution, spelling, grammar, rhetoric, literature, history, botany, philosophy, arithmetic, algebra, geometry, and such other high-grade studies as the boards may prescribe, is entitled to a first-class or high-school certificate. Since the 1st of October, 1890, no certificate can issue to any new applicant to teach in the public schools who has not passed a satisfactory examination in the study of the nature of alcoholic drinks and narcotics and their effects upon the human system, in connection with the several subjects of relative physiology and hygiene.

MAINE.

System: State superintendent, superintending school committee, school agents, supervisors, districts, towns. A town may, at annual meeting, determine the number and limits of school districts, may change the same; school in small district may be suspended; remote parts of town may be omitted in districting. Towns may abolish school districts, choose school agents, empower district agents to employ teachers; towns shall raise money for the support of schools. School committee shall make rules and regulations for the distribution and preservation of school-books and appliances. On school-book or appliance being injured or lost by pupil, his parent or guardian shall make good the damages. A city or town may provide for instruction in industrial or mechanical drawing in either day or evening schools.—**Assessors** or city officers shall make report to state superintendent under oath of—1st, the amount voted by the town; 2d, the amount of moneys payable to the town from the state; 3d, the amount of money expended for schools; 4th, the amount of school moneys unexpended; and shall answer other inquiries.—**State Superintendent** shall furnish blanks, make a return to the state treasurer; no money appropriated for public schools shall be paid except upon written order issued upon a proper voucher. State superintendent is appointed by the governor, with the advice and consent of the council. The superintendent shall keep an office at the seat of government, preserve reports, exercise general supervision of schools, obtain information, take necessary measures to hold state educational conventions, may hold county institutes, publish abstracts of the proceedings of such conventions, prescribe studies to be taught, make report to governor and council annually, compile, publish, and distribute amended school laws; may issue circulars of information, prepare blanks.—**Town** at annual meeting shall choose superintending school committee of three, or shall choose a supervisor of schools. A town failing to choose a committee or a supervisor forfeits not less than $30 nor more than $200. Towns may make by-laws concerning truants, and appoint prosecutors to complain of violation of by-laws. Truant children may be placed in suitable institutions. Compulsory education is required. Free high schools may be established. —**School Districts** are corporations. School-district meetings are called by the agent, upon a written application of three or more voters, stating the reasons and objects. When there is no agent, or when he neglects, it may be called by municipal officers or by a justice of the peace, and the district may determine the manner of notifying future meetings. School district may choose a school agent. The district has power to raise money for erecting, repairing, renting, purchasing and removing school-house, for land, apparatus, appliances, water, and for inclosing grounds. They may locate school-house, dispose of school property, regulate admission to schools, instruct superintending school committee or supervisor when school shall commence. They have power to allow the school-house to be used for religious worship or other similar purposes. District having county graded schools may choose a committee to superintend the expenditure of money. A minority on money questions may appeal to town. School districts may be formed from two or more towns.—**Superintending School Committee** shall designate by lot one of their number to hold three years, and another two years; and the third member shall hold office one year; and each member elected thereafter holds office three years. They shall appoint time and place for examination of teachers, employ teachers, issue certificates, or render valid by indorsement any graded certificates issued to teacher by normal-school principal, county supervisor, or state superintendent. They shall direct the general course of instruction, and select a uniform series of **Text-Books**, not to be changed for five years, purchase books, examine schools, dismiss teacher for cause. They shall expel any obstinately disobedient and disorderly scholar, after a proper investigation of his behavior, if found necessary for the peace and usefulness of the school, and restore him on satisfactory evidence of his repentance and amendment; exclude persons not vaccinated, classify scholars, make annual report, make annual statement.—**Powers and duties of School Agents**: They shall call school meetings, provide fuel and utensils, make reports, procure insurance. If one neglects, special agent may be employed. Shall return account, and return under oath a list of all the school children. Person teaching without **Certificate** forfeits all money contracted for. No teacher's certificate shall be valid for more than one year without the approval of the superintending school committee annually indorsed thereon. Disturbing school or injuring school or school property, liable to a penalty.

MARYLAND.
(Compiled by Hon. E. B. PRETTYMAN, State Superintendent.)

System: State board education, county school commissioners, district school trustees, county examiners. — **Boards** of county school commissioners have care of school property. They may examine charges against teacher, annul certificate, from which appeal lies to the state board education. — **District School Trustees** have charge of schools, furniture and apparatus, attend to repairs, employ teacher subject to confirmation of county school commissioner. They may suspend or expel pupil for cause, and appeal lies to board county school commissioners. — **Teachers** must have certificate from county examiner, or from principal of state normal school, or life certificate from state board of education. First-grade certificate, on examination, may be given by examiner or president of state normal school. State normal-school diploma is equivalent to first-grade life certificate. One who has been a teacher seven years, five years in Maryland, may have, if the state board of education grants it, a life certificate, which may be revoked for cause. We have provided for an annual examination of applicants for life certificates. — **Text-Books**: School-books shall be nonsectarian. County school commissioner may adopt and purchase text-books for the county. — **County Examiner** examines teacher, gives certificates — first grade and second grade good for five years, unless revoked. Any person disturbing public school during session shall be fined or imprisoned. Effect of alcohol and narcotics must be taught.

MASSACHUSETTS.

(Compiled by the Hon. J. W. DICKINSON, Secretary State Board.)

System: State board of education, secretary state board, normal schools, towns, superintendents.—**State Agents of the Board:** The board employs six agents. Five of these are appointed for a general inspection and examination of the public schools of the state, for conferences with school committees and teachers, for instruction in teachers' institutes, and for lectures before the people on subjects connected with public instruction. One is employed in directing and supervising the drawing required by the statutes to be taught in the public schools. Through the observations made by the secretary and agents of the board, the condition of the public schools in all parts of the commonwealth may be known at any time. The knowledge thus obtained furnishes the basis of all school legislation. Each one of the agents has a certain part of the state assigned to him as his field of work.—**Secretary** state board shall have general supervision, attend meetings of teachers when directed by the board, obtain information, make reports, send out blanks.—**Town** may elect school committee of three persons, or a number divisible by three. Committee shall appoint a secretary and keep a record; shall select and contract with teachers.—**Teacher** must have certificate. Committee may issue certificates, dismiss teachers, visit schools, require Bible to be read when not against conscientious scruples; no sectarian books to be used. Shall prescribe text-books and studies. They may purchase, at the expense of the state or town, text-books to be used in the schools, to be loaned pupils free of charge, and may purchase apparatus for the use of the schools. The school committee has charge and superintendence of the use of the school-house.—**Text-Books** may be changed by vote of two-thirds of the whole school committee. Town may require the school committee to appoint a superintendent; union districts may employ a superintendent. The school-house is located by town meeting, and land may be condemned for school-house and the owner may have trial by jury. Persons disturbing school shall be fined. Teachers shall instruct as to effects of narcotics and alcohol. Compulsory education is required.

MICHIGAN.

(Compiled by Hon. FERRIS S. FITCH, State Superintendent.)

Townships are divided into districts by township board of inspectors. Inspectors alter boundaries of districts in their discretion. District has three officers — moderator, director, and assessor, one elected each year; term of office three years. Annual district meeting held first Monday in September, and special meeting may be called on six days' notice. Districts with more than one hundred children may organize as graded-school districts, with a board of five.—**District Board** reports taxes, manages school funds, purchases and leases sites and builds school-houses, employs teachers, prescribes text-books and course of study, and establishes all necessary regulations for management of schools, and makes annual report.—**Director** provides all necessary appendages, and keeps school-house in repair. Director draws and signs warrants upon township treasurer for all moneys raised for district purposes, payable to assessor of district, and orders upon assessor for moneys to be disbursed by district.—**Text-books** adopted by district boards. Physiology must have certain portion devoted to effects of stimulants and narcotics on the human system. Books once adopted not to be changed within five years. District may vote to supply free text-books.—All **Contracts** with teachers must be in writing, and signed by majority of board. Contract with person not holding certificate not valid.—Three grades of certificates granted by **County Board of Examiners** — first grade for four years, second grade for three years, third grade for one year. All questions for county examinations must be prepared by superintendent of public instruction. Life certificates granted by state normal school, state university, and state board of education.—**Rules** for government of school to be made by district board.—**State Superintendent** has general supervision of schools, apportions primary-school interest fund, conducts institutes, appoints visitors to chartered educational institutions. County commissioner of schools has general supervision of schools of county, and grants certificates to teach.

MINNESOTA.

System: State superintendent of public instruction, county superintendent, common, independent and special districts, high-school board.— **Common-School District** is a body corporate. School districts are common-school districts, independent school districts, special school districts. Every district may hold title to its property. Sites may be acquired by condemnation. A new district may be formed by the county commissioners, proper steps being taken; and they may change boundaries.—**Women** may vote and hold office.—**District Meeting** may appoint moderator, adjourn, elect director, clerk and treasurer, and if necessary choose clerk *pro tem.;* designate or change site, vote a tax to purchase or lease a site, to build, hire or purchase a school-house, keep in repair and provide the same with furniture and appendages, procure fuel and purchase school apparatus.— Common-school district **Board of Trustees** is director, treasurer, and clerk. It has power to lease or purchase a site for school-house designated by the voters. Shall build, hire or purchase a school-house with funds provided for that purpose, and when directed may sell or exchange site of school-house. The trustees of any common school, independent, special, or free-school district may, when petitioned therefor by a majority of the legal voters of the district, permit the school-house in their district to be used for purpose of worship or such other purposes as will not interfere with use of school-house for school purposes.—The **Board of Trustees** shall hire teachers and contract with such only as have certificates, but no contract shall be made with any teacher who is related by blood or marriage to any member of the school board without the concurrence of all the members of the board of trustees. The board of trustees may sue on contracts made with them officially to enforce a liability or a duty enjoined by law in favor of such officers of the district; to recover damage for an injury to their official rights or property.—**Independent Districts** elect six as board of directors, called "The Board of Education——;" they elect superintendents, establish schools, provide buildings, purchase or erect school-houses, purchase sites for same, purchase, sell, or exchange school apparatus, furnish fuel for schools, take care of the property of the district, procure insurance and make ordinary repairs upon the same, prescribe text-books, and appoint three school examiners. Examiners may give teachers' certificates.—**County Superintendents** shall examine and license **Teachers,** annul certificates for cause, visit and instruct schools and advise teachers, conduct one teachers' institute a year; aid the school officers. The county superintendent may issue three grades of certificates: first grade, valid in county for two years; second grade, valid in county for one year; third grade, valid in a given district for only six months. They may renew certificates. No person shall receive a first-grade certificate who has not taught school for three months. The diploma from either the elementary or advanced course of study of the state normal school shall be valid as a certificate of qualification of the first grade to teach in the public schools of the state of Minnesota for a period covering the time of the student's pledge of service, namely, two years from date of graduation. At the end of two years' teaching, the diploma of such graduate may be indorsed by the president of the normal school from which it was issued, and by the state superintendent of public instruction. Such indorsement shall make the diploma of the elementary course a valid certificate for five years from its date, and the diploma of the advanced course a permanent certificate of qualification.

MISSISSIPPI.

(Compiled by Hon. J. R. PRESTON, State Superintendent.)

System: State board of education, superintendent of public education, county superintendents, districts.—**State Board of Education** consists of secretary of state, attorney general and superintendent of public education.—**Superintendent of Public Education** has general supervision of the schools, prescribes rules and regulations, presides over meetings of state board, solicits reports, preserves books, apportions state fund, makes reports, keeps a record, and is not to be interested in school-books.—**State Superintendent** shall require reports from county superintendents, prepare blanks and forms, confer with county superintendents, give opinions.—**County Superintendent** appointed in certain counties, elective in all others. Candidates to be examined. He shall have an office, keep record, preserve reports, and shall not teach school.—**Board of Education** shall appoint county superintendent in appointive counties, shall decide appeals from county superintendents or from decisions of state superintendent, and their decision shall be final; may suspend county superintendents for neglect of duty. (This is not to apply to elective county superintendents.) May remove county superintendents for neglect of duty, drunkenness, incompetency, or misconduct. They shall audit claims, fix expenses of state superintendent's office, and regulate the course of study.—**County Superintendents** shall employ teachers recommended by local trustees, holding certificates; they shall examine reports, fix salaries, enforce course of study adopted by the board of education and uniform text-books, visit schools, distribute reports, annually make report, file a list of teachers with chancery and municipal clerks, and keep a record. They may remove teacher for cause. May revoke teacher's license. They are not to speculate in warrants.—**School Board** shall consist of one member from each supervisor's district, appointed by superintendent, subject to ratification by the board of supervisors. The superintendent shall be president of the board. There shall be three **Trustees** for each school district. They shall select teachers; they may suspend or expel pupils for misconduct, visit, provide fuel, protect school property, arbitrate disputes, from which an appeal lies. They cannot use money not appropriated for the purpose. Trustees of separate school districts may prescribe and enforce rules, manage property, enforce study and **Text-Books** adopted by authority, appoint librarian, enforce rules of library, exclude sectarian, partisan or immoral books, suspend or expel pupils for misconduct, visit, furnish blackboards and furniture; elect superintendent, if one is required, and a principal; elect teachers and fix their salaries; impose fines and penalties for neglect. All teachers must have license from county superintendent. All trustees have power to exclude children of filthy or vicious habits, or suffering from contagious diseases. Two first-grade teachers, with the county superintendent, constitute **Board of Examiners.** First-grade license, with general average of 85, valid for two years; a license of first grade, with general average of 90, good for three years; and a second three-years license, obtained after the expiration of the first, shall be renewable in the county as long as the holder continues to teach. Teaching five years under first-grade license exempts from further examinations.—**County School Board** appoints text-book board to adopt series of text-books, which may be changed every five years. Pupils must comply with the regulations, pursue required course of study, and submit to the authority of the teacher. Any pupil injuring the school property is liable to suspension or expulsion; and their parents or guardians are liable for all damages. Any person abusing teacher in presence of school, liable to fine. Any person disturbing public school is liable to fine. Institutes held annually in each county; conductors selected by board of examiners from a list appointed by state board of education. Board of examiners may apply 20 per cent. of surplus institute fund to purchase of works on teaching, which shall be held in charge by superintendent for use of teachers.

MISSOURI.

(Compiled by Hon. L. E. WOLFE, State Superintendent.)

District Organization: The control of the country districts is under a board of three directors, one chosen each year for a term of three years. The control of city, town and village districts is under a board of six members, two of whom are chosen every year for a term of three years. Special meetings of the board must be called by the president.—**District Boundaries:** These are changed by the qualified voters at the annual April election. When the districts or parts of districts affected fail to agree, an appeal may be made to the county commissioners, whose decision is final.—**District Boards:** (*a*) Powers—To contract with qualified teachers, issue warrants, provide necessary rules and regulations for the government, organization and grading of the school. (*b*) Officers—In country schools, president and clerk; in town schools, president, secretary, and treasurer.—**Contracts**—**Warrants:** Contracts must be in writing, signed by president and teacher, and by the secretary or clerk when the teacher's certificate is filed. Certificate must be in force for the entire time the contract is made. Contract must be by order of the board.—**Warrants:** Warrants are issued by the board upon the teachers' fund, building fund and incidental fund, and in no case to exceed the income provided for the year beginning on the first day of July and ending on the thirtieth day of June.—**Text-Books:** The Missouri school-book commission, in September, 1891, contracted with publishers to supply text-books in the common branches for the state of Missouri for five years. A penalty is imposed upon boards of education for permitting the use of any other text-book in the same branches and of the same grade.—**Teachers' Contracts:** Each party is equally bound by the contract; neither party to the contract can dismiss school without the consent of the other party. The rules and regulations of the board, if presented to the teacher when the contract is made, become part of the contract. The burning of the school-house renders the contract void.—**Teachers' Certificates:** Three grades of teachers' certificates in the common branches are issued by the county institute board of instructors and examiners at the annual monthly institutes. Second- and third-grade certificates are valid in the county for one year each; first-grade certificates are valid anywhere in the state for three years; state certificates, in the common branches and in the twelve higher branches, are issued by the state superintendent upon examination, and are valid in the state for life.—**Pupil—Punishment—Rules:** "The board shall have power to make all needful rules and regulations for the organization, grading and government in their school district — said rules to take effect when a copy of the same, duly signed by order of the board, is deposited with the district clerk, whose duty it shall be to transmit, forthwith, a copy of the same to the teachers employed in the schools."—**Powers and Duties of Superintendents, State and County:** It is the duty of the state superintendent to examine teachers and issue state certificates; to prepare blanks for school officers, have them printed at the state's expense, and annually sent out to county commissioners for distribution; to annually apportion to the counties the public school moneys; to make an annual report; to interpret the school law, and to take general charge of school interests. Only two counties in the state have county supervision, which has been adopted by a vote of the people in accordance with the local-option law on the subject; all the other counties have a county commissioner, who annually distributes school blanks, decides district boundary contests when appealed to him, makes an annual report to the state superintendent, interprets school law, and is a member of the county institute board of examiners and instructors.

MONTANA.

(Compiled by Hon. JOHN GANNON, State Superintendent.)

System: State superintendent, county superintendent, districts, trustees, clerk.—**State Superintendent** adopts course of study, rules and regulations for schools, uses a seal, makes reports, prepares forms, and visits schools.—**County Superintendent** visits schools in his county, distributes school information, reports annually, enforces course of study, enforces rules and regulations in examining teachers, keeps record, may appoint trustees to fill vacancies, and ascertains school boundaries. —**Trustees** may employ teachers and employés, and fix compensation; enforce rules of state superintendent; enforce course of study adopted; provide for furniture and supplies; suspend or expel pupil; rent, furnish, repair, and insure school-house; build or remove houses, and purchase or sell lots when directed by vote; hold property; provide books for poor; require pupils to have books; exclude sectarian literature; require teacher to keep register; require teacher to make report, appoint district clerk; and provide evening schools.—**District Clerk** shall provide school supplies, keep school-house in repair, and keep an accurate record. Takes annual census of all children. Separate schools for colored children.—**Teacher's Certificates** from county superintendent for one, two, and three years; first grade three years, second grade two years, third grade one year. Valid in other counties on being registered with superintendent and indorsed. Teachers have power over pupils to and from school and on the play-ground; may suspend pupils for cause. No school officer shall be interested in a contract. Compulsory education is required.

NEBRASKA.

System: State superintendent, county superintendent, district board, district officers, board of education of cities. State superintendent may organize teachers' normal institute, visit schools, decide disputed points, prescribe forms, print school laws, annually report, apportion funds.—**County Superintendent** shall examine teachers, may indorse certificates from this and other states, may grant teachers' certificates, may revoke for cause, must keep record, visit schools, advise teachers.—**Teacher's Certificate:** First grade two years, second grade one year, third grade six months or less. Graduates of colleges and universities, having certificate of first grade, teaching three years in high school in this state, entitled to professional certificate. State superintendent may grant professional state certificate. State normal school may grant certificate. State board of education may grant to students from state normal school three-year certificate and life certificate, but life certificate will lapse after three years' failing to teach. **District Board** shall grade scholars, adopt course of study, make rules, suspend or expel pupils for one term. No officer shall be party to a contract. Board of education of cities may appoint committee to examine teachers; may grant or revoke certificates; and no one shall be interested in a contract. **Text-Books**: School district required to purchase text-books necessary; contract for term of years, not to exceed five; pay for books out of district fund; books loaned to pupils free. This includes school supplies.

NEVADA.

State Superintendent apportions money, makes reports, prescribes forms and blanks, visits each county.—**County Superintendent** apportions money, visits schools, supervises the school interests, distributes blanks, keeps reports, makes reports, presides over institutes, appoints trustees where voters fail to elect, draws warrants for school-books for poor children, and may appoint deputy.—**Trustees** provide maps, furniture and appendages, books for poor children, arrange studies, employ teachers, suspend or expel pupils, apportion fund, establish union school, levy tax when needed.—**Teacher's certificate**: County superintendent appoints two others, making board of examiners, who grant certificates—first grade three years, second grade two years. May grant a county certificate on presentation of a life certificate from any state, or a California state normal-school diploma if not over five years old. Those holding graduation diploma of a state university are entitled to first-grade certificate for life.—**Text-Books**: State board of education prescribes uniform series of text-books, not to be changed oftener than once in four years.

NEW HAMPSHIRE.
(Compiled by Hon. J. W. PATTERSON, State Superintendent.)

System: State superintendent of public instruction, school districts, common and town school board.—**State Superintendent** appointed by governor for two years; has general supervision and control of the educational interests of the state; prescribes forms and blanks, receives and distributes documents and reports, annually makes report, visits, organizes, superintends teachers' institutes.—A **Town** is a single district for school purposes, provided that special districts previously existing may retain their organization; they are corporations. Districts may hold and dispose of property, may raise money to procure site, to build, purchase, rent, repair, and remove buildings, to insure, to provide shade trees, furniture, books, maps, charts, apparatus, and pay debts; may hire money for building school-house, not exceeding four-fifths of the cost, payable in five years; school district may establish high school, or two or more districts adjoining may establish high or public school. A district may contract with an academy to furnish instruction to its scholars. A special district may be united to a town district. Annual district meeting is to be between the 1st of March and the 20th of April. Officers of a district, when not otherwise provided for, shall be: Moderator, clerk, school board of three persons, treasurer, one or more teachers, and such other officers as the voters may think necessary. District may locate a school-house by vote, or by a committee appointed. No committee can bind the district beyond the amount of money voted. Ten or more voters aggrieved with location of a school-house may appeal to the school board; and ten or more voters may appeal to the county commissioners to determine the location, if dissatisfied. Location of school-house shall not be changed in five years, unless appeal is prosecuted. School-house site may be condemned.—**School Board** shall select and hire suitable and competent teachers; may prescribe rules for attendance upon schools; shall purchase text-books and other supplies required to be used in the public schools, and shall loan the same to the pupils free of charge.—**Text-Books** or series of text-books on one subject shall continue in use for five years after introduction, unless price is unreasonably raised. School board may annually change one text-book or one series of text-books which has been in use five years. Sectarian or political books cannot be used. Scholar may be dismissed by the school board for misconduct, or for refusing to conform to the reasonable rules of the school, not to attend until restored by the board. District may make by-laws concerning compulsory attendance, and anyone violating such by-laws shall be punished. District may elect or appoint superintendent of schools, etc. School boards may appoint truant officers, who shall enforce the laws and regulations relating to truants and children between the ages of six and sixteen. Teachers of public schools have the right to attend teachers' institutes. Parents required to send children to school between the ages of eight and sixteen. The normal school a part of the educational system of the state.

NEW JERSEY.
(Compiled by Hon. A. B. Poland, State Superintendent.)

State Board of Education may make by-laws, rules and regulations, appoint county superintendent, decide appeals from state superintendent.—**State Superintendent** has supervision of schools, apportionment of school-money, prepares blanks, decides disputes, suspends or revokes teachers' certificates with consent of state board.—**County Superintendent** examines and licenses teachers, fixes boundaries, which must be approved by state superintendent, divides and unites districts, forms new districts, supervises schools in the county, and may appoint trustees on failure to elect. Appeals from county superintendent are to the state superintendent.—**District Clerk** keeps building in repair, provides fuel, obtains blackboard supplies.— **Board of Trustees** may employ and dismiss teachers and employés; make rules and regulations; may, under vote, erect building, buy land, and borrow money. They may rent, furnish, and repair buildings; purchase property; may enforce regulations of the state board; may prescribe uniform text-books, suspend or expel pupil, provide books, call special meetings of the voters of the district, and permit school-house to be used for other purposes.— **Teacher's Certificate** of state board good for any part of the state as long as the certificate is valid by the terms thereof, for that grade. County board of examiners may grant certificates. Highest grade entitles the holder to teach in any part of the state; any certificate lower than the highest entitles the holder to teach in that county. **State Board of Examiners** may grant certificate. Corporal punishment cannot be inflicted in the state. Compulsory education required in this state.— **State Superintendent of School Census** appoints census enumerators and reports to state board of education the census by school districts.

The board of trustees of the State Normal School and the board of trustees of the N. J. School for Deaf Mutes have been abolished, and their powers and duties transferred to the state board of education. The state board of education now consists of the trustees of the school fund, who are the governor, secretary of state, attorney general, comptroller, president of the senate and the speaker of the assembly, and one member from each congressional district, appointed by the governor; not more than four of whom shall belong to the same political party. These eight members are appointed for five years. School districts are authorized to provide free text-books for the use of the scholars, and to pay for the same by special district tax; also to purchase flags for the school-houses, the money to be raised in the same manner. All poll taxes for school purposes are abolished. Any county raising $100 for the purpose of establishing a teachers' library may receive a like sum from the state, and yearly thereafter $50 from the state by raising a like sum. All school-houses over two stories in height are required to have outside fire-escapes and some means of extinguishing fires. District clerks who refuse or neglect to perform their duties are liable to a fine of $20. The law providing for six trustees in large districts is abolished, and only five are allowed. The notice stating that the question of increasing the number of trustees from three to five can only be posted upon the written petition of one-fourth of the legal voters of the district. All orders issued by district trustees bear interest from date, when the township collector has no funds to pay the same; such interest to cease when said collector gives public notice of his readiness to pay the orders. The proceeds from all sales of riparian lands now go to the state fund instead of the school fund; the latter fund remains intact, however, and the interest can only be used as heretofore. Additional free scholarships in the State Agricultural College are established, equal to one from each assembly district, the expense to be paid from the income of the school fund. Applicants are examined by the county and city superintendents, on the first Saturday in June; the questions for which examination are prepared by the authorities of the college and approved by the state superintendent. The age for admission to the deaf-mute school has been raised from five to eight years.

NEW MEXICO.

(Compiled by Hon. AMADO CHAVES, Territorial Superintendent.)

Territorial Superintendent recommends text-books, prepares forms, reports, and has general supervision.—**County Superintendent,** with two persons appointed by the judge of the district court, constitute examining board; issues teachers' certificates of three grades.—**School Directors** shall provide sites, school-houses and fuel, pay teachers and interest on school bonds, and may levy taxes. May provide supplies and appendages for schools. No warrants shall be issued to exceed the levy for one year. They may employ teachers, and shall control and manage the schools.—**Compulsory Education** is required. Books for poor children may be furnished. Board of education may adopt uniform **Text-Books** and contract for the same, to be sold to the counties for cash. Shall not be changed for four years.—**Board of Education** in cities may elect their officers except treasurer, make their rules, organize system of graded schools, establish high school, and control school property. No sectarian teaching is allowed.—**Teacher** must pass examination on the effects of alcohol on the system.

NEW YORK.
(Compiled by Hon. A. S. DRAPER, State Superintendent.)

District — Organization — Alteration — Meetings: In the cities the schools are administered as provided in special acts of the legislature. In the country the school district is the unit of organization, and may have one trustee or three; in union districts, from three to nine trustees. Districts may be altered by county commissioners. District meetings are held upon call of the trustees.—**Powers of District Boards**: Their powers are somewhat limited. Aside from the power to care for the property and employ teachers, they must ordinarily get authority from district meetings. These meetings can only exercise powers conferred upon them by statute.—**Contracts — Supplies —Warrants**: Answered above; it is a crime for a trustee to be personally interested in any agreement to which he is officially a party.—**Text-Books**: Trustees in the union districts and meetings of the electors in the smaller ones may designate text-books. Once designated, text-books cannot be changed for five years. There is no state or county uniformity in text-books. —**Teachers' Contracts**: Teachers must be employed for fixed terms of not less than ten weeks in duration. They cannot be dismissed in the course of a term of employment except for a cause approved by the state superintendent. They must be paid as often as at the end of each calendar month. When a contract is made, the trustees must give the teacher a written memorandum setting forth its terms.—**Teachers' Certificates**: These are only issued upon written examinations supplied by the state superintendent, and under regulations prescribed by him.—**Pupils—Punishment—Rules**: The school age is from five to twenty-one. Corporal punishment is not prohibited, but has practically ceased. Pupils must submit to the discipline of the school or be debarred its privileges.—**Powers of Superintendent, State and County**: The powers of the state superintendent probably exceed those of any other similar officer in the country. He is a judicial officer so far as all school controversies are concerned, and his determination of them is final, and cannot be called in question by the courts. He prescribes the regulations for the government of the eleven normal schools and the one hundred and twenty teachers' training classes, the school libraries, etc. The institute conductors are appointed and directed by him. He regulates the proceedings of the county commissioners. The last-named officers have general supervisory powers. They may require new school-houses to be built, may require additional furniture to be purchased, may revoke the certificates of teachers, etc. In short, they may do almost anything which experience has shown to be necessary to good school administration.

NORTH CAROLINA.

System: State board education. State board recommend text-books for term of three years. County board to supervise their introduction. No sectarian or political books are to be used. Price of books recommended by state board education. —**Superintendent of Public Instruction** has general supervisory power. Justices and county commissioners elect **County Board of Education** of three persons. The county board settles controversies, decides boundaries, prosecutes suits by the instruction of state superintendent. Commissioners and justices elect county superintendent; and county board and county commissioners may remove county superintendent. County board may lay off the counties into districts. Separate schools for white and colored. Text-books for primary and intermediate courses, one-fourth to consideration of alcohol and narcotics, and high grades twenty pages.—**Teacher** must pass an examination on these subjects before obtaining a certificate.—**County Superintendent** may issue certificate: average of 90 per cent., first-grade certificate; 80 per cent., second-grade; 70 per cent., third-grade, valid for one year in county where issued. County superintendent may suspend teacher for cause, visit schools, and superintend schools.—The **School Committee** of each district shall purchase, hold, sell and transfer sites; shall prosecute suits. School committee may employ and dismiss teachers and fix pay; shall have care of school-houses; receive site by donation; may condemn lands for site. Teachers may dismiss pupils for willful and persistent violation of the rules of school. School committee may contract with teacher of private school having first-grade certificate. It is a misdemeanor to willfully disturb any school. Partial third-grade certificates are abolished. For cause, the county superintendent may revoke a teacher's certificate. He may, for cause, discontinue school. Conductor of county institute with the county superintendent may grant first-grade certificates for three years. Applicant must have studied books on school economy, and theory and practice of teaching. At the close of teachers' county institute first- and second-grade certificates shall be issued. They may be revoked for cause.

NORTH DAKOTA.
(Compiled by Hon. JOHN OGDEN, State Superintendent.)

System: State superintendent of public instruction, county superintendent of schools, district school boards.—**State Superintendent:** General supervisory power; prepare lists of books for school libraries; prepare and furnish all blank forms needed; prepare questions and prescribe regulations for county examinations; issue state certificate upon examination; prescribe courses of study for all public schools and normal schools; provide regulations for institute, appoint conductors and prescribe course of instruction; prescribe course of reading for reading-circles; convene and confer with county superintendents; decide appeals; apportion state tuition fund.—**County Superintendent:** Supervisory power in counties; advise teachers and record visits; convene teachers in reading-circles; meet with school officers; decide matters in controversy; carry out instructions of state superintendent; conduct examinations; hold institutes.—**District School Boards:** Three directors, elected, one each year; treasurer elected biennially, not a member of the board; clerk appointed by the board, not a member of the board; manage schools in district; control property; establish schools; purchase library; employ teachers; levy taxes; make enumeration; no officer shall be interested in any contract or school-book supplies.—**School Districts:** Based upon township plan as to area, and upon district plan as to government; compulsory education; special districts provided for cities, towns and villages.—**Teachers:** No person shall be employed who has not a valid certificate; county superintendent issues three grades according to ratio of correct answers—first grade three years, second grade two years, third grade one year, valid in county where issued; first grade valid in any county when indorsed by the county superintendent; first-grade certificate may be renewed once without examination. State certificates, professional for life and normal for five years, valid throughout the state, issued by state superintendent. Shall attend institutes; shall pursue reading-circle course; shall teach physiology and hygiene, including temperance teaching; may suspend pupil.—**School Funds:** State tuition fund apportioned to all districts on basis of enumeration of children over six and under twenty years of age; consists of two-mill general tax, one dollar and a half poll tax, interest on invested permanent school fund, rental of school lands, net proceeds of fines, penalties and forfeitures; special fund raised by district local taxation; districts may issue bonds.

OHIO.

(Compiled by Hon. O. T. CORSON, State Superintendent.)

Board of Education for township district, divided into sub-districts, consists of township clerk and one director for three years, from each sub-district. The clerk of the township is *ex officio* clerk of the board, but has no vote except in case of a tie. Notice of election to be given for six days in three or more places. Board of education shall hold regular meetings quarterly and from time to time specially.—**District Board** of education in a district may build, enlarge, repair and furnish school-houses, purchase or sell sites, rent rooms and provide apparatus.—**Township Board** education shall furnish fuel, build and repair fences, plant shade trees, and provide other conveniences. Questions of change of site, or erection of new building, are determined by the township board of education.—**Pupils** may be suspended by superintendent or teacher only until time to convene the board of education; no pupil expelled except by two-thirds vote of the board of directors, and not until the parent has had an opportunity of being heard, and no pupil shall be suspended or expelled beyond the current term. The board of education of the district may appoint superintendent, suspend superintendent, hire teachers and employés, and fix salary. No contract can be made for a longer time than that for which a member of the board is elected. Any appointee may be dismissed for cause. No teacher, in township districts, can be employed prior to the annual election for school officers in April, for a term to commence after the current school year. School-book law of 1891 provides that when the state school board has accepted proposals and adopted **Text-Books** the school commissioner shall make out a list. Board of education shall purchase books and sell to scholars at not exceeding 10 per cent. advance.—**Compulsory Education** is required.—

Board of Examiners to be appointed in city district of the first class are to be appointed by board of education of district. County board of examiners is three persons, appointed by probate judge. County board of examiners may grant certificates for one, two and three years in the county, except in city and village districts, which have board of examiners. Examiners may grant certificates for five years to those who have been three years engaged in teaching, twelve months in one place. Examiners may revoke certificate for cause. Teacher who has not a certificate, and who is not qualified to teach physiology and hygiene, cannot be employed. Examiners in city district may examine teachers. Board may grant certificates for one, two and three years. Teachers must give instruction on the effects of alcohol. State board of examiners may issue life certificates.

OREGON.
(Compiled by Hon. E. B. McElroy, State Superintendent.)

Territorial Divisions, consisting of state, county, cities and towns, school districts.—**Officers**: *State Board of Education*—Governor, secretary of state, and state superintendent of public instruction. *Powers, etc.:* Members hold office by virtue of elective official position; hold semi-annual meetings at the state capitol on the first Monday in January and July; sit as a board of examination at their semi-annual meetings; may establish a state board of examination; have power to grant state certificates and diplomas; prescribe rules and regulations for the general government of public schools; have power to make decisions on appeals and other powers of general and special supervision; serve for a period of four years. State superintendent of public instruction, county superintendents, city superintendents, county board of examiners, directors and clerks of city and town districts, directors and clerks of school districts in general.—**Institutions** in general: Graded schools in cities and towns, normal training-schools, ungraded district schools, city institutes for teachers under supervision of city superintendents, county and local institutes for teachers under supervision of county superintendents.—**Higher and Special Institutions** of learning: State University, at Eugene City; State Agricultural College, at Corvallis; State Normal Schools, at Ashland, Drain, Monmouth, and Weston; School for the Blind, at Salem; School for Deaf and Dumb, at Salem; Orphans' Home, at Salem; Orphans' Home, at Portland.—**State Divisions:** Establish schools; provide for a uniform system of public instruction, text-books, taxes, etc.; provide for state board of education; elect state superintendent of public instruction; establish benevolent and special schools; provide for the management of school funds; establish universities, colleges, and professional schools.—**County Divisions:** Elect a county superintendent; secure uniformity in text-books and other features of school work under the general laws of the state.— **City Divisions**—*Cities of 10,000 Inhabitants:* Have local and general control of schools; employ city superintendents, teachers, janitors, etc., and fix their compensation; prescribe course of study; make rules and regulations for government of districts; lease and build school-houses, buy and lease lands, furnish apparatus, furniture, levy taxes, make annual printed report, fix rates on tuition, etc., for school purposes. —**School District Divisions:** Districts are formed in the villages, towns and country for the purpose of extending, localizing and permanently establishing educational facilities; school districts are public corporations; school districts are organized under the provisions of the general statute.—**State Superintendent of Public Instruction:** Serves for a period of four years; is elected by the people; has general supervision of public schools; makes biennial reports to the legislative assembly; is secretary of the state board of education; is authorized to hold meetings of county superintendents; annotates and compiles all school laws ordered published; issues letters and circulars of information, explanation and construction to county and district school officers; holds biennial institutes for teachers in each judicial district; attends county institutes when practicable; holds a state teachers' association annually; makes decisions on appeal from school officers, etc.; prepares uniform series of blanks, registers, forms, rules and regulations for use of public school officers and teachers; visits educational institutions of the state, and secures statistics of same when possible; issues, quarterly, uniform series of questions to the several county superintendents for examination of teachers; visits, as far as practicable, every county in the state annually in the interests of education.—**County Board of Examiners:** Is composed of the county superintendent and two competent persons. They hold public examinations quarterly, and issue three grades of county certificates—first, second, and third—that continue in force three years, two years, and one year, respectively; they may sit as a board of appeals, and may consider all questions that will advance the best interests of the county public schools. —**County Superintendent:** Serves two years; is elected by the people; establishes school districts; makes apportionment of school funds; makes an annual financial report to county court; makes an annual report to superintendent of public instruction; examines teachers, and issues certificates; may revoke certificates obtained by fraud, etc.; is chairman of board of county examiners; holds an annual institute for the teachers under his supervision; visits schools annually; holds local institutes; hears, examines and decides appeals from district officers, teachers, and others; receives reports from district officers and teachers; may arrange a course of study for county schools; has an advisory power in the location of school-houses, selection of teachers, etc.; is *ex officio* chairman of board of arbitrators for division of school property; votes for state uniform series of school-books once in six years.—**District Directors:** There are three for each district; they are elected by the legal voters in the district, and serve for three years; they employ teachers and assist them in the government of the school; they audit all claims against the district and draw all orders; they locate, establish and provide schools; they may levy taxes for buildings, furniture, school-sites, apparatus, etc.; examine and correct assessment rolls; they may levy rate-bills under conditions; they have entire control of the district schools, within certain limits; they must enter into a written contract in employing teachers; they have power to locate school-houses; they must prosecute any person for willfully injuring school property; they issue calls for regular and special meetings; they can dismiss teachers only for good cause shown, and the teacher may take an appeal; two directors constitute a quorum.—**District Clerks:** There is one for each district; they are elected by the people, and serve one year; they must give bonds; the clerk is custodian of all school funds; the clerk is *ex officio* treasurer, and pays all warrants; they make out assessment rolls and collect taxes; they make an annual census of the district; they must keep correct accounts of all meetings and other business; they must make annual reports to the county superintendent; they receive, examine, approve and file teachers' reports.—**District Organization:** County superintendents organize school districts, upon petition from legal voters. Upon notice by county superintendent, of organization, three notices are posted in district, calling for meeting of citizens in ten days to organize; meeting organizes by the election of three school directors and one clerk.—**Text-Books:** A uniform state series of school-books adopted every six years by vote of county superintendents and members state board of examiners.—**Contracts** are made with teachers by boards of directors for specified terms of teaching and salary, etc.—**Rules and Regulations** for the government of public schools and school officers are made by the state board of education. These rules include and govern under the following heads: Appeals, Teachers' Examinations, Pupils, and Classification of Text-Books.

PENNSYLVANIA.

System: Directors and controllers, state superintendent, county superintendent, city, borough and township superintendents, districts, cities, boroughs, and townships, and independent districts. — **State Superintendent** decides disputes between boards of directors, gives advice, makes annual report, removes county superintendent for cause, prescribes forms, and generally superintends. — **County Superintendent** shall visit school, supervise county schools, grant **Teachers' Certificates** and revoke for cause, giving ten days' notice to the holder and to the directors and controllers of the district. County, city and borough superintendents shall issue two grades of certificates; one provisional, good for one year in the locality where issued; the other professional, good in the locality during the term of the officer issuing it and one year thereafter.—**State Superintendent** may grant permanent certificate on recommendation of board of directors, committee, and superintendent; and it shall be valid in the county where issued, and good for one year in any other county, without re-examination. It may be revoked for cause. Certificate of scholarship and teacher's state certificate may be granted by state normal school. Sectarian works may be excluded; scriptures should be read in school. — **Books** may be purchased and supplied free of cost for use in the public schools. Not to be changed oftener than once in three years. Directors not to furnish supplies; school officers not to be agent for books. — **School Directors:** 1. Organize within ten days after the first Monday in June. 2. Establish a sufficient number of schools for all the children above the age of six years that may apply for admission. Attendance is voluntary. 3. Fill vacancies in the board. 4. Levy tax for school and building purposes and appoint collector. 5. Select sites for and erect school-houses. 6. Fix length of school term, which cannot be less than five nor more than ten months. 7. Appoint teachers and fix their salaries. 8. Grade the schools when necessary. 9. Direct what branches shall be taught. 10. Decide what text-books shall be used, which, when adopted, can be changed only once in three years. 11. Visit the schools. 12. May dismiss teachers for sufficient cause. 13. Elect superintendents. 14. Make annual reports to superintendent. 15. Pay all expenses by drafts on the treasurer. 16. Publish annually a financial statement.

RHODE ISLAND.

(Compiled by Hon. THOS. B. STOCKWELL, State Commissioner of Public Schools.)

Two of **State Board of Education** are elected annually, for three years.—**Commissioner of Public Schools** elected annually. He shall recommend, and, with the board of education, bring about uniformity of text-books. He is to advise with school officers, visit and inspect schools, conduct institutes, apportion school-moneys, and act as executive officer of the state board of education.—**Towns** may maintain schools with or without districts. Towns may be divided into districts. Towns may provide for school-houses for districts. School committee shall be elected for three years, one-third each year. Its school committee shall appoint a superintendent for schools of town.—**District** may sue and be sued; may purchase and hold property; may build, purchase, hold and repair school-houses, and supply same with blackboards, maps, furniture and other necessary and useful appendages, and may insure its property. Districts annually elect moderator, clerk, treasurer, collector, and one or three trustees, and may fill vacancies. If district neglect to organize, or fail for six months to employ teacher, the school committee may provide a teacher. The district may devolve its powers on the school committee.—**Meeting** annually, April in each year. Special meeting may be called on request of five electors, stating the object; and if trustees neglect, the school committee may call it. Notice of annual meeting given by publishing in a newspaper of district, or by publishing in two or more public places five days. No person can vote on tax unless liable to pay tax. Joint school district may be established.

by school committees of the two towns. The joint district has all the powers of a single school district, and is under the supervision and regulations of school committee of the town in which located.—**Trustees** of school district have care of property; shall employ one or more teachers for fifty pupils in average daily attendance; provide school-rooms and fuel; visit twice a term and see that pupils have books, and if not provided shall furnish them at expense of district. School committee of town meet at least four times a year; determine and alter districts; locate school-houses; examine teachers for the town; visit twice a term; make rules for attendance, also classification of pupils, text-books, instruction and discipline under direction of commissioner of public schools. May suspend incorrigible pupils. Change of **Text-Books** in any town may be had by two-thirds vote of school committee; not more than once in three years, unless the board of education consents.—**Teacher's Certificate** given by school committee of town, or by some one appointed by said committee, or by trustees of normal school; if signed by the committee, is good in the town for one year, or for such portion of time as specified therein.—**School Committee** may dismiss teacher refusing to conform to their regulations.—**Appeals** from school committee, district meeting, or trustees, are to the commissioner of public schools.—**Compulsory Education:** Children from seven to fifteen years of age must attend twelve weeks some public school, unless the private school is approved by the committee, where teaching is in English. Religious school may be approved. No child between ten and fifteen years shall be employed in any factory or mercantile house except in vacation, unless he has attended school at least twelve weeks in the year preceding his employment.

SOUTH CAROLINA.

(Compiled by Hon. W. D. MAYFIELD, State Superintendent.)

School Officers: State superintendent of education, elected by the people for two years; four members of the state board of examiners, appointed by the governor for two years; county school commissioners, one for each county, elected by the people for two years; two members of the county board of examiners, appointed by the state board of examiners for two years; three school trustees for each school district, appointed by the county board of examiners for two years.—**Powers and duties**: The *State Superintendent*—To give bond and take oath; has general supervision; to visit and report visits; to secure uniformity in the use of text-books; to prepare, have printed and distribute blanks, blank books, instructions, and school law; to collect school-books, apparatus, maps and charts; to certify copies of papers and official acts under official seal; to hold school property in trust; to prescribe regulations to enforce statutes; school commissioners to conform to his instructions; county treasurer to report to annually; is *ex officio* a member of the boards of trustees of all state educational institutions; to report annually the condition of the state educationally—the amount of money spent and for what purpose, the number and condition of school-houses and property, the number in attendance in the public schools for the year and what studying, by sex and race, etc. *State Board of Examiners*—The state superintendent is *ex officio* a member and chairman, and he with the four appointive members constitute the board, and his clerk is the secretary of the board and keeper of its records; are an advisory, appellate and review body; all appeals to be made through the county board of examiners, in writing; to adopt rules and regulations for its own government; to prescribe and enforce rules for the examination of teachers; to prescribe a standard of proficiency before county board of examiners, which will entitle persons examined by such boards to certificates to teach; to prescribe and enforce the course of study in the free public schools; to prescribe and enforce, as far as practicable, the use of a uniform series of text-books in the public schools, except in the city of Charleston—a series adopted not to be changed within five years, without permission of the general assembly;

to grant state teachers' certificates on examination, on recommendation of institute faculties, and diplomas from state chartered institutions; to meet regularly in April and October of each year, and at any other time upon the call of the chairman or request of a majority of the board; (a majority of the board constitutes a quorum;) to appoint members of county boards of examiners; and to use the seal of the state superintendent. *County School Commissioners*—One for each county, elected every two years; governor appoints in case of vacancy; takes oath; gives bond in the sum of $2,000; to visit schools, note course of study, condition of school-houses, etc.; to aid in improvement of teachers and encourage associations; to report annually to the state superintendent the educational condition and standing of his county, giving all required statistics; to report annually to the presiding judge; to be paid a salary and traveling expenses; to keep and use a seal; his consent necessary for the sale of school property; teachers to furnish him with statistics; must countersign teachers' pay certificates before they can be paid; to be provided with an office, etc.; to administer oaths, free of charge, touching all school matters; to report to his county treasurer by Feb. 1st the appropriation of the school fund of his county, by school districts, based on the average attendance of the districts, except the poll tax, which remains in the district where collected; not to be interested in school claims, under penalty; county treasurer to report to monthly; to report quarterly to the comptroller general the names and amounts of all claims approved by him for the quarter, and to attend on the annual settlements of the comptroller general with the treasurer.—The *County Board of Examiners:* The county school commissioner is *ex officio* a member and chairman, and he and the two appointive members constitute the board; are an advisory and appellate body; to hear and determine all local controversies, with right of appeal from to state board; may recommend the purchase of school apparatus; to appropriate funds for the holding of teachers' institutes;

to see that the branches are taught; to hold examinations of teachers, under regulations of the state board, and grant teachers' certificates to those found qualified on examination, and on diplomas from state chartered institutions, good for two years; to meet in April and October of each year and at such other times as the chairman or a majority of its members may call a meeting; to keep a record of its acts; may change school districts or form new ones for convenience or necessity; to limit school term to school fund; to fix pay of school commissioner, county auditor acting in the place of school commissioner for this purpose; former to regulate teachers' salaries; to appoint school trustees and have general jurisdiction. *School Trustees* —Board consists of three, appointed by the county board of examiners; hold school property in trust; give bond in certain cases; may purchase school apparatus when recommended by the county board; to see that the branches are taught; meet at the beginning of the scholastic year, and as often as may be necessary; have general jurisdiction, subject to the county board; to provide sites and school-houses; employ teachers having certificates, and fix their salaries, subject to the county board, and discharge them; call public meetings; sell school property, with school commissioner's consent, and report; to transfer pupils; cannot go in debt; teachers to report to monthly; must not teach; at least two must sign every warrant, pay certificate, for any purpose, on the county treasurer against the school fund, which must be countersigned by the county school commissioner before it can be paid; to administer oaths, free of charge, touching school matters; all claims to be sworn to by the payee before approval by them; not to buy or be interested in school claims; to report list of polls to auditor; auditor to report list of polls to them, and the treasurer to report to them a list of all polls collected.—**School Fund:** The school fund consists of a poll tax of one dollar on each male individual between twenty-one and fifty years of age, which must be applied to educational purposes in the district where collected; and a tax on all taxable property in the state. This tax cannot be less than two mills, but may be as much more as the legislature may levy. The amount raised in each county from this source remains in the county where collected, and is distributable among the school districts of the county in proportion to the average attendance of the districts. These are constitutional provisions, and cannot be in any way altered or changed except by constitutional amendments voted by the people.

SOUTH DAKOTA.

(Compiled by Hon. A. G. SOMERS, Deputy State Superintendent.)

The present school law was enacted at the second session of the legislature of South Dakota, and went into operation March 9, 1891. Prior to its enactment two school codes were in force in the state. One, governing about forty counties, provided for so-called township districts, which were divided into sub-districts containing one school each; the other, governing the remaining counties of the state, provided for a school-district system, of which each district contained but one school. The present law upon taking effect did not change the boundaries of school corporations, but abolished sub-districts. All school corporations are now called school districts. As a result of the adoption of the present law, school districts are unequal in size, some containing but one school, while others contain two or more, as the district was formerly under the school-district or school-township system. The present code may be called a compromise between the two systems just mentioned, and was adopted with a view to effect uniformity in the administration of the school law of the state. Provision is made in the law whereby the large districts — school-township districts — may be cut up into smaller ones of one school each, and smaller districts consolidated into a large one equal in area to the civil township. Provision is also made for changing boundary-lines between adjacent districts. Districts containing two or more schools hold four stated or regular meetings each year for the transaction of business;

districts containing but one school hold one regular meeting of the board annually; but provision is made for calling meetings of the voters at any time, who may instruct the board relative to the management of the school. Special meetings of the electors of a school district may be called, as occasion requires, to vote upon the question of issuing bonds, selecting school-house sites, building or hiring school-houses, etc. The law is defective in not providing for election details, but will no doubt be remedied at the next legislative session. The care, control and general management of the schools devolve upon the school boards. For districts governed by the general provisions of the act, the school board consists of three — a chairman, a clerk, and a treasurer. These officers are elected for a term of three years, but their terms are so arranged that one goes out of office and his successor is elected each year. In cities and towns governed by the provisions of chapter 9 of the act, the governing board is styled a board of education, and consists of three, except that in cities and towns divided into wards, one member shall be elected from each ward. The school board is empowered to make all necessary repairs to the school-houses, out-buildings, and appurtenances, and furnish fuel and all necessary supplies for the school. The board makes all contracts on behalf of the district. Teachers' contracts are required to be in writing, and must be signed by at least two members of the board, and the teacher. The school board of each district determines what text-books may be used in the schools, except in such counties as have adopted uniformity of text-books as provided in chapter 104, Session Laws of 1891. In such counties the county board of education selects the text-books. All persons giving instruction in the public schools of the state governed by the school laws of 1891, except specialists mentioned in section 13 of chapter 2, are required to hold a certificate of qualification, either from the state or county superintendent. All children between six and twenty years are of legal school age. School boards are required to coöperate with teachers in the government and discipline of the schools, and may make proper rules and regulations for the same. They may temporarily expel from school any pupil for insubordination and disobedience. County superintendents exercise a direct supervision over the schools within their jurisdiction, except in towns of more than one thousand inhabitants. The county superintendent is the organ of communication between school officers and the state superintendent of public instruction, whose supervision is for the most part advisory. The state superintendent has appellate jurisdiction over cases determined by the county superintendent.

TENNESSEE.
(Compiled by Hon. W. R. GARRETT, State Superintendent.)

System: State superintendent, county superintendent, district school directors.—**State Superintendent** appointed by the governor, confirmed by the senate. Duties are: To collect and dispense information; to inspect; to supervise the administration of schools; prepare forms and blanks; have printed school laws; to appoint agents to examine the schools in the county; require county superintendent to report; to prescribe the mode of examining and licensing teachers, and their qualifications; preserve documents; report to the comptroller the scholastic population; and report to the governor.—**County Superintendent** is elected by the county court biennially; may be removed for misconduct or inefficiency, charges having been made in writing. Has supervision of schools in the county; visits teachers and district directors, to promote their interests, to suggest changes in text-books, and to see that directors make reports; to perform such duties in regard to examination of teachers and issuing certificates to them as are required of him by the state superintendent; to report to the county trustee the scholastic population; to make annual report; to keep record.—**District Directors:** Three elected in each district. Duties: To explain and enforce the laws and regulations; employ teachers, and dismiss them for incompetency, improper conduct, or inattention; to suspend or dismiss pupils when the prosperity and efficiency of the school make it necessary; to use the school fund apportioned; to see that the census is taken; to hold regular meetings as prescribed and special meetings when called by the chairman or by any one of the members; to keep separate white and colored schools; to control public-school property. No state or county officer can be interested in a school contract.—**Contracts** with teachers must be in writing.—**Teacher,** for cause, may suspend pupil from attendance on school until the case is decided by the board of school directors, which shall be with as little delay as possible. State board of education controls normal schools; has no other powers. Cities, incorporated towns, and municipal corporations of the class called taxing districts, have power to establish boards of education, and to establish and maintain graded high schools.

TEXAS.

(Compiled by Hon. J. M. CARLISLE, State Superintendent.)

Districts: One hundred forty-five counties have school districts; the commissioners' court fixes the boundaries. Change by majority vote of each district affected by the change. Citizens meet on the first Saturday in June and elect three trustees, who must be able to read and write. Notices are sent out by the commissioners' court as for other elections. Seventy-five counties have no fixed districts. They are called community counties. The citizens of each community petition the county superintendent each year for a school, and that certain named persons be appointed trustees. The patrons of any school are not limited as to territory. There is no continued organization. —**Powers of District Trustees:** They contract with teachers, determine the number of schools in the district, the location of each, and when schools shall open and close; they manage the schools, subject to the regulations of the county and state superintendent; they approve all vouchers; they are not allowed to create deficiency debts; they can dismiss teachers, but the teachers so dismissed may appeal to the county and state superintendents; they may employ assistant teachers. In cities, towns, and taxing districts, the trustees have increased powers as to the general management of the schools, and are not limited as to the salaries of teachers.—**Contracts, Supplies, Warrants:** The trustees contract with teachers, subject to the limitation as to salaries and certificates fixed by law and the approval of the county superintendent. The contracts of cities, towns, and taxing districts are not required to be approved by the county superintendent. They buy all supplies, make repairs, and have school-houses built. They cannot, under the law, create deficiency debts for teachers' salaries or other purposes. All warrants must be approved by the county superintendent, and his permission must be obtained before warrants for supplies, repairs, or buildings, are drawn.—**Teacher** cannot contract until he has a valid certificate. In the rural schools and in the non-taxing towns salaries are limited to the grade of the certificate held—third grade $30, second grade $50, first grade $75. They may receive tuition collected from pupils over and under school age, and from those who attend from other districts, or this may go for extending the school term. —**Teachers' Certificates:** Each county has an examining board—three teachers with first-grade certificates; questions are furnished by the state superintendent. Examinations are held quarterly. These certificates are good only in the county in which they are issued. A third-grade certificate is good for one year, a second-grade for one or two years, according to the grade made, a first-grade good for one, two or three years, according to the grade made. A summer normal institute is held in each senatorial district each year. First- and second-grade certificates are issued, good for two years. Questions are prepared by the state superintendent, and graded by a state board appointed by him. State certificates are granted once a year on specified subjects, papers being graded by a state board. Life certificates are granted to B. S. and A. B. graduates of first-class colleges, provided each candidate has taught five years in Texas.—**Pupil**—**Punishment**—**Rules**: The rules are left to local trustees. A pupil may be suspended for the remainder of any school year on account of incorrigible conduct.—**State Superintendent**: He may issue directions in all cases wherein the law makes no provisions, or when hardships or delays will result without such rules. He is the executive officer of the state in all educational matters. He has power to withhold the compensation of teachers and school officers until the required reports are made. He submits forms for reports, hears appeals from the rulings and decisions of the county superintendents, and acts as secretary of the state board of education.—**County Superintendent**: He has the general supervision of all the schools in his county; he visits all the schools, approves all vouchers against the school fund, and makes a report to the state superintendent.

VERMONT.

System: Superintendent of education, town superintendent, towns, districts; superintendent to have general supervision; shall hold teachers' institute in each county during his biennial term; shall visit, lecture, advise. Graduate normal school holding ten-years' certificate, teaching 200 weeks, may obtain a renewal good until revoked. Graduate of highest course of normal school in another state may obtain certificate to teach in any county. Towns may be organized into districts and may be divided into districts, or several towns may unite and form a district.—**District at Annual Meeting** elect a moderator, clerk, collector, treasurer, one or three auditors, and a prudential committee of one or three persons, and may elect the collector of town taxes.—**Prudential Committee** employ teacher, remove him when necessary, and may adopt measures not in conflict with town superintendent. Prudential committee, when not prohibited by vote, may permit use of house for religious or other purposes. Schools may be maintained under the town system. Town central school system for advanced pupils may be adopted. Town system may be abolished. School age is five to eighteen years. Compulsory education is required.—**Text-Books** may be changed every fifth year. Any town or district may purchase and hold text-books for use in its schools if it so votes in a meeting warned for that purpose. The county supervisor and county board of education are abolished, and town superintendents restored. The state superintendent and governor shall appoint in each county an **Examiner of Teachers**, and fill vacancies. Examiners to consult with town superintendents and hold suitable number of examinations of teachers in spring and autumn; may employ suitable person to examine; shall issue certificates on examination papers and report of person conducting examination; if examiner is unable to issue certificate, state superintendent may. No person to teach without certificate; exception as to principal of highest department in graded schools; teachers to be not less than seventeen years of age. Three grades of certificates to be issued by examiner: first grade to one teaching forty weeks, with examination papers of grade required by state superintendent, good for five years in any town in the state; second grade to one who has taught twelve weeks, and whose examination papers are of grade required by state superintendent, and good for two years in any town in the state; third grade limited to a particular school and not to exceed one year. Examiner may be removed by state superintendent and governor for cause.—**Superintendent of Education** shall prepare questions for examination and blanks for teachers' certificates, and fix the standard required.—**Town Superintendents** may issue permits to teach a particular school for a single term, not to be renewed more than three times to anyone. Town superintendent of each town shall have power to dismiss any teacher who is incompetent. Nothing in the above shall interfere with existing arrangements of such towns as may be acting under the town system of schools; and the chairman of the school directors shall perform the duties of the town superintendent. School districts hold annual meeting on the last Tuesday of March.

VIRGINIA.

(Compiled by Hon. JOHN E. MASSEY, State Superintendent.)

Each county is subdivided into school districts; three trustees for each school district constitute district school board; district trustees of a county constitute county school board. Each district board elects from its members a chairman and a clerk.—**Duties of District School Boards:** Explain and enforce school laws, rules, regulations, and observe same; employ and dismiss teachers; suspend or dismiss pupils; decide who may receive text-books free (refers to indigent pupils); see that school census is taken; hold regular meetings; call meeting of people for consultation in regard to school interests of districts; to make estimates of school funds; manage and control school property of district; make reports to county superintendent; to visit schools, etc.—**District Boards** make contracts (written) with teachers, purchase supplies, and issue warrants in payment of teachers' salaries and incidental and other expenses. —Under the constitution, the state board of education provides for uniformity of **Text-Books.** The state board prescribes a list of books from which county and city school boards select. (State board is composed of the governor, superintendent public instruction, and attorney-general.)—**Teachers** elected by district boards; must hold certificate issued by superintendent of county or city in which they purpose teaching; elected by district boards from list licensed by county or city superintendent; must enter into written contract with district board. Schools free to all persons between the ages of five and twenty-one years residing within district; white and colored pupils taught in separate schools.—**State Superintendent**—Duties: Chief executive of school system; see that school laws are faithfully executed; use all proper means to promote a desire and appreciation of education among the people; determine true intent and meaning of the school laws and regulations, etc.; prepare blank forms, registers, etc.; require reports; inspect schools; decide certain appeals; file decisions and official papers; apportion state school funds; submit annual report to board of education, etc.—Duties of **County and City Superintendents:** Explain school system; sub-apportion school funds; examine teachers and grant certificates; promote efficiency of teachers; assist in organizing district boards; visit and examine schools; decide appeals and complaints; administer oaths and take testimony in matters relating to public schools; require reports from district clerks, etc.; keep records of official acts; make annual report to superintendent public instruction, etc.—**County and City Treasurers** collect and disburse school funds. All school funds are paid out on warrants of district school boards. State school funds are apportioned on basis of school population.

WASHINGTON.
(Compiled by Hon. R. B. BRYAN, State Superintendent.)

System: State superintendent of public instruction, state board of education, county superintendents of common schools, board of directors, district clerk for each district.—**State Superintendent** shall have general supervision over all matters pertaining to the common schools; shall report to the governor biennially, prepare forms, travel and visit the different counties, cause to be printed the common-school laws; shall be *ex officio* president of the board of education; shall biennially call a convention of county superintendents; apportion state school fund; shall require a report from state and private schools; shall keep a directory of school officers and teachers; shall file all records and papers, decide points of law submitted by county superintendents, or on appeal from the county superintendents—and his decision is final unless set aside by a court of competent jurisdiction; may employ clerk.—**State Board of Education:** Four persons appointed by the governor, with the superintendent of public instruction, shall constitute the state board of education. They shall adopt uniform series of **Text-Books** once in five years; may reject proposals, (publisher must give bond); shall prepare a course of study; use a seal. They shall sit as a board of examiners, and grant state certificates and life diplomas.—**State Certificates** shall be granted to such as shall satisfy the board that they have taught twenty-seven months, nine months in the public schools of the state, and must pass a satisfactory examination in the branches required, or file a certified copy of a diploma from some state normal school, or of a state or territoral certificate from any state or territory the requirements to obtain which shall not have been less than those required by this state. State certificates are valid for five years, and may be renewed or may be revoked by the board. Life diplomas are granted to such as have taught successfully ten years, not less than one of which shall have been in the common schools of this state. They may be revoked for cause. The board must prepare questions for county examinations.—**County Superintendent** shall have general supervision of the county, visit schools, enforce rules and regulations and course of study adopted by the state board, keep record, administer oaths, preserve manuscripts of examination; teachers may appeal to the state superintendent. County superintendent makes annual report, keeps transcript of boundaries, shall endeavor to harmonize boundaries, may appoint directors and district clerks to fill vacancies and for new districts, apportion school funds.—**Teachers' Certificates** are: First grade five years, second grade two years, third grade one year. Board of examiners may issue certificates without examination to graduates of state normal schools, or to holders of state certificates or life diplomas from other states.—**Board of Directors** for school district, three in number. They shall have power to employ and discharge teachers and employés; shall enforce rules and regulations of the superintendent of public instruction and state board; shall provide supplies; rent, repair, furnish and insure, build or remove school-houses; purchase or sell real estate when directed by vote of district; may hold title to property for district; may suspend pupil for cause; shall exclude immoral or sectarian books; may authorize use of school for other purposes. Appeal may be taken from their decisions to county superintendent.—**District Clerk:** Elected in each district. He shall keep records, take census, note attendance at schools, exclude Indians and Chinese, note defective youth, report names of children, enrollment, teachers' wages, text-books used, etc., etc.—**Text-Books** not to be changed in less than five years.—**Complusory attendance** is required. Party abusing teacher or disturbing school or school meeting is liable to punishment.

WEST VIRGINIA.

System: State board of education, state superintendent, county superintendent, school districts, district trustees, board of education of district.—**Board of Education** may determine number of teachers, and salaries.—**Teachers:** Teachers' certificate — first grade not less than $25 per month, second grade not less than $22 per month, third grade not less than $18 per month.—**Board of Education** of a district or independent district is a corporation, and succeeds to the rights of former township and district boards; may prosecute suits; is liable for the claims of predecessors; shall receive and hold property. Board of education appoints secretary. Board of education determines and locates schools, changes boundaries. Appeal is taken to county superintendent. Teacher must have temperate habits and good morals. Effects of alcohol and narcotics are to be taught. Teacher may be removed for incompetency, neglect of duty, intemperance, profanity, cruelty, or immorality. Trustees may exclude pupils having diseases; may suspend or expel pupils disorderly, refractory, indecent, or immoral; but all the trustees must have had notice, and two must concur, and this is subject to revision by the board of education.—**County Board of Examiners:** Composed of county superintendent and two experienced teachers. All applicants for teachers must be examined. First-grade certificate, average 90 per cent.; not less than 75 on any one branch; good for four years.

Second-grade, average 80 per cent.; not less than 70 on any one branch; good for two years. Third-grade, general average of 70; not lower than 60 on any one branch.—**State Board of Examiners** can grant certificates to graduates of state normal school or state university. (First class is twelve years, and second six years.)—**Text-Books** adopted by state, furnished pupils for cash. Te be enforced in any school district, when the board of education concur.

WISCONSIN.
(Compiled by Hon. O. E. WELLS, State Superintendent.)

School Districts are formed and altered by town boards. Every district is deemed duly organized when any two of the officers elected at the first meeting consent to serve. The time for holding the annual meeting is fixed by statute, and occurs on the first Monday in July. Special district meetings may be called by the clerk, upon the petition of any five legal voters of the district. Six days' notice is required for a district meeting. —The **District Board** represents the district in all business transactions, and exercises a general control over the property of the district. The board is composed of a clerk, director, and treasurer. No act is valid unless voted at a meeting of the board. The clerk keeps all records, takes the census annually, and makes all reports. The director countersigns all orders, and represents the district in actions by and against it. The treasurer is the custodian of the district's funds, and pays out the same only on the order of the clerk, countersigned by the director. The board *only* has power to bind the district by contract. All necessary supplies are furnished by the board.— **Text-Books** may be purchased by the district and loaned to pupils, if the legal voters so decide at the annual meeting. Otherwise the pupils furnish the books. The board determines the text-books to be used. The board makes all contracts for the services of teachers. Only duly qualified teachers can enter into contracts to teach public schools. Certificates granted by the proper authority, and diplomas of normal schools, state university, and colleges, located within the state, when countersigned by the state superintendent, are the only evidence of the legal qualification of teachers. The contract is required to be in writing, and a copy of the certificate must be attached thereto. The schools are free to all children between the ages of four and twenty years. Residents of the district between the ages of twenty and thirty years may be admitted by the board, free of charge. The board has power to make all needful rules for the government of schools, to suspend or expel pupils who persistently refuse to obey the rules established.—The **State Superintendent** has general supervision over the public schools of the state. He prescribes courses of study for high schools, examines and determines all appeals, apportions the income of the school fund, and is a member of the board of regents of the normal schools and state university. The county superintendent examines and licenses teachers, visits schools, conducts institutes, and advises teachers and school boards in all matters relating to schools.

WYOMING.

(Compiled by Hon. STEPHEN T. FARWELL, State Superintendent.)

System: State superintendent, county superintendent, school districts.—**State Superintendent** shall have general supervision, may grant certificates, and regulate grade of county certificates.—**County Superintendent** may grant teacher's certificate, good for two years; shall determine appeals from decision of district courts. An appeal from county superintendent to board of county commissioners, and from county commissioners to superintendent of public instruction, is granted on formation of school district.—**District Meeting** may fix the site, vote money, purchase or lease school-house; build, rent or repair school-house; furnish supplies; direct sale of property; delegate these powers to district board.—**Compulsory Education** is established; effects of alcohol and narcotics are required to be taught.—Superintendent may grant **Teach-**

ers' **Certificates**: Sec. 3908. The superintendent of public instruction shall also have power to grant certificates of qualification to teachers of proper learning and ability, to teach in any public school in the state, and to regulate the grade of county certificates. Sec. 3914. He shall examine every person offering himself or herself as teacher of public schools, and if in his opinion such person is qualified to teach a public school, shall give him or her a certificate authorizing him or her to teach a public school in his county for one year. Whenever practicable, the examination of teachers shall be competitive, and the certificate shall be granted according to the qualifications of the applicant. Sec. 3916. The county superintendent of any county in the state may, if in his opinion the interest of the schools will be as well served, grant a certificate to any person of requisite ability and qualification for two years or during his term of office, or may renew a certificate previously given to such person, without a re-examination.—**Text-Books** (Constitution): Sec. 11. Neither the legislature nor the superintendent of public instruction shall have power to prescribe text-books to be used in the public schools. Adoption and use of text-books (Laws of 1888): Sec. 3. At the expiration of the period of five years for which the books now in use are adopted, the county superintendents and city superintendents of schools in the state shall meet at a call of the state superintendent of public instruction to adopt a series of text-books, and the books thus adopted shall be the only legal text-books to be used in the public schools of the state for the ensuing five years.—Authority of the board to **Admit or Remove Scholars**: Sec. 3037. The district board shall have power to admit scholars from adjoining districts, and remove scholars for disorderly conduct; and when scholars are admitted from other districts the district board may, in their discretion, require a tuition fee from such scholars.

Teachers' Certificates.

I am indebted to Hon. Geo. W. Winans, State Superintendent of Kansas, who had issued a circular note of inquiry on the subject of the effect of a teacher's certificate in states other than where issued, and the responses received by him are set out below:

Alabama.—Applicants must pass an examination. Nothing said in the law about diplomas from other states. (School Law.)—Jno. G. Harris, State Sup't.

Arkansas.—"Life certificates are granted upon examination alone. No credit is given to the applicant for any similar document granted by any other state or any college."—J. H. Shinn, State Sup't.

California.—Certificates are granted, without examination, to holders of state normal-school diplomas and state life diplomas. (Circular.)—J. W. Anderson, State Sup't.

Colorado.—The state board of education may, upon the recommendation of the state board of examiners, grant state diplomas, without examination, to persons holding a diploma from some other state. (Circular.)—N. B. Coy, State Sup't.

Connecticut.—"The board does not think it has authority to give credit for certificates granted in other states. If we had authority we probably would not accept them."—Chas. D. Hine, Sec'y.

Delaware.—"No credit is given to certificates granted in other states."—C. C. Trudal, Sup't of Kent Co.

Florida.—"Certificates from other states are considered as evidence of proper character to a degree, but certificates are not issued upon them."—Albert J. Russell, State Sup't.

Georgia.—"I have no authority under our law to recognize diplomas or licenses from other states."—S. D. Bradwell, State School Commissioner.

Illinois.—"State certificates shall only be granted upon public examination, in such branches and upon such terms and by such examiners as the state superintendent and the principals of the state universities may prescribe."—Henry Raab, State Sup't.

Indiana.—"Our state board does not give credit to state certificates issued by other states."—Hervey D. Vories, State Sup't.

Iowa.—"A state certificate from another state may be accepted in place of the examination in academic studies. The candidate, however, will be obliged to submit his credentials to the board of examiners, together with proof of at least eighteen months' successful work in Iowa. He will also be obliged to pass an examination in theory and art of teaching, or such branches as the board may designate."—J. B. Knoepfler, Pres. State Board of Education.

Kansas.—"The law does not recognize such certificates or diplomas. They are of no value in this state."—Geo. W. Winans, State Sup't.

Kentucky.—"No credit is given to these certificates and diplomas granted in other states."—Ed. Porter Thompson, State Sup't.

Louisiana.—"Our law makes no provision for the issuing of life certificates. Teachers have to undergo examinations by the committees appointed by parish boards for that purpose."—W. H. Jack, State Sup't.

Maryland.—"No certificates are granted in this state upon examinations taken in other states."—E. B. Prettyman, State Sup't.

Massachusetts.—"By law, no certificate from another state is accepted as sufficient."—J. W. Dickinson, Sec'y.

Michigan.—"It has never been the practice in this state to grant certificates on examinations held in other states, or to indorse certificates granted in other states."—Ferris S. Fitch, State Sup't.

Minnesota.—"The certificates of other states are not honored in this."—D. L. Kiehle, State Sup't.

Mississippi.—"We issue no life licenses, and do not recognize those of other states."—J. R. Preston, State Sup't.

Missouri.—"The state superintendent of Missouri is not permitted, in granting state certificates, to take into consideration diplomas and certificates from other states."—L. E. Wolfe, State Sup't.

Montana.—"Under our statute we cannot issue term certificates or life diplomas to teachers upon examination."—John Gannon, State Sup't.

Nebraska.—"Our statutes do not authorize the granting of state certificates on similar documents granted in other states."—A. K. Goudy, State Sup't.

Nevada.—Upon presentation to the state board of a life certificate of any state, of any state normal-school diploma, the board may grant a state certificate without examination. (Circular.)—Orvis Ring, State Sup't.

New Hampshire.—"No state certificates are issued."—H. L. Huntrep, Clerk for Sup't.

New Jersey.—"The state board may indorse the diploma of another state when the requirements for such certificates are equivalent to those required in this state."—E. Q. Chapman, State Sup't.

New York.—"The state superintendent is authorized by statute to indorse state certificates from other states."—A. S. Draper, State Sup't.

North Carolina.—"This state issues no life diplomas. All certificates are issued upon examination."—S. M. Finger, State Sup't.

North Dakota.—State certificate will be granted only upon examination. (Circular.)—John Ogden, State Sup't.

Ohio.—"So far our board has not recognized the state certificates granted in other states as authorizing their holders to a certificate from our board without examination, although the taking of such a position has been frequently discussed in our board meetings favorably."—James W. Knott, Clerk.

Oregon.—"We recognize state papers from other states of an equivalent grade with those issued by our board here."—E. B. McElroy, State Sup't.

Rhode Island.—"We have at present no system of state certificates."—Thos. B. Stockwell, State Commissioner.

South Carolina.—"Certificates from other states are not recognized in this state."—W. D. Mayfield, State Sup't.

South Dakota.—"Our school laws make no provision for recognition of certificates issued in other states."—Cortez Salmon, State Sup't.

Texas.—"We have no law by which we can recognize examinations held in other states."—J. M. Carlisle, State Sup't.

Vermont.—"We do not issue either term certificates or life diplomas."—Edwin F. Palmer, State Sup't.

Virginia.—"Diplomas and certificates from other states are not recognized in Virginia."—John E. Massey, State Sup't.

Washington.—"Applicants filing a certified copy of a state certificate, the requirements to obtain which shall not have been less than those required in Washington, may be granted certificates or diplomas. (School Laws, page 10.)"—R. B. Bryan, State Sup't.

West Virginia.—"Other states are not included in our law,

and their state certificates do not have any force within this state."—B. S. Morgan, State Sup't.

Wisconsin.—Applicants must pass successful examination. (Pages 93 and 94, School Laws.)—O. E. Wells, State Sup't.

Wyoming.—"Certificates granted in other states are not valid in Wyoming."—S. T. Farwell, State Sup't.

INDEX.

A.

	PAGE
Abandonment—building	21
Absence—rules	174, 175
Acceptance—building	22
Accident—pupils; expelling	198
Admission—pupil	171, 172
Adoption—text-book	301–312
Aiding—religious (see Parochial)	157–170
Alabama—	
Laws	331
Tax	228
Alteration, district	54–80
Annual meeting	117
Apparatus—	
Officer	146
Supplies	225
Appeal	5–10
District alteration	57, 58, 63, 74
District organization	86
Funds, apportionment	96
Location site	200
Pupil, residence	194
Superintendent	217–219
Superintendent, county	145
Superintendent, state	6, 214
Appendages	30–33, 225
Apportionment, funds	92–98
Mandamus	93
Suit	93
Superintendent, state	94, 96
Appropriation, funds	98, 99
Arbitration—	
District alteration	57
Suits	209
Arizona—laws	333
Arkansas—	
Laws	334
Tax	228
Assault—pupil; punishment	177
Asylum—	
Aiding	158
Funds	95, 112
Attorney—contract	44

B.

	PAGE
Ballot—election	134, 135
Bible, text-book, 164,170,171,176,	198
Bill exchange—contracts	46
Board education—term	154
Boarding teacher	51
Bond	10, 16, 92
Builder's	18, 21
Funds	100–102
Official, liability	137–143
Surety	227, 228
Books (see Text-books)	296
Boundary—	
District	81, 87
See District Alteration	54–80
Officers, powers	145
Building—	
Contract	16–28
Control (see Building, use)	28–30
District organization	82
Election	91
Repairs	30–33
Use	33–36

C.

	PAGE
California—	
Laws	336
Tax	229
Certificate, teacher's	262–274
Changes—building	18
Chart—supplies	225
Chinese pupil	173
Classification pupils	40
Clerk—	
Liability	140
Qualification	148
Records	195, 196
Vacancy	154
Collector—qualification	147
Colleges—universities	317–321
Colorado—	
Laws	337
Tax	229

(405)

Colored school 36– 44
Commissioner—
  Officer.. 136
  Qualification................................. 146
  Term 153
Committee—
  Building 17, 22
  Qualification................................. 147
Compensation — teacher...... 274– 279
Condemnation—
  Site... 201
  Site, meeting 124
Connecticut—
  Laws 339
  Tax.. 230
Constitution—
  District alteration 62
  Funds... 100
  Statute... 208
  Use of funds................. 157– 170
Contract—
  Altering... 227
  Attorney 44
  Building 16– 28
  District alteration............. 61, 65
  Notes.. 45, 46
  Officers.. 143
  Officer interested....................... 46
  Officer, liability 48
  Power....................................... 48– 50
  Ratification.................................. 51
  Site.. 201
  Suit.. 210
  Teacher........................... 280– 289
  Time 132
Conveyance — site....................... 202
Corporation.................................... 53
  District alteration 77– 79
Costs — officer's liability............. 138
County superintendent—(see Appeal)........................... 217, 218
Crime—
  Disturbing school 54
  Indictment 133

D.

Damages—(see Pupil; Punishment.)
  Negligence, building................ 33
Debts—
  District alteration.....62, 64, 65, 68
                                 73–75, 77– 80
Delaware — laws........................ 339
Director—
  Qualification................................ 149
  Vacancy... 156

Discharge and dismissal—
  Pupil 173– 175
  Teacher......................... 289– 294
Dissolution, district.................... 82
District—(see minor sub-heads, as Contracts, Sites, etc.)
District alteration........... 66, 54– 80
  Appeal.. 74
  Boundary............................. 71, 72
  Contracts...................................... 61
  Corporation................................. 77
  Debts..................................... 64, 65
  Mandamus.......................... 71, 73
  Notice.................................... 62, 63
  Suit... 70
  Title... 61
District boundary 81
District dissolution 82
District library............................. 82
District organization............ 82– 88
  Appeal 86
  Boundary..................................... 87
  Defects................................... 84, 85
  Evidence....................................... 85
  Quo warranto............................. 86
  Record 86
  Tax.. 84
District suits.................................. 209
District union 89, 90
Disturbing school — (see Laws)... 54

E.

Election — (see Voters)............. 323
  Bond 10
  Building.. 91
  Notice.................................... 91, 92
  Officer................................. 134– 136
  Site...................................... 203, 204
  Superintendent, county.......... 135
Evidence — record............. 195, 196
Execution — judgment........ 114– 116
Exemption — tax (see Tax, each state)........................ 228– 262
Exhibitions — building............. 34
Expulsion, pupil 173– 175

F.

Fees — (see Officer, compensation.)
Fence.. 31
Fence — supplies........................ 225
Fines — funds............................... 101
Florida—
  Laws 340
  Tax.. 230
Free — text-book 269

INDEX. 407

Funds—
  Apportionment............ 92– 98
  Appropriation.......... 98, 99, 113
  Bonds................................. 100
  Constitution 100
  Control............................... 144
  District alteration 66
  Fines 101
  Interest.............................. 102
  Investing........................... 102
  Judgment; payment............ 99
  Liability............................ 137
  Liquor................................ 103
  Loan...................... 103–108, 113
  Officer............................... 109
  Sectarian schools........... 157– 170
  Use 110–112, 128
Funds, use—constitution 100
  Orphans................................ 95

G.

Georgia—
  Laws................................. 341
  Tax................................... 231
German text-book.................. 299
Grammar school..................... 113

H.

Hall—building........ 17, 20, 21, 23
High school............................ 113
Holiday, religious 200

I.

Idaho laws............................. 342
Illinois—
  Laws 343
  Tax.................................... 231
Indiana—
  Laws 344
  Tax.................................... 233
Indictment—officer 139
Industrial schools—aiding.. 159– 170
Injunction—
  Building............................... 29
  Site................................... 204
Inspector—election 136
Institute—teacher 295
Interest—
  Contracts............................. 46
  Funds................................ 102
Iowa—
  Laws 345
  Tax.................................... 233

J.

Janitor—contract.................... 49
Joint high school.................... 113
Judgment—
  Execution 114– 116
  Funds................................. 99
  Mandamus................. 115, 116
Justice peace 209

K.

Kansas—
  Laws................................. 347
  Tax 235
Kentucky—
  Laws................................. 349
  Tax 235

L.

Laws—
  Alabama............................ 331
  Arizona............................. 333
  Arkansas........................... 334
  California.......................... 336
  Colorado........................... 337
  Connecticut....................... 339
  Delaware........................... 339
  Florida.............................. 340
  Georgia............................. 341
  Idaho................................ 342
  Illinois.............................. 343
  Indiana............................. 344
  Iowa................................. 345
  Kansas.............................. 347
  Kentucky........................... 349
  Louisiana.......................... 350
  Maine............................... 353
  Maryland.......................... 356
  Massachusetts................... 357
  Michigan........................... 358
  Minnesota......................... 359
  Mississippi........................ 361
  Missouri........................... 363
  Montana........................... 364
  Nebraska.......................... 365
  Nevada............................. 366
  New Hampshire................ 367
  New Jersey....................... 368
  New Mexico..................... 370
  New York......................... 371
  North Carolina................. 372
  North Dakota................... 373
  Ohio................................ 375
  Oregon............................. 376
  Pennsylvania..................... 380
  Rhode Island 381

Laws—
  South Carolina.......................... 382
  South Dakota........................... 386
  Tennessee............................... 388
  Texas................................... 389
  Vermont................................. 391
  Virginia................................ 393
  Washington.............................. 394
  West Virginia........................... 396
  Wisconsin............................... 397
  Wyoming................................. 398
Legislature—
  Apportionment........................... 93
  District organization................... 88
  Funds, use.............................. 110
  Powers............................. 53, 116
Liability—
  Officers............... 48, 132, 137– 143
  Teacher................................. 296
Library, district......................... 82
Lien, mechanic's.......................... 116
Liquor—
  Funds................................... 103
  License................................. 101
Loan—funds.......................... 103– 108
Location—see Building; see Site.
Louisiana—
  Laws.................................... 350
  Tax..................................... 237

M.

Maine—
  Laws.................................... 353
  Tax..................................... 239
Mandamus—
  Apportionment........................... 93
  Colored pupil....................... 39, 41
  District alteration................. 58, 73
  Funds........................... 96, 97, 112
  Judgment................................ 116
  Officers................................ 144
Maryland—
  Laws.................................... 356
  Tax..................................... 237
Massachusetts—
  Laws.................................... 357
  Tax..................................... 237
Mechanic's lien........................... 116
Meeting—
  Annual.................................. 117
  Notice............................. 118– 127
  Officers' powers........................ 145
  Records........................... 195, 196
Michigan—
  Laws.................................... 358
  Tax..................................... 240

Minnesota—
  Laws.................................... 359
  Tax..................................... 240
Mississippi—
  Laws.................................... 361
  Tax..................................... 240
Missouri—
  Laws.................................... 363
  Tax..................................... 241
Moderator; qualification.................. 148
Montana—laws.............................. 364
Mortgage—see Funds, loan...103– 108
  Release................................. 138
  Suit.................................... 212

N.

Nebraska—
  Laws.................................... 365
  Tax..................................... 242
Negligence—
  Damages................................. 32
  Officers, liability............... 142, 143
Negro—see Colored Schools.
Nevada—laws............................... 366
New Hampshire—
  Laws.................................... 367
  Tax..................................... 243
New Jersey—
  Laws.................................... 368
  Tax..................................... 245
New Mexico laws........................... 370
New York—
  Laws.................................... 371
  Tax..................................... 247
Notes—see Contracts; Warrants.
  Contracts.......................... 46, 49
  Officers, liability..................... 141
  Supplies................................ 226
Notice—
  District alteration......... 66, 67, 69
  Election........................... 91, 92
  Meeting........................... 118– 127
  Site.................................... 205
Normal school............................. 127
  Building................................ 18
North Carolina—
  Laws.................................... 372
  Tax..................................... 252
North Dakota laws......................... 373

O.

Oath, officer—see officer; qualification................... 146– 149
Oath—officer.............................. 129

Officer	128–156
Bond, official	149
Commissioner	136
Compensation	129–132
Contract	132, 133
Election	134–136
Funds	109
Interested, contract	46–48
Intoxication	150
Liability	32, 48, 132, 137–143
Liability, negligence	142, 143
Mandamus	134
Oath	127
Power	143–146
Pro tem	129
Qualification	146–149
Quo warranto	150
Removal	150, 215
Secretary state board	134
Site	205
Suit	212
Surety	226, 227
Tax	151
Term	151–153
Treasurer	154
Vacancy	154–156
Women	328
Ohio—	
Laws	375
Tax	252
Orders (see Warrants)	324–328
Order — contracts	45
Oregon—	
Laws	376
Tax	253
Organization, district	82–88
Orphans — fund, use	95
Outbuildings	31

P.

Parochial school	157–170
Party — suit	209–213
Pennsylvania—	
Laws	380
Tax	253
Petition — district alteration	54–80
Piano supplies	224
Private school—	
Aiding	157–170
Building	34–36
Funds	111–112
Property — title	312
Prudential committee	146, 152
Liability	139
Suit	212, 213
Vacancy	154

Public school funds	110–112, 127, 128
Punishment, pupil	176–191
Pupil —	
Admission	171, 172
Chinese	173
Dismissal and expulsion, 7,	173–175
Punishment	176–191
Residence	192, 193
Text-book	299, 300
Tobacco, use	199
Tuition	192–194
Purchasers, bonds	14, 15

Q.

Qualification, officer	146–149
Quo warranto —	
District organization	83, 86
Officer	150

R.

Railroad —	
Bonds	13
Funds, loan	103
Ratification	25–27
Building	20
Contract	49, 51
Recitals — bond	15
Record —	
Amendment	197
Evidence	195, 196
District organization	86
Treasurer	154
Refunding bonds	12
Religion (see Bible, Parochial, Text-books) —	
Aiding	157–170
Building	34, 35
Holiday	200
Meetings	34
Removal, officer	150
Residence, pupil	192, 193
Rhode Island —	
Laws	381
Tax	254
Rules and regulations	197–199, 296
Absence	174, 175
Pupils	172–175

S.

Salary—see Officer, compensation.	
Sale, site	206
Secret society — colleges	172
Sec'y state board — constitution	134
Sectarian — funds	100, 111, 112, 157, 170

410 PUBLIC SCHOOL LAW.

Separate schools — see Colored.
Settlement, treasurer 154
Site —
   Appeal........................... 5–, 10
   Bonds............................... 13
   Building...................... 200– 208
   Condemnation...................... 201
   Contract........................... 201
   Conveyance........................ 202
   Election 203, 204
   Injunction......................... 204
   Lease.............................. 202
   Meeting............................ 126
   Meeting, notice 122
   Notice............................. 205
   Officers........................... 205
   Place.............................. 205
   Sale............................... 206
   Tax................................ 206
   Title.............................. 207
   Trust.............................. 208
South Carolina —
   Laws............................... 382
   Tax 255
South Dakota laws 386
Statute — constitution............... 208
Studies —
   Rules 197– 199
   Text-books............... 174–176, 299
Suits.................... 30, 209– 213
   Attorney........................... 45
   District........................... 209
   District alteration 70
   Party 209– 213
Sunday school — building ... 34, 35
Surety........................ 226, 227
   Funds; loan........................ 104
Superintendent, county....... 217, 218
   Appeal.................. 6, 8–10, 145
   Compensation................ 130– 132
   District alteration 57– 59
   Funds.......................... 97– 99
   Liability.......................... 141
   Term........................ 152, 153
Superintendent schools........ 128, 130
                                      219– 223
   Qualification 147, 148
Superintendent, state......... 214– 216
   Appeal........................... 5, 74
   Apportionment...................... 94
   Contract, attorney 44
   Normal............................. 128
   Power.............................. 130
Supplies..................... 224– 226
   Contract........................... 48
   Warrants.................... 324– 328

T.

Tardiness — rules..................... 197
  (See Punishment; Rules and Regulations.)
Tax —
   Alabama............................ 228
   Arkansas........................... 228
   Building.................. 17, 20, 24
   California......................... 229
   Colorado 229
   Connecticut........................ 230
   District alteration 55
   District organization.............. 84
   District union..................... 90
   Exemption (see each state)..260– 262
   Florida............................ 230
   Funds; use......................... 112
   Georgia............................ 231
   Illinois........................... 231
   Indiana............................ 233
   Iowa............................... 233
   Kansas............................. 235
   Kentucky........................... 235
   Louisiana.......................... 237
   Maine.............................. 239
   Maryland........................... 237
   Massachusetts...................... 237
   Meeting.......... 119, 123–125, 127
   Michigan........................... 240
   Minnesota.......................... 240
   Mississippi........................ 240
   Missouri........................... 241
   Nebraska........................... 242
   New Hampshire...................... 243
   New Jersey......................... 245
   New York........................... 247
   North Carolina..................... 252
   Officers..................... 137, 151
   Ohio............................... 252
   Oregon............................. 253
   Pennsylvania....................... 253
   Rhode Island....................... 254
   Site............................... 206
   South Carolina..................... 255
   Tennessee.......................... 255
   Texas.............................. 256
   Trespass.................... 313, 314
   Utah............................... 257
   Vermont............................ 257
   Virginia........................... 257
   Washington......................... 259
   West Virginia...................... 260
   Wisconsin.......................... 260
Tax-payer; officer................... 148
Teacher — (see Teacher, compensation; Teacher, contract).

INDEX.

Teacher—
  Appeal.................................. 7
  Certificate......... 262–274, 400– 403
  Compensation ... 274–279, 289– 294
  Contract 51–52, 280– 289
  Discharge 289– 294
  Institute................................. 295
  Liability................................ 296
  (See Pupil, punishment; Rules and Regulations.)
  Officer; qualification................ 148
  Officer; removal 150
Tennessee—
  Laws..................................... 388
  Tax 255
Term—
  Officer............................ 151– 153
  Time 296
Texas—
  Laws..................................... 389
  Tax 256
Text-book—
  Adoption 296, 297, 301– 312
  Appeal..................................... 7
  Change............................ 297, 298
  Free 299
  German 299
  Officer................................... 129
  Pupil.............................. 299, 300
  Rules 197
  Studies 174–176, 299
Time—term........................... 296
Title—
  District alteration 61
  Property 312
  Site............................... 203, 207
Town—
  Corporation........................... 313
  Site...................................... 313
Treasurer—see Officer, liability... 313
  Bond.................................... 129
  Compensation................. 130, 132
  Liability 137– 141
  Officer.................................. 154
Trespass 313
  Site...................................... 208
  Suit...................................... 203
Truant—
  Officer.................................. 151
  School 314– 316
Trust 316, 317
Trust—site............................ 208
Trustee—
  Liability....................... 137, 141

Trustee—
  Liability; penalty.................... 140
  Officers' powers 146
  Term 152
  Vacancy................................ 155
Tuition—pupil 192– 194

U.

Union district.................... 89– 90
Universities...................... 317– 321
University—
  Nebraska............................... 128
  Pupils................................... 172
Use—
  Building.......................... 33– 36
  Funds........................... 110– 112
Utah—tax............................. 257

V.

Vacancy—officer............... 154– 156
Vaccination—constitution 323
Vermont—
  Laws.................................... 391
  Tax 257
Virginia—
  Laws 393
  Tax 257
Void—
  Bonds.................................... 16
  Building contract..................... 25
Vote—contract 50, 51
Voters 293
Voters—women 329

W.

Warrants—
  Building................................. 25
  Supplies 225, 324– 328
Washington—
  Laws.................................... 394
  Tax...................................... 259
West Virginia—
  Laws.................................... 396
  Tax...................................... 260
Wisconsin—
  Laws.................................... 397
  Tax...................................... 260
Women—
  Officers................................. 328
  Voters 329
Wyoming laws....................... 398

www.ingramcontent.com/pod-product-compliance
Lightning Source LLC
Chambersburg PA
CBHW050845300426
44111CB00010B/1135